Labour's Lost Leader

Labour's Lost Leader

The Life and Politics of Will Crooks

Paul Tyler

I.B. TAURIS
LONDON·NEW YORK

Revised paperback edition published in 2013 by I.B.Tauris & Co Ltd
6 Salem Road, London W2 4BU
175 Fifth Avenue, New York NY 10010
www.ibtauris.com

Copyright © 2013, 2007 Paul Tyler
First published in hardback by Tauris Academic Studies, an imprint of
I.B.Tauris & Co Ltd, 2007

The right of Paul Tyler to be identified as the author of this work has been asserted by the author in accordance with the Copyright, Designs and Patent Act 1988.

All rights reserved. Except for brief quotations in a review, this book, or any part thereof, may not be reproduced, stored in or introduced into a retrieval system, or transmitted, in any form or by any means, electronic, mechanical, photocopying, recording, or otherwise, without the prior written permission of the publisher.

ISBN: 978 1 78076 046 9

A full CIP record for this book is available from the British Library
A full CIP record for this book is available from the Library of Congress

Library of Congress catalog card: available

CONTENTS

Acknowledgements vii
Abbreviations x

Introduction 1

PART ONE: LOCAL ACTIVIST AND LABOUR PIONEER 1852-1907

1　Will Crooks of Poplar　17
2　Guardian of the Poor　41
3　Unemployment and the Poor Law　67
4　Woolwich and independent Labour representation　100

PART TWO: LABOUR PIONEER AND MEMBER OF PARLIAMENT 1903-1921

5　Member for Woolwich　125
6　Role in Parliament and the General Elections of 1910　153
7　Returns to the Parliamentary Fray　175
8　War and Peace　194

References and Notes 225
Bibliography 261
Index 273

ACKNOWLEDGEMENTS

The life story of Will Crooks has a Dickensian resonance. He was a cockney lad born into abject poverty, and experienced the rigours of Poplar Workhouse and Poor Law school. Nearly forty years later Crooks became Chairman of the Poplar Board of Guardians, the very board that had given him shelter as a boy, during the depressing time of his young life. He entered Parliament in 1903, and later became a Privy Councillor in 1916. This monograph is a pioneering biography of a significant Labour figure, and an important reinterpretation of the early trade union and labour movement 1887-1921. The study of the public life of this influential, but controversial, Labour leader, has drawn upon material not uncovered before. Historians have not told Crooks' story, and have failed to recognise his significant contribution to the Labour cause in any way. This book remedies this.

This study is based on my doctoral thesis, and taken as a whole is the result of nearly twenty years study, which began with an undergraduate extended essay on the 1903 Woolwich bye-election in 1987, and ended with the research for this book. I do not apologise for the time it has taken for me to complete my research on Will Crooks. He did not leave any personal papers, except for a few letters that are in private hands, and a number of pamphlets in the British Library of Economic and Political Science. Using George Haw's two books *From Workhouse to Westminster* (1907) and *The Life Story of Will Crooks MP* (1916) as points of reference, I began an extensive search for primary material — digging out and accessing a large amount, especially newspaper articles by and about Crooks, reports of his political activities, and his Parliamentary speeches.

I have been greatly encouraged to publish my findings by a number of colleagues to whom I owe an enormous debt, and who in numerous ways helped me through the writing, and the complexities of publishing a biography on Will Crooks. My supervisors Professor Denis Judd, Dr. Dennis Dean, and my two examiners, Professors Michael Newman and John Shepherd, all encouraged me to publish my thesis as a book. Further, I am greatly indebted to the History School, University of North London (London Metropolitan University) for funding my research studies for ten years, and for granting me a number of bursaries. I am also grateful to Brian Roper, Vice Chancellor, and London Metropolitan University for a financial contribution towards the publication of this book.

My interest in Will Crooks received wholehearted support from members of the Crooks family, who commented on drafts of my thesis over a number of years, and offered hospitality and friendship, especially Len and Maureen Byott, David Viner, Jeff Williams, Joan and John Skelton, Crooks' great-grandsons and granddaughter, their wives, husbands, and partners. I owe a huge debt of gratitude to Crooks' great-grand children, Ray Jefford, the Crooks family historian, and Sue Spier, who both put me in touch with other members of the family, and gave me access to private papers in the families possession. Thirty members of the family came together in March 2003 for three days to celebrate the centenary of Will Crooks victory in the 1903 Woolwich bye-election. Civic receptions were organised in Tower Hamlets and Woolwich, and a Labour Party dinner arranged in the families honour.

I would like to thank a number of institutions, which I frequently visited, for their professional help and support. Chris Lloyd, Malcolm Barr-Hamilton, and David Rich at Tower Hamlets Local History Library; Julian Watson, Barbara Ludlow, Francis Ward, and Jenny O'Keefe at the Greenwich Local History Library, Blackheath; Beverley Burford, and Chris Foord at the Greenwich Borough Museum; Ron Roffey for allowing me to search the Royal Arsenal Co-operative Society (RACS) Archives and Library. In 2004, the Local History Library and the Museum both closed, and came together in the Greenwich Heritage Centre, Building 41, Artillery Square, Royal Arsenal, Woolwich. The RACS Archives pertinent to Woolwich, and the Royal Arsenal, were deposited later.

I am also most indebted to Stephen Bird at the Labour History Archive and Study Centre, Manchester; Christine Coates, and Briget Collins at the TUC Collections, London Metropolitan University; Richard Storey and Christine Woodland at The Modern Records Centre, University of Warwick. I have also received kind, and generous support from the staff of many libraries, record offices, and organisations throughout this and other countries. British Library; British Library of Political and Economic Science; Canadian National Archive; Guildhall Library; Hoover Institute, Stanford University, USA; House of Lords Record Office; International Institute of Social History, Amsterdam; London Metropolitan Archives; Marx Memorial Library; National Library of Canada;

National Newspaper Library, Colindale; National Records Office; Sydney Jones Library, University of Liverpool; University of London; Working Class Movement Library, Salford. My thanks also go to John Edmunds and Peter Carter at the General, Municipal, Boilermakers and Allied Trade Union (GMB), for their support and hospitality.

I have received invaluable help from learned colleagues, and I would like to thank Professor Mark Bevir, Dr. Alan Clinton, Dr. Chris Cook, Professor David Howell; Professor Keith Laybourn, Dr. David Martin, Dr. Roland Quinalt, Malcolm Starrs, Professor John Tosh, Dr. Dan Weinbren, and Professor Chris Wrigley. I would like to thank my publishers I. B. Tauris, especially Dr. Lester Crook, my Commissioning Editor, who saw that my original thesis showed potential as a book, and for encouraging me to write it. And my Subject Editor, Elizabeth Munns, who showed patience and fortitude throughout the time it took to produce this book. Further, I would like to thank the following for copyright; Sue Donnelley, British Library of Political and Economic Science (Lansbury, Beveridge and Passfield papers); Dr. Maureen Watry, Sydney Jones Library, Liverpool University (Glazier Papers); Sue Spier, Mylor Bridge, Falmouth (Crooks Papers); Jeannine Sudworth, Independent Labour Publications, Keir Hardie House, Top Moor Side, Leeds (Francis Johnson Collection), and Claire Willgress, Fabian Society, London (Fabian Collection).

Although this book is dedicated to Will and Elizabeth Crooks, it saw the light of day because of Denis Judd, my PhD Director of Studies, who has been my tutor, mentor and friend for the past twenty years. Some fourteen years ago, he said to me: 'Go away and write it' - the thesis, and later the book. Little did I realize what a sojourn it would be. In addition, I must apologise to my long-suffering comrades and friends, especially Councillor Peter Brooks, and John Austin MP, who have had to live with Will Crooks and me for the past twelve years. I hope this book not only repays the debts I owe, but goes some way in accommodating those who have been waiting for this biography. Finally, I am indebted to my soul mate and good friend Christine Ojera for her indefatigable and steady support throughout.

ABBREVIATIONS

ASE	Amalgamated Society of Engineers.
BOT	Board of Trade.
BL	British Library.
BLPES	British Library of Political and Economic Science.
BWL	British Workers' League.
CVLU	Colne Valley Labour Union.
GHC	Greenwich Heritage Centre.
HMM	History of the Ministry of Munitions
ILP	Independent Labour Party.
LHASC	Labour History Archive & Study Centre
LCC	London County Council.
LGB	Local Government Board.
LMA	London Metropolitan Archive.
LMU	London Metropolitan University.
LPL	Labour Protection League.
LRC	Labour Representation Committee.
LTC	London Trades Council.
LU	London University.
MAB	Metropolitan Asylum Board.
MBW	Metropolitan Board of Works.
MRC	Modern Record Centre, Warwick University.
NEC	National Executive Committee.
NFWW	National Federation of Women Workers.
NTWF	National Transport Workers' Federation.
OF	Ordnance Factory.
Parl. Deb.	Parliamentary Debates.
PLP	Parliamentary Labour Party.
PLEC	Poplar Labour Election.Committee

PLL	Poplar Labor League.
PLRA	Poplar Liberal Radical Association.
PRC	Parliamentary Recruitment Committee.
PU	Poplar Union of Poor Law Guardians.
RACS	Royal Arsenal Co-operative Society.
RCF	Royal Carriage Factory.
RGF	Royal Gun Factory.
RL	Royal Laboratory
SDF	Social Democratic Federation.
TEB	Technical Education Board.
THLHL	Tower Hamlets Local History Library
TUC	Trade Union Congress.
WLP	Woolwich Labour Party
WLRA	Woolwich Labour Representation Association.
WTC	Woolwich & District Trades Council.

INTRODUCTION

The aim of this book is to examine the political life of Will Crooks of Poplar, a leading pioneer of the trade union and labour movement, who has been overlooked by modern historians. In order to rectify this, the career of Will Crooks will be examined both at the local and national level. This study aims to assess what effect his participation was to have on the trade union and labour movement in a Poplar and Woolwich context during the struggle for independent Labour representation and his contribution towards the emergence of the Labour Representation Committee (LRC), and the consolidation of the Labour Party. The record indicates that Crooks was at the forefront in the pioneering days of Poor Law reform and the campaigns against unemployment both locally and nationally. He was a party activist for thirty years. It is against this background of progressivism that Crooks' contribution to the development of the Labour Party will be examined and assessed. He fervently believed that it was his sacred duty to serve the people, and help bring about the emancipation of the working-class. Crooks believed that the workers had to put right the wrongs done to them, they 'had to seize it as a sacred obligation.' If they did not 'they committed a crime against their own class, and against common humanity.'[1]

While Labour historians have concentrated their attention on the lives of leading activists, such as John Burns, Keir Hardie, George Lansbury, Tom Mann, and Ramsey MacDonald, they have neglected to explore the important and enabling contributions of other pioneers of the trade union and labour movement.[2] Most notably, Will Crooks (Cooper), Pete Curran (Gasworker), Robert Banner (Compositor), and Fred Hammill (Engineer). Historians need to recognise that Will Crooks played an important part in the creation of a Labour culture in Poplar, especially towards the strengthening of Fabian socialism, trade unionism, religious nonconformity, and the level of political awareness in the area. For example, Susan Pennybacker and Kenneth Brown both wrongly describe Crooks as the Labour 'councillor for Woolwich.'[3] The question of whether Crooks was a Labour man politically active in Woolwich, or a Radical in Poplar, is crucial to an understanding of Crooks' early public life; what events nurtured his radical outlook, and his subsequent worldview.

By changing his political environment, the socio-political perspective is obscured, confused, and therefore misunderstood. One of the aims of this book is to correct this view, and at the same time present a revision of orthodox thinking on the emergence of Labour. Further, this approach will help explain and clarify any ambiguities historians may feel about Crooks' place within the radical tradition of Labourism.

The radical tradition of Labourism emerged from a continuous chain of ideas and efforts, founded upon the Reform movement of the 1820s; the political radicalism of Mazzini and the Young Italy movement of the 1830s and 40s; Chartism, and its recovery at a lower level in George Julian Harney's Society of Fraternal Delegates, and Ernest Jones' International Committee. The influence of the European Revolutions of 1848, and the development of Trade Unionism in the 1850s and 60s were an integral part of this progression. Similarly, also, the popular radicalism of John Bright and Gladstonian Liberalism, together with the founding of the Socialist societies in the 1880s, and the advent of New Unionism in 1889 were of major significance in the evolution of nineteenth century political ideas and organisation. For example, Biagini and Reid 'maintain that popular radicalism not only survived after 1848, but remained a major political force, with a substantial impact both on the Gladstonian Liberal party and on the Labour party in its formative years.'[4] It is essential to recognise this development of radicalism, especially the early period 1830-1848, often ignored by Labour historians, which saw political émigrés from France, Germany, Italy and Poland imbue the notion of class-consciousness and solidarity with the European working-class.

It was important in influencing the internationalist ideas of the early Labour pioneers such as Hardie, Crooks, Shackleton, and Henderson. It helped inform them, and underlined the necessity of working-class unity in the common struggle for liberty, freedom, and emancipation. Ramsay MacDonald later wrote; 'the colonial and world policy of a democratic State' must be founded upon 'internationalism', and 'humanism'.[5]

Crooks typified this tradition. His view was complex and idiosyncratic. He borrowed from, and was influenced by, the various strands of internationalism, radical liberalism, Fabian, and Socialist thought. The important difference about Hardie, Shackleton, Henderson, and Crooks' stance on social and political issues was that they were infused with strong Christian values. Crooks was a Congregationalist, and a follower of Joseph Mazzini, whose religio-radical writings appealed to Crooks' religious principles. Crooks said: 'There is a book that has had much to do with the saving of my life ... The Life of Joseph Mazzini', written 'more than sixty years ago'. [6] Mazzini's message defined Crooks' political vocation, his duty to serve the people.

Both Mazzini's beliefs and that of the Congregationalists merge on the ethical position of Mission and Duty. For example, Mazzini said: 'Life is mission: duty, therefore is the highest law',[7] especially in the struggle against despotism. 'The source of your Duties is in God. The definition of your duties is found in his Law. The progressive discovery and application of this law is the mission of Humanity.'[8] Crooks saw his mission towards humanity as that of reforming the social condition of working people, especially the poor. Although Mazzanian radicalism influenced Crooks on issues such as poverty, education, women and the family, Empire and war, whenever he approached the question of monarchy his radicalism passed into a profound and reverent conservatism. Crooks' position on war is important because it informs the stance taken by him during the Great War. His views were obviously influenced by Mazzini, who believed democracy carried within it 'the gift of the obligation to life, and if need be readily to die for one's country.'[9] It influenced Crooks' position on both the conscription campaign during the Great War, and the Military Service Acts of 1916. Lloyd George, who had studied the writings of Mazzini, wrote in *The Times*: 'I doubt whether any man of his generation exercised so profound an influence on the destinies of Europe as did Mazzini. The map of Europe as we see it today [1922] is the map of Joseph Mazzini.'[10]

The central aim of both Mazzini's and Crooks' life was to 'make democracy alike in thought and action religious.... it was the idea of political equality ... the claim for political justice.'[11] In other words, religion and politics were inseparable. It cannot be over-emphasised that Christianity was the driving force that underpinned Crooks' radicalism. With George Haw he would have agreed: 'There never will be a universal freedom, or universal brotherhood, nor universal peace on this earth, except by the faith in the Universal Father.'[12] Crooks' commitment to the cause of humanity was unshakable. He said: 'The agitation of the Labour Party was a holy agitation', and when things did not go according to plan it didn't shake his faith in God 'any more than to-days fog shakes my faith in the sun.'[13]

What characterised Crooks' life and values, besides his religiosity, were his formative experiences, which were shaped by the poverty and deprivation of London's East End. It was this environment that had taught him to approach political and social issues from a practical point of view. From the time Crooks entered public life, as a Trustee of the Poplar Vestry in 1886 he was always the pragmatist. There is no doubt Will Crooks was always an emotional, rather than an intellectual, activist. He was not ignorant of theory, nor did he despise it, but he knew it was not his strength.

Since Crooks was one of the earlier Fabians, it can be assumed he had some grasp of socialist political theory. He thought that within the political distribution of class power that was his world, the intellectual activist already had proportionately more power and recognition than those with working-class experience. Therefore given the circumstances, Crooks felt that he could best serve the interests of the working-class through what he considered the greater value of 'common sense' and practicality. It is likely that what contact he had with middle-class theorists, such as Sidney Webb, George Bernard Shaw, Graham Wallas, and Edward Pease, was to lead to a rather deferential acceptance of those elements of liberal theory that most suited him. In Crooks' case, it seems that the Fabians themselves gave priority to political expediency over ideological purity, which confirmed the validity of his approach.[14]

Will Crooks was a member of the Fabian Society for thirty years. In December 1910, he gave the Fabians their first electoral victory when he regained the Woolwich seat after losing it in January.[15] It is also important to recognise that Crooks, like his contemporary Thomas Burt (the Lib-Lab MP for Morpeth), was accepted to a great extent 'among the middle and upper classes, in industry as well as governing circles' because of his policies on industrial affairs. He was always a staunch advocate of conciliation, and supported 'a strike only after all other avenues to settlement failed. Compromise and practicality were for [Crooks] the norms in politics.'[16] This was in spite of Crooks' attempt to draft a bill on industrial relations in 1911, which was received unsympathetically by both trade unions and industry. He put a poorly drafted bill before the TUC, which was for him an uncharacteristic tactical error. It is important to be aware that Crooks was not an opportunist. He sincerely believed that everything he did was in the interests of furthering the cause of Labour. He made mistakes, but unlike most politicians, he was usually the first to admit them.

Not since George Haw published his two biographies of Crooks (1907 and 1916) nearly one hundred years ago has there been any meaningful research into his life.[17] The constituencies of Poplar and Woolwich have not been examined in any detail since Paul Thompson's *Socialists, Liberals and Labour* (1967). It is the only notable study of the London progressive movement, the nature of which precluded a detailed analysis of the influence of independent labour representation on the trade union and labour movement in Poplar. Since the publication of Thompson's work, the early Poplar movement has attracted little attention from Labour historians, apart from John Shepherd, who in his biography, *George Lansbury*, looks at the involvement of Lansbury and Crooks as Poplar Guardians 1893-1907. Although Noreen Branson examines Poplarism and the Councillors' Rate Revolt of 1921, she neglects to recognise that the 'Poplarism' of the 1920s had its roots in the actions of the Poplar Guardians of the 1890s and 1900s. Shepherd acknowledges this link.[18] It is necessary, therefore, to set the record straight by extending the debate around issues previously neglected, especially regarding the struggle for independent labour representation in Poplar 1891-1893, in which Will Crooks played a leading role.[19]

In all probability, historians have ignored Crooks' involvement in the trade union and labour movement because he was seen as part of a past generation, older than most of his Labour contemporaries and not worthy of particular note due to the seemingly localised nature of his politics. Nothing could be further from the truth. Crooks was a standard bearer of welfare reform. He was known nationally as the man responsible for humanising the Poor Law. It was Crooks who drew to the attention of both the Tory and Liberal Governments that they had a responsibility towards the unemployed, old age pensioners, and the children of the poor. He was responsible for placing the welfare of the working-class in the political domain. His early work helped lay the foundations of what was to become the Welfare State. It is worth pointing out that reformers such as Crooks were debating old age pensions and labour exchanges well before they were implemented in 1908-09.[20]

On the issue of welfare reform, for instance, historians, by default, usually give the credit to Beveridge, a notion that is misleading. Beveridge was an academic, who viewed poverty and unemployment from a theoretical perspective, and 'first directly encountered the problem of poverty whilst he was employed at Toynbee Hall', Whitechapel, 1903-5.[21] During this period the Webbs, and the Warden of Toynbee, Canon Barnett, introduced him to the problems surrounding unemployment. By comparison, Crooks had lived through and experienced poverty and the exigencies surrounding unemployment for over fifty years, long before Beveridge promulgated his theories on the subject. In other words Beveridge's ideas on social reform in the Edwardian period were based on, and owed much to, the pioneering work done by those reformers such as Crooks, who were active in the 1880s and 90s.

Will Crooks' formative years and his involvement in the local politics of Poplar and London 1852-1907, together with his election as MP for Woolwich in March 1903, are examined and discussed in Part One. The recurrent themes throughout this period were Crooks' tireless agitation at the local level against poverty and unemployment, and the campaign for the implementation of independent Labour representation. These demonstrations and protests underline the significance of his contribution towards Labour politics. The support that Crooks received from reformers and trade unionists in the district will be examined to determine what role he played in bringing them together. Questions will be asked; such as in what way was his campaigning style different? Why was it successful, why did a group of Radical Liberals, led by Crooks, and supported by the London Fabians and the New Unions split with the Poplar Liberal and Radical Association (PLRA) over the demand for independent Labour representation?

It will become evident that Crooks' political activity, and the creation of a Labour culture in Poplar, through Crooks' 'College' (the regular Sunday morning meetings at East India Dock Gate), was largely responsible for disseminating a culture based on trade union and labour values. One objective of this study is to show that these meetings were to concern themselves with the task of improving Poplar's environment, and eradicating impoverishment. The Dock Gate meetings, as will be shown, were responsible for placing the issues of poverty, destitution, and unemployment high on the political agenda of New Unionism. This research seeks to appraise the political ideology of Crooks during this transition, and examine his conversion from Radical Liberalism to Fabianism 1891-93. Further, the study aims to show that Will Crooks and the Poplar working-class Fabians were the chief organisers who led the movement to introduce independent Labour representation into the district. They provided the platform and focus that achieved a separate Labour identity, distancing it from the more moderate PLRA. The object of this discussion is to demonstrate that the left Fabian group in Poplar was atypical of Fabianism. They did not believe in permeation but in the organisation of a separate Labour Party, and were led by working-class trade union organisers, such as Ben Tillett, Tom Mann, John Burns, and Will Crooks.

The study shows that in the 1890s and even in the early 1900s, a 'Labour' man could do more for the cause locally than at a national level. As Keith Laybourn and other historians have argued, 'local politics can affect the attitudes of national parties and that to ignore the local perspective is to disregard a vital component in the make-up of national politics.'[22] The agitation for independent Labour representation in Poplar 1891-93 exemplifies this view. The Liberal Party came under local pressure nationally because of the emergence of Labour societies, who put forward the proposal of independent representation. Although there are a number of local studies on the ILP, the contribution to the development of independent Labour representation by local Fabian Societies has been ignored, possibly because of adherence to the orthodox view put forward by some historians that the Fabian Society had no place in the British political tradition. A study of the political agitation in Poplar challenges this view.

Since Crooks 'College' also agitated for the beginning of the construction of the Blackwall Tunnel, its contribution towards the pressure for a vehicular tunnel will be examined. It is argued that the construction of the tunnel not only provided work for the unemployed, but also facilitated the dissemination of radicalism on both sides of the river Thames by enabling activists to attend trade union and political meetings. For example, after the tunnel was opened in May 1897, the trade union and labour movement in Poplar helped the progressive movement in the Tory stronghold of Woolwich to improve its political organisation. In addition, the Poplar Labor League gave financial support to the Crooks Parliamentary Maintenance Fund in 1903. This link between the Poplar Fabians and the Woolwich trade union and labour movement is significant. A theme elaborated upon during the discussion around the campaigns in Poplar and Woolwich for independent Labour representation. The development of the Woolwich trade union, progressive and labour movement, and the Woolwich by-election of 1903, will be the subject of investigation to show that political activists in Woolwich were aware of the influence of the Poplar Labor League upon the politics of Poplar.

The replacement of the Metropolitan Board of Works (MBW), by the London County Council (LCC) with the Local Government Act of 1888 (which left the Vestries and District Boards virtually unaffected), has been the topic of a number of studies by contemporary and modern historians.[23] Crooks' municipal career typifies this transformation; his introduction into, and participation in, elected public service began as a Poplar Trustee in 1886. Crooks' election to the Poplar Vestry in 1889, and his contribution to the development of Progressive and Fabian politics in the London County Council (LCC), especially its Progressive administration 1892-1907, is given close attention, especially his work on the Bridges, and the Parks and Open Spaces Committees. Also investigated are Crooks' involvement in the work of the LCC Technical Education Board 1893-1904, together with his terms of office on the Poplar Board of Guardians 1893-1907, Mayor of Poplar 1901-2, and the Metropolitan Asylums Board 1898-1904. The campaign around the building of the Blackwall Tunnel and the Fair Wages Clause in a Poplar and Woolwich context is discussed in detail using primary sources. It is argued that the construction of the tunnel, together with other building projects, was the catalyst that made possible the fair wage movement, and the campaign for a Works Department to oversee the implementation and regulation of fair wages in the contracts of the LCC. Historians of the LCC have failed to acknowledge this, and by omitting Crooks and the Poplar trade union and labour movement from their studies have failed to perceive a fundamental contribution towards LCC policy.

The part of the book on the Poplar Guardians concentrates on the successful enterprise of Crooks and Lansbury, namely their efforts to humanise the Poor Law, and eradicate 'Bumbledom' from the workhouse. In this context, it is important to recognise that they both brought to the Board something that had been seriously lacking in their deliberations in the past - an understanding of working-class culture, and a commitment to change things for the better. Will Crooks and George Lansbury helped immeasurably to improve living conditions in the workhouse, provided education for children in their care, and set an example to the other guardians of how to treat poor people with dignity.

It is important to recognise that the Poplar Guardians did not involve themselves in the administration of unemployment relief until after Crooks and Lansbury were elected to the Board in April 1893. The local focus of this study will investigate Crooks' contribution towards Poplar's unemployment problems 1892-1905, and the administration of the Poor Law, including the setting up of the London Unemployed Fund in 1904. As early as 1892, Crooks urged Poplar's local authorities to deal with the distress that had arisen from a serious contraction of local industries. He argued that local vestries, local boards, town, and county councils should be allowed, and even encouraged to co-operate with boards of guardians in dealing with the distress. Public works should be introduced to alleviate the distress caused by unemployment, and the stigma of pauperism should not be attached to relief. To understand Crooks' commitment to the problem of unemployment at both the local and national levels, it is important to discuss the Unemployed Workmen Act of 1905, and note the local employment and unemployment schemes that followed as a result of its implementation. Crooks' agitation in parliament — after fifteen years of unrelenting struggle to make the State admit a duty to the unemployed — was finally realised when the Balfour government implemented the Unemployed Workman Bill.[24]

Will Crooks was able to adapt to work with varied interests, while remaining grounded in the local community and its concerns. He was able to exploit a vast range of committees and commissions that came into existence in the 1890s to investigate and alleviate unemployment. Crooks' vision of how to change society came not from abstract theory but from real experience, especially on issues relating to the viability of the Poor Law, and what could be done on a voluntary, private scale for the unemployed.

Thus, Crooks presents a valuable study of shifting public opinion between 1893-1905.

The story of the development of the Woolwich labour movement, and how in the late 1890s, with the support and backing of Will Crooks and the Poplar Fabians, revolves around the campaign for independent Labour representation, which saw Crooks elected Labour MP for Woolwich in 1903. It will explain that the political groundwork and agenda in Woolwich was put in place by a labour movement that were mindful of Crooks' leadership, and the part played by the 'College' in the Poplar militant experience 1891-93. His selection was based on a familiarity with his work of serving the interests of the working-class at both the local and municipal level. The Arsenal Gates meetings provided the focus for educating the workingmen of Woolwich. Many historians accept the importance of industrial conflict in creating the climate for independent political action by the working classes.[25] In Poplar, such conflict was the Dock Strike of 1889. The agitation for the eight-hour day in the Arsenal, followed by the engineers' lockout, was the precursors to the eventual realisation of independent Labour representation in Woolwich. Historians have not considered the link between the Poplar and Woolwich labour movement, which enabled Crooks' election in 1903. This study will show that the Woolwich labour movement saw Crooks' selection as central to the development of independent Labour representation in the district.

Although Crooks' instinct was always to protect the weak, the helpless and unfortunate, his judgement was sometimes flawed. He was too trusting of other people's motives to help the poor. This was not helped by his ingrained habit of seeing the best in a man's conduct, and not his worst.[26] This weakness is exemplified by the mistake he made of remaining Chairman of the Poplar Board of Guardians after his election to Parliament. The majority of guardians were members of the Liberal and Conservative parties, and were out to 'take advantage of [Crooks'] relaxed attention to bring discredit on the Boards' administration.'[27] They were instrumental in calling upon the Local Government Board to hold a public enquiry accusing Crooks and Lansbury, the two most prominent Labour guardians, of maladministration in 1906. 'They were actually held up to reproach and ridicule for faults and follies committed by colleagues who had bitterly opposed their policy at every step.'[28] Crooks resigned after being found not guilty of any offence by the Enquiry.

The mistake Crooks made in trusting his fellow guardians made him bitter, and suspicious of their motives in relieving pauperism. This can be seen as a contributory factor that influenced Crooks' future attitude towards people, namely Liberal and Tory politicians, whom he may have respected, but did not trust, especially after the events of 1906. Will Crooks' cynicism towards hostile guardians surfaced sometime later when he referred to them as 'little tin gods'.[29] He believed their only interest was to preserve the status quo, and stifle Poor Law reform. This outburst was characteristic of him, but as William Barefoot, Crooks' agent 1905-21, explains there was another side to Crooks' nature that was not perceptible to his casual friends:

> With all ... his humour there was a deep strain of sadness in his nature, which made him a peculiarly lonely man. The formative influences of his life, his early struggles, and the loss of loved ones, all tended ... to drive him within himself. Though a great conversationalist, there were outside his family, but a few intimate friends — they can be counted on one hand — who knew the real man.[30]

These insights into the individuality of Crooks' makeup, given that he was a deeply religious man, reveal how his unwavering and personal belief in God sustained and galvanised him throughout the trials and tribulations of public life.

Discussion in this part of the project has focused on the political development of the trade union, radical and socialist movements in London, and upon Will Crooks' activities within these movements. Nevertheless questions of national political issues have not been ignored, especially regarding those policies that determined and influenced the movement's response to the Irish Question, unemployment, social and economic reform, free trade, imperialism, the franchise, and independent Labour representation.

The themes of unemployment and poverty take up a large part of this investigation. Throughout this study, it will be shown that the resolution of these issues was for Crooks of national urgency, and after 1903, when he was elected to parliament, he was in a stronger position to resolve and continue his agitation against them. Crooks brought to Woolwich and the LRC important skills that he had learnt in Poplar. He was an accomplished political leader, negotiator and conciliator, and an experienced Poor Law chairman, administrator, and school manager. For example, in Poplar 1887-92, Crooks led the campaigns for independent Labour representation and the building of a tunnel at Blackwall. He also through negotiation secured an improved scheme of wages for the tunnel workers: 'It was owing to Mr. Crooks' efforts that a revised schedule of wages was adopted. The result of this was that the contractors paid an additional £26,000 in wages.'[31] Later as the Member for Woolwich, Crooks' leadership qualities proved invaluable to the Arsenal workers in their agitation against the War Office over the issue of discharges. It was through this protest that he demonstrated to his constituents how extra-parliamentary agitation together with parliamentary pressure could bring about positive results in the face of political opposition.

Crooks believed that the War Office, namely the Ordnance Department, conspired with private interests to undermine direct labour in Woolwich Arsenal. It began, according to Crooks, in 1901, and culminated in the 'Shell Scandal' of 1915, with the creation of the Ministry of Munitions; partly due, it is argued, to Crooks' disclosure of the War Office's incompetence and secrecy. By concentrating on the important issues that affected his constituents and the working-class in general — unemployment, low pay, education, old age pensions, and temperance — it will be shown that Crooks' contribution was significant, in both the local and national contexts, in bringing the aspirations and needs of the working-class and the Labour Party together.

Will Crooks' early ideas on unemployment and the role of Labour suggest that he was a man ahead of his time. He believed the government of the day should be responsible for the unemployed, and provide financial help through the exchequer. Given this, in 1893, he appealed to A. J. Mundella (President at the Board of Trade), pointing out that the government should reclaim land that would provide work for the unemployed: 'just the kind of work to absorb unskilled labour'. [32] His recommendations were realised sixteen years later when the Liberal Government implemented the Development Bill, a clause of the 1909 'People's Budget'. In connection with employment schemes, Crooks believed a Department and Minister for Labour ought to be created to officially register the unemployed, and administer work schemes with the support of local guardians and councils. This was the essence of Crooks' argument in the House of Commons during 1904, when along with Keir Hardie; he recommended the setting up of a Labour Ministry to deal with the unemployment problem.[33] A Ministry of Labour was finally set up in December 1916, with John Hodge (Labour MP for Gorton) as Minister.[34]

Part Two of this study examines Will Crooks' parliamentary and extra-parliamentary activities 1903-1921. At the beginning, the MacDonald/Gladstone electoral agreement of 1903 — they met to formulate an electoral arrangement between the LRC and the Liberals — will be discussed to determine whether Crooks' victory at the Woolwich by-election played an influential part in the negotiations. The parliamentary debates around the Licensing Bill of 1904, the General Election and Trades Disputes Act of 1906, the Unemployed Workmen Bills of 1907-8, and the Old Age Pensions Act of 1908, will be assessed to determine if Crooks was able to influence the important issues of the day, especially those that shaped national politics. The General Election of 1906 is examined to establish whether the pact between the LRC and the Liberals delivered and held together in the provinces. Crooks' role in the consolidation of the Labour Party will also be assessed to determine if he was able to sway the leadership upon the important issues of the day, especially those that shaped national politics. Crooks' extra-parliamentary agitation on behalf, and in defence of, Government workers, especially those that worked in the Woolwich Arsenal, will be a recurrent theme throughout this part of the study. The Arsenal discharge campaigns of 1907-8 will be examined in detail to show that Crooks was alert to the interests and needs of his constituents, and voiced their demands in the House of Commons.

Following this, the People's Budget of 1909, and the general elections of January and December 1910, provide the focus of analysis. Crooks' response to these events will be addressed. Why, for instance, did he welcome the budget, and call for the abolition of the House of Lords? Also the continuing debate on unemployment, and Crooks' contribution, will be examined to discern how far the Liberals kept their promise of introducing a new unemployment policy in 1909. Will Crooks' world cruise, taken for health reasons later that year, meant he was away for the January election – which he lost, only to regain the seat again the following December. This raises the question, was Crooks' absence from Woolwich a significant factor in his defeat? Both Woolwich elections are examined to establish whether Crooks' campaigning style was the secret of his success.

The events of the Constitutional crisis 1910-11, the Votes for Women agitation 1910-14, the Labour unrest 1911-14, and the Irish Home Rule crisis 1912-14, have shaped, and formed, a significant body of the political historiography of this period. However, very little, if anything, has been written about how backbench Labour MPs represented their constituents and the interests of the working-class. It is against this backdrop of political disorder, that the story of Will Crooks' contribution towards ameliorating the social conditions of the working-class, especially the poor, will be viewed. It is important to note that in this period, although Crooks did not contribute to the major debates in any significant way, except on the minimum wage and industrial unrest. He continued to campaign in Parliament on issues that were central to the needs of working people, such as the minimum wage, unemployment, the Poor Law, the feeding of school children, wages, and conditions of Government workers, Old Age Pensions, Elementary Education, and Army and Navy Estimates. This is not to say that Crooks did not have a position on the important questions of the day. He did, but there is no record other than in newspapers and Parliamentary debates on which to base an examination. Thus an investigation of the portentous events of 1911-1914 will help to determine where Crooks stood on them and will further enable an analysis of whether his contributions influenced Labour Party policy throughout this period.

Will Crooks' loyalty to the Government during the Great War will be examined, his patriotism towards the recruitment campaign 1914-15, and his support for the Military Service Bills of 1916; the recruiting campaign included a fifteen-month speaking tour of the country, and a visit to the Front in July 1915. These activities will be found crucial to the understanding of Crooks' patriotic Labourism, and his support for the war effort in the face of disapproval from both the local and wider trade union and labour movement. This criticism also included his brief dalliance with the British Workers' League 1916-17.

Early in 1915 Crooks disclosed the Shell Scandal, and the shortage of the manufacture of munitions. He insisted that the War Office was diverting work away from the Arsenal in favour of private interests. The historiography of this episode has neglected to record Crooks' involvement in publicising this scandal. Will Crooks' input in this dispute was more important than historians have indicated. Throughout the War, he continued to represent the concerns of workers, soldiers, children of the poor, and old age pensioners in the House of Commons. Historians of the period 1910-18, both contemporary and modern, have written little, if anything, about how Labour backbench MPs functioned. They have tended to concentrate their political and historical studies at the macro level — an approach detrimental to explaining how Labour MPs, such as Crooks, and their constituents viewed national political decisions locally. Evidence will show that Crooks was more than just a good constituency MP. He supported and spoke at meetings organised by religious, temperance, trade union, women's, Labour party, electoral reform, and Irish (Home Rule) organisations, throughout his parliamentary life. In addition, the period before the First World War is often looked upon as a golden age, an alleged *belle époque*, but contrary to this perception it was a period of political turmoil, that can only be described as disorderly, and violent. It was a time in which the Lords and women rebelled, there was unprecedented industrial unrest, and Ireland was on the brink of civil war over Home Rule.

It is probably because most historians have tended to focus upon the wider issues such as the Labour unrest, and the Home Rule Crisis, that the matters, which Crooks promoted, have been overlooked. 'Bread and butter' questions were for him crucial, but it seems that for most political historians these did not fit comfortably into national politics. The internecine strife of the Liberal party, with its emphasis upon the political differences between Lloyd George and Asquith, and the intrigues surrounding the questions of Coalition Governments dominate their studies. For them, it seems, the everyday social question was humdrum by comparison. This is probably the explanation why there is nothing on record of any importance that gives an insight into Crooks' feelings on the Liberal leadership. The Liberal Governments of 1906-15, together with Coalition, are looked upon as

Governments of social reform, but little is said about how they were pressured, harassed, and cajoled from below by people such as Crooks to put their ideas on social change into practice. It is the aim of the study to examine this, and to look at the problems and frustrations Crooks faced when trying to voice his concerns. His argument that there was an inextricable link between unemployment, low pay, poverty, and education, will be examined to see whether Crooks' ideas had any lasting influence upon social reform.

Throughout Crooks' public life, he was dogged by ill health – due mainly to physical exhaustion, which was brought about by his overwork in representing the interests of the working-class. During the war, Crooks' health was undermined and finally shattered. His platform work and constant travelling, as well as a major operation, coupled with the shock he suffered from the Germans' bombing of a school in Poplar, were the major causes of Crooks' worsening physical condition between 1917 and 1921. Crooks often attended Parliament against doctors' orders so that he could put forward the concerns of his constituents. Even though he was a shadow of his former self by 1918, Crooks proved to be dependable. Irrespective of his debilitating illness the Woolwich party in recognition of his loyalty and faithful service to the Labour cause, supported his candidature in the 'coupon election' of 1918. It is clear that throughout this period, Crooks struggled physically to fulfil his Parliamentary duties and that after the summer of 1917 his civic work and platform speeches ceased. Will Crooks' voice was to be heard no more in public. He finally resigned the Woolwich East seat in February 1921, and died the following June. Overall the significance of the work of Crooks and others is not so much what they achieved as what they prevented. Given the overwhelming conservative and traditionalist nature of the average working-class person (and Crooks epitomised an average working-class person), who were politically cautious, it is perhaps fitting that he played, with others like him, an important role in ensuring that the Labour movement played a part in the continuity of the British political system rather than becoming a catalyst for revolutionary upheaval.

PART ONE

Local Activist and Labour Pioneer 1852-1907

1

WILL CROOKS OF POPLAR

The district of Poplar is located on the Isle of Dogs peninsular opposite Greenwich, on the north bank of the river Thames, approximately two miles up river from Woolwich. The district covered three and half square miles. It was surrounded and intersected by various waterways, and extending about four miles from north to south and nearly one mile from east to west. With the opening of the West India Docks in 1802 and East India Docks in 1806, the district at the beginning of the nineteenth century concentrated on port and riverside industries. With the coming of the railway in the 1840s, Poplar's economy underwent a marked change. It gradually lost the predominance of sea borne and riverside activities as factories and workshops expanded after 1870-80.[1] From a port and dock area, the district evolved into a mixed economy in which manufacturing played a more significant role.

Poplar, unlike other neighbouring districts, was scarcely affected by the sweatshop system, and not at all by Jewish immigration, as the 1901 Census shows.[2] In both of these respects, Poplar differed from other parts of the East End. Moreover, not only did one find highly skilled labour in large numbers in the shipbuilding and metal trades, but side by side with these skilled workers was a large mass of low paid unskilled workers, general and dock labourers, and casual workers.[3] By 1880 most of the industry carried out in Poplar was not in the small workshops typical of the East End, but in large factories such as Spratts, and Bryant and May, which at peak times each employed nearly two thousand workers.[4] By 1900, industrial workers who were employed in factories numbered 90 per cent in the area. 'Poplar came in third place in London in this respect after Woolwich and Greenwich.'[5]

A Nonconformist minister, William Lax, who lived in the district, said it was an area 'almost exclusively inhabited by the poor, by those who suffer the meaner miseries of London life', calling it a 'desert unrelieved by any middle class oasis'.[6] The statistics confirming the general state of poverty at the end of the nineteenth century all show the same thing; the area was typically proletarian.[7] Charles Booth's survey of poverty and unemployment in 1889 shows that nearly nineteen per cent of families in Poplar were poor or very poor, and also the income of these families was largely reliant on a male workforce who were employed either casually on a day-to-day basis, worked irregularly, or were dependent upon low paid labour.[8] Given Booth's argument, the condition of employment in Poplar was largely to blame for the level of poverty.[9] Ben Tillett, secretary of the Tea Operatives' Association during the 1889 Dock Strike, who gave a vivid description of the poverty and squalor of living conditions in the area, endorsed this view. He spoke of the dockers being laid off for three to six months a year because of a depression in trade:

> ... a capitalist complains of depressed trade; let them come down to the back streets and slums where the "Dockers" live, and they will see, in the misery and squalor, where the depression is felt. It strikes me they would sing another tune then.[10]

This area of deprivation was the focus of public attention between 1888-91, when the district was pivotal to New Unionism. The movement began with the Matchgirls' Strike at Bryant and May in 1888, followed in 1889 by the great Dock Strike, during which time 'The Wade's Arms', Jeremiah Street, Poplar, was the headquarters. The area was again brought into the public gaze in 1906, during the dispute over its administration of the Poor Law between the Poplar Guardians and the Local Government Board.

FORMATIVE AND EARLY YEARS

Will Crooks was born into poverty in a little one-roomed house on 6 April 1852, at 2 Shirbutt Street, Poplar, not far from Gough Street, where he lived most of his adult life, until his death in 1921. He was the third of seven children, the son of George and Charlotte Crooks. His early years were dominated by want and sorrow. To make things worse when Crooks was three years old, his father, who was a ship's stoker, lost his arm in a steamship accident. This accident forced his father to give up work, and this mishap, according to Crooks, was when the family's privations began. 'We were so poor', he said, 'that we children never got a drop of tea for months together. It used to be bread and treacle for breakfast, dinner and tea, washed down with a glass of water.'[11] With his father unable to work, it fell to Crooks' mother to strive to keep seven children as well as their father. In order to clothe and feed the family Charlotte Crooks suffered the ignominy of being at the mercy of the sweating trade for a long time, at least six years. Crooks recalled: ' "I can picture her now as I used to see her when I awoke in the night making oil-skin coats by candle-light in our single room,' and he vowed: "Wait till I'm a man! Won't I work for my mother when I'm a man!" '[12]

Crooks' mother broke down under the terrible strain, and since there was no other means of keeping them, she turned to poor relief. The family was summoned before the Board of Guardians, and five of the children were taken from home, young Will included, and put into the Poplar workhouse together with their disabled father. Crooks remembers the fateful day when: 'I went with my mother to a board of Poor Law guardians, holding on to her skirt, and heard a homily read by the Chairman ... [who] pointed at me, a giant figure of eight years old, and said, "It is time that boy was getting his own living." I was terrified ... I hate that board of guardians to this very day.'[13] His mother remained outside the workhouse with the eldest and youngest of the children. Three weeks after entering the workhouse Crooks was sent with his younger brother to the Poor Law School at Sutton. Years later he recalled, 'every day spent in that school is burnt into my soul.' In addition he said, 'I may truly say that I commenced my acquaintance with the outside world by entering the workhouse door!'[14]

Crooks returned to Poplar after leaving the confines of the school at Sutton. While he was away the family had moved into a small house in Crawford Yard, off Poplar High Street, next door to the entrance of the casual ward, with the main workhouse building at the back. This was to be Crooks' home for the rest of his boyhood. It was here that he witnessed a bread riot in 1866. Sights such as this made an early impression on him, together with his experiences in the workhouse and the workhouse school at Sutton. This was, perhaps unwittingly, Crooks' start in the study of the old Poor Law system. It was during these early years Crooks made a vow that someday he would champion the lot of the inmates, especially the children. He was later to say: 'So you may be sure I have always had in my heart a very warm corner for the workhouse child; and I hope I have never failed in doing all I possibly could to ameliorate his lot.'[15] Just thirty years later Crooks became Chairman of the Poplar Board of Guardians, the very board that had given him and his brothers and sisters shelter at the youthful stage and dark times of their lives.

Will Crooks' work in regard to the Poor Law was perhaps the most important phase in his life. He was different from other poor law reformers in that he spoke from experience. He had seen the system from the inside. His bitter encounter with the Poor Law in early childhood had filled him with the resolve to bring about its change; especially in the way it treated children. Crooks spoke out about how Victorian 'Bumbledom' associated children with family misfortune. Why should little children be asked to carry the domestic burden? They should not go in front of the guardians, he argued. 'All his Poor Law work [was] guided by the desire to prevent the breaking up of homes ... which flow directly from his personality ... and from his own home life.'[16] In addition, whenever Crooks broached the subject of unemployment, he championed the sanctity of the home, pointing out that the burden falls heaviest upon the wife. Crooks succeeded as a social reformer because he spoke in a language with which the working-class could identify. They knew his antecedents, and trusted him. This empathy with the working-class was the main reason why Crooks was elected on numerous occasions at both local and national level to represent them.

Even before he left school Will had gone to work to assist in supporting the home. After school, a local milkman employed him, giving him sixpence a week. Then he got 'promotion' into the grocery business (after school hours again), and there he received two shillings a week and some food. He had not yet realised his great aim of having done with school by acquiring regular all-day employment. This came in due course, before he was eleven years old, when he left the George Green (Elementary) School in East India Dock Road. He began working twelve hours a day in a blacksmith's shop in Limehouse Causeway for five shillings a week. Will said of the job: 'Although I stopped with him two years — in a smithy certainly not "under a spreading chestnut tree!" — I cannot truthfully affirm that I ever really settled down to the job as a be-all and end-all.'[17]

When Crooks was fourteen years of age, his mother took him away from working for the smithy 'when she found out he was not to be taught the business but to be merely a smiths' labourer, and she apprenticed him to the trade of a cooper'. This meant a reduction in wages. He would receive two shillings and six pence a week, instead of the six shillings he was earning with the smithy. Crooks' mother sacrificed the difference in wages in his best interests, because, as Haw points out: 'She was as determined that her boys should learn a trade as they should learn to read and write. "The sacrifice of a few shillings a week," says Crooks, "which mother made in order that I should learn a trade was only one of many things she did for me as a boy ... I really don't know how she managed to feed us all, after losing my three-and-six a week." '[18] Given the sacrifices that she made, it is necessary to recognise that Crooks' mother was a leading motivation in his life, and one of the reasons why he became a social reformer. It was the sense of unfairness aroused in him as a boy, when he witnessed the heartbreaking struggle with poverty that his mother had to endure. It was to characterise Crooks' abiding hatred of the old Poor Law system.

It was not long before he joined the coopers' union. It was during Crooks' apprenticeship that he was introduced to 'social and political matters' by a friendly workman, who encouraged him to read by lending him books and papers, and inspiring him with an enthusiasm for the teaching of John Bright. This period in the life of Will Crooks was significant. It shaped his future world outlook. His three-year apprenticeship marked the beginning of his political education in the fundamentals of radical liberalism and social reform. Even at home, Crooks was nicknamed 'Young John Bright':

> An uncle, looking in on the eve of the General Election of 1868, said jokingly, "Now young John Bright, tell us all about what is going to happen." Nothing loath, Will delivered a long speech on the political

situation, and foretold, among other things, that the Liberals would sweep the country, and one of their first acts would be to disestablish the Church of Ireland. The prophecy, needless to say, was fulfilled.[19]

Crooks after serving his apprenticeship became a master cooper, and for a couple of years he was employed as a journeyman.

On 10 December 1871, Crooks at the age of nineteen married Matilda South at St. Thomas's Church, Bethnal Green. His wife was the daughter of Thomas South, an East London shipwright. They had ten children 1871-91, but four of them died. Crooks said, 'the wife and myself had very dark hours sometimes, especially in the early years of our married lives.' [20] The first years of married life on a full journeyman's wage were reasonably comfortable, but Crooks' principled stand as a trade unionist led to his dismissal. He refused to use inferior timber on a job. In addition, he rebelled against certain conditions of work and objected to excessive overtime. Crooks' trade union activities earned him a reputation as a troublemaker, and after his dismissal, he was unable to find work in London: 'Every shop and yard in London was closed to him. Word had gone round that he was an agitator.' [21] Crooks 'got work at the docks and could of easily have become a 'ticket man'; but he was so sickened by the sight of men fighting for a job that he decided he must get back to his own trade.'[22] Finally, in 1876, he tramped to Liverpool to seek regular work. To his dismay, he could not find any, and thus began what was a depressing experience, which involved tramping about until there were no shoes on his feet or money in his pockets and nowhere to get lodgings.

Eventually he secured a job and sent for his wife and youngest child. 'But the little one pined and died within a month ... the couple left Liverpool on the night of the funeral', and returned to London.[23] Crooks recalled: 'It was the most miserable railway journey of his life.'[24] Unable to find work in London, he tramped to Liverpool a second time, and secured work in his own trade. Soon afterward, he found permanent employment in Poplar. Crooks, who was unemployed for several years, said of his experience:

> It is enough for you to know that I have gone through as bad a time as any man can have whilst thinking of the ones at home wanting help at a time when he cannot help himself ... Liverpool proving such 'a frost', I came back to Poplar, and got regular work at last. I had now seen much of the world; I knew the difficulties and heartbreaks for the poor man; so I began to take a deep and absorbing interest in movements calculated or intended to improve the conditions of labour for him, to make him a better citizen, to raise the poor and needy to more comfort and congenial environment.[25]

This period of unemployment and impoverishment together with his childhood experience in the workhouse were indelible episodes in his life, and helped nurture his future radicalism. Later, he founded Crooks 'College'; a series of Sunday morning meetings outside East India Dock Gates where he drove home to his working-class audience the lessons on the poverty of life, unemployment and low pay. The electors of Poplar saw in him someone who would stand fast and represent them, and they rewarded him. He fondly says:

> I have belonged to Poplar all my life — so far as residence goes ... I belong to Poplar still, and I expect I shall belong to Poplar till I die. I fancy I have stood for and represented Poplar in just about every available capacity open to the ordinary citizen, seeing that I have done duty on its Board of Guardians, on the Borough Council, served as its Mayor, sat on the L.C.C ... the district I love so much and know so well.[26]

It is of significance not only to understand the ideological make up of the man, Will Crooks, but to appreciate that by his activity and example he helped create a Labour culture that was principally to concern itself with the task of eradicating impoverishment, improving Poplar's environment, and the electorates' expectations of its representatives. He was largely responsible for placing the issues of poverty, destitution, and unemployment high on the political agenda of the new unions. According to Tom Mann and Ben Tillett:

> ... poverty in our opinion, can be abolished, and we consider it is the work of the trade unions to do this ... the real difference between the "new" and the "old" is that those who belong to the latter, and delight in being distinct from the policy endorsed by the "new," do so because they do not recognise, as we do, that it is the work of trade unionists to stamp out poverty from the land.[27]

This concern with poverty served to give Crooks the justification to agitate for trade union action for the abolition of long hours, sweating, all forms of overwork, conditions of privation, and its corollary unemployment. These in essence were the convictions that underpinned the New Unionism, and Crooks immersed himself in this struggle. He became one of the half-dozen Labour leaders who led the Dock Labourers' Strike in 1889.

POPLAR RADICALISM AND CROOKS 'COLLEGE'

Before discussing Crooks 'College', it is important to understand the political developments both nationally and locally that brought about its establishment, and their relevance to the origins of the Poplar radical and progressive movement, towards which the 'College' played a determining and significant role by helping to radicalise Poplar's electorate 1887-93. The split in the Liberal party over the Irish question, together with the Liberals' subsequent defeat in the General Election of 1886, had a significant impact upon the development of radicalism in Poplar.[28] This schism in the Liberal party created confusion in Poplar among Liberal supporters. Evidence shows that abstention from voting in the general election by dissentient Liberals reduced the majority in favour of Sydney Buxton, the Liberal candidate, quite considerably, and the majority of Liberals, who did vote, voted Conservative. In 1885, Green secured over 65 per cent of the vote, and in 1886, Buxton managed only 50.7 per cent; the Conservatives increased their vote by 15 per cent. [29] London returned sixty-two members. Of these, eleven were Liberal, and only two were returned in the East End, in Poplar and Whitechapel, where seven seats were contested.[30] These events brought about a significant change in the political milieu of Poplar. A radical culture emerged that ultimately resulted in the development of a campaign for independent Labour representation, led by Will Crooks.

During the years of opposition 1886-92, the Radicals, including Crooks, struggled inside the Liberal Party trying to bring it over to their point of view. The problem was that Ireland blocked the way. Nationally, William Gladstone, in his old age, was almost fully engrossed with the question of Home Rule.[31] He believed it would be difficult for other questions to gain proper attention until the Irish question was resolved, and liberties restored to the Irish people. Thus, it was because of the Liberal party's intransigence on the Irish question that the London Radical Clubs detached themselves from this programme, and allied themselves with the socialists, who insisted upon and pledged a great deal more. This impasse over Irish affairs was problematic for the radical movement, because what the working-class and casual poor really wanted was relief from unemployment and social degradation.

The cyclical trade depression of 1884-7, and the severe weather in the winter 1886-7, led to serious unemployment riots in Central London on 9 February and 'Bloody Sunday' on 13 November 1887. These events helped to promote middle-class alarm, and influenced the belief in the necessity of working-class involvement in poor law relief, and the need to enlist the co-operation of the working classes themselves. The new Liberal approach was outlined by Arnold Toynbee, when he stated: ' "I would say, abolish outdoor relief under the poor law, because outdoor relief lowers wages, degrades the recipient and diminishes self reliance. I would have this done with workmen themselves sitting as poor law guardians." ' [32] This new Liberal development of Poor Law administration was one reason why a progressive Radical agenda was implemented in Poplar from 1888. The other was because of the limit of Liberal tradition, a pre-occupation with the Irish question. It was because of this inclusive agenda that the old Liberal/trade union alliance came under pressure from the ideological challenge of socialism from Marxism and Fabian socialism, and their attempts to build broader labour organisations based on independent labour representation.[33] The Socialist Democratic Federation

(SDF) and the Fabian Society took advantage of Liberal concentration on the Home Rule issue, which had left the way open for them to develop the support of the local working-class.[34]

The Poplar Liberal Radical Association (PLRA) response was to organise a programme of education that would unite the trade union and labour movement in support of progressive, political, and social reforms. This was to prove an inadequate response to appease the left Radical group in the Association. The group became disillusioned and concerned that the PLRA was still not addressing the distressing conditions of the working-class or working-class representation, and joined the socialists. This left a Moderate rump in the Radical Association who resisted the socialist challenge and independent Labour representation.

To understand the unity of purpose around the need for political and social reform in Poplar in this period it is necessary to be aware of the multi-faceted network of socio-political relationships that existed between the trade unions, the labour movement, and the progressive clergy. The progressive clergy in both Poplar and Woolwich played its part in the development of independent labour. They supported trade unions and councillors in their campaigns for housing, work for the unemployed and for old age pensions, and acknowledged rather than led local political feeling. Paul Thompson endorses this view. It was the clerical support in Poplar and Woolwich which 'help to explain why these were the first areas in London to maintain successful independent Labour Parties.'[35]

The progressive clergy in Poplar demonstrated their political support for reforms that would benefit their parishioners by sending numerous delegates to the PLRA Council. Seven clergymen were honorary officers of the Radical Party.[36] The clergy who served this area and those who were active in the labour movement felt that they could not withhold support from their parishioners in their struggle against abject poverty. The Rev. James Adderley, a local clergyman, speaking of the casual labourers and their predicament, said it was impossible to preach the gospel to empty stomachs, 'the message of Christ was only half given if it did not touch the social problem.' For the progressive clergy the social problems of the area could only be addressed by radical reform; they saw the Radicals as upholding Christian and moral values. Adderley was a Christian Socialist who had committed himself to the political socialists,[37] and was a friend of Ben Tillett and Will Crooks.

Crooks epitomised the radical position put forward by the progressive clergymen. He believed that it was the duty of workingmen to improve themselves, and this could only be done by 'a solemn mission to prove that we are all sons of God, and brethren to Him. You can only prove this by improving yourselves, and fulfilling your duty.'[38] It was Crooks' Nonconformist beliefs together with his Mazzinian radicalism that underpinned his ethical and political outlook. It was this message of duty and mission that formed the basis of his lectures to those workingmen who attended Crooks 'College'.

Two events in midsummer 1888 were to influence the future left Radical agenda, and determine their political priorities. In July, the movement for New Unionism began when the match girls at the Bryant and May match factory at Bow went on strike. This dispute was significant in that it influenced and set in motion a series of events that was to emerge and transform the relationship between trade unions and the employer. It is important to recognise that the Matchgirls' Strike also set an example to the men of what can be achieved by strong organisation. Following this, in August, the Local Government (County Council) Act of 1888 was passed, which meant that the proposed London County Council (LCC) could levy local rates, and poor relief would be transferred to the LCC, who would be elected by ratepayers. This legislation empowered workers to influence the progressive working-class voter. The County Council would also be responsible for the maintenance of roads, bridges, and lunatic asylums.[39]

The Local Government Act and the Matchgirls' Strike were milestone events in Poplar, and for the broader trade union and labour movement in London. In Poplar, they were central to a fundamental change in its political culture. Poplar became the hub of the New Unionism where Sundays and weekday evenings were entirely devoted to the purpose of spreading these principles. In this, Crooks 'College' made an important contribution towards the new union creed, and to 'home rule all round', which was part of the Progressive agenda for the implementation of local government.[40] The *Morning Leader* said Poplar's municipal life began with Crooks 'College':

> The birth of Poplar's new municipal life took place round the East India Dock gates one Sunday morning, when, from a stand backed by trade union banners, a short, but wide-beamed man, like a skipper, with a black beard and truculent eyebrows, and a voice cyclonic with denunciations, which alternately awoke dead enthusiasms, shook men with laughter, or made them very quiet with a story of brave endurance in a mean street ...[41]

'The area in front of the gate had become a Speakers' Corner of the East End, long used as a rallying point and place of public oratory by trade unionists and politicians.' [42]

Since there are no extant records dating the beginning of the 'College', it can be assumed that it was established in August/September 1888 to respond to the needs of campaigning on a progressive municipal programme, a manifesto that would return Progressive candidates to the LCC in January 1889. At the same time, it enabled the left Radical group, within the PLRA, to reassert their claim of support for social reform, and thus form an alliance with the socialists.

What was significant about Crooks 'College' was that it created a political movement that was distinct and different in its campaigning strategy and tactics. It disseminated useful knowledge, on citizenship, on trade union organisation and other information connected with the workplace. Issues of the day and politics in general were discussed and acted upon. It became the focus for independent labour representation and led to a strong Labour offensive from 1891 with the emergence of the Poplar Labour Election Committee, which succeeded in getting Crooks, and Kaye elected as Guardians in 1893.[43] The 'College' agitated for the commencement of the construction of the Blackwall Tunnel and started the campaign for the footway tunnel under the Thames between the Isle of Dogs and Greenwich. It began the Poplar Free Library movement, and the demand for a Poplar Technical Institute and recreation ground. The policy to reform Poor Law administration, caring treatment for workhouse inmates, especially children, and the idea of a farm colony system in England, originated outside the East India Dock Gate.[44]

The priority for the PLRA in this period was to decide their manifesto and candidates to represent Poplar in the forthcoming LCC elections. At a meeting of the Radical Council during October 1888 a policy platform for the LCC elections was agreed, which included local government for the people of London, and a progressive policy in all matters of interest and importance to them. This included free education, the equalization of the poor rate, control of gas and water, reform of Poor Law administration, control of open spaces, and to secure the early completion of the Blackwall Tunnel;[45] reforms that were addressed by Will Crooks in his future capacities as Guardian, London County Councillor and Member of Parliament.

As the electorate was limited to ratepayers (householders with a one-year residential qualification and lodgers who occupied lodgings worth £10 a year, subject to one-year residential qualification), the Radicals needed to campaign and broaden their influence upon the voter, thus promoting their candidates. To this end, Crooks 'College' took the campaign to the workers. By teaching them the advantages of municipal reform, and the need to eradicate poverty and social deprivation, they would become involved in the debate in the trade unions, the workplace, and with their peers. The 'College' also gave lessons on public speaking to workingmen and women, and provided the platform for their first experience. In other words, the 'College' educated and empowered workers to influence the progressive working-class voter. It instilled in its supporters a self-assertive mission.

Two members of the PLRA Council, John McDougall, a flour mill manager, and the Hon. Richard Grosvenor, the eldest son of Lord Grosvenor (later 1st Duke of Westminster), were unanimously selected to stand as Poplar's Progressive candidates in the forthcoming elections in January 1889.[46] The Poplar LCC elections were not a great success for the Radical Party. William Bullivant, Conservative and Unionist candidate, a wire rope manufacturer, topped the poll with over one-third of the vote. The result was Bullivant, 2,925; McDougall, 2345; Lananton, 1363 votes.[47] John Lananton, who was a member of both the PLRA Council and the old Metropolitan Board, split the Progressive vote by refusing to give way to the PLRA nominees. The *East End News* reported that 'the consequence was that the Hon. Richard Grosvenor was left behind.' [48] Grosvenor was subsequently elected an Alderman of the LCC. That two-thirds of the electorate had voted for Liberal and Independent Liberal candidates suggests that the lectures at Crooks 'College' and the left Radical groups' educational strategy was a success.

FROM RADICAL TO FABIAN

New Unionism, the founding of the Gasworkers' Union, and their struggle for the eight-hour day, and the Dock Strike of 1889, have been fully chronicled by a number of historians.[49] While Will Crooks' contributions and involvement in these movements have been largely neglected, if not ignored by modern historians. Therefore, it seems appropriate to discuss Crooks' importance as a Radical Liberal, his pivotal position as a leading Fabian working-class pioneer, and his involvement in this movement, together with his contribution to New Unionism within the broader labour agitation in Poplar.

On Sunday 18 August 1889, the meeting of Crooks 'College' took on an added significance. At the dock entrance, there were a number of speakers including Will Crooks. After the meeting those men who had come to listen marched from East India Dock to the Victoria Dock gates and then continued to march in procession to the St. Katherine and London Docks. They invited the Labour Protection League and the United Stevedores' Protection League to abstain from helping the London Dock Companies, whilst refusing to work off the shore with those dock labourers who went in against them.[50] The quality of the organisation enabled a historic victory to be won. The leaders of the strike were successful in breaking down sectional barriers between organisations representing skilled and unskilled workers, arranging picket duties, keeping public opinion informed and sustaining the morale of strikers by organising marches and rallies daily.[51] The discipline of the men earned the understanding and respect of all sections of the community. Will Crooks' biggest contribution in all this was the political education of thousands of men who had learnt at Crooks 'College' that their behaviour, sense of discipline, and responsibility could lead to a new era.

Although Crooks worked hard doing a twelve-hour shift, from six in the morning until six at night, he used to go down to the docks to speak to the men after work to help as much as he could to urge them on in their dispute. Often he would not reach home until midnight or after. It was more common that after addressing the strike's outdoor meetings he would spend until dawn at the organising office even though he had to be off to work again at six in the morning. Crooks' commitment was such, speaking in all weathers and seldom taking his clothes off, that after the Strike, he was hospitalised with rheumatic fever, which nearly brought him to his grave. He was in the London Hospital, Whitechapel Road, for over three months. [52] Crooks' work was held in such high regard by his employer, the brewer Carrington, that during all the time 'not only did his employers pay him his full wages, but they never allowed a single week to pass without one, at least, of them coming to see him personally in hospital.'[53] The imbursement of sick pay is possibly the first time in the history of industrial relations that such an arrangement occurred. Most historians of the 1889 Dock Strike have sadly neglected Will Crooks' contribution to this historic triumph.

In September 1890, the employers at the docks stood firm against what they saw as the 'corporate tyranny' of New Unionism. They formed the Shipping Federation 'for the purpose of maintaining liberty of contract and resisting the new union methods of coercion, more especially the tactics adopted by the National Amalgamated Sailors and Firemen's Union ... who assisted the new union[s] by threatening to strike against the employment of non-union officers.'[54] The employers' first counter-attack 1891-3 was crucial on the waterfront.[55] It created serious setbacks for new unionism, such as a reduction in membership. Thus, the offensive launched by the employers halted the forward march of the new unions. It is argued by John Saville that the whole period throughout the decade of the 1890s and well into the new century was an age 'of a developing counter-attack by the propertied classes against the organisations of working people'.[56] It was mainly the old societies that benefited most from the membership explosion, sustaining and increasing their membership after the economic boom crumbled at the end of 1891.[57]

The counter-attack, along with Liberal obstinacy, helps to explain the beginning of the agitation for independent Labour representation. The trade unions and the Fabians campaigned together to combat the hostility of the employers and the Liberal party, and their message to the working-class was that there was no difference between them. They both served the interests of monopoly and privilege. This solidarity between the local trade unions and the Poplar Fabians formed the background against which Crooks 'College' successfully organised the campaign for labour representation. The 'College' advocated: 'Trade Unionism as a principle applicable to every department of labour.'[58] Thus, the 'College' played an important part in bringing both the industrial and political societies together in a concerted effort to expose the belligerent and inflexible attitude of the forces of opposition. Given this, in all probability, Crooks 'College' would have advocated that the LCC, as part of its municipal reforms, ought to take over the Port of London, which as Gillespie points out was a 'long political controversy ... following the Dock strike of 1889.'[59]

During 1891, Colne Valley and Poplar were going through a similar process of political change, albeit different in character. It is argued, by David Clark, that Colne Valley Labour Union's (CVLU) break with the Liberal party 'drew its personnel and ideas, from advanced Liberalism'. Such was the case among the Poplar trade union and labour movement. He further argues that the CVLU 'was encouraged by the antipathy of the local Liberal Association towards the demand for separate Labour representation.' At this time, the Liberals, nationally, were trying to undermine the Radicals' argument for independent representation because it would weaken their hold on working-class support.

The PLRA was against independent Labour representation, mindful that a split in the working-class vote had cost them a seat in the LCC elections of 1889, and they wanted to remedy this in the forthcoming elections in 1892. In spite of Liberal enmity, the advanced Liberals and their supporters in the CVLU and the Poplar trade union and socialist alliance, continued to put forward the aim that the 'prime objective ... was to establish a movement to procure the election of representatives of the working-class movement.'[60] Although ideologically the CVLU held similar views to those of the Poplar movement on Labour representation, organisationally and environmentally it was very different, as Bill Lancaster points out in his study of radicalism and socialism in Leicester. In the 'Colne Valley ... political activity [was] undertaken in unique circumstances. The valley had an unusually low level of trade unionism for an area noted for its lack of religious participation, and, more important, was physically made up of small towns and villages with no focal centre.' By comparison, Poplar's political setting was more akin to that of Leicester, where 'the debate on socialist strategy ... was carried out against a backcloth of large, popular trade union organisations.'[61]

Crooks played a significant and important part in the development of the College's strategy and tactics. He brought to it a political outlook that was different in purpose and character, a position that was deeply rooted in the needs of Poplar's working-class. To serve those needs he felt, along with others, that they had to overcome the hegemony of the local Liberal party, which only voiced concern for the workers when it suited them; when they needed working-class support at the ballot box. What was different about Crooks is that he was able to draw on a broad base of working-class support. At the 'College', when he spoke of the needs of the working-class, he taught them how to organise and campaign to accomplish social reforms, which would be favourable to them. Ann Stafford points out, 'he taught sound practical stuff; if Will talked about a fair day's pay, he also talked about a fair day's work ... he saw everything in terms of practical problems which individual men and women really [had] to face', and he kept alive through the 'College' the hopes of 'hundreds of men and women, who might otherwise have foundered in despair.'[62] It was this rapport with the Poplar working-class that set Crooks apart from other local reformers, together with his leadership qualities in the political and industrial spheres, which enabled him to represent all sections of the progressive movement, including the clergy.

It was no accident that between January 1891, when Will Crooks joined the Fabian Society,[63] and March 1893, when he resigned from the Radical Party,[64] the Poplar trade union and labour movement had distanced itself politically and organisationally from the PLRA over working-class representation, claiming only working men understood and could serve Labour's interests. Crooks felt, as Adelman describes, that instead of Radicalism taking over the Liberal Party, the party was swallowing up Radicalism.[65] In Poplar, the left Radical group withdrew from the PLRA, led by Crooks, and helped set up the Labour Party. Thus began a phase of working-class militancy that was to culminate in Poplar having independent Labour representation, and the election of representative candidates of the Poplar Labor League. Crooks with other working-class Fabians, led this transition, and the 'College' at the Dock Gates became a focal point. Another significant factor, which underpinned the development and success of the 'College' in this period, and helped characterise Crooks' role in the Poplar movement, was his selection by the Philanthropic Coopers to the London Trades Council (LTC) in February 1891.[66]

If further backing of Crooks' approach to local politics was needed it was provided by the LTC. Earlier, in November 1890, the LTC had set up a lecture bureau and 'offered to send speakers free of charge to help in propaganda or in forming unions where organisation was unknown.'[67] This transformation in the Trades Council's approach to local politics enabled educational organisations such as the 'College' to promote progressive ideas that would benefit the working-class. It is worth noting that Ben Tillett, Fred Hammill, and Bill Steadman, who helped Crooks organise at the 'College', were also members of the LTC, and had been party to the debate on education, and thus helped to influence the LTC in its deliberations. Possibly because of this, the successful propaganda work of the 'College' inclined the Council to make the decision that it did. Tillett and Hammill were also responsible for the organisation of the lecture bureau.

Despite the success of the new trade unions, the geographical dissemination of both socialism and independent labour politics was patchy in London. Even after the Great Dock Strike of 1889, there was little working-class backing for a break with the Liberals.[68] In some of the outer, more industrialised suburbs, Woolwich, West Ham, Poplar, and Battersea, the growth of a more homogenous working-class did provide a footing for the advent of labour politics in the 1890s.[69] For example, 120,000 men worked in the metal and engineering industry centred on Woolwich and Poplar. In West Ham alone, the docks, railway workshops, and the engineering and chemical industries employed over 20,000 men, which exceeded that in many provincial industrial towns.[70]

John Shepherd argues that 'despite the challenge of independent labour and socialist politics ... the organised labour movement remained ... virtually unshakable in its connections with Gladstonian Liberalism and the Liberal Party.'[71] This may have been the case in the provinces, but in London, it was different. After a miserable showing at the polls in 1895, the Liberals decided in 1899 'to examine the special problems of the metropolis, where, despite a thriving Progressive policy on the LCC, the Liberal record had – for a decade – been abysmal.'[72] It is noteworthy that when the Liberal Party distanced itself from Gladstone Liberalism in the LCC elections in 1889 by campaigning on a Progressive/Radical platform they did much better.

THE FABIANS AND THE POPLAR LABOR LEAGUE

During January 1891, the Fabians introduced the 'People's Free Lectures' under the auspices of the Educational Committee of the Tower Hamlets Co-operative Society.[73] By facilitating the lectures, the Fabians hoped to educate the workingman as to why he should support the trade union and labour movement's involvement in political action. The recruitment of working-class support for the Labour cause in Poplar had become paramount for the Fabians. Working men in Poplar supported the Fabian Society because they had nowhere else to go, apart from the SDF, who believed revolution was the only way forward. The attraction of Fabianism for many reformers, according to Cole and Postgate, was that it managed to articulate a socialist ideology in terms that its current programme made a potent appeal to many who were not socialists.[74]

In March 1891, Fred Butler, a friend of Crooks, who helped organise the Dock Gate meetings, and Ben Tillett, joined the Fabians.[75] Tillett supported the Poplar Fabians by encouraging workingmen who attended the 'College' to join a trade union, and helped educate his fellow trade unionists by getting them to read Fabian literature. At the Dock Strike 'College' meeting on Sunday morning, 16 August, Will Crooks advocated the claims of representation of Labour in Parliament. At this meeting, the agitation was initiated to run Labour candidates in every constituency irrespective of Liberals and Tories - thus beginning the agenda of putting forward Labour candidates on independent platforms. Will Crooks and the Poplar working-class Fabians were the organisers, and led the movement for independent Labour representation in Poplar. Crooks 'College' became the focus of militant working-class Fabianism, which achieved a separate Labour identity, distancing it from the Poplar Liberals and Radicals. This was achieved by setting up the Poplar Labour Election Committee (PLEC).

At the annual meeting of the National Liberal Federation (NLF), on 2 October 1891, Gladstone outlined the Newcastle Programme.[76] Although Irish Home Rule was the first priority, it included one-man one vote, tax reform, free trade in land, and the rights of labour. The labour measures and those pertaining to social reform were not seen as concessions (by the Left Radicals) that served the interests of the industrial working-class, but as a statement of intent, in the run-up to the general election of 1892. It was a platform designed to influence the working-class voter. The NLF, who in the past had influenced Radicalism in the Liberal Party was now patronised by the party leadership, and had become assimilated into the Gladstonian Party.[77] This development emphasises why Crooks defected to the socialists, because the Liberal Party was absorbing Radicalism.

Perhaps it was coincidence, or it may have been a response to the Newcastle Programme that the London Fabian Group met ten days later to discuss reorganisation. The origins of the Poplar Labour Party began at this meeting, when the London Fabian Group split into two distinct groups. One comprised of Hackney and Essex, the other Poplar and the East End.[78] According to Pelling, the latter group was made-up of predominantly working-class constituencies.[79] This change fundamentally transformed the future political make-up of Poplar. It did, as Tanner points out, when referring to British socialists, provide 'the opportunity of merging an indigenous popular radical tradition (which formed their own initial background) with newer socialist ideas, giving them an altered form and substance.'[80]

Will Crooks took the chair at the first meeting of the (new) Poplar Group of the Fabian Society, which met on 9 November at the Co-operative Rooms, Poplar. Hubert Bland, treasurer of the Fabian Society, was invited to speak on 'Socialism'.[81] It was no coincidence that Bland was invited. He was anti-Liberal, and a left-wing Fabian, who expressed distinct dissatisfaction with permeating the Liberal Party with socialism. Bland believed in independent labour action, and in the formation of an independent Socialist political party. He argued:

> This permeation of the Radical left, undoubted fact though it is of present day politics ... there are two possible and tenable views as to its final outcome. One is that it will end in the slow absorption of the Socialist in the Liberal Party.... Accordingly ... there will come a time, and that shortly, when the avowed Socialists and the much socialized Radicals will be strong enough to hold the balance in many constituencies, and sufficiently powerful in all to drive the advanced candidates ... further than his own inclination would take him. Then, either by abstention or by actual support of the reactionary champion at elections, they will be able to threaten the Liberals with certain defeat. The Liberals ... will thus be forced to make concessions and to offer compromises; and will either adopt a certain minimum number of Socialistic proposals, or allow to Socialists a share in the representation itself.[82]

This was a view similar to that held by Crooks and the PLEC.

The Poplar Fabians had gained control of the open-air meetings at Crooks 'College' during 1891, thus reducing the political influence of the PLRA by poaching their platform, and promoting vigorously independent Labour representation around the theme of 'The Rights of Labour'. This episode undermined the Radical agenda, and created latent tensions between Labour and the Radicals. The rancour between them finally emerged over working-class representation. What rankled with the PLRA was that they felt betrayed by Crooks, a member of the Council since 1887, because he was obviously responsible for the College's change of political allegiance. They never forgave him, and frustrated his every move to seek political office locally. Thus began the fundamental break with the PLRA. Divisions about working-class representation began with the LCC election in 1892, and culminated in a split in 1893, over the Guardian elections.

In early December, Edward Pease on behalf of the Fabian Executive expressed his concerns to Will Crooks about the credentials of Jack Helps, who was the chairman of the Sunday morning meetings. Crooks replied; 'Have known J. M. Helps for years he is a straight man has helped us a great deal at the Dock Gates he is Branch Sec of the Dockers Union and worth knowing.'[83] Since Helps was not a Fabian, Pease wanted an assurance that he was the right man for the job, and that Helps would not compromise Fabian issues. These letters represent how important to the middle-class Fabians the 'College' was. The 'College' enabled the Fabian programme, providing a platform for working-class empowerment, and an opportunity to recruit in an industrial area.

On 28 December, the Poplar Fabian Group convened an organisational meeting in the Co-operative Rooms to set up the Poplar Labour Election Committee. The evidence shows that the setting up of this committee by trade union and labour activists supported the view that the time had arrived when labour should be more directly represented on the London County Council, and that a 'permanent organisation with power to add to their number' be set up that distinctly represented working men. Nominations were invited from every Trade Union in the district, 'after which a meeting would be held ... to make the final decision.' The meeting nominated Will Crooks and Tom McCarthy of the Dockers' Union to go forward as Labour nominees for Poplar, at the next County Council elections. Alf Graham (secretary of the Poplar Fabian Group) was elected secretary. The meeting adjourned until 5 January when the Poplar Labour Election Committee was formally constituted. [84]

Its first executive committee comprised of Alf Graham, secretary, Rev. H. A. Kennedy, treasurer, and local representatives of the London Trades Council; the Engine Drivers' and Firemen's Union, the Waterman's Society, the Dockers' Union, the Philanthropic Coopers' Society, the East London Plumbers' Union, the Federated Trades and Labour Unions and the

Gasworkers' Union. In addition, a number of trade associations subscribed to the Wages Fund through their branches,[85] and the London Trades Council Labour Representative League 'expressed willingness to co-operate with the committee.' [86] Will Crooks moved a motion that further endorsed the decision made by the Committee at the previous (December) meeting:

> That every trade in the district of Poplar be invited to nominate a candidate to stand for the next County Council election, and to submit such nominations to a special delegate meeting for final selection, and that the selected candidate, if elected to the County Council; be paid a fair remuneration for his services.[87]

This meeting was held at Poplar Town Hall on 25 January 1892, at which Will Crooks was 'selected at a thoroughly representative meeting of Trade Unionists of Poplar, to which eighty-seven branches in the immediate neighbourhood had been invited to send delegates.'[88] The vote in favour of adopting Crooks was unanimous.

A wage fund for Crooks was discussed at a meeting of the Millwall branch of the Dockers' Union on 1 February. The meeting considered how were they going to get the money to pay Will Crooks to represent Labour on the LCC. It was proposed and accepted that what was required was 3,000 men to pay the small sum of one penny per week, which would realise the needed amount of £150 per annum.[89] The problem for workingmen in this period was that Council meetings were held during working hours. This meant that men would attend in peril of losing their job, hence the necessity of a wage fund for the representatives of Labour.

It is of particular significance that the 'old' unions representing engineers, boilermakers, stevedores, railwaymen and ironfounders also contributed to the fund. They belonged to a long-standing tradition of popular radicalism, argues Reid in his article on Old Unionism. He concludes that the old unions used this tradition as a progressive basis for the repudiation of state socialism.[90] This was not the case in Poplar where craft unions alongside new unions through the trade union, Labour, and progressive movement committed themselves to collectivist action, based on a programme of achieving parliamentary representation by gradual intervention and state socialism. Other evidence that negates Reid's view is that put forward by Sidney Webb, who said, when referring to the 1892 LCC election and the trade unions:

> ... for the first time in the history of democratic institutions in this country the great trade unions took an organised part in an ordinary political election, not only on behalf of their own members, but also of those Progressive candidates who were running a Socialist Programme.[91]

Further, he said, 'the programme of the progressives bore a suspicious resemblance to a certain Fabian tract on the Government of London.'[92] London voted eighty-four to thirty-four in favour of the Progressives.[93]

During the period January/February 1892, there was concern in the PLRA whether Crooks was the most suitable workingman that they should send to the LCC. The Radicals were considering a possible compromise with the Unionists, to allow Bullivant and McDougall to run together for the Council unopposed. A 'handful of Labour men protested against Poplar being disfranchised on the Council, and forced the [PLRA] ... to agree to support a Labour Candidate.' These Labour men, including Crooks, were members of the Radical Council, and were the 'connecting link' between the Radicals and a much larger force supporting independent Labour representation organised by the Election Committee. It was agreed that Will Crooks, and John McDougall, stand on a joint Progressive and Labour platform for the forthcoming LCC election. The Will Crooks LCC Wage Fund was probably crucial to this decision, because on receiving a statement from Alf Graham that Crooks' 'salary was for the greater part guaranteed, opposition to his candidature practically ceased.'[94]

In addition, the PLRA could not ignore the Labour Party's protestations, given that Lord Salisbury's Conservative and Unionist Government had almost fulfilled all their legislative commitments during a six-year parliament, and a general election was imminent. The support of Labour was critical if Sydney Buxton's slender majority was to be defended, if not increased. The PLEC met with the London Trades Council Labour Representative League on 2 February: 'After a long discussion, it was resolved that a branch of the League be formed to co-operate with the ... Committee in returning Mr. Crooks to the County Council.'[95]

'The Fabians were not inspirers of the Labour Party', writes Hobsbawm, 'they kept aloof from the labour movement ... opposed the formation of an independent party of labour', and therefore had no place in the British political tradition.[96] The evidence throughout this study contradicts this view. Hobsbawm in this case allows tendentious generalisations, when describing the Fabians, to replace rigorous analysis of their contribution towards the creation of the Labour Party. This elitist 'democratic' centrist approach, with its emphasis on the Fabian leadership conveniently ignores 'To Your Tents, O Israel', published in November 1893, by G. B. Shaw and Sidney Webb: 'It announced their disillusion with the Liberals ... and proclaims the need for a Labour Party rooted in trade unions.'[97]

Mark Bevir, in his article on Fabian Permeation argues, 'the triumph of the revisionists ... Hobsbawn and McBrier ... dismiss the Fabians as vehemently as Shaw once extolled their virtues.... On the revisionist view, the Fabians stand condemned as elitist and irrelevant: elitist because they ignored the grass-roots of working-class politics in favour of the high politics of the day.'[98]

Given this, therefore, Hobsbawm's statement obscures the fact that it was the rank and file members of the Fabian Society, active trade unionists such as Will Crooks, Fred Butler, Ben Tillett, Bob Banner and Fred Hammill, who pioneered independent Labour representation, and helped the Poplar and Woolwich Labour Parties to emerge. It is important to remember that during this period political affiliations were fluid. Robert Banner and Hammill, for example, while still members of the Fabian Society, helped establish the Woolwich ILP in 1894, and took the organisational skills that they had learnt in the Poplar Fabian agitation with them. This link between the Poplar Fabians and the Woolwich trade union and labour movement is significant.

On 29 March 1892, the second annual meeting of the East London Fabian Group of the Fabian Society was held at the Poplar Town Hall. Sidney Webb presided.[99] It was at this meeting that Webb explained the attitude of other organisations towards the Society, on the question of class, and responding to the annual report said:

> It was sometimes supposed that the Fabian Society was purely a middle-class organisation, working for middle-class purposes; but he thought that the character of that demonstration showed that was not the case. It was also demonstrated that the methods and objects of the Fabian Society appealed not only to the middle classes, but to mechanics, artisans, and labourers, and that the Society could take root in purely industrial districts better than some bodies which claimed to be the sole representatives of social democracy. [100]

Will Crooks, speaking in the debate, said of the working people of Poplar: 'They very well knew in Poplar that the Fabian Society was a respectable body of Socialists. The programme was the people's programme, and they asked the men in a position to carry out to do so, or else they would go.'[101]

Besides Sidney Webb, there were other members of the Fabian middle-class literati (Executive) present, namely Graham Wallace, Edward Pease, and George Bernard Shaw. Evidence shows that there were workingmen present from both the craft and new unions, including Bill Steadman of the Bargebuilders' Union; Bob Banner of Woolwich and the London Compositors' Society; Harry Orbell of the Dockers' Union; Harry Brown of the Gas Workers' Union; and Will Crooks of the Coopers' Union.[102] This is contrary to the claims of Adelman, who believes the Fabians were anti-union through arrogance and an obsession with political 'permeation'.[103] The evidence that negates this premise is provided by the Fabian Tract *How Trade Unions Benefit Workmen,* 'Every workman and workwoman in the country ought to Join a Trade Union.' [104] The statements by both Hobsbawn and Adelman show that they failed to understand the underlying contradictory nature of Fabian politics, particularly the difference between those members of the rank-

and-file, such as Crooks, who supported independent Labour representation, and a leadership who were divided over the issues of independence, and the permeation of the Liberal party.

THE RADICAL SPLIT

In May 1892, a benefit in support of the Wages Fund for Crooks was held at the Queen's Palace, Poplar. At this meeting Will Crooks, speaking of the eight-hour day, stated Labour's frustrations, '... if the Liberal and Radical Party shirked that important question, the Labour Party would not. If the men in the House of Commons could not frame an eight hours day Bill, let them clear out, and they would make one themselves.'[105] Crooks was voicing the sentiments held by his Labour colleagues, that the official Liberals were not bothered whether their candidates were Liberal or Radical as long as they were elected. He was of the opinion that the official Liberals were no more their friends than the Tories, and when the Liberals supported Fabian candidates, especially in LCC elections, they pretended that they were glad to see them get in. The only interest the Liberals had for the working-class was in their vote.

In January 1893 the Independent Labour Party (ILP) was established, but failed to make any impact in London according to David Howell. He states that the only branches left of any significance by 1898 were in St. Pancras, Fulham, and Woolwich.[106] For example, the ILP tried to organise in the East End but to no avail. At a crowded meeting in Limehouse on 13 March 1893, Keir Hardie urged the workingmen of Limehouse to form an Independent Labour Party. The meeting was disruptive, and interspersed with threats of violence. J. Steward Wallace, Liberal MP, represented the workingmen of Limehouse in Parliament. Hence, the workers not only saw the meeting as an attack upon him, but also were resentful of Labour interfering in their affairs. The meeting resolved itself into a faction row.[107]

The problem for the ILP in London was to make headway politically with a working-class who were wedded to the Liberal Party, and to compete organisationally for working-class support that was already committed to Fabian and SDF organisations. The Liberals managed in London to contain Labour within the broad framework of LCC Progressivism, 'a proposition admitted by the ILP with its shift towards compromise in the LCC elections of 1901.'[108] Even in Poplar where the tensions and rift between bourgeois Liberalism and working-class Radicalism were evident, the ILP failed to organise because Labour representation was already established.

During February 1893, the PLEC met on a number of occasions to nominate Labour candidates and draft an election manifesto for the forthcoming Guardian elections.[109] Finally, on 21 February, at the Co-operative Hall, Poplar, at a meeting of Trade, Labour, and Temperance Societies, Will Crooks and Harry Kaye of the Dockworkers' Union were selected along with five other delegates to represent the Poplar Labour Party.[110] The controversy surrounding working-class representation between Labour and the Radical Party culminated in a fundamental split during the selection of Poor Law Guardian candidates. The 'battleground' of accusation and counter-argument was bitter. It was the subject of recrimination and acrimony in the *East End News* for over two months. It began at a meeting to celebrate the anniversary of the Poplar Labour Party's success at the 1892 London County Council elections. A 'tremendous demonstration' was held at the Poplar Town Hall on 5 March 1893.[111] Will Crooks in his opening remarks as chairman said:

> ... although the workmen of Poplar respected their member, Mr. Sydney Buxton, they that night made a declaration of war against both the Liberal and Conservative Associations of the districts. The cause of labour was before any other question, and the Independent Labour Party was determined that as the power of the workers had made itself felt at the London County Council election, their whole force should be directed in sending to Parliament men who were pledged to the Labour Programme.[112]

The meeting pledged unanimously to secure the return of Labour candidates at the Guardian elections at the head of the poll.[113] Pete Curran rebuked the Liberals for their opposition of Labour candidates, and for putting forward the middle-class McDougall. He said, 'he did not regard Mr. McDougall as a Labour representative ... other constituencies in the West End ... would suit him better'.[114]

In a letter of 11 March 1893, to the *East End News*, Will Crooks publicly stated the Labour Party's position in relation to the Liberal and Radical Association. In doing so, he spelt out the reason for the dispute was that the Liberals refused to throw out the right to veto Labour nominees. The Labour Party as the representatives of working men considered they had a right to run Labour candidates whether it met with Liberal approval or not. In addition, given that the property qualification had been lowered to £5, 'not one of the chosen candidates of the Liberal Association comes within the category.'[115] In other words, Labour men were being ignored. Crooks continued, 'but we mean to have a share of workmen on all our Local Boards, whether the Liberal and Radical Association ... like it or not.'[116]

This public statement by Crooks gave notice to the electorate that the Labour Party was going to put forward its own candidates in the Guardian elections, and at the same time, it served as a challenge to any opposition from the PLRA. Crooks' strategy for success, from the outset of the campaign for independent representation, was based on both strong personal support and an immovable commitment by the Poplar trade union and labour movement to see Labour men returned to local government.

Clearly the PLEC felt that they had more chance of winning on a local platform, putting forward a programme of Poor Law reform independent of Liberal support, than they would have done on a municipal platform at the LCC elections. As far as the latter elections were concerned, it would have been political suicide to subject their supporters to defeat, and it could have meant the possible demise of Labour in Poplar. Therefore, it was felt a more prudent tactic, by Crooks and the PLEC, to measure their electoral support locally, and thus allow Labour to determine more easily the strengths and weaknesses of its support, and establish future strategies accordingly.

Crooks' public statement had the desired effect. It provoked the PLRA. Responding to the letter in the newspaper, Henry Ley, a member of the Radical Party, stated that the letter was all about 'fighting' and 'that such wild talk should not be necessary over the election of a few men to serve as dispensers of our charity to the poor'. He thought it irrelevant 'whether a Guardian is a navvy or a baronet, provided he is honest.' [117] Ley further states he was balloted along with Crooks on the Radical list, after having tied with him 'for bottom of the poll.' [118] He believed the Labour Party was being badly led in parting with the Radicals on this matter. Alf Graham, secretary of the PLEC, writes on 17 March; 'I have no desire to rush into print over the severance of the *unnatural alliance of labour, and Gladstonian Parties*.' Henry Ley, by admitting Crooks was bottom of the poll, only serves to prove that the Labour Party had been forced out of the Radical Party by 'the action of a majority attending their Council meetings, and cannot themselves be accused of separation.'[119] Graham saw Buxton's general election victory in 1892 as a Labour success. According to him it was the 'Labour men who ... created a winning policy at the last County Council elections, followed by a *Labour victory* at the general election.'[120]

At the outset of Labour's challenge in Poplar, the Liberal caucus hoped that by undermining the threat they would be able to maintain the status quo and continue their past dominance at the ballot box, which was after all, their prime objective. No assistance was given, or any expected from the Liberal Party during the hustings for the Guardian elections.[121] The *East End News* reported 'never before were there so many votes.... The 1965 votes given to Will Crooks in Poplar, and the 1430 votes for the Labour Candidates in the Bromley division' show that the Election Committee 'working in conjunction with the Liberal and Radical Association is now past discussion and reconsideration.' [122]

Will Crooks served his time 'as a Radical activist, and then split with them, thus beginning a period of accusation and acrimony with his former associates. Nevertheless, he remained strongly attached to many Liberal policies, and still viewed Liberals as preferable to their Tory counterparts.'[123] The latter view anticipates Crooks' support for the Progressives on the LCC 1892-1907; a period during which he remained strongly attached to his Liberal past. As Lawrence has shown in his essay on the limitations of party in Wolverhampton: 'Labour activists ... retained broadly the same political outlook as their Radical forebears ... it was the political context within which they operated which had undergone a sea-change.'[124] Such was the case with Crooks.

2

GUARDIAN OF THE POOR

In the 1880s, London was a municipally underdeveloped city, with its markets, docks and tramways, gas, water supply and some of its bridges and parks in private hands, and the police force remaining under the supervision of central government.[1] Since 1855, the Metropolitan Board of Works (MBW), as a unitary municipality, a two-tier metropolitan system, had administered London. The MBW was indirectly elected through the District Board system, and its members were nominated by local Vestries and co-opted onto the Metropolitan Board. Members were rarely, if ever, opposed for re-election, 'security of MBW tenure, turned the Board into a municipal gerontocracy. In 1885 at least sixteen of forty-six members were over sixty-five, and five over seventy ... against an average of forty-six for the directly elected members of the first London County Council in 1889'.[2] Allegations of corruption bedeviled the MBW throughout its thirty-three years because of this inclusive representation, and also by excluding the scrutiny of ratepayers — 'the MBW had earned its nickname the "Board of Perks".'[3]

The most important attribute of the London Local Government Act 1888, which brought into being the LCC, was the new directly elected first-tier authority consolidating municipal and county powers, 'it was the capital's first democratic metropolitan authority'.[4] The Liberal/Radical Progressives who controlled the LCC for its first eighteen years were entrusted with the responsibility of reforming London's municipal administration, and introduced a municipal agenda that incorporated the provision of gas, water, electricity and transport, and included public health reform, slum clearance, urban regeneration through street improvements, parks and the public utility of open spaces and other amenities.

The lack of London's municipal utilities and the need for social reform was the subject of debate in the re-constituted Liberal and Radical Associations in the 1880s.[5] In August 1888, the London Liberal Associations pledged themselves:

... in all matters of interest and importance to the people of London ... the adjustment of the incidence of Rates; the equalisation of the Poor Rates; the control of the Police; the abolition of City privileges; the utilisation of endowments; the control of Gas, Water, Markets, and Hackney Carriages; the control of the Metropolitan Asylums; the reform of Poor Law Administration; the reform of London Local Government; the abolition of the Coal Tax; the reform of the Register; the abolition of Aldermen; and the control of Open Spaces.[6]

The constituency Associations affiliated to the Radical Union, including the Poplar Liberal and Radical Council, endorsed these sentiments.

The PLRA added proposals relevant to the locality, '... and the improvement of Thames communications east of London Bridge; and who shall pledge themselves to use every effort to secure the early completion of the Blackwall Tunnel for vehicular and foot traffic'.[7] Whilst being aware of the demand for extensive structural and environmental improvements the Progressives knew that they would need to address the day-to-day problems facing working-class London, and advance the concerns of London labour if they were to remain in control of the LCC. Will Crooks described how this was achieved when he spoke of bringing the County Council into the workingman's home:

> We not only protected poor tenants from house spoilers and extortionate water companies, we gave a helping hand to the housewife. We saw that the coalsacks were the proper size, that the lamp oil was good, the dustbin emptied regularly, that the baker's bread was of proper weight, that the milk came from wholesome dairies and healthy cows, that the coster in the street and the tradesman in the shop gave good weights in everything they sold.[8]

Crooks was selected Chairman of the Public Control Committee in 1898.[9]

VESTRYMAN AND COUNTY COUNCILLOR

Shortly after the LCC elections in April 1889, Crooks was elected to the Vestry of the Parish of All Saints, Poplar.[10] At his first meeting, he was elected a Trustee. This position included hearing reports from committees on the social and economic life of the parish. The remit was parochial business, namely to sign cheques to the Guardians of the Poplar Union and to the District Board of Works. Crooks saw himself as representing the interests of workingmen on the Vestry, and as such saw his duty as monitoring the Board's financial dealings closely on their behalf. For example, in August 1889, he sent a letter to the *East End News* complaining that the Trustees of the Vestry had not seen fit to increase the wages of bath and washhouse employees: 'I do hope the workmen of Poplar will watch how the Vestry deals with the question. Will they shelve it and allow the Local Board of Works to increase the pay of its clerical assistant from £300 to £325 per annum without a protest.'[11] Crooks was identifying with the workmen of Poplar. Although a Trustee, the letter was giving notice to his fellow Vestrymen where his sympathies lay.

In January 1891, Crooks 'exposed a great valuation scandal' which he said 'will, no doubt, prevent its repetition.'[12] The case in question involved William Joshua Rundell, architect and Chairman of the Trustees in 1890, who was appointed to the position of valuer, to value factory properties for the Quinquennial Valuation List in March 1890.[13] On 30 December 1890, Crooks sent a circular to Poplar's ratepayers, the contents of which were published in the *East End News*:

> Important to Poplar Ratepayers!... At next Thursday's [1 January] trustee meeting cheques amounting to £900 for payment of the professional valuers for the quinquennial assessment are announced to be signed. It is generally known that one of the valuers [Rundell] has done absolutely none of the work, and yet is making an application for £300 as a share of the plunder, for which no service whatever has been rendered. If you permit this to be paid, you will have to pay your share of it in increased rates... I intend to oppose this payment, and shall be glad of your attendance and support ...[14]

At the Trustee meeting on 1 January, held at Poplar Town Hall, Crooks was late, and the cheque was signed before he had the opportunity of taking action to oppose it.

On arrival, he moved a resolution to defer payment of the cheque until the next meeting of the Trustees. In support of deferment, he said: 'I am, as an elected Trustee, a man looked to watch the public expenditure — am I wrong in going about to make enquiries? (Cries of "No.") I should be the last man to stir in this matter if I did not believe in my heart there was ground for so doing (Applause).... It has been suggested I have been party to a job — to keep out of the room until the cheques were signed.'[15] The resolution was narrowly carried, 54 voting in favour of deferment, 51 against.[16]

At the next meeting on 29 January, Crooks argued that Rundell had not carried out the contract entered into with the Trustees. He had not presented a proper list for which he was to be paid, and had appointed a deputy to do the work. Crooks said: 'Even if he had presented that list he would object on the ground that Mr Rundell had no right to appoint a deputy to do the work. The man who had acted as his deputy already held a sinecure office in the parish at £300 a year.'[17] After a long discussion, it was felt that because the cheque had been signed, the Trustees could not legally withhold it. The motion to withhold the cheque was lost by a large majority.[18]

What happened at both of these meetings? Why was Crooks undermined politically when it was clear he had taken the correct decision of exposing financial malpractice, and why did his fellow Trustees close ranks when it was made public? Was it part of a Liberal ploy to taint, and thus hinder, the Fabian agenda, given that they felt betrayed by Crooks, who had joined the Fabians that month? This meeting reveals some of the tensions, the internecine polemics, between the Liberals and Radicals in the PLRA, and Crooks. It was the beginning of the phase of working-class militancy in Poplar, when the left Radical group withdrew from the PLRA, and helped to establish independent Labour representation in Poplar.

On 7 December 1891, Crooks, who continued to expose the Trustees misappropriation of public funds, was appointed to a Special Committee of the Trustees to look into the financial affairs of the Board. The following week, at the Special Committee meeting the Churchwardens and overseers were censured for not presenting an explanation for the 'item £89 10s. for "attendance of officers", etc., in connection with the preparation of the list of voters for the parish.'[19] Will Crooks and the Committee demonstrate that no one was above suspicion of predatory gain from the public purse, not even the Church. It was this critical attitude of Crooks towards Tory and Liberal bureaucracy in Poplar that endeared him to the local ratepayers.

By 1892, when Crooks was elected to the LCC, he had already made a reputation as a Labour councillor. He was seen as representing working-class interests, and of defending the already overburdened ratepayer by drawing the deliberations of the Trustees to public attention. Crooks made sure Vestry meetings were reported in the local newspaper, advocating that the Trustees should be made accountable when it came to sound economic administration and financial control. He was of the view that it was of the utmost importance that such details should be open to public scrutiny.[20] Crooks also 'proposed and secured the insertion of a Trade Union Wage Clause in the Trustees' Local Contracts' that benefited local workers.[21] In 1896 the Poplar Labor League reported: 'In connection with the quinquennial valuation [1895] of the Union, he [Crooks] occupied a unique position for a Workmen's representative, viz: the chairman of the revision Committee of the valuation lists of Bow, Bromley and Poplar, this work occupied 38 sittings.... This is how our Member spent his holiday during the vacation of the County Council.' [22]

Crooks was requested by the trade union and labour movement of Poplar to represent them in the 1892 LCC elections, and they were prepared to pay his wages. As Crooks states in his election address: 'Sufficient funds will be raised to enable me to *give my whole time* to the work of the Council.'[23] For example, one of the objects of the PLEC was that their funds were devoted to paying Will Crooks' (the Labour representative on the LCC) wages. 'This is the only source from which he derives wages'.[24] Crooks together with John Burns of Battersea helped pioneer paid Labour representation. As well as his work on the Trustees the ratepayers of Poplar recognised the significant part Crooks played in the Blackwall Tunnel and the Free Library campaigns through Crooks 'College', and duly elected him to represent them on the County Council in 1892. Will Crooks and John McDougall (Liberal candidate) put forward a joint Progressive and Labour programme, which considered both the Radical tradition and *The Fabian Municipal Programme,* which was issued for the LCC election in 1892: [25]

Full-Self Government for London, Home Rule for London.
Municipal Ownership.
Economical and Efficient Administration.
Better Housing.
Trade Union Wages, Good work, and No Subcontracting.
The Eight Hour Day, Direct Employment of Labour.
Increase in Wages, Equalization of Rates.[26]

Crooks and McDougall were both elected with 3,465 and 3,713 votes respectively on 5 March 1892.[27]

This local progressive alliance, two wings of progressivism; consisting of Labour organisations and their affiliated trade unions and Liberal and Radical Associations, were commonplace in London's local elections; Liberals and Labour worked together as an incremental force.[28] This collusion between reformist organisations was taken as a model for what at national level such co-operation could achieve.[29] Woolwich was unique in London in this period because there was a lack of any attempt, or any need, for the trade union and labour movement to collude with the Liberals locally or nationally. Crooks was the Council's first Labour member, although some historians mistakenly think that it was John Burns, possibly because he sat on the Labour bench. While the Battersea Labour League supported Burns' candidature to the LCC in 1889, he stood as a social democrat. As Chris Wrigley points out, Burns 'stated definitely that he would not stand as a radical candidate, nor as a labour candidate, but simply as a social democrat'.[30]

The 1892 County Council election campaign was held against the background of an impending General Election, which added to political controversy and bitter party warfare.[31] A 'good deal of the electoral controversy on the elections ... turned on the housing question and the closely allied one of local taxation ... a readjustment of local taxation to do away with the unfair burden placed on occupiers as against ground landlords.' [32] The result of the election was the return of eighty-three Progressives, as against thirty-five Moderates, with nineteen Aldermen being elected by the first meeting of the Council.[33] The Liberals were jubilant. John Davis gives one possible reason why, 'in ... good years ... Progressive landslides reduced the Council Moderates to a West End rump, which itself made the development of a Moderate municipal policy less likely.'³⁴ The most likely reason for jubilation was a result that endorsed the Liberal agenda, and inspired their expectation of forming the next government at the coming general election. The *Star* and *Daily Chronicle* supported the Progressives' interests throughout the election, warning the electorate of what to expect from a Moderate administration. The *Daily Chronicle*, wrote:

> The interests which keep *London poor, ill-governed, divided into isolated administrative cells, in which jobbery can flourish at its will*, are determined to leave no stone unturned to restore the reign of vestrydom which the Council replaced.... Only let the people of London know the alternative to a Progressive majority on London's second Council. The Vestry gang are ready to seize on the Vestry which escaped them three years ago [My italics].³⁵

W. T. Stead's Radical journal *Review of Reviews* reported: 'The victory of the Progressives in the London County Council election was very brilliant and a very satisfactory piece of work ... The Moderates were simply wiped out ... they richly deserved their defeat.'³⁶

Crooks took his seat on 15 March, and Ben Tillett, secretary of the Dockers' Union, was elected an Alderman.³⁷ At the next meeting on 22 March, Crooks was selected to the Bridges, Parks and Open Spaces, and the Public Control Committees.³⁸ Besides being responsible for the upkeep and maintenance of London bridges, the Bridges Committee was responsible for the Woolwich Free Ferry (opened in 1889); Crooks was elected to the Woolwich Ferry Subcommittee. The remit was not only to keep the steam ferry in good repair but members were also responsible for sustaining and reviewing staffing and wage levels.

Whilst on the LCC Crooks continued to support Liberal candidates in three-cornered fights against independent Labour. Paul Thompson states that this continued 'even after his election as a Labour MP', and that the 'Labour group on the LCC made no pretence of independence'.³⁹ In a private letter to Ramsey MacDonald, Crooks complained that the Labour Bench of the LCC was not seen in support of the Labour candidate in South Hackney, during the 1898 LCC hustings. He wrote: 'I did not succeed today so well as I should have liked.' ⁴⁰ This seems to endorse Thompson's statement about the Labour group, but does nothing to help explain Crooks' political behaviour.

The problem of Labour members speaking on Liberal platforms was an issue that plagued the Labour Representative Committee (LRC) after its formation in 1900, and Crooks was not the only offender with whom MacDonald had to deal. What is revealing about Crooks' political stance, especially in relation to LCC elections, is that he wanted to remain independent of the Progressive whip, and at the same time, have the option of supporting it if he thought Labour support was weak in a given election. What seemed to others a contradictory position Crooks possibly explained as political expediency. He would have supported a Progressive candidate in local elections if he was of the opinion Labour was fighting a lost cause. Crooks' axiom was that it was better to support the devil you know than let in the Tory.

Blackwall Tunnel

The Bridges Committee during this period was involved in the process of negotiating, signing, and sealing a major contract of £871,000 for the construction of a tunnel at Blackwall. Work started on sewage relocation in early 1892, and a schedule of wages in the contract was adopted later.[41] To understand and appreciate the tensions involving the Metropolitan Board on the one hand, the Local Government Board (LGB), the LCC, and the frustrations of the Poplar working-class on the other, we need to look at the campaigns that took place around the Thames Communication Movement.

Public meetings, petitions, and deputation after deputation had waited upon the MBW urging the claims of the ratepayers for communication across the river Thames. Eventually the Board did apply for and obtain an Act of Parliament enabling them to build a tunnel. A Bill was before the House of Commons in 1884, a Bill enabling the MBW to 'make a new means of communication across the River Thames by means of tunnel or subway.'[42] This enterprise never began. A second Bill, The Thames Communication (Blackwall) Act of 1887 was taken more seriously, and a tunnel was later constructed by the LCC.

Although the campaign for the construction of a tunnel was centred on both sides of the river, the Poplar experience, including the contribution of Crooks 'College', needs investigation since it demonstrates a better understanding of Crooks' role in the agitation. The 'College' was an important forum in educating, and politicising local working people around the need for a vehicular tunnel, which would give them easier access to work. Further, it is probable that the 'College', given its political prescience, put forward the idea that the tunnel would not only provide work for the unemployed, but would also facilitate the dissemination of radicalism on both sides of the river, by enabling activists to attend trade union and political meetings. For instance, after the tunnel opened in May 1897, the trade union and labour movement in Poplar helped the progressive movement in the Tory stronghold of Woolwich to develop and organise.

During 1887-1892, Crooks 'College' was at the forefront of organising public meetings at Poplar Town Hall on the Blackwall Tunnel. These meetings sent petitions and delegations to the Metropolitan Board urging them to draw up a contract, and petitions and letters were sent to the LCC exhorting its construction. Crooks was able to call on the support of his fellow Radicals, trade union activists and organisers, and his friend Sydney Buxton MP, to take action around the campaign for a tunnel at Blackwall. For example, the Metropolitan Board meeting 15 March 1889 received two delegations, one from the Poplar Trustees urging that the work of constructing the tunnel should begin, and the other from Bromley St. Leonard. The delegation from Bromley urged that the work on the tunnel should begin immediately. They could not afford to wait until the new County Council came into working order. Lord Rosebery, who became the first Chairman of the LCC, aware that tenders would be laid before the MBW that day with reference to the construction of the tunnel, wrote:

> ... as the responsibility would devolve upon the Council it seemed to them that the Metropolitan Board should not enter into so important a contract as this, and thereby fetter the action of the Council ...The letter from the Local Government Board stated that the President deemed it inexpedient, and expressed a hope that the Board would not proceed to bind their successors — the new London County Council — in a matter of such importance ... the question should be left open to be dealt with by the new Council. [43]

The Board ignored these interventions. They saw the actions of the LGB and the provisional LCC as intimidatory, and agreed that Sir Wheatman Pearson's company, Pearson & Son, would construct the Blackwall Tunnel, and passed their decision on to the LCC.[44] The Council responded that they did not hold themselves bound by the acceptance of Messrs. S. Pearson & Son's tender for the Blackwall Tunnel by the Board on 15 March.[45]

Sydney Buxton, speaking at a public meeting on 18 March, at the Poplar Town Hall, moved a resolution that 'characterised the opening of tenders by the Metropolitan Board on the previous Friday as a solemn farce ... [a] fatuous folly in regard to the tunnel.'[46] The motion also supported the Provisional LCC, who would probably be making an application to the Local Government Board, asking that the duties of the Metropolitan Board be wound up earlier than agreed. He continued by saying that the MBW 'had opened tenders, not for the tunnel that was wanted,' a passenger tunnel and a vehicular tunnel, designed to take both passengers and vehicles.[47]

Sydney Buxton reported that Charles Ritchie, President of the Local Government Board, appealed to the Metropolitan Board not to adopt the tender in the last period of their life. They ignored him. Ritchie then said: 'If you persist in this conduct we will, under the Act of Parliament which gives us power, put an end to your existence some ten days before you would otherwise expire.'[48] Buxton also pointed out that because the Board's engineer (Edward Bazalgette) had resigned, it was better to leave the drawing up of plans to the County Council, who had pledged themselves to proceed with a passenger and vehicular tunnel.[49] The inhabitants of Poplar, Bow and Bromley petitioned the LCC in March 1889, on this issue.[50]

The delay in a decision about any scheme of communication across the river, according to the LCC, was to be expected. They had to investigate, appreciate, and understand what was being suggested. The contracts that had been accepted by the Metropolitan Board needed to be scrutinised to see if they met the Council's criteria. If not they would need amending. In April 1889, the Council employed an eminent engineer to report on the practicality of the proposed scheme, as it was necessary to carry out what was best for the ratepayers of London, because building a tunnel would be a costly business, and would affect the rating considerably. At the meeting of the LCC on 18 June 1889, the Bridges Committee reported: 'That the Blackwall Tunnel take precedence of all other schemes of trans-communication' across the Thames. [51] 'They wanted to meet the constant cries which came to them from the different Boards in the East End of London by showing that they were doing something.' [52]

At last, in February 1891, the agitation by Crooks 'College', and the London progressive movement was successful. The long-deferred realisation of the hopes of the inhabitants of east and south-east London seemed to be at hand. The LCC agreed to invite tenders for the construction of the tunnel, and instructed the Chief Engineer, Alexander Binnie, to prepare to draw up specifications and draw up a contract.[53] Pearson & Son's tender for the contract was signed and sealed in November 1891.[54]

It is important to this discussion to acknowledge that the construction of the tunnel together with other building projects was the catalyst that made possible the trade union wage rate movement and the campaign for a Works Department to oversee the implementation and regulation of fair wages. Historians of the LCC, both contemporary and modern, have failed to acknowledge this, and by omitting Crooks and the Poplar trade union and labour movement from their studies have neglected to apprehend a fundamental contribution towards LCC policy. This omission changes the focus, and limits the scope of expanding historical knowledge — how did the influence of socialism in the constituencies impact upon the Council and municipal reform?

The Fair Wage Clause

It was significant that leading trade unionists such as Will Thorne, Pete Curran, Ben Tillett, and Tom Mann, trade union officials who represented the interests of the general labourer (most of whom were paying into the Crooks, Burns and Steadman Wages Funds), were identified with or affiliated to the Poplar Labour Committee. Curran, Tillett, and Mann, who were members of the Fabian Society in the early 1890s,[55] believed in a policy of collectivist socialist action. Therefore it can be plausibly assumed that they discussed with Labour members of the LCC the urgent need for a minimum wage, an agenda for inserting a fair wage and hours clause into LCC contracts, especially the setting up of the LCC Works Department with their Fabian friends on the Bridges Committee, Will Crooks and Bill Steadman. A strategy of agitation was put forward, including the idea of a LCC Labour bench to make progress on an agreed agenda. This agitation, co-ordinated by the Fabian caucus to pay trade union wage rates in the construction of the tunnel, began at the beginning of 1892, and 'continued the practice of paying fair wages that had been inaugurated by the London School Board following a campaign by the London Society of Compositors.'[56] John Burns during this period had strong ties with the Fabians. He formally joined the Society in 1893.[57]

In February 1892, the Bridges Committee received letters of complaint from the Gasworkers' and General Labourers Union, and the Navvies, Bricklayers' Labourers and General Labourers' Union, stating that Messrs. Pearson & Son, contractors for the Blackwall Tunnel, were not paying the recognised rate of wages to navvies and labourers.[58] Both of these unions were affiliated to the Poplar Labour Election Committee, and thus party to the agreed agenda on fair wages. Will Crooks and John Burns responded to the complaints by trade unions of low wages at a meeting of the Woolwich Ferry Subcommittee held on 1 April 1892. The subcommittee resolved that the Bridges Committee be recommended to inform Pearson & Son 'that 6d. an hour must be the minimum wage paid by them for adult labour employed in connection with the works of the tunnel.'[59] Pearson met with the Bridges Committee on 26 April, and a scale of wages was proposed and agreed.[60]

The LCC Labour members responded to trade union concerns over wages by constituting the first meeting of the Labour bench of the County Council, held at the Dockers' Union offices, Mile End Road, on 26 April 1892.[61] The meeting 'declared for direct employment of labour in municipal workshops. The L.C.C. Works Department ... was the result.... minimum wage of sixpence an hour for labourers and ninepence for artisans, with a maximum working week of fifty-four hours.... retiring pensions for workman as for officials. This ... soon became practical politics on the County Council.' [62] The Labour bench was formed to formulate, oversee, and progress the implementation of these policies.

Burns' and Crooks' discussion with trade union officials was productive. The Fair Wages clause originated as an amendment to insert a fair wage and hours clause in contracts by way of schedule. It was moved by John Burns at the LCC Council meeting on 3 May 1892:

> That all contractors be compelled to sign a declaration that they pay the trade union rate of wages and observe the hours of labour and conditions recognised by the London Trade Unions, and that the hours of labour be inserted in and form part of the contract by schedule, and that penalties be enforced for any breach of agreement [63]

Will Crooks supported the amendment in his maiden speech at County Hall.

He defended the enforcement of trade union wages: 'No contractor had ever been ruined by paying trade union rates of wages. The best wages had always meant the best workmen. Trade unions were anxious that the surplus labour of the country should be employed, and they only asked the Council to fix a minimum rate of wages. The sooner the Council employed men direct the better.'[64] The original motion was withdrawn in favour of the amendment; the debate went on for weeks, with amendment after amendment by the Moderates being thrown out. Finally, it was decided to set up a Special Committee to look into the issue on 31 May, and to report back.[65]

On 26 July, the Special Committee was 'unable to report to the Council on the main question before the recess',[66] (26 July - 27 September). A report was finally placed before the Council on 16 December, and was passed with various minor amendments.[67] The LCC Fair Wages Clause was the first time that trade union rate of wages, hours of labour and conditions of work were included in contracts by any public authority. It was first employed in the Blackwall contract. When work started on the tunnel, Crooks and the Poplar Labour Committee worked to further:

> ... the direction of getting concessions for workmen, and preventing isolated disputes during the progress of the work. A Blackwall Tunnel United Trades' Committee was formed consisting of Delegates from all grades of labour employed. Deputations waited upon ... the Bridges Committee.... Although all the demands of the men were not conceded owing to the contract having been taken under the Fair Rates of Wages clause, many concessions were granted. [68]

The secretary of the Trades Committee was Alf Graham, secretary of the Poplar Labor League.[69]

The Works Department was established in 1893. Professor McBriar while discussing the influence of the Fabians in the LCC writes, 'the Works Department was the very storm centre of the dispute about Municipal Socialism in London. The establishment of this Department was thought to mark the point where Radicalism crossed the boundary into Socialism, where it passed from mere public ownership to public management and the 'direct employment of labour'. The Fabians ... saw it as the outcome of the Trades Unions' 'fair wages' policy.' [70] Crooks was elected to the Works and Stores Committee in May 1893.[71] The Moderates were so against the Works Department that they abolished it in 1908.[72]

From the time he joined the Council to May 1897, when the Prince of Wales went to Poplar to open the Blackwall Tunnel on behalf of Queen Victoria, Crooks was among the keenest of the public men engaged in carrying this great engineering feat through. So satisfied were his fellow County Councillors with the practical work he did at Blackwall, that on its completion they elected him Chairman of the Bridges Committee in March 1899.[73] In this capacity, he steered through the Council and through a Committee of the House of Commons two other schemes for tunnels under the Thames, one for foot traffic only between Greenwich and the Isle of Dogs, and the other for general traffic between Shadwell and Rotherhithe. The *Municipal Journal* said of him:

> Mr. Will Crooks, more than any other man, has made Londoners acquainted with the tunnel. His popular lecture on the Blackwall Tunnel has been given in all parts of London to all kinds of audiences ... Mr Crooks himself has been identified with the construction of the tunnel. As one of the representatives of the Poplar district, he has turned his membership of the Bridges Committee to good account by giving to the tunnel his special attention ... The workmen had just cause to bless the Poplar County Councillor. *It was owing to Mr. Crooks's efforts that a revised schedule of wages was adopted. The result of this was that the contractors paid an additional £26,000 in wages.* (My italics).[74]

This demonstrates Crooks' statement, made in his first speech to the Council, that no contractor ever lost by paying the trade union rate of wages.

At this time: 'He refused an offer from the progressives to become vice-chairman of the County Council'. When this occurred is not clear, but probably it was in 1900, after he had fulfilled the role of Chairman of the Bridges Committee. If Crooks had accepted this offer, he would automatically have been Chairman of the LCC the following year. Further to this, again it is unclear when: 'he also refused a managerial post in a coopering works, then, as ever, preferring complete independence.'[75]

It is clear from the evidence of the LCC offer that Crooks was a more prominent figure than previously acknowledged by historians. Obviously, Crooks' colleagues on the LCC were impressed by his leadership qualities, and his grasp of complex legislation, or they would not have offered him the position of Vice-Chairman. He must have thought about the proposal, but refused it, realising that he would be tied to the Progressive platform. It was not his political style to be burdened with a post that would restrict his independence, and compromise the Labour cause.

In her study of the LCC, *A Vision For London,* Susan Pennybacker writes: 'It is said that the LCC's greatest achievement ... was the elaboration of an innovative labour policy.... the practices of paying fair wages ... It pursued a policy of 'direct labour' ... which led to the opening of the LCC Works

Department.'[76] While acknowledging the substance of her argument, it is important to recognise that this achievement was brought about by Labour members. John Burns and Will Crooks were the pioneers of the Fair Wages Movement and the LCC Works Department. The above evidence suggests that they were able to bring about political change by campaigning within the Council Chamber through the Bridges Committee, and by organising a well co-ordinated political lobby outside.[77] The reason why local government had become increasingly involved in trade unionism since 1889 was because municipal public utilities and services swelled the number of publicly employed manual workers in this period. They were now operating under a large working-class electorate therefore it would be advantageous politically to avoid damaging disputes and stoppages.[78] Hence the Fair Wages clause.

During 1895, political conditions changed. The Liberal government was defeated, and the Progressives lost twenty-four seats to the Moderates on the LCC. For three years 1892-1895, the Liberal government had failed lamentably to legislate on its electoral promises. It had failed to respond to working-class criticism in the solving of growing unemployment, and placed Irish Home Rule again before the Labour Question. Thus, the working-class was even more convinced that the Liberals' interest in the working-class was their vote. Now that the Irish Question was out of the way (the Second Irish Home Rule Bill was defeated in 1893), the Conservatives and Unionists promoted the spectre of militant socialism and collectivism, and the fear of destructive class conflict. The Conservatives were returned in July 1895, as the largest single party. The party balance on the LCC was even with fifty-nine Moderate and Progressive (Liberal and Labour) councillors, but the Progressives held on to power with a majority of five Aldermen.[79]

The Progressive losses were partly due to a concerted campaign by the Liberty and Property Defence League, London's militant ratepayer organisation, which supported the right of freedom, *laissez-faire* principles, attacking municipal socialism,[80] and partly because the Liberal government was reluctant to set in place sweeping measures in local finance for the sake of the LCC. This was seen as no different from Tory obstruction. John Davis explains: 'Whatever advantages the Progressives gained from their stance at the local level, their militancy encouraged their opponents to renew the battles in Parliament, where LCC initiatives were most vulnerable.'[81] Crooks was returned top of the poll in Poplar with 3052 votes.[82]

Parks and Open Spaces

While on the Parks and Open Spaces Committee Will Crooks campaigned to get a number of his proposals for parks for the poorer districts of Poplar, Bromley and Bow carried through. Crooks firmly believed in reclaiming open space and wasteland, and in providing a healthy environment for the residents of the district, areas where children could play safely. This agitation of reclaiming open space culminated with the opening of the Island Gardens on the Isle of Dogs (located directly opposite Greenwich Pier), Bromley Recreation Ground, and the Tunnel Gardens at Poplar, in 1895, 1900 and 1902 respectively.[83]

An area of reclaimed marshland, almost the only portion of riverfront of the Isle of Dogs that was not used for wharfage or commercial premises, was purchased from the Earl of Wemyss in November 1884.[84] It was cleared and landscaped to form a park, Island Gardens, which was opened by Will Crooks, Chairman of the LCC Parks Subcommittee for the district, in August 1895.[85] Among the official delegation at the opening ceremony on 3 August were Sydney Buxton MP, and representing the LCC were John McDougall, John Burns and Ben Cooper. McDougall said the Island Gardens was 'the end of six years labour' by Crooks. Both Burns and Cooper paid tribute to his energy and zeal. Burns stated, '... Poplar was to be congratulated on its representatives, for the district was singularly fortunate in having such ... conscientious men to represent the electors.' Crooks said 'he was present that day to carry out what he had thought of as a little child ... [on] an excursion to this spot in his childhood.' He appealed to local residents to treat the area as if it was their own 'private property', and make it a safe place for mothers to send their children. [86]

A new site for a recreation ground for Bow and Bromley was agreed by the LCC in May 1889. At a cost of £6,000, it was agreed to purchase a piece of land for the purpose of a public open space at Grace Street, Bromley.[87] Ben Cooper opened Bromley Recreation Ground on 14 April 1900. In his address Cooper thanked the LCC for providing the recreation ground 'including the gymnasium ... it was the first open space provided in that district, which with a population between 70,000 and 80,000, had had no recreation ground for its people.' Crooks, whilst congratulating the residents of Bow and Bromley on their new open space, stressed the usefulness of the gymnasium to the children of the district. [88]

The land that was designated Blackwall Tunnel Gardens in August 1902 was purchased initially by the Bridges Committee, and was being 'held for the purpose of widening the tunnel approach or of constructing a second tunnel when either ... may be found necessary.'[89] Will Crooks, who proposed the scheme, suggested 'that the land should not be allowed to remain waste and unoccupied, and that until the time came for widening the tunnel the place should be utilised as a recreation ground.'[90] John Piggott, Chairman of the Parks Committee, and Will Crooks, the Mayor of Poplar (1901-1902), opened the Gardens officially on 30 August.[91] Crooks was complimented by John Piggott, when he said, '[Crooks] had persevered with his pet scheme until at length the boys and girls of Poplar had got their Tunnel playground (cheers).'[92] John Burns supported a vote of thanks for the admirable work done for Poplar by Crooks. There is no doubt that Crooks was highly regarded by his constituents for the way he served Poplar, and his desire to improve the environment of the poor in the East End impressed his colleagues on the LCC.

Crooks saw the achievements of the LCC Parks Committee as complementary to the work he did on the Technical Education Board in providing elementary technical education. He saw both as contributing towards the social amelioration of working-class districts in London. Crooks was especially concerned with the education and welfare of the children of Poplar. He believed '[it] was as important to develop muscles as of mind.' [93] Haw explains: 'It had long been a grievance to the working-classes of London that nearly all the parks lay in the West End and the suburbs.' [94]

The Technical Education Board

Will Crooks was appointed to the TEB Education Subcommittee in May 1893. It was to report to the LCC 'as to the best manner of proceeding to carry out the subject of the reference to the Board.'[95] The Council had expressed the opinion that every district of London ought to be adequately provided with technical education of every grade rising from the school to the workshop and the university, and that the existing institutions were co-ordinated, and further provisions made where it was necessary to improve them.

In March 1894, Crooks was appointed to the TEB's Domestic Economy Subcommittee, on which he served for ten years, and the Secondary Schools and the Higher Education Special Subcommittees. He was also selected to the Scholarships Subcommittee in 1895, on which he remained until 1904.[96] Andrew Saint states: 'The working man who made most practical impact on the TEB was Will Crooks ... an LCC member who seems to have viewed his role on both the Council and the Board in 'localist' terms, as a means to furthering the interests of Poplar.' [97]

The Domestic Economy Subcommittee's work included funding free scholarships to schools that taught Cookery, Laundry work, Housewifery and Needlework, and Dressmaking, in the Boards schools, Polytechnics, and Institutes. The scholarships were means tested, 'no candidate whose parents are in receipt of an income from all sources of more than £400 a year will be qualified to hold a Training Scholarship.' A Scholarship was awarded by competitive examination.[98] The Committee was also accountable to the Board for the welfare and salaries of its domestic economy teachers. The Scholarships Subcommittee was responsible for the election of scholarships in Science, Art, and Technology, and the scheme of work in the delivery of the syllabus in these subjects in all the Board's institutions. The Committee also monitored those institutions which had been awarded grants for improvements to make sure they kept to the conditions of the grant.[99]

Although a technical education institution for Poplar was one of the demands of Crooks 'College' in the late 1880s, it remained unrealised until it was taken up by the TEB in 1896/7. This came about when the Committee for the Promotion of Technical Education in Poplar (CPTEP) was advised by Crooks to approach the Board regarding the promotion of technical classes in Poplar. He consulted with the Board on the Committee's behalf. Subsequently in February and October 1896, the CPTEP wrote to the TEB, informing them that there was growing public demand in Poplar for a scheme of work to deliver technical education in 'chemistry, electricity, drawing (including mechanical), carpentry, plumbing, cookery and dressmaking.' The Board was also informed that classrooms at George Green School would be made available, and were asked for 'financial assistance to carry out ... the ... scheme of work.' The Science, Art and Technology Subcommittee (SA&T) at a meeting in October 1896 responded to the letters from George Ford, secretary of Poplar Technical Education Committee: 'Enquiries are now being made as to the possibility of securing financial co-operation with the Board in the establishment of a technical institute in Poplar.' [100]

In April 1897, the SA&T recommended that 'the secretary of the Board be authorised to negotiate for the purchase ... of premises at the rear of George Green's schools ... for the purpose of a technical institute, on the understanding that all agreements are made subject to confirmation by the Council.'[101] The Council meeting in June supported the TEB recommendation for the purchase of houses in East India Dock Road as a suitable site for the Poplar technical institute. The Council were also informed that the Poplar Board of Guardians were willing to help financially in the purchase of the rear portion for the 'storage and purification of boiler feed water'.[102] As Chairman of the Guardians, Will Crooks was influential in the negotiations with the LCC. The Guardians 'having secured a sum towards the building ... was negotiating for the purchase of house property for this purpose ... a prohibitive price was asked ... while Poplar still waits for its children to be technically educated.'[103] The LCC sealed the purchase of the site in April 1900. [104]

The Council gave the approval to build in July 1901. The Technical Institute was to be mainly devoted to marine engineering, navigation, naval architecture, and commercial classes. The main object of the institution was to provide courses of training for the Board of Trade certificates, and suitable courses of instruction for those engaged in marine engineering, repair shops, and shipbuilding yards. [105] The LCC Works Committee erected the building. The work was entrusted to the LCC Education Committee when the TEB was wound-up in March 1904. The Institute, which was opened in January 1906, became known as the Poplar School of Marine Engineering and Navigation.[106] Crooks was reported as saying: 'If posterity remembers me ... as the man who brought the School of Marine Engineering and Navigation to Poplar I shall be satisfied.'[107]

POOR LAW GUARDIAN

Will Crooks was elected to the LCC in March 1892, and afterwards he was elected along with George Lansbury to the Poplar Board of Guardians in April 1893. This is contrary to what is inferred by George Haw, who was of the view that Crooks was elected to the Poplar Board of Guardians in August 1892, six months after his return to the London County Council.[108] Crooks' election to the Guardians, it can be argued, was the key to all other public posts he held. It was during 1893-1907 that he gained expertise in administering to the poor and aged through the Poor Law, and acquired the skills necessary to deal with unemployment.

The election of Will Crooks and George Lansbury to the Poplar Union, that covered the parishes of Bow, Bromley St. Leonards and Poplar,[109] had been made possible because the property qualification of £40 for rent had been lowered to £5, and was soon to be abolished.[110] They were joined by three other working-class Guardians,[111] including 'Harry W. Kaye, of the Transport Workers, cashier for the Dockers' Union.'[112] They remained in a minority for some years, but by acting jointly, and putting forward cogent argument, they became the motivating force within the Board. In 1897 Crooks became Chairman,[113] a post he held until he resigned it in 1907. Crooks and Lansbury brought to the Board something that had been seriously lacking in their deliberations in the past - an understanding of working class culture. It was said among Crooks' neighbours:

> ... nothing happens in Poplar without someone running to Will Crooks about it. His little house ... was the gathering ground of all kinds of deputations and of troubled individuals seeking advice on every subject under the sun. He was a court of appeal in family troubles as well as on public questions.[114]

G. K. Chesterton, the author and critic, visited Will Crooks at home on a number of occasions, and in his book on Charles Dickens said of him, he was a good man 'honest and responsible and compassionate'.[115]

The working-class representatives who were elected to the Poplar Guardians were to sweep away the old regime of 'Bumbledom' and make 'the Poplar Union a model among Poor Law authorities, and one frequently recommended by the Local Government Board'.[116] When he joined the Guardians, Crooks was elected to the Assessment Committee, which was the Committee that dealt with the rating considerations of the Union, and he was selected its Chairman in 1895.[117] His selection so soon to such a responsible position by the Board showed that his fellow Guardians, irrespective of their political allegiance, respected his honesty and commitment towards everything he did. He 'soon proved ... the best administrator among them'.[118]

At the beginning of his public service in 1892, Crooks became a widower when his wife who had been bedridden during the Dock Strike, suffered a relapse and died. This left Crooks to look after six children, the youngest only a baby. As well as carrying out his new duties on the LCC, together with other commitments to help the Labour movement, he had to be both mother and father to his children. This carried on for some twelve months until he married Elizabeth Coulter (née Lake), an asylum nurse, who lodged with his mother. The wedding took place in Poplar Parish Church in 1893.[119]

Poplar Workhouse
During the 1906 Local Government Board of Inquiry, Corrie Grant MP, who was the Board's legal representative, asked Crooks what were the conditions like in the workhouse at the time he became a Guardian. He replied, 'the condition of things in the House was almost revolting Dirt, empty stores, inmates without sufficient clothing, many without boots on their feet, and food of the worst possible description.'[120] George Lansbury, writing later, states, '... the mixed workhouse at Poplar was for me Dante's *Inferno*. Sick and aged, mentally deficient, lunatics, babies and children, able-bodied and tramps all herded together in one huge range of buildings'.[121] Conditions in the workhouse were so bad in 1893, it was said that many of the workhouse inmates preferred to go to prison.[122]

In 1894, the reforming Guardians first turned their attention to the Poor Law officials in the workhouse, especially the senior staff, who were paid large salaries. It seemed that even once kindly officials could be brutalised by the Poor Law system, argued George Lansbury. They soon discovered that the road to promotion and increased salaries was economy, at the expense of the poor, but this was no excuse for corruption.[123] On examining the stores and accounts, Crooks and Lansbury discovered that officials were buying stock inferior to what was recorded and they pocketed the difference. A Committee of the Whole Union was appointed on 7 February 1894 to consider matters connected with the management and discipline of the Workhouse. They reported in a letter of 25 April, that they had '... received reports respecting deficiencies ... in the suits supplied to inmates ... it had been the practice of the Master to obtain a particular kind of unbleached calico, not in the contract, for making men's and women's underclothes.'[124]

The Master, Mr Deason, was unable to account for the discrepancies. After hearing of Deason's carelessness in 'estimating the amount of goods likely to be required under contract', it was felt that the work of management had outgrown his capabilities and he was asked to resign on health grounds, this to take effect from 24 June 1894. George Lansbury asked for copies of the returns and reports about the alleged irregularities in the Stores Department of the Workhouse. This was moved by Lansbury and seconded by Crooks. It was resolved that copies of the Returns of Clothing and Clothing Materials together with copies of the Officers' Report and the Reports of the Special Committee, be forwarded to the LGB. [125]

The LGB official inquiry took place in October 1894. A report concerning the findings was sent to the Guardians in early December. It stated that the clothing store was practically empty, and that inmates were wearing underclothes 'little better than rags together with socks and stockings that were worn out.' The Guardians were paying more than the contract price for cloth, and had been for some twenty-one months. The Master's Registration Book shows it as being in contract. Fraudulent intent, the misappropriation of goods for cash, was not proven against Deason. The report stated that the situation in the Workhouse had been unsatisfactory, especially the serious aspect of mismanagement, when dealing with clothing in the Medical Officers' Report on 16 March 1893. Where the question of health was involved, Deason seems not to have taken immediate action to increase clothing. [126]

The ill-fitting blue uniforms were abolished. It was also resolved that flannel shirts and vests and bodices and drawers for the aged and infirm men and women should be supplied. The humanising of the institution was not enough for Crooks and Lansbury. The working-class Guardians wanted to keep people out of the workhouse altogether, and believed it was better to pay them out-relief enabling them to maintain their dignity. In the workhouse, the food was improved. Cocoa was introduced, and butter replaced margarine and fresh meat for stale. Crooks instigated a workhouse bakery, which insured cheaper better bread and tasks that are more enjoyable for the inmates. A letter was received on 10 March 1894 from the LGB enabling the Guardians to supply female inmates in the Workhouse with dry tea, sugar and milk, besides the tea prescribed by the Dietician. [127]

George Lansbury was elected Chairman of the Poplar Board of Guardians and Will Crooks was re-elected to the Assessment Committee on 2 January 1895.[128] Trade union agreements, conditions of employment were strictly adhered to, and where possible, were improved upon. In 1897 George Lansbury moved that Labour Day on 1st May should be observed as a public holiday in the Workhouse and that where possible all those employed by the Guardians be allowed a holiday without loss of pay.[129] A year later, the General Purposes Committee observed that the wages of the Assistant Tailors employed at the Workhouse were considerably below the minimum rate recognised by the trade union. They agreed to increase the weekly rate from 30s. to 36s. per week.[130]

The Poplar Guardians were not just concerned with the distress created by unemployment, but with providing education to the children in their care, who were there, largely, as the result of unemployment. The financial maintenance of those children placed in the Forest Gate School District by the Guardians was the responsibility of the Metropolitan Community Poor Fund. The management of the school was the Guardians' responsibility, having elected representation on the School Management Board.[131] Children in the Forest Gate Schools District chargeable to the Poplar Union had increased from 358 to 583 between 1884-1894, an increase of nearly 63 per cent.[132] Proposing the future dissolution of the Forest Gate Schools District, the managers wrote on 24 December 1895, offering to sell the site and buildings to the Poplar Union. The content of the communication was sent to the Local Government Board so they could deliberate on the fairness of the terms offered by the management.[133] A letter from the management of the school in January 1896 asked what arrangements the Guardians had considered for the accommodation of the children chargeable to the Poplar Union, should the Forest Gate School District be dissolved. Crooks moved that the Local Government Board be informed 'that this union is not desirous that the dissolution of the School District should be proceeded with ... terms of purchase offered to the Board considered not equitable'.[134]

When the Guardian representatives on the School Management Board retired after their three year tenure was completed in 1896, it was resolved unanimously that Crooks serve as a manager, with four others, to represent the Poplar Union for three years, ending 25 March 1899.[135] In December 1898, the LBG issued an order for the dissolution of the school.[136] This date was brought forward to October, after the Whitechapel Union withdrew their children on 2 October 1897.[137] George Lansbury states in his memoirs that 'we bought out Whitechapel and took over the school'.[138]

Conditions in the Workhouse had improved immeasurably since the reforming Guardians took office. When Henry Chaplin MP, President of the LBG, made a surprise visit to the Workhouse on 14 April 1897, he made the following entry in the visitors' book: 'I have had the greatest satisfaction in visiting this establishment, which appears to be as complete and well managed in all aspects as could be desired.'[139]

The Metropolitan Asylum Board

After his visit to the Poplar Workhouse, Chaplin showed his support for the Poplar Poor Law policy by inviting Crooks to sit on the Metropolitan Asylum Board (MAB); he took his seat in May 1898. A Labour man, nominated to this select body by a Conservative Cabinet Minister, must have raised eyebrows. This was the first time a workman had been appointed to such a position. Walter Long, Chaplin's successor, as President of the Local Government Board, twice re-nominated Crooks to the Asylum Board. It was the largest hospital authority of its kind in the country, caring for nearly 7,000 people. [140]

Crooks became a member of the Children's, Contracts, and Park Hospital Committees. He was Chairman of the Children's Committee (CC) for three years 1901-3, [141] also in 1901 he was appointed Chairman of the LCC Industrial and Reform Schools Committee.[142] These posts provided him with further positions with which to serve the distressed poor, and to help neglected children. At his first CC meeting in May, he was elected to the Subcommittee responsible for visiting children's seaside homes in Herne Bay and Margate. Crooks resigned his position on the Board in June 1904. [143]

It was discussed in October 1898 as to whether the CC should provide houses for those remand children in the care of MAB. It was current practice to remand them to prison or the care of the workhouse.[144] Crooks argued the case that: 'These children want keeping as far as possible from both prison and workhouse.... We ought to put them in small homes and give them school-time and play-time, like other children, until their cases come before the magistrates again.' [145] In January 1899, the CC, on the instruction of the Board, 'with regard to the provision of accommodation for remand children', decided to purchase three houses in Peckham, subject to approval of the LGB. Two weeks later, negotiations to buy were broken off, without explanation. In March 1889, the Committee recommended that the Board purchase a house in Camberwell Green; the decision to buy was referred to the LGB, who agreed to the proposal. [146]

Crooks led a deputation of Board members to the London magistrates at Bow Street, urging 'them in future to commit all remand children to the Homes.' The magistrates were supportive of the scheme, but explained it was their duty to uphold the law, and that young offenders must be sent to the workhouse. 'We'll alter the law then,' was Crooks' reply. 'For I am determined these youngsters shall be no longer sent to the workhouse.' Crooks approached the Home Secretary, Charles Ritchie, and explained the Board's proposal, and pointed out that the Juvenile Offenders' Bill (1899) was before Parliament at that very moment, 'and that the insertion in that measure of an additional clause ... would keep remand children away from the workhouse for all time'. Crooks' suggestion became law the following month.[147] In May the Board agreed to provide, three remand institutions, one in Camberwell, south of the Thames, and two, north of the river in Hampstead and Pentonville. These remand centres provided accommodation for 150 children at any one time, and the magistrates now felt justified in sending about 80 per cent of remand cases to their parents. [148]

Thus Crooks' commitment to his constituents, especially the children of the poor, is beyond question. He paid special attention to his first LCC electoral pledges, a tunnel between Greenwich and Blackwall, the employment of direct labour, strict enforcement of the Fair Wages Clause, 'whilst giving every attention to the general work of the Council and the interests of the District.'[149] He represented the interests of the working classes, who formed three-quarters of the ratepayers of Poplar. Thomas MacKinnon Wood (LCC Progressive), in a speech at St. James's Hall in January 1898, stated 'Messrs. Crooks and McDougall have made more attendances at the Council and Committee Meetings during the past year than 35 Moderate Members together.' For example, in the year 1898/99, Crooks' attendance at LCC meetings, Committee and Subcommittees numbered 340. He attended 75 meetings of MAB, and 200 meetings of the Poplar Guardians, Committees, and Subcommittees. Sometimes he attended sixteen meetings in a week, not including public meetings. [150]

POPLAR ENQUIRY 1906

In the period 1898-1905 the Poplar Guardians pursued a policy of humane assistance; adequate out-relief to the aged poor, and unemployed, which was not tolerable to the old order of Poor Law administrators, nor some officials of LGB. The practices of the Poplar Guardians met with resistance from the Municipal Alliance (Conservative/Unionist) and the Local Government Board. Locally, many ratepayers resented the money that the Guardians spent on poor people. Their opportunity came to denounce the Guardians at the Poplar Enquiry, which was set up by the LGB in 1906, to enquire into the payment of out-relief to the unemployed by the Poplar Board. The Guardians were accused of 'exploiting all the legal loopholes in the Poor Law in order to use their relieving powers to the fullest possible extent.'[151] The Municipal Alliance representing ratepayers had accused the Guardians of being 'guilty of wasteful and deliberate extravagance, and instead of administering the Poor Law with judgment and discretion, they have unduly fostered and increased pauperism in the district.'[152]

Leading Poor Law officials argued that the Guardians had undermined the central principle of deterrence, which was the spirit of the 1834 legislation.[153] The enquiry excited such widespread interest throughout the country that it stands out prominently in the early twentieth century history of Poor Law Government. It marked the public trial of a humane plan of treatment of the poor inaugurated by the Poplar Board, as against the old system, which reeked with harshness and injustice. The Guardians had revolutionized the old official treatment of the aged and infirm, and children of the poor. It had introduced an altogether new system of dealing with the able bodied, the object being to keep unemployed men in a physical condition to perform a day's work when it was available.

The resistance against the Poplar Guardians turned into outright attack in 1905 when the Liberal Government appointed John Burns as President of the Local Government Board. He ordered an enquiry into the running of the Poplar Union and nominated the reactionary Chief Inspector James S. Davy to conduct it.[154] Davy was known for the maintenance of poor law orthodoxy, of upholding the 'moral code of 1834', which underpinned the Victorian Poor Law system. The enquiry was seen by Crooks and Lansbury as a direct attack to challenge the reformers' work at Laindon and Hollesley Bay, and if possible convict the Poplar Union as a whole of misadministration, waste, and corruption, and they were of the opinion that the LGB had decided upon the outcome of the enquiry before it had even begun. Crooks stated in the *Pioneer*: 'Who demanded the Enquiry? In the first place, it must be borne in mind that *the enquiry was demanded by the Poplar Board of Guardians*.' (My italics). It can be assumed from Crooks' statement that the Guardians insisted upon an enquiry as a means of putting their system on trial, which they hoped would exonerate them from any wrongdoing. Although the Guardians for a long time had submitted to criticism, innuendo, and condemnation, they did not fear publicity. The Board expected no mercy, and it got none.

According to Crooks those that supported the enquiry represented the 'monied and capitalist classes, who see in the working of the system, and its consequent preservation of the manhood of the nation, a shrinkage in the field of their exploitation of the workers.' Further: 'Arrayed against the Guardians are all the forces conceivable in the shape of the Municipal Alliance and the other representatives of monopoly whose sole desire is to squeeze the manhood out of the people, and render still true the old adage "once a pauper, always a pauper".'[155] Crooks and Lansbury's ruling principle was that they were being true Guardians of the poor, and not merely Guardians of the Poor Rate.

Lansbury ascribed to the Local Government Board a perpetual malicious intent. He attacked those people on the Board as persons who wished to inflict suffering and humiliation on those that lacked money and would go a very long way in trickery and obstruction to punish local authorities who tried to be humane. Lansbury's underlying concern was that Burns wanted to undermine his standing on the Central (Unemployment) Body, and his Chairmanship of the Working Colonies Committee, which supported the Hollesley Bay scheme. Burns was 'hostile to the idea of labour colonies, and under his Presidency the Local Government Board soon declared Hollesley Bay *ultra vires*'.[156] Corrie Grant MP represented the Board of Guardians at the enquiry. The proceedings lasted twenty days between 7 June and 26 July; Crooks gave evidence for three of them. [157]

There had long been animosity between Crooks and Burns: Beatrice Webb was the main troublemaker. She befriended Burns for selfish reasons: 'With John Burns we are very friendly, but this is only because he is jealous of Macnamara and Crooks and has an old grudge against MacDonald.'[158] This animosity stemmed from MacDonald and Crooks' attempt to cut the grant of whisky money made by the TEB to the London School of Economics (LSE) in 1898: 'While Sidney and Beatrice Webb were on their tour of the United States'.[159]

The Webbs founded the LSE in 1895 with money left as a bequest to the Fabian Society by Henry Hutchinson. They saw themselves as the parents of the School and their child was under attack from the TEB; Sidney Webb was the Chairman of the TEB 1894-1904. What had this friendship between Burns and the Webbs have to do with the enquiry? John Burns and Beatrice Webb were political opportunists, who both had hidden political agendas. They knew that an enquiry into the affairs of the Poplar Guardians would be politically damaging for Crooks and Lansbury. Beatrice Webb in her diary records what Burns thought of Crooks; 'Crooks ... "would be ... out of Parliament" if he [Burns] were Providence.'[160] Crooks had not endeared himself to Burns, he had challenged and criticised his handling of the Poor Law, especially on how it should be implemented, in the House of Commons, ever since Burns had taken office. Burns for his own part was of the opinion that Crooks was a corrupt politician. Beatrice Webb questioned this: 'Or merely a demagogic sentimentalist?'[161]

Burns had betrayed his former socialist loyalties, according to Crooks and Lansbury. In 1907, Lansbury wrote a bitter attack against Burns over the issue of Hollesley Bay in *The Times*. In it, he said: 'To become the first working-class Cabinet minister, Burns had "carved his way to power ... by the unsparing use of the scalping knife and the tomahawk". He had outlived his early faith and "stepped from the ranks of the workers and become one of the bitterest opponents of all those principles and ideas by the preaching of which he obtained place and power".'[162] It seems that Burns wanted to make an example of Crooks and Lansbury for personal reasons to soothe his political ego, even though these two radical reformers represented a minority group of ten to twenty-four on the board.[163]

The majority were Conservatives and Liberals. Crooks and Lansbury's political clash with Burns over how the Poor Law should be delivered; especially regarding the payment of out-relief to old age pensioners and the unemployed, lay behind, and did much to distort the proceedings of the enquiry against both men. The Labour men saw the procedures of the enquiry as favouring the prosecution. For fifteen out of the twenty days that the enquiry lasted the Inspector allowed the Municipal Alliance practically to direct proceedings.

The enquiry exonerated the Union of any corruption or maladministration, and did much to enhance the reputations of Crooks and Lansbury; George Lansbury was elected as the MP for Bow and Bromley in the December 1910 election. Will Crooks resigned from the Poplar Union, accepting the usual vote of thanks on 3 April 1907.[164] He felt that it had been a mistake to carry on after his election to Parliament because there was less time to attend to the affairs of administration, but he was asked to remain. 'He little thought that some of those who had pressed him to stay would take advantage of his relaxed attention to bring discredit on the Board's administration.'[165] The Moderate Alliance had underestimated the loyalty of the people of Poplar, who stood by their Labour member in the Borough Council Elections that closely followed the enquiry:

> To them an insult to Crooks was an insult to Poplar. The Borough Council Elections followed soon after the inquiry, the Alliance throwing all its weight into

the local campaign. In nearly all the other London boroughs the Progressive and Labour men were badly beaten. In Poplar the Labour Party went back larger in numbers and backed by a stronger vote of the electors than they had ever before. Lansbury defeated the Chairman of the Alliance.[166]

The Conservatives took control, following the London County Council elections on 2 March 1907, and while Progressive and Labour seats toppled throughout London, Crooks was re-elected for Poplar, topping the poll with 3,504 votes, 'though the Alliance strained every nerve to oust him.' [167]

One casualty of the LCC elections was George Lansbury, the Woolwich Labour candidate, who came bottom of the poll with 7,611 votes, beaten by Municipal Reformers, although the combined Labour vote increased by 1,640 votes over the LCC Election figures of 1904.[168] Earlier, in November 1906, Lansbury had defeated the Chairman of the Municipal Alliance in the Poplar Council elections. To save face, 'the Alliance put on its list several Progressives'. ' "That," said Crooks at the time, in an interview in one of the daily papers, "is the answer of the people of Poplar to the slanders and misrepresentations levelled against us. The people of Poplar know the truth about the Inquiry; the people of London do not — they only have the Yellow Press version." '[169]

On 8 November, the Davy Report on the Poplar Poor Law Enquiry was presented to the House of Commons in the form of a Parliamentary paper. The following day Crooks sent a letter to the Press. In it, he complained that the report was unfair, and that it contained prejudices and misstatements: "Do you think it's fair," he asked:

> that a relief officer [Davy] should be sent down to make such an inquiry who has already made up his mind on the merits of the case?...to-day I have been told by members of all parties that the report is not only wicked but brutal.... I propose to appeal ... to the public.... If the public upholds this insult to the poor I shall be painfully surprised. [170]

Crooks was quite happy to accept the challenge thrown down by the Local Government Board. He was quite adamant that he was not going to change his policy of humanising the Poor Law, a cause that had taken up the greater part of his life.

Crooks was true to his word, he appealed to the public. While sections of the press were still being aggressive towards him, he addressed great meetings throughout the country. His appeal to the public had the support and confidence of working people all over England. Crooks was seen as the man who had stood up against the Poor Law system and the Government's vicious assault on Poplar's Poor Law policy. 'At Chesterfield he addressed an open-air meeting of twenty thousand Midland miners, where his reference to his Poor

Law policy was cheered to the echo.' There was the same fervour when he attended the Cleveland miner's annual gathering. This enthusiasm continued at public meetings in Newcastle, Burton, Huddersfield, Rossendale, Stockport, Batley, Sunderland, Penarth, and Bradford. At Crooks' indoor meetings, 'there were rarely fewer than two thousand people present. Often he spoke to audiences of four and five thousand.' [171] A crowd of over two thousand turned out at a Labour rally at the Drill Hall, Woolwich. It was Crooks' first public meeting in Woolwich since the report was published.

The emphasis of his message was always the same; the only thing he and Lansbury were guilty of was that they had endeavoured to take care of the aged and unemployed paupers, those people who were unable to look after themselves, and make their lives a little happier. Was this wrong? Crooks would ask. People knew they could depend on him to champion the bottom-dog.

3

UNEMPLOYMENT AND THE POOR LAW

After the great strike of 1889, and the formation of the Dockers' Union in 1890, casual labour on the docks was greatly reduced. The consequence of this was that between five and six thousand men were without work, and were forced to find employment in the manufacturing and the service sector. In his report on the Poplar Union in 1906, James Stewart Davy, Chief General Inspector of the Local Government Board, wrote: 'There is no doubt that there has been within the last twenty years a considerable change ... Poplar ... is becoming less a port than a manufacturing town. The large ironworks and shipbuilding trade had moved elsewhere, and the conditions of the shipping trade have changed to materially affect the work of the dockers.' At the same time the matchmaking, jam making, confectionery and other trades that were 'largely dependent on casual labour had been started in the union'.[1]

The Royal Commission on Labour 1893-4 stated that in its view: 'The continued demoralisation of the riverside population of East London by the system of casual labour, constitutes ... the gravest of all the problems that the metropolis presents.'[2] For example, the Census Returns of 1901 (London County Council) show that 'occupations filling a large place among Poplar male residents are those of clerks, railwaymen, carmen, seamen, dockers, dealers in food, and — by far the largest class — casual menials (general labourers) and men in the engineering and metal trades.'[3] Although factory employment in the engineering trade increased by 10 per cent 1901-1904, the census and factory figures show that the better and more regularly paid men lived outside Poplar; contributing little, if anything, to the local economy. By comparison, the men who lived in Poplar were largely dependent upon employment that was casual.[4] It has been estimated that in 1901, about 29.9 per cent of the male workforce were unskilled, and 25.3 per cent semi-skilled.[5] It was this emphasis on the importance of casual labour that largely produced the problem of unemployment that the Poplar authorities had to deal with; firstly in the winters of 1892-5, secondly in the depression of 1902-5, and thirdly in 1908.

The principle that directed Crooks in all his dealings with the unemployed was his belief that 'the only sound way to help an unemployed man ... is by work rather than by relief. The condition he imposed on the provision of such work was that it must be useful. He would have nothing to do with "works" provided only as "relief." Work that is not useful can never relieve'.[6] In other words, he saw work for relief as base and demoralising. The workingman needed employment that paid earnings, work that was meaningful. Local authorities should provide 'work which had a definite public advantage'.[7] He believed 'as the poor belonged to the Empire, so the Empire should look after them'. As the problem of unemployment was a national one the government should initiate legislation giving local authorities the power of combination and organisation to provide useful work, the cost of which should be met wholly or in part by the government.[8] Will Crooks was steadfast in the belief that the government of the day should be responsible for the unemployed, and should not leave the responsibility of dealing with it through the rates to local authorities, especially those districts that suffered from exceptional distress from the want of employment, such as Poplar. This fundamental tenet guided him throughout his agitation on behalf of the unemployed.

UNEMPLOYMENT RELIEF 1892-95

With the development of a factory-based economy, plus the decline of traditional trades, Poplar's economy was vulnerable to wide fluctuations. This was its fundamental weakness, and led to irregular employment which was the underlying cause of working-class poverty, 'itself a result less of low wages than recurring unemployment'. Here was a permanent and apparently irreducible mass of unskilled workers that were exposed to the disheartening effects of changes in the labour market and recurrent under-employment.[9] This was further exacerbated between 1892-5, by severe winter weather in conjunction with an acute depression of trade, causing constant distress and unemployment in the poorer districts of London, especially in the East End. The winter in 1895 was particularly severe when 'the Thames was immobilised by blocks of ice' and the Port of London came to a standstill.[10] The great frost set in on 24 January, and lasted over three weeks. On Thursday 8 February 'after the tide began to ebb ... the river between London-bridge and the Tower was almost covered with a solid field of ice', and on the following Sunday 'when the tide was slack, the whole distance between London-bridge and the Surrey Commercial Docks was a solid mass.' For example, on 8 February the temperature at Greenwich, across the river from Poplar, was 12 degrees Fahrenheit (-11 degrees Celsius). [11]

Historians do not look at Crooks in any detail in this period. For example, Haw in *Workhouse to Westminster* while describing Crooks' guiding principles for dealing with the unemployed 1892-1905, is somewhat sketchy, and chronologically vague.[12] While Ryan and Keith-Lucas in their articles on 'Poplarism' briefly discuss the Poplar Guardians' attitude towards unemployment and the Poor Law in the 1890s, the emphasis of their studies is the role of Crooks and Lansbury as Guardians of the Poor after 1903.[13] On the other hand, Harris in *Unemployment and Politics* examines in detail the social problem of unemployment in London between 1886 and 1914, and discusses the reaction to new ways of investigating the unemployment problem, and the difficulty of social administration.[14] Again, unemployment is examined in a Poplar context but Crooks does not play any significant part. Therefore, it is important to revise the evidence of historiography, and examine the role of Will Crooks.

Crooks was, by example, able to convince other progressives that local authorities could be persuaded to provide work for the unemployed. His contribution towards the needs of the unemployed in the winter 1892-3, especially his influence in persuading the Poplar District Board of Works to provide work for the unemployed, exemplifies this, and needs to be examined in detail. It is significant that the Poplar Guardians did not involve themselves in the administration of unemployment relief until after Crooks and Lansbury were elected to the Board in April 1893. Will Crooks' requests to the local authorities urging them to find work for the unemployed in periods of exceptional distress was not without precedence. In March 1886, the President of the Local Government Board (LGB), Joseph Chamberlain, sent a Circular Letter to the Board of Guardians, entitled *Pauperism and Distress,* stating:

> In districts in which exceptional distress prevails, the Board recommend that the Guardians should confer with the Local Authorities, and endeavour to arrange with the latter for the execution of works on which unskilled labour may be immediately employed.... expenses may be properly defrayed out of borrowed moneys, the Local Authorities may rely that there will be every desire on the part of the Board to deal promptly with the application for the sanction to a loan.[15]

Crooks saw the opportunity during the period of extreme distress in the winter 1892-3 of implementing the Chamberlain circular. He urged local authorities, and the trade union and progressive movement, to test it. Crooks was ideally placed to lobby on behalf of the unemployed; he was a Poplar Trustee, London County Council representative, delegate to the London Trades Council, and a member of the Poplar Labour Election Committee. In addition, his position in the wider London progressive movement earned him the reputation between the London working-class as an implacable agitator on behalf of the poor and unemployed.

In September 1892, Crooks made a strong appeal to the London progressives 'for prompt action to cope with the unemployed question, and prepare for the distress, which would undoubtedly increase as the severe weather approached.'[16] The PLEC, of which Crooks was an executive member, wrote to every trade and labour union in the district asking them for a return of the number of unemployed members, and the general state of trade. They sent a resolution to all Cabinet ministers urging them to instruct 'all local authorities responsible ... to push on without delay all necessary work ... for the purpose of alleviating the present distress, which must become intensified as winter approaches'. A resolution was also sent to the LTC requesting them 'to send a deputation to the heads of Government Departments for the purpose of urging useful public work'.[17] Subsequently on 20 October the LTC requested Henry Fowler, President of the Local Government Board (LGB) 'to issue to all local government bodies a circular urging them to carry out at once all useful work in their respective districts, in order to mitigate, as much as possible, the distress through want of employment'. The LTC also sent 'a communication ... to every vestry and local government board in the metropolis urging them to set up temporary labour exchanges with the object of registering the unemployed and possibly finding work'.[18]

Crooks, encouraged by the support afforded to him by his colleagues in the trade union and labour movement, was not content to let the problem of unemployment rest without pressing for urgent measures to be put in motion by local authorities, especially those with responsibilities for Poplar. For example, at the Poplar Trustees' meeting on 29 October, Crooks brought forward a motion requesting the Trustees 'to urge upon the Local Board [of Works] the desirability of pushing all necessary work, with a view to giving occupation to some of the great army of the unemployed'.[19] He also wrote a letter to the Local Board of Works in his capacity as LCC representative endorsing the Trustees' position. Crooks suggested that the Board do what it can 'to push forward all the work possible during the coming winter, and thus enable some men to find employment who would otherwise be starving'.[20] On 1 November, Crooks was invited to address the Board on the business of the letter. He explained:

... that the movement which he wished to support was a national one, and that he did not wish to take any course which would bring the unemployed to the district or to London ... He was not advocating the cause of the loafer or ne'er do well, and had reasons to believe there were a great many unemployed of the genuine working class ... He repudiated the suggestion of putting men on at a low wage, but would prefer that work should be spread over a number of unemployed by different parties of men, having worked say three days a week at a proper rate.[21]

The issue was referred to the Works Committee, which would meet on 7 November; Crooks was invited to attend. On 14 November 1892, Henry Fowler reissued the Chamberlain circular and asked local authorities to inform him of the progress of local works.[22] The Fowler circular endorsed the deliberations of the Board, and further served to endorse providing work for the unemployed.

At the next meeting of the Board of Works on 15 November, a deputation was received representing twenty-one organisations, consisting of delegates from trade and labour unions, and local associations. The delegation was led by J. A. Murray Macdonald, Radical Liberal MP for Bow and Bromley, and included George Lansbury of the Gasworkers' (Bromley E Branch), and the Rev. H. A. Kennedy of the PLEC. They were of the 'opinion that the present distress is abnormal ... and ... that the distress will become greater after Christmas.' Their demand was for work for the unemployed; including the cleansing of streets, the laying out of a disused burial ground, and setting out open spaces.[23]

The Chairman of the Works Committee reported on the meeting to consider how the Board could help unemployed men. He said 'they had given the matter careful consideration, and had the advantage of the attendance of Mr. Crooks, who showed that 30 per cent of the labouring population of Poplar were out of work.'[24] The recommendation was to employ no more than a hundred men on cleansing, and repairing roads, at the same rate as those men already employed. 'The same men not to be engaged more than three days a week if other applicants present themselves' and only those resident in the district for twelve months would be considered.[25] The recommendations to the Board were agreed upon unanimously. It was also decided to set up a Special Committee of the Board on the Unemployed to help carry out the adopted recommendations and deal with the men who were already registering for work. It was reported during the meeting that over 600 men had registered as unemployed at the Board offices.[26] Crooks was unable to attend at the start of the meeting due to LCC business but arrived before the close with Ben

Cooper, his friend and colleague who sat on the LCC Open Spaces Committee with him.[27]

The Board of Works had thus agreed to employ no more than one hundred unemployed men. The number to be allotted to the districts of Poplar was dealt with by the Special Committee, forty to Poplar, forty to Bromley, twenty to Bow.[28] 'Numbers ranging between seventy-three and ninety-two daily were put on to sweep roads from November 17th to December 24th.'[29] The rate of pay was four shillings a day for ten hours; the same men were employed for three days a week, and the daily average number of men employed was seventy-eight.[30] The ratepayers opposed the course being pursued by the Special Committee, and 'urged ... the desirability of taking land upon which the unemployed could be engaged in preparing stone for the repair of the road.' In other words, the unemployed should be engaged breaking stones. The Board meeting of 29 November agreed to leave this letter of complaint on the table.[31]

It can be seen but for Crooks' untiring advocacy for a scheme to meet the needs of the unemployed, it is doubtful whether such a scheme would have seen the light of day. The evidence shows that his administrative skills and knowledge of the issue under discussion were influential when lobbying for action on the issues of reform, especially those conditions that surrounded the poor, poverty, and unemployment. Crooks' tactics were effective on two fronts, at the regional level through the LTC, and at the local political level with the support of Crooks 'College' and the PLEC. It is not clear Crooks participated in the debate at the Delegate Meeting of the LTC on 20 October 1892.[32] Probably he did, and urged the meeting to lobby Fowler to reissue the Chamberlain circular. By putting pressure on the LGB to implement an official directive to local authorities, the London trade union and labour movement could pursue their aim of dealing with the problem of unemployment legitimately. It was not only the LTC that lobbied Fowler, the metropolitan local government authorities organised resolutions, and delegations, calling upon the LGB to issue a recommendation in support of their finding useful work for the unemployed. A feature of the agitation was that local trustees, vestries, and boards of guardians organised numerous conferences on unemployment.

The Mansion House Conference on the Condition of the Unemployed was convened in the winter of 1892 at Toynbee Hall, to consider the question of distress in the East End. Because of the deliberations, an Executive Committee was formed to deal with the distress among waterside labourers of East London. The Rev. Marmaduke Hare, Rector of Bow, the Rev. Arthur Chandler, Rector of Poplar, and Sydney Buxton MP were the Poplar representatives.[33] The Conference reported that their independent inquiry exactly confirmed the conclusion of John Burns in his article in the December issue of the *Nineteenth Century*. 'Taking London as a whole there is about the average number out of work for this time of year; but taking groups of trades and districts, as the extreme East-End, things are nearly as bad as 1886.' [34] In an earlier publication on Unemployment, John Burns had discussed the altered outlook of the unemployed labourer in 1893:

> The unemployed labourer to-day is not a replica of the out-of-work of a few years back. His predecessor was a patient, long suffering animal, accepting his position as beast of burden with a fatalistic taciturnity, looking upon his enforced idleness as inevitable, and with blind submission enduring his lot ... Mute, inarticulate, unenfranchised, he escaped observation because he had no vote, no political, no municipal influence.[35]

The growth of the labour movement — to some extent — had changed all this, through education, trade unionism, socialist propaganda, and the struggle involved in the extension of the franchise.

This had been the case in Poplar since the establishment of Crooks 'College' in 1887. It is important to note that the campaign to build the Blackwall tunnel had succeeded by November 1892, and the LCC Fair Wages campaign was at its height. Crooks 'College' and the PLEC were central to these campaigns, and the question of unemployment was an integral part of the debate on the direct employment of labour. Crooks' intervention on behalf of unemployed workers was an example of the action that they had come to expect from him. After all he had lectured to them often enough on the subject of unemployment at the East India Dock Gate and at Poplar Town Hall. John Burns further said of the unemployed worker: 'His eyes are now open, and the Samson of labour has pulled from them the bandage that class rule, apathy, and his own ignorance and drunkenness had placed upon him.'[36]

In the winter of 1893, Will Crooks became a member of the Poplar Relief Committee. It became possibly the most productive committee for relieving distress in the metropolis. Twelve years later, according to George Haw, it became the basis of the Workmen Unemployment Act. 'It represented co-operation between a committee of citizens and the local authorities.'[37] Crooks said of it, 'he has never known a committee to equal it in the completeness and thoroughness of its investigations.'[38] The Relief Committee was started at the suggestion of the Christian Social Union, of which Canon Scot Holland was chairman, 'and was designed to meet, in some small measure, the exceptional distress that had unhappily prevailed during the past winter.'[39] Crooks joined at the request of the Rector of Poplar (Rev. Arthur Chandler). He describes how at the first meeting his influence profoundly transformed the committee, from one controlled by the clergy and social workers, to a workmanlike body.[40] Crooks told them their first duty was to broaden their position:

> You will never do anything so long as your committee is confined to gentlemen like these, he told the clerical chairman [Chandler]. What you need is to get hold of trade union secretaries and the secretaries of the friendly and temperance societies and members of working men's clubs. They will soon discriminate between the waster and the deserving man. The waster is always boasting that parsons are so easily deceived.[41]

After this recommendation to widen its ranks, the Committee's constitution was changed to include representative workingmen, local clergy, the secretary of the Charity Organisation Society (COS), and others.[42] 'It ... gave relief in cash and kind from a fund (£500) raised by the Bishop of London.'[43] Towards the end of March, Chandler wrote to the *East End News*, praising the workingmen members on the Committee for their 'zeal and judgement.... Their action has convinced me that municipal bodies in general, and Board of Guardians in particular, would be immensely strengthened by the presence upon them of ... working men.'[44] This letter was significant because it can be seen that Chandler was supporting Crooks' candidature for election to the Poplar Guardians in April, and by association endorsing the PLEC's electoral platform and the Labour split with the Liberals; subjects that dominated the correspondence in the *East End News* during this period.[45]

In 1893 Crooks appealed to both the Thames Conservancy and the Board of Trade in September and November respectively concerning his scheme to 'help in allaying the threatened distress of the coming winter by reclaiming the [Thames] foreshores' between London Bridge and Woolwich. [46] He said: 'It will give employment to thousands of men, will not interfere with existing industries, and will show a good result for the outlay.' Crooks realised that work provided for the unemployed by local authorities could not cope with the situation, and what he was 'mostly concerned for ... what can be done at once.'[47] After putting his scheme forward in the press and at numerous public meetings,
he was urged to put it before A. J. Mundella, President at the Board of Trade. He pointed out to him:

> ... that under the Foreshores Act of 1866 the Board of Trade had power to reclaim land. Again, under an Act of 1857 the Thames Conservancy could reclaim miles of foreshore in and below London. I showed that this was just the kind of work to absorb unskilled labour, and supplied

examples of the success of reclaiming land on the banks of the Forth and the Tay and on the Lincolnshire coast. [48]

This letter epitomises Crooks' belief that the government of the day, especially a Liberal one, should be responsible for the unemployed, and provide financial help through the exchequer. There is no extant record that shows this scheme was acted upon.

The Poplar Relief Committee met again in the winter 1893-4. They were strengthened by the addition of Sydney Buxton as treasurer, and by members of the Board of Works and Board of Guardians. It also divided into two committees, one dealing with charitable relief, and one with employment assistance. During November 1893, Will Crooks received an offer of £1000 for the unemployed from Mr. A. F. Hills, chairman of the Thames Shipbuilding Company on condition that the local authorities did likewise. The Relief Committee put the offer before the Local Board (Crooks claimed that he persuaded the Board to accept), who 'agreed to do its part, provided that it should have full control of the works'. The Relief Committee was given the task of investigating applications and recommending suitable men. In addition, the Committee's work was extended to include the districts of Bow and Bromley.[49] During the winter of 1894, the paving of the Bow Road with wood provided the main relief work, and the total cost of relief work was over £15,000. Hills later 'expressed disillusionment with this method of relief'. Crooks later stated 'although there was a loss of 10 per cent upon the work ... this was more than saved to the rates by the subscription list that had been raised.'[50]

In November 1894, Crooks chaired an unemployment conference organised by the Poplar Guardians in the Board Room, Upper North Street. The Metropolitan Board and West Ham Guardians were invited to consider calling on Henry Chaplin, President of the Local Government Board to use his powers 'to form the several Unions and Parishes of the Metropolis and West Ham into one district to be called the London Unemployed District ... that such district when formed should at once take in hand the question of establishing farms near London'. [51] In their reply, the LGB stated that they were considering the matter but there was a need for a specific plan, a proposal and details of the scheme's management were necessary; the Board promised to give the matter their full consideration. [52]

The Guardians' support for the unemployed did not stop there. On 22 January 1895 Crooks led a deputation of the unemployed to meet with the District Board of Works, urging upon them the necessity of putting in hand at the earliest moment all work that could be undertaken by the unemployed, work that would not interfere with the labour market. Crooks and Lansbury organised a lobby of a full meeting of the District Board the following week. The Board offered the men a day's work immediately, and promised that their case would be referred to the Works Committee. The following day, 1 February, one thousand unemployed men attended the Guardians' meeting at North Street, Poplar. There was a further 1,000 outside who were unable to get in. A resolution calling for a further meeting of the unemployed the following Saturday was carried. Reporting to this meeting the Poplar Special Committee on the Unemployed stated that they had agreed to set up a labour colony, and were to visit a site near Laindon, Essex. Laindon and Hollesley Bay colonies were eventually set up in 1904-5.[53]

In response to the unemployment deputations the Guardians called an Extraordinary Meeting on 15 February to discuss out-door relief. It was resolved to open in each Parish of the Union, Poplar, Bow and Bromley, labour yards to provide work. After receiving the accounts for expenditure on running the labour yards between 19 February and 9 March, it was resolved to spend a further sum of £1,000 on out-door relief, and after that the labour yards were to be closed. Crooks supported the closure of the stone yards; Lansbury and the SDF group on the Board opposed it. [54] William Beveridge points out that '1895 is the year of guardians' stone yards, and of their final condemnation as a means of dealing with the unemployed.'[55]

There was a violent reaction to the closure: 150 men entered the workhouse demanding relief. Crooks was accused publicly of 'doing nothing for the working classes who paid him for his services'. He was also threatened with his life. At a meeting at the Dock Gate, both Crooks and Lansbury denounced one another over the closure. Lansbury and the SDF accused Crooks of being 'a thorough reactionary ... now he was in league with the Liberals and Radicals again he had to do just as his paymasters, the capitalists and sweaters told him to do.' Crooks said in response: 'He was for Labour pure and simple. He was under the thumb of no body of men — who might if one chanced to differ with them, demand his instant resignation — as were Lansbury and Goult to the SDF.' 'This conflict between Crooks and Lansbury was less concerned with stone yards as such — both disliked them — than over the nature of their response to popular pressure.' [56]

Crooks felt that many of the men employed at the Poor Law stone yard were not really in need of relief.[57] They were loafers, recruited by Lansbury and the SDF, who had been advised to harass Crooks, and to use every means to intimidate the Guardians.[58] In the context of this row, it is important to recognise that Crooks was seen by his constituents as an honest man who put their needs first. The object of bullying him into making a decision which he did not agree with must have seemed disreputable to them. Crooks was obviously annoyed at the political attitude of his critics, and their sectarian posturing, which was anathema to him because it was politically divisive, and did nothing to help the 'respectable' able-bodied workingman. A friend and colleague John R. Clynes MP, gives an example of how Will Crooks would have responded to this censure in a biographical sketch. He said, 'when his mood was altered to condemnation or wrath it made his censure the more emphatic and cutting.'[59]

In February 1895, the General Purposes Committee of the Poplar Union inspected a number of farms in Essex with the intention of negotiating the purchase of one of them. A provisional contract was entered into for the purchase of Dunton Wayletts Farm. It was felt that an immediate application be made to the Local Government Board for authority to purchase such land for poor work 'in connection with poor relief.' In June, the LGB responded to the Union asking for full particulars of the proposal to buy the farm. The Guardians were asked to submit draft regulations for their approval. The suggested instructions were sent for approval on 3 July 1895, plus they estimated the cost of erecting buildings at £4,000. Henry Chaplin wrote to the Poplar Union on 7 August stating that the proposals submitted to purchase was 'in excess of the statutory limit and the enactments in question do not empower the guardians to provide buildings for the use of the persons employed.' Subsequently, the Guardians dropped the scheme. The government was also lobbied in January 1896; a letter was sent to the Prime Minister, Lord Salisbury, urging the government to bring forward measures dealing with the question of unemployment during the coming session of Parliament. The records show that Crooks and the Poplar Union examined every possibility in their quest to initiate relief schemes for the unemployed. [60]

THE WINTERS OF DISTRESS 1902-5

Unemployment, which had remained fairly low since the mid-1890s, began to rise during the years of the Boer War 1899-1902, 'at the same time real wages tended to fall, making the army a more attractive prospect', according to Richard Price. He further points out that during the war recruitment figures and the time of high unemployment show a definite trend, 'it should be noted that the time of highest unemployment — the winter of 1902 — was also the time of greatest working class recruitment.' [61] Unemployment steadily declined between 1894 and 1899, then increased every year until 1904, when according to Board of Trade figures it stood at 7.1 per cent.[62] The post-war depression according to Elie Halévy cannot be accounted for solely by the sudden demobilisation of 200,000 men in the army. For it began, 'not with the restoration of peace [May 1902], but in 1900'. He hypothesis's that the depression can be explained demographically. That at the beginning of the twentieth century there was an abrupt influx of labour which industry was unable to assimilate, due to a birth rate that had realised its maximum twenty years before, and a death rate that had constantly declined over the same period. Also according to Halévy, 'the most characteristic feature of these two or three years of depression was the chorus of complaints raised by the employers.... Surely the true explanation is the warlike policy of the Government and the sudden increase in taxation.' [63]

During the distress of the 1890s, the Poor Law had ceased to fulfil its proper function of administering relief, especially to the able-bodied poor. There were the usual calls in 1902-3 upon the government to intervene, and extend the powers of the local authorities 'to grant a sufficient sum of monies from national funds', and 'to extend powers to Boards of Guardians to assist those in distress by Poor Law relief without inflicting political disfranchisement.'[64] According to Harris, 'even if ... proposal[s] for the abolition of disfranchisement had been accepted it is unlikely that poor relief would ever be acceptable to the bulk of the unemployed', because as stated above the 'stigma of pauperism' meant more than just forfeiture of the franchise. The franchise was a politically contentious issue between the conservatives and the radicals. The radicals accused the conservatives of intentionally encouraging the poor to accept relief in order to get them struck off the electoral register, while conservative critics accused the guardians of yielding to popular pressure. [65]

In 1902, Crooks stated in the *East End News* that some causes of the present distress were preventable, and for this the Government was to blame, particularly Joseph Chamberlain, the Colonial Secretary:

> We are supposed ... to have a Government of business men; at least the Colonial Secretary says so. Yet they rush the soldiers home as soon as possible instead of waiting until spring, which would have been the proper course. The consequence is that the normal slackness which is usual in winter time among such trades as building, excavating, and so on, is added to not only by men who have returned from serving with the colors but also by many others who found employment upon the large fleet of transports which were used.[66]

Furthermore, he could not see the practicality of the Government appealing to 'patriotic' employers to find work for the 'home-coming Tommy'. 'If then, they discharge Jack to find work for Tommy the case is just as broad as it is long.'[67]

In other words, the employers had only so much work, and government intervention only served to transfer the needs of one class of workingman to another.

When the Poplar Borough Council superseded the Board of Works in 1900, powers were transferred to the Borough, including the responsibilities of inquiring into cases of distress and effecting methods of relief. Moreover, in 1902 an Act was introduced into Parliament legitimising expenditure on labour bureaux out of the rates.[68] In November 1900, Will Crooks stood as a Labour candidate in the Council elections. He was elected topping the poll in North West Ward with 723 votes.[69] Subsequently Crooks became Mayor of Poplar in November 1901, and thus became the first Labour Mayor in London. The procedure was that the Mayor was elected on a show of hands and on this occasion, no clear winner emerged, so the outgoing Mayor drew lots and declared for Crooks. It is often thought that Crooks was the obvious choice but the record shows that the Borough Councillors did not think so. They were split down the middle, because half of them were against Poplar being represented by a workingman Mayor.[70]

It was the desire of most public men to be Mayor in Coronation Year. Crooks declined to accept a salary. He was now ideally placed — Chairman of the Poplar Guardians, Borough Mayor, Poplar's representative on the LCC — to influence decisions made by the local authorities to find work for the unemployed in line with the Chamberlain circular, and execute Henry Fowler's recommendations. Thus, Crooks became a leading member of both — Guardians and the Council — controlling authorities of rate support relief in the district.

Will Crooks' influence, and the control that Labour exercised, especially upon the Poplar Guardians, evoked alarm, and consternation among middle-class critics. So much so, that Crooks' involvement in Poplar's administration of the Poor Law was attacked in *The Times* on 22 September 1902. The content of the article 'Municipal Socialism' was both disparaging and vindictive towards Crooks, and the working-class people of Poplar. The article blamed the ordinary middle-class elector as being 'too apathetic to go to the trouble to record his vote', and it was because of this apathy that Labour and Socialist influences controlled large interests in Poplar, 'some of the largest and most important industrial undertakings to be found in any one district in or around London'. Furthermore, the newspaper declared that:

> ... if they would only vote [the middle-class] — to return really capable and desirable representatives, possessed of some idea of the value for money, able to control large interests, and having some degree of scruple in not

acquitting themselves of their public duties in the personal interests of the people that elect them [71]

Crooks and his Labour colleagues were accused of being unprincipled, undesirable, and incapable as representatives, devoid of any idea as to the value of money, and was an obstacle in the way of vested interests.

Crooks' response was immediate. He accused the paper of 'yellow journalism' and said that the article 'has very discourteously given quite unnecessary advertisement and moreover recorded a lengthy statement of inaccuracies', and that it was full of 'unjustifiable errors ... relating to Poplar and the action of its local authorities'. He pointed out that the LGB had approved Poplar's Poor Law administration, and that the Board had insisted that boards of guardians in England and Wales amend their workhouse dietary scales 'up to the level of Poplar'. Crooks further pointed out that trade unionists on public bodies 'can and do discharge their duties irrespective of partisan feelings that are supposed to actuate them', unlike the present Government, who find soft jobs for their friends, 'whether they have the capacity or not ... no such charge has ever been proved against the Labour representatives of Poplar.' [72]

The 1902 article in the *Times* was an isolated one. Overall, the Establishment preferred to ignore what was going on in Poplar, while comfortable profits from local industry continued to go to people in rich parts of London. Unwittingly the article helped boost Will Crooks' popularity, and it could have played, although there is no direct evidence to support it, an important part in promoting Crooks' adoption in December 1902, when he was invited to contest the Woolwich Parliamentary seat for Labour.

The Relief Schemes

During the winter of 1902-3, the accommodation in the Workhouse at Poplar was inadequate for the number of persons requiring indoor relief so that immediate steps became necessary to relieve the pressure. It was reported that, in September 1902, there were 1,372 inmates and this number increased to 1,568, being in excess of 253 over the certified number in December. A temporary workhouse at Hackney was secured and used to deal with the overcrowding; 130 able-bodied inmates were transferred to Hackney from Poplar. As soon as the approach of summer caused the number of inmates of the Poplar Workhouse to decrease sufficiently the temporary workhouse was closed. While this measure met the difficulty for the time being, it was a distinct failure as a way of providing adequate employment for able-bodied inmates. [73]

During this period, the scarcity of riverside work and the return of the soldiers from South Africa combined to cause a considerable amount of distress. The churches and Salvation Army opened soup kitchens and a farthing breakfast depot. The clergy set up distress funds, and appeals to the press to assist increased. To come to terms with the situation, Crooks played an important part in bringing together the trade union, labour movement, and the progressive clergy in Poplar. He also — in early December — took on the added responsibility of becoming one of the treasurers of the *Daily News* East End Relief Fund, which raised over £7,000, of which £2,500 was spent in Poplar. [74]

On 15 December 1902, he attended the Poplar Trades Council meeting, and a public meeting — both held in Bromley — to discuss the organisation of unemployed work schemes. In addition, the Mayor at the request of the Guardians convened a conference on 19 December of aldermen, councillors, guardians, the members of Parliament for the district, and other progressive representatives at the Council offices, Poplar. The meeting was convened to consider what steps should be taken to alleviate the terrible distress. It was emphasised at the meetings that the unemployed question was a national one that should be dealt with by Parliament. The Government was urged to find funds to enable local authorities to find work for the unemployed. Ben Cooper, chairman of the Trades Council, stated 'such work not to be of a local, but a national character', and this would help to lessen the poverty and suffering that existed. He also informed the meeting that the LCC were doing all they could by introducing schemes to alleviate the scarcity of work. Councillor Job Bellsham at the unemployment meeting in Bromley suggested that the proper solution was for the Government to 'recognise unemployed labour by the establishment of national farming, workshops, etc. It was also pointed out by Stopford Brooks, the Radical Parliamentary Candidate for Bromley, 'England had miles and miles of uncultivated land ... thousands of men might be employed ... if only the Government were ... to cultivate the land themselves, the distress in the towns would not be half so bad.' [75]

At the borough conference it was reported that the Council had already approved giving employment to 400 extra men three days a week for a month; further works were proposed, and 'registers of unemployed workmen had been opened at the Council depot.'[76] An appeal was issued for subscriptions to the East End Relief Fund, and an executive committee appointed to administer the fund through committees, five members from Poplar, and five from Bromley.[77] In addition, the Guardians had recently — on the initiation of Will Crooks — taken an area of land at Shenfield, as a site for a new school where some road making would have to be carried out. It was decided to offer work immediately, as far as subscriptions to the relief fund permitted, to as many men as possible. The result of this exercise — for the Guardians — of finding useful work for the unemployed, and relieving their families at the same time out of the fund proved 'satisfactory and successful.' [78] The success of the Shenfield experiment influenced the way the Guardians dealt with the problem of unemployment and poverty in future periods of distress. The Guardians sealed the issue by buying a farm at Laindon in 1903.

It is important to note that although Will Crooks was heavily committed and able to influence decisions made in Poplar, he was always aware of the broader picture in London and in the country as a whole. As was pointed out above, he believed the problem of unemployment was a national one, a view held strongly by other reformers, and that the Government should take on the responsibility of bringing about measures enabling local authorities to deal with it. Since the Government obstinately refused to act upon representations made by trade unions, boards of guardians, and local councils, on how the present unemployment problem could be dealt with by the introduction of a national scheme. It was decided to invite all the administrative authorities in London to attend a conference on 13 February 1903, organised by the LCC, 'and if necessary, to call a further Conference of all public bodies throughout the United Kingdom.'[79]

Probably, Will Crooks and Sir John McDougall, Chairman of the LCC (elected November 1902),[80] had discussed the problem of the government's intransigence on the unemployment question, and how best to confront their obdurate attitude with other leading members of the Labour bench on the LCC: John Burns, James Ramsay MacDonald, Bill Steadman, and Sidney Webb. Therefore, in the likelihood that these discussions did happen, it was most probable that they decided to call for a conference on unemployment by lobbying support for a resolution to this effect at the Council meeting 16 December 1902,[81] in the hope of bringing pressure to bear on the Government. After all Crooks and McDougall were the LCC representatives for Poplar, and were committed, along with their colleagues on the LCC, to do all in their power to bring about relief for the unemployed of London.

According to the record, it is obvious that the Conference was initiated by Poplar, by Crooks and McDougall with the support of both the local Council and Guardians. Not only were Crooks and McDougall responsible for moving the resolution calling for an unemployment conference at the December meeting of the LCC, but also the main resolutions suggested at the Conference were from the Poplar Council, and the Guardians. Crooks' political blueprint and influence can be identified throughout both resolutions, so much so that Crooks himself could have written them. Considering the inestimable influence he had on both bodies he probably did. The resolution of Poplar Council suggested this:

That the Government be urged to take steps immediately to undertake certain extensive work of public benefit to be carried out in convenient sections to giving workmen permanent employment away from large cities and to aiding them in times of exceptional distress, such works to include afforestation, reclamation of the foreshores, and making of a national road round the coast, etc.[82]

The Poplar Guardians suggested that the resolution was amended to include river improvements, and the establishment of agricultural communities.[83]

Will Crooks had long held the belief — before his letter to Mundella in 1893, that the government should be responsible for organising public works for the unemployed, especially the reclamation of the foreshores of the river Thames, and the establishment of work farms. Therefore given Crooks' influence, dedication, and his commitment to this proposal, it should come as no surprise that the resolution was finally adopted following supportive speeches by him, and Councillor Alex Main of Poplar Borough Council.[84] At this meeting several suggestions were discussed on how to deal with the present lack of employment, and recommendations were ultimately referred to a Committee consisting of fifteen members, who agreed to 'present their report at a second meeting of the Conference, held at County Hall, on 3rd April 1903.' Crooks and John Burns were unanimously elected on to the Committee, and were joined among others by MacDonald, Steadman, and the progressive clergyman, Canon Escreet of the Woolwich Guardians. The report was subsequently presented and approved by the LCC Council on 27 October 1903.[85]

Without waiting for the commencement of another winter the Guardians in July 1903 asked the Local Government Committee to consider the desirability of the establishment of a 'country workhouse' for the able-bodied men where farm work could be undertaken. While this correspondence continued, George Lansbury and the Guardians received an offer of land from Joseph Fels, an American soap magnate; land to be used for home colonisation, and for the purpose of the employment of able-bodied males. Fels discussed the offer with the Guardians, offering the land at a peppercorn rent for three years with the option of purchase at the original price. [86]

Upon receiving the Board's approval in November, it was agreed to buy Dunston Farm, near Laindon in Essex.[87] The Guardians obtained formal possession of the farm on 5 March 1904.[88] It was agreed to order the erection of buildings at Laindon after the General Purposes Committee had reported to the Guardians,[89] and provision was made for the appointment of staff 'subject to the approval of the Local Government Board', which was subsequently granted; the LGB also fixed the maximum number of people to be maintained at 100. The Poplar Guardians, according to one historian, 'was the pioneer of the modern farm colony in this country. For nearly a dozen years the Guardians pleaded with the Local Government Board to be allowed to take a farm.'[90] Joseph Fels with the help of the Guardians and the London Unemployment Fund established the labour colony at Hollesley Bay in February 1905; its administration was taken over by the Central Unemployment Body set up under the Unemployment Workmen Act of 1905.[91]

At the end of November, the Mayor of London revived the Mansion House scheme, which had been dormant since 1895. It was financed by a fund of £4,000, and relief work was arranged with the Salvation Army at Hadleigh Farm, and at Osea Island Farm, near Maldon. The relief works were kept open from 17 December 1903 to 24 March 1904. During this period 467 men, heads of families representing 2,500 persons, received relief who were resident in the four East End boroughs of Stepney, Bethnal Green, Poplar, and Shoreditch.[92] According to Harris the 'Mansion House scheme 1903-4 was important because its decentralised administrative structure was copied by subsequent schemes and because it attracted a new generation of social reformers to the study of unemployment'; people such as William Beveridge and Percy Alden.[93] What Harris neglects to point out is that the Mansion House Fund helped ease the financial pressures brought on by the depression of trade in the East End boroughs, and therefore the boroughs did not have to find work and provide relief for those people who were helped by the Fund. The Mansion House scheme for example, sent seventy-seven men from Poplar, to Osea and Hadleigh, and at the same time maintained their families at home, at a cost of approximately £924.[94] During this period the Poplar Committee, which had a fund of £653, sent thirty-one men to Shenfield at a cost of £23. 5s. Also the local Council during the winter of 1903-4 distributed a dole of about a sovereign apiece in employment relief to 3,000 unemployed men at a cost to the borough of £20,000, of which £17,000 was specially raised by a loan.[95]

WALTER LONG'S SCHEME: DEPUTATIONS AND PETITIONS

During 1904 unemployment averaged 5. 9 per cent peaking in December at 7. 1 per cent. During 1905 it fell, gradually, to five per cent. In the period 1902-1905, it was over fifty per cent higher than the average over the previous decade. The worst affected areas were the North-east of England and London.[96] The clamour for State intervention to deal with the national question of unemployment increased in this period. It culminated with the SDF calling for a special parliamentary session to deal with unemployment at the end of 1904. [97] Meanwhile both the ILP and LRC had taken up the issue, and the TUC in September 1904 — for the first time in seven years — debated the problem of unemployment. The TUC agreed the best way to co-ordinate the attempts of local authorities to combat distress was to direct its Parliamentary Committee to press the Board of Trade to set up a special department. However, as Harris points out, 'it was local pressure that persuaded the Government to take action', and eventually bring in the Unemployed Workmen Bill on 18 April 1905. [98] It was local pressure by the Poor Law and municipal authorities, and in particular, the part played by Will Crooks, with others, that put the Bill on the Parliamentary agenda.

In 1904, throughout London and in the provinces, the local boards of guardians and councils convened unemployment conferences to induce the Government to take up the unemployment question, and introduce legislation giving local authorities further powers of combination and organisation in the provision of useful work, the cost to be met by the exchequer.[99] Delegations from these conferences were sent to lobby Walter Long, the President of the Local Government Board (1900-1905), and urged him to take some remedial action to alleviate the distress; Will Crooks with other MPs had also waited upon Long in deputation.[100] As significant was a national campaign of public meetings and demonstrations aimed at putting pressure on the central government organised by the trade union and labour movement, to win the hearts and minds of the working man. It was believed by the proponents of this agitation, Crooks being one of them, that if workmen of this country were united in realising they had power and influence behind them, they would undoubtedly gain the attention of Parliament. This action obviously had the desired effect because later, when Long gave evidence to the Royal Commission on the Poor Law, he admitted 'that one of the decisive factors behind his decision to legislate had been that many local authorities were constantly drawing his attention to their unemployed and the need to take some action':[101]

> There were crowds besieging the offices of the Relieving Officers and Boards of Guardians in London, in Leeds, in Liverpool, in Birmingham, and all our great cities where the unemployment difficulties arose in acute form; the Boards of Guardians could hardly sit in some places without safeguarding their doors, which was besieged by a crowd of people demanding relief.[102]

Therefore, on 6 October 1904, Walter Long 'announced that, because the situation in London was giving rise to some concerns, he had decided to hold a conference of metropolitan Poor Law guardians on October 14'.[103]

Some members of the ILP greeted Long's announcement with mixed feelings. W. F. Black, for example, in the *Labour Leader*, stated that the conference would be ineffectual because with Mr. Long's present attitude of mind, 'and the general calibre of the men who will attend ... any hope of something practical, or permanent, or on a large scale, resulting from the conference, may be dismissed from our mind.'[104] It will become clear that his comments were misplaced.

The conference was convened by Long allegedly to discuss proposals with the metropolitan authorities, but, in fact, he outlined his own scheme for the unemployed. He was eager to find a middle course, but not bind the Government to a loosening of the Poor Law or any unalterable obligation to find work for the unemployed and thus relieve distress.[105] The scheme, proposed by Long, which according to him would deal with unemployment more systematically than ever before, included the setting up of local Joint committees, composed of representatives of borough councils, boards of guardians, and charitable organisations. A central committee was to be created made up of delegates elected from each joint committee, and of people nominated by the LGB. The Board would fund the administrative expenses of the new central committee out of the common poor fund, but 'he was not prepared

to suggest that provision for ... employment ... should come out of Imperial funds'.[106]

Long also stated temporary unemployed workmen who were employed on borough relief works, and not relieved by the guardians, would not be disenfranchised as long as they met the London minimum residential requirement of six months, and that the scheme would be organised along similar lines to that of the Mansion House Fund.[107] He further stated that the work provided by the borough councils 'must not be intermittent but continuous'.[108] In other words, in future the employment of casual labour should not be considered in any relief works proposed by the boroughs. The Lord Mayor, John Pound, appealed for public funds to finance the scheme; this realised £50,000, 'and a loan of £20,000 at 2 per cent was floated on the stock market in January 1905'.[109] It is not necessary to examine the scheme further, because a detailed analysis of it is chronicled in the reports of the London Unemployment Fund, and discussed by Beveridge.[110]

It was a scheme welcomed by Crooks. He had been urging the LGB to implement something like it for ten years, since November 1894, when the Poplar Guardians called for the London Unemployed Districts. Both Crooks and Lansbury were delegates to the Conference, and Crooks in the concluding speech said:

> ... the Conference was under an extraordinary debt of gratitude to the President for making the suggestions he had done ... He asked the

Conference to pass a vote of thanks — not an ordinary vote, but a heartfelt expression of their thanks — for calling that historic meeting, which was a precedent for all time, and would remain as an effort of a President who might have had great predecessors, but who had had the moral courage to create a precedent which was for the benefit of the people.[111]

Although Crooks publicly acclaimed the President for his endeavours, privately he was undeniably worried about the immediate necessity of relieving the present distress in Poplar. Even Walter Long had admitted that no single locality would be able to meet the expense of its own unemployed.

Crooks was sceptical whether the richer boroughs, without an unemployed problem, would contribute financially towards the poorer districts of London when the Central Committee was set up. The success of Long's scheme depended on voluntary and public contributions, and not on State funding. Crooks by contrast believed in direct taxation as a means of redistributing wealth. He advocated this in the House of Commons in 1903, and believed that since it was created by the working-class, it was the Government's responsibility to deliver financial support for the unemployed as only Parliament could legislate on what should be a local, a county, or national charge.

On Sunday 16 October, two days after the Conference at the LGB, Crooks spoke at a demonstration that was organised at the East India Dock gate, which called upon the Prime Minister to summon Parliament to pass legislation in favour of metropolitan authorities organising the unemployed, the expense of which should be distributed throughout the whole of London. Crooks stated that Joseph Chamberlain deserved to be impeached 'as a traitor to his nation ... he floated his fiscal proposals, and because of that the wealth, which was admitted existed, was not brought out and spent'. Chamberlain, according to Crooks, was responsible 'for at least one half the poverty, and the lack of employment existing in Great Britain today', and given the chance he would say it in the House of Commons.[112] Crooks' acrimonious outbursts against Chamberlain were mostly borne out of his opposition to Tariff Reform and his frustration with the Balfour Government, who always came up with the excuse that time could not be found for Parliament to legislate on the unemployment question.

On the question of Tariff Reform, Crooks did not claim to possess the cultivated intellect that was required to understand all that was put forward in support of fiscal reform. He believed there was no justification for it 'except to cover up the delinquencies of those who were responsible to the nation for other things'.[113] It would mean that every penny of the workman's wages that was spoken for already, plus the increased price of food — the real meaning of

Tariff Reform — would make the rich richer and the poor poorer. It would serve the interests of capital rather than those of labouring men. As far as the Government was concerned, Crooks often pointed out, they could find time to watch Harrow and Eton play cricket, and disappear on the glorious twelfth to shoot grouse, but they were unable to find time for those out of work.

At the first meeting of the Poplar Joint Committee on 2 November — Crooks was an *ex-officio* member — it was decided that the 'three day system should be dropped', and replaced by continuous employment relief as opposed to casual; in line with Long's recommendation.[114] On 16 November, Arthur Balfour acknowledged receipt of the Guardians' resolution calling for an autumn session of Parliament. The Guardians responded on 21 November.[115] Crooks, as Chairman of the Board, wrote a long letter to Balfour, pointing out that although Walter Long's scheme was put forward for dealing with the unemployment question immediately, the committee was still to be set up, and meanwhile the Guardians had to deal with the unemployment problem. He suggested that if either the Premier or a representative could privately attend a relief meeting of the Board they would find ample evidence to support a session of Parliament. Crooks also supplied official figures showing the exceptional level of distress that was 24 per cent in Poplar.

He further 'pointed out that the Guardians' request for an Autumn Session was supported by fifty-six other Poor Law Unions and no fewer than eighty municipalities throughout the country.'[116] Will Crooks told a deputation who attended the meeting that the next thing the Guardians 'would have to do was consider whether it was possible to work under Article 10 of the Local Government Orders.' He went on to say 'the people must be fed first' irrespective of their becoming disenfranchised. [117]

Meanwhile, during November Crooks' tireless work for the unemployed and the poor was recognised by both his contemporaries and the Government. He was elected vice-president of the Poor Law Unions' Association,[118] and later was nominated by Walter Long, along with Bill Steadman, to the Central Executive Committee of the London Unemployed Fund. Other members of the executive committee included George Lansbury, and Charles Grinling of the Woolwich Guardians.[119] Will Crooks became a member of the Works Committee, and Lansbury (Chairman), Grinling, and Steadman members of the Working Colonies Committee. The Working Colonies Committee managed the more permanent Labour Colony at Hollesley Bay, the site that had been offered to the Central Committee at its first meeting (25 November 1904) by Joseph Fels.[120]

A response to Crooks' letter was received from Balfour on 28 December, and put to the Guardians, who met two days later. Balfour believed that the

Guardians should wait and see how Long's scheme developed, now it was actually working. On the subject of a special session of Parliament he said:

> I think we should abstain from placing exaggerated hopes upon anything which may be immediately accomplished by Parliament, because organised effort would be paralysed till the decision of Parliament was known; and between the beginning of our debates, and the moment when their result could be embodied in a working shape, much preventable suffering would inevitably have occurred.[121]

Crooks and the Guardians were unhappy with Balfour's reply, notably his reluctance to grapple with the problem of unemployment. They felt that 'while Mr. Long's scheme, in a general way, shows a departure in the direction' of approaching the unemployment problem in London, 'it has no power to enforce contributions from anyone.' In his reply to Balfour, Crooks included this point, and on the subject of Parliament said:

> ... they are certainly of the opinion that if Parliament and the Government really desire to grapple with this great evil, they could in a short time, and with the expert appliances at the disposal of the Government, set in operation a great deal of work useful to the nation. They, therefore, sincerely hope their previous representations will be acted upon ... that the matter shall be laid before the next meeting of Parliament.[122]

He also informed Balfour of their present plight. They had reached a stage where something must be done immediately.

The Guardians were now receiving numerous applications for outdoor relief, and were spending £690 per week, 'borne entirely by the local rates, which stand at 10s. in £, and will considerably increase by the addition of this extra relief.'[123] The Guardians also probably realised that Balfour's reticence in calling Parliament together was due to the difficulties he was having with the supporters of Tariff Reform. His party was hopelessly divided on the fiscal question. For Balfour the motivation, above all the skirmishing over fiscal reform, was the need to keep his majority intact, and by not calling Parliament together on the unemployment question Balfour reduced the risk of an irrevocable split in the Unionist party. In December, Long and Balfour corresponded privately with each other, to discuss the implications of the London scheme. Long wrote to Balfour stating that he was:

very strongly of the opinion, and have been for sometime, that there is every justification for a fresh Inquiry [Poor Law] indeed I have more than once suggested that something of the sort was inevitable ... I happen to know that the Radicals are trying to get credit both for what we do and for what must be the logical outcome of our policy ... I am naturally anxious they [Radicals and Socialists] should not get credit they do not deserve ... It is of course obvious that the experience gained by these Central Committees must be of material assistance to us in deciding what form an inquiry should take.[124]

Balfour's reply to Long reveals his concern with financing the scheme: 'you may be driven to give certain London areas facilities for obtaining money on loan'. Balfour was also noticeably anxious about a precedent being set, because he asked: 'Was anything of this kind ever done for the employed before ... can we now do it for West Ham unless we are prepared also to do it for any district in the country?'[125]

The problem of whether national or local government should bear the financial cost of any relief system was not only the root cause of the clash over Long's scheme, but the clash with Conservative ideology.[126] Balfour was more than ever anxious that private charity and public appeals should pay for unemployment schemes, and that local authorities should not be given the powers to raise funds through the rates to finance them. Balfour saw rate support for local unemployment schemes as one of the main reasons behind the demand for an autumn session of Parliament.

In Public Demand
Since becoming MP for Woolwich in 1903, Crooks' workload had increased enormously, so much so, that in early January 1905, Crooks suffered a nervous breakdown, complicated by rheumatism. Haw points out that the 'demands made upon him to address public meetings in other parts of the country became terrific after Woolwich.... The Labour Party ... had his first consideration always.' For example, in 1904 Crooks told George Haw, that he was booked to speak at thirteen meetings 'at different places within the next fortnight, and I've just got a pressing appeal to speak at another within the same time.' Will travelled thousands of miles on draughty trains, in all weathers to speak at public meetings, as well as attending Westminster, carrying out his duties on the Metropolitan Asylum Board; the Guardians; the London Unemployment Fund, and the Poor Law Union.

In addition, Poplar re-elected him to the LCC with a majority of 1600 in 1904. The only position he gave up was that on the Poplar Borough Council in

November 1903. Crooks had often said that he would rather die serving labour, than have done nothing at all. It was almost a prophetic statement because the breakdown nearly killed him — it affected him for life — his health was never the same again, suffering throughout the remaining years from nervous pain for weeks on end, depriving him of sleep and rest. Yet, he still refused to relax his efforts on behalf of the people 'at our end of town' as he fondly called the people of Poplar and Woolwich.[127]

Will Crooks' demanding itinerary, and the lengths the LRC would go to in securing his availability, is put into perspective, by looking at his invitation to speak on unemployment in Liverpool on 25 and 26 January 1905. Crooks was invited by the LRC Executive Committee to be present and move an unemployment resolution at a: 'Special Conference on Unemployment for Wednesday afternoon and Thursday morning January 25th and 26th.' [128] Will jumped at the chance. 'Yes,' he replied.[129] Meanwhile Jim Middleton, assistant secretary of the LRC, had written to members of the LRC executive suggesting that Crooks be invited to speak at the LRC Demonstration after the Conference in Liverpool. Pete Curran replied 'certainly book Crooks for Liverpool if you can get him'; [130] J. H. Clynes agreed 'it would be advisable to secure Mr. Crooks.'[131] Whilst David Shackleton, who agreed with the proposal, pointed out there could be a problem: 'Crooks is booked to speak at Bolton.'[132] On 31 December, Crooks received a letter from Middleton asking him if he could speak at the LRC Demonstration in Liverpool on the evening of 26 January.[133] Crooks replied the following day: 'Thursday 26th I am booked to speak for Mr. Gill at Bolton (secretary of the Bolton Operative Spinners, and Labour MP for Bolton 1906-12), Wednesday 25th or Friday 27th I could do for you but not Sat 28 as I am in Exeter.' [134]

To make sure that there would be no clash of dates, MacDonald arranged with Gill and Crooks to move their meeting to Wednesday evening (25th), so that Crooks could speak at both the Liverpool and Bolton meetings. Crooks would then speak at the Liverpool Special Conference on Wednesday afternoon, travel to Bolton in the evening, return to Liverpool the following day, and then go on to Exeter. MacDonald had been under pressure from the Liverpool trade union and labour movement to secure the services of Crooks at the demonstration to support their parliamentary candidate. For example, J. Stephenson of the Engineers said getting Crooks to speak would make the meeting a success: 'Liverpool is a place that needs some work put into it, and this will be the best opportunity we will have for quite a long time.'[135] Altogether, in four days, Crooks spoke at four meetings, a round journey of around 750 miles, and this is only one example. But what makes this particular occurrence even more poignant is that he left his sick bed to fulfil his promises, and suffered a relapse as a consequence.

Will Crooks' outlook reflected the experiences he had gained by living among the poor people of Poplar. He understood the poverty they lived in because he remembered his childhood, and the experience of being out of work himself in the past gave added credence to his speeches on unemployment. This is probably why there was such a demand to hear him. Not only did he know what he was talking about, but also he put forward constructive arguments on how the Government could help in alleviating the problem of unemployment. People wanted to hear Will Crooks, MP for Woolwich, the Labour member who was at the forefront of Parliamentary agitation against unemployment and poverty. Audiences warmed to this affable cockney, and admired his absolute genuineness in his connection with the working classes. He told them they held the key to parliamentary reform in speeches filled with humour, pathos, and wit. If Crooks was engaged to speak at a meeting anywhere, it was guaranteed that the hall would be packed, hence Pete Curran's comment to Middleton 'certainly book Crooks for Liverpool *if you can get him,'* (my italics). This statement sums up Crooks' busy schedule, and the difficulty organisations, including the LRC, had in securing his services.

THE UNEMPLOYED WORKMEN ACT OF 1905

At the Conference in Liverpool in January 1905, Crooks stated that the LRC should make the question of unemployment 'so inconvenient that it would have to be mentioned in the King's Speech when Parliament met'.[136] This proved to be the case. An Unemployment Bill was announced in the King's Speech to a newly assembled Parliament on 14 February 1905. The Bill would include the setting up of machinery to deal with unemployment.[137] Alas, Crooks was not there to hear it.[138] He was still recovering from the relapse he suffered after his speaking tour of Liverpool, Bolton, and Exeter at the end of January. It was some five weeks later, in March, that Crooks began his public duties again.[139]

The clash with Conservative ideology greatly bedevilled the history of the Unemployed Workmen Bill, specifically the controversial proposal of a rate aid clause, and the raising of money for the new scheme out of the rates. It also caused discord in the Conservative party and the cabinet. Before Walter Long left the LGB to become Chief Secretary of Ireland on 14 March,[140] his memorandum in support of the principle of rate aid was discussed by the Balfour cabinet on 2 March. At this meeting, Lord Salisbury had prepared a counter memorandum, arguing against the idea. According to him, 'it involves principles so novel that they ought only to be adopted upon the most conclusive evidence.'[141] However, when Gerald Balfour (who had succeeded

Long at the LGB), introduced the Bill under the ten-minute rule on 18 April, it still contained the controversial clause. He said 'it seems to me it would be impossible to set up statutory bodies, permanent bodies for statutory duties, and leave them entirely dependent upon voluntary subscriptions for their maintenance.'[142]

The scheme, which Balfour outlined, was compulsory for the London boroughs. It involved replacing the local London borough joint committees with distress committees, supervised by a central body. The local committees would not be empowered to provide work, they would only be responsible for investigating applicants, and passing on those suitable to the central committee, who would be responsible for finding them work. The central committee would also be responsible for the establishment of labour registries and bureaux in the localities. The scheme was to be financed by each borough contributing the equivalent to a rate of one halfpenny in the pound, to be raised to one penny at discretion of the LGB.[143] The organisation outside London was to be optional.[144] Crooks thought that this proposed measure was 'exceedingly dangerous, and the Bill will have to be amended ... we cannot accept any measure that will leave the question optional in the provinces, and make us deal compulsorily with our Unemployed in London.' He pointed out that people who now come into London looking for work 'will be intensified if the Bill goes through the House' in its present form.[145]

The Bill was condemned by Conservatives and generally welcomed by radical and labour representatives. The richer London boroughs saw it as being too much akin to socialism. According to Haw, 'one of the bitterest opponents of the measure, Sir William Chance ... described it as "a Poplar Bill framed to meet Poplar's needs." So it was. For Poplar's needs just then were the needs of the unemployed.'[146] Members of the Labour Group were divided, Burns opposed the Bill, Crooks and Henderson supported it, as did Hardie and MacDonald, with reservations.

The Bill's guiding principles were based on those which Crooks and the Poplar Guardians had been advocating for years, which were in essence an extension of the Long scheme. Crooks saw that at last the government had conceded state responsibility for the unemployed; it equalised the rate burden among the London boroughs, unified them for the purpose of tackling the unemployment problem, and removed the disenfranchise penalty on those who received help.[147] Both the Balfours were quick to stress that it was not their intention to establish the principle of state aid. The clause had been incorporated into the Bill precisely to avoid giving such an impression. Brown contends that this contrary interpretation of the clause 'must help explain the government's subsequent reluctance to persevere with the Bill'.[148]

Apprehension as to the government's belief in the Bill was beginning to surface within the labour movement by mid-May, prompted by the Prime Minister's unwillingness on '19 April and again on 8 May to name the day for the measure's second reading.'[149] This fuelled rumours that the government was going to drop the scheme. Because of the government's prevarication, patience was also wearing thin among the unemployed workers throughout the country, who were organising to march on London, much to the alarm of Crooks and MacDonald. They believed that disorganised bodies of the unemployed would seriously threaten the chances of securing support for consideration of the unemployment problem. Organised meetings and marches on the other hand were a different issue. MacDonald and Hardie were of the opinion that organised marches by the LRC and ILP would best increase the prestige and standing of the labour movement.[150]

Crooks and Hardie Fight for the Bill

In moving the second reading of the Unemployed Workmen Bill on 20 June, Gerald Balfour said that the object of the Bill was to deal with a limited class of the unemployed; those people that honestly desired to work, but because of no fault of their own were unable to do so. Therefore this class would receive more 'suitable treatment under the Act than under the Poor Law'.[151] In other words, the Bill would include the genuine workman, and exclude the loafer; legislation based on principles, which Crooks had been agitating for since 1892. During the debate, Walter Long stated that: 'It was because he desired to maintain the existing Poor Law system that he supported the Bill.... He would have never have made himself responsible for the scheme of last year if he had thought it would weaken the foundations on which the Poor Law system rested.'[152] He recommended the use of farm colonies, something that the Poplar Guardians had been pleading for fourteen years and the LCC had been advocating since October 1903. Crooks congratulated both Balfour and Long for dealing with a difficult problem. Speaking to the amendment of Sir George Bartley (Islington North), Crooks said:

> The Amendment spoke of the proposals of the Bill as being detrimental to the interests of the poor. Could anything be more detrimental to the poor than keeping them without food.... What was wanted was to lift the people up and prevent them becoming a charge on the Poor Law.... There were millions of acres of land in this country upon which men could be employed.... The Bill now before the House had met the terms of the resolution which was adopted by the London County Council.[153]

Crooks was quietly confident that the Bill would be acceptable to the trade union and labour movement in its amended form.

The Bill had been amended to include compulsory compliance by the county boroughs, and the payment of wages at the standard rate of skilled labour per hour, which 'would be attained by reducing the hours [per week] rather than reducing the pay per hour.'[154] What must have given Crooks most pleasure was the retention of the clause that farm colonies would be maintained out of the rates. 'What they [Labour members] wanted' said Crooks in defence of the farm colonies clause, 'was to have the necessary capital to start with for the payment of fair wages; and in a very short time these farm colonies would be self-supporting.'[155] Personally Crooks did not ever think the Bill 'was a great one, but it did admit a principle' of setting up machinery to deal with unemployment, and allowed the creation of farm colonies. He said at this moment he would be satisfied 'if the Government would pass the measure.... I would be content with the skeleton of a measure like this one.'[156]

Crooks must have been exasperated by the Government's evasiveness. It was obvious that they were under pressure to withstand attempts being made by the bill's opponents to drop the measure. The day after the second reading, for example, the government was criticised by the *Graphic*, who claimed that 'happily there is good reason to believe that the Government will recognise the dangers that lurk in this hastily drafted measure and will prudently allow it to drop.'[157] The Government yielded to this pressure, because on Monday 3 July, Crooks and Hardie were told by the Prime Minister that the Government was abandoning the Workmen Bill, 'to clear the way for the Alien's Bill.'[158] Crooks called it shameful for the House to 'waste its time on a Bill like that. It was abominable!'[159] It seemed to Crooks that the Government was using procedure as a 'pretext for shutting us out altogether'.[160]

Crooks and Hardie felt the bill was still worth fighting for. Crooks believed it was better than nothing at all. It is probable that the Labour Group, especially Crooks, Henderson, and Hardie believed that in the circumstances extra-parliamentary pressure should be brought to bear to make the Government see reason. Agitation had worked in bringing the plight of the unemployed to the LGB's notice. Perhaps they should persevere with a programme of organised meetings and demonstrations in the hope of changing the Government's parliamentary agenda.

The rumours of the bill being dropped, plus the fact that the unemployment index still stood at a high 5.2 per cent at the end of July,[161] probably accounted for the success of the programme, because throughout the country over one hundred meetings took place, the largest of them in Liverpool, Portsmouth, West Bromwich, Burnley, Merthyr, and Derby.[162] The campaign culminated with a demonstration and rally in London on 9 July, organised by the LRC.[163]

The wives of unemployed men in Poplar and Edmonton continued the agitation in support of the Bill on 17 July, by lobbying both Arthur Balfour, and the leader of the opposition, Henry Campbell-Bannerman. A large meeting of over 500 women, some with babies in arms, was organised at Caxton Hall by George Lansbury, before the two delegations left to meet Will Crooks at the Houses of Parliament. The deputation to Balfour was introduced by Crooks, and 'urged him [Balfour] to pass the Unemployment Bill during the present session, or failing that to call an autumn session for the purpose.' Balfour's response was brief and evasive. He said: 'I can tell you that we will do all that is possible to get the Bill forward — if not in the form in which Mr. Crooks would like it, yet in some other we will do our best.'[164] The deputation that met Campbell-Bannerman received a more positive response. He told them:

> As to the Bill, he thought its prospects ought to look very favourable that day ... during the afternoon an announcement had been made in the House of Commons which released a considerable part of the time which remained of the present Session; and he thought nothing perhaps, had a greater claim upon that time so released than the Bill in which they were interested.[165]

He added that as far as he was concerned there would be 'no impediment put in the way of proceeding with this legislation'.[166]

Campbell-Bannerman's last comment must have come as a welcome relief to Crooks, because in the past it had needed all the tenacity of Crooks and Hardie to persuade members of the Liberal Party not to oppose the second reading of the Bill. According to Crooks, the Liberals seemed to be too fearful that the Government might gain credit by its measure instead of being anxious to remedy a national evil.[167] For all Balfour's promises, obstacles were still placed in the way of the Bill's progress. The Government offered all sorts of excuses why the Scotch Education and the Redistribution Bills should be taken before the Unemployment Bill. For example, Crooks, Keir Hardie, and Henderson were told by the Prime Minister that the 'Government did not consider the measure was one of urgent public importance.' Crooks states 'we retorted that surely the desire of men to earn their daily bread must be business of most urgent public importance, of the greatest possible importance certainly to the British House of Commons.'[168] On 31 July, Balfour relegated the Unemployment Bill to the House of Commons' waste paper basket, when he omitted the Bill 'from the list of those which were ... to go through before the session ended.'[169]

On 1 August, just when it seemed that the Bill would to be left to die, a riot of unemployed workers in Manchester — Arthur Balfour was the MP for Manchester East — caused a prompt *volte-face* by the Government. According to Brown: 'It was no coincidence that on 2 August, the day after the Manchester riot, the government began manoeuvres to withdraw from the difficult position it now found itself.'[170] Gerald Balfour stated that the Government would introduce the Bill, as an experiment for three years — he had previously announced the Bill would last for ten years — while a royal commission investigated the Poor Law, and the problem of impoverishment and distress. This statement was in stark contrast to that of his brother, who had announced the Bill's omission from the list of measures to be settled before the end of the session.[171]

By 7 August, the amended report and third reading of the Bill had passed the Commons, withstanding two attempts by Hardie to 'reinstate the rate aid clause.' [172] Obviously, Hardie was bitterly disappointed, and withdrew his opposition in deference to Crooks. He said:

> he was against the Bill as it stood, and would divide against the Third Reading were it not that some of his colleagues did not agree with his view. The hon. Member for Woolwich, whose practical experience of the working and administration of the Poor Law entitled his judgement to carry weight, believed the Bill would be helpful, and in deference to that opinion he was prepared to yield his own judgement.[173]

The *Daily News*, reporting the story of the passing of the Unemployment Bill, bears witness to Crooks' skill in keeping the Bill alive: 'At the end of last week its chances seem to have disappeared. Today it has passed Committee and Monday will see it through the Commons. The member chiefly responsible for this is Mr Crooks, who has shown undoubted subtleness as a Parliamentary tactician.'[174] What he personally thought of the Unemployment Bill is disclosed in a letter to MacDonald on 14 August '... you will find the Revolution will be through the administration and many things are possible under this precious act.'[175]

Speaking at the National Liberal Club on 20 November 1905, Crooks further endorsed the measure. 'The Act itself I consider ... to be of the most revolutionary character that this or any other Government has ever passed.' [176] Distress Committees – twenty-nine - were set up in every London borough in September and October 1905, comprised of nominees from local guardians, borough councils and charitable organisations. Each Distress Committee nominated two delegates to the Central Unemployment Body (CUB), which was convened in November 1905.[177] Crooks and Beveridge were both co-opted to the CUB at the head of the poll.[178]

Although Crooks saw the Bill as an administrative 'revolution', he was aware that problems would arise due to the scheme's financial limitations. Its administration was to be funded out of the rates, but wages were to be paid out of public contributions. Almost immediately, after the Bill was passed the Prime Minister was confronted with a campaign to call an autumn session of Parliament 'to introduce new legislation on unemployment'.[179] As part of this campaign Elizabeth Crooks and a deputation of unemployed from Poplar — organised by the Borough Council — was received by King Edward at the opening of Kingsway-Aldwych junction on 18 October.[180] The King was presented with an address that called for an autumn parliamentary session. It also drew to his attention the plight of the 3000 men in Poplar, who had signed the unemployment register at Bromley depot, [181] and were unable to find work because of the lack of public funds.

On 6 November, Crooks and Lansbury at the head of a triple deputation of women workers from Poplar, Southwark, and the Central Workers' Committee, plus 5,000 unemployed, marched to see Arthur Balfour, to demonstrate and appeal for funds to alleviate their misery and despair.[182] Harris states 'the women's demonstration was by no means ineffective' because Balfour 'urged his supporters to contribute generously to the fund opened in the name of Queen Alexandra.'[183] This appeal realized £150,000, which proved sufficient for the needs of the Distress Committees in the winter 1905-6. The Liberal Government in 1906 voted £200,000 to the Distress Committees for the winter 1906/7. Haw claims: 'Poplar had done its work. The women had marched to victory'.[184] It is important to note that the Poplar women's political agitation; mass deputations to the House of Commons to question MPs on unemployment happened some time before the suffragettes adopted the practice.[185]

It has been shown that for eleven years Crooks and the Poplar Guardians had advocated a work scheme, including the use of farm colonies, similar to that implemented by the Walter Long scheme in 1904. It was Crooks' commitment to the cause of the unemployed, and his will to succeed against the odds, which were important in making the Government recognise its responsibility to the unemployed. It was without doubt due to his persistence and skill that the

Unemployed Workmen Bill was guided — albeit in emasculated form — through the House of Commons.

4

WOOLWICH AND INDEPENDENT LABOUR REPRESENTATION

Woolwich was an industrial town by 1800. Although it covered less than twenty square miles, its growth was due to a large extent to its long association with the military, especially the development of the Royal Arsenal, earlier known as the Woolwich Warren, which dates from 1671 when it was an ordnance storage depot.[1] Advances in weaponry and equipment for the Army required more production space and a more efficient Ordnance Depot, resulting in establishing the Royal Gun Factory for the manufacture of rifled breech loading ordnance in 1857. The Royal Arsenal expanded most notably in the mid-nineteenth and early twentieth centuries to accommodate Army requirements. By 1914, the Arsenal extended some six miles down river to Erith.[2] The Arsenal, Siemens cable works, G. A. Harvey, engineers, and the Dockyard, by the turn of the century used as a War Department store, were the principal employers. By 1901, the Woolwich Parliamentary Constituency, which included North Woolwich, supported a population of 130,927, including soldiers in barracks.[3] 'A ... feature of Woolwich was', according to Donoughue, Bernard, and Jones:

> its self-contained isolation from the rest of London. The majority of the population were employed within Woolwich, and there was little commuting into the centre, eight to nine miles away. Woolwich was very much a separate community with its own civic life, very untypical of London, and similar to isolated mining communities in the Welsh valleys.[4]

After the opening of the Blackwall Tunnel in 1897, and during the Boer War (1899-1902), an influx of skilled workers, including many Nonconformists from the North Country and Scotland, attracted by the prospects of employment in the Arsenal, had its effects on the social composition of the borough. These immigrants became members of an Arsenal workforce that was strongly unionised, and constituents of a relatively stable community, where workingmen's clubs took an active part in local politics, and 'by London standards nonconformity was strong. These factors seemed to suggest a basis for a strong Liberalism, but this was not the case.' Liberalism failed to capture Woolwich in the 1890s, which led to a strong Tory working-class vote, and Woolwich in this period was a rare example of 'Tory Democracy'. This weak nature of Liberalism worked eventually in Labour's favour, and 'could be viewed as a promising basis for socialist growth'.[5]

During 1899-1901, over four thousand people moved into the area, a population growth of 5.7 per cent, a large number of who were employed in the Arsenal.[6] During the war, the Arsenal employed 20,015 workers, approximately 17 per cent of the total population of the Woolwich Borough.[7] This statistic does not take into consideration Charlton, a district in close proximity to Woolwich Arsenal, with a population growth of 8.3 per cent between 1899-1901, which was greater than that of Plumstead.[8] From the mid 1880s until the early 1900s, Tory businessmen dominated Woolwich civic life, being in control of the local vestries, the Board of Works, and subsequently the Borough Council. Edwin Hughes, who held the Woolwich parliamentary seat 1885-1902, was a local solicitor and magistrate. Also, in this period the alliance between the trade unions and the Liberal Party weakened, and finally withered away. Because of the demise of the Liberals, the Tories were able to fill the political vacuum, and win workingmen to their cause. Crooks helped break Woolwich's political and geographic isolation, and thus the Tories hold on the district. Booth's social survey of the area in 1902 claimed: 'Each year Woolwich tends to become more and more working class.'[9]

THE DEVELOPMENT OF INDEPENDENT
LABOUR REPRESENTATION

In November 1868, a small group of engineers employed in the Arsenal formed the Royal Arsenal Supply Company, which later changed its name to the Royal Arsenal Co-operative Society Limited (RACS) in February 1872, and became an important element in the growth of the movement for independent Labour representation in the 1890s. In 1878 a RACS Education Committee was formed. This development was significant in the formation of political education in Woolwich in the 1890s.[10] The contribution of the Educational Committee was significant in the growth of political education in Woolwich in the 1890s. That the Society's origins were in the Arsenal, led to the adage that local political activity came out of the barrel of a gun in the Arsenal. 1883 saw the emergence of the Women's Co-operative Guild, whose aim was to better the conditions of working women. By 1888 there were three Guild branches affiliated to the Royal Arsenal Society, Erith branch, founded in 1884, Charlton in 1887 and Plumstead in 1888.

In the 1880s, the main centres for working-class politics were the local workingmen's and radical clubs. As Paul Thompson points out, besides a strong Engineers' Club, 'there was the Woolwich Radical Club founded in 1880, the Plumstead Radical Club which split off in 1887, the Woolwich Labour Club formed in 1898, and the Dockyard Labour Club and Abbey Wood Club formed in the 1900s.' Of these six clubs, along with the RACS, the 'first four all built impressive premises', and became the focus for propaganda work, putting forward a distinctive political programme of labour demands. The Clubs helped to break down sectional barriers between different crafts and grades and became an important element in the growth of the independent Labour representation movement in the 1890s. Sixteen branches of ASE held their meeting at the Engineers' Club. [11]

During this period, trade union organisation was strong in Woolwich at a time when the movement in London was notably weak. The ASE membership more than doubled between 1885 and 1891. In July 1889, Woolwich No. 4 branch of the Gasworkers' Union was founded with the help of Pete Curran, a bosom friend of Will Thorne.[12] Curran worked in the Arsenal, driving a steam hammer on the night shift; he was victimised and sacked in a dispute in the Arsenal over an alteration of working conditions and became an official of the Gasworkers' Union.[13] In addition, during the great Dock Strike, the South Side Labour Protection League (LPL) was established to organise dockworkers on that side of the river,[14] and by November, the LPL claimed 14,000 members and twenty-three branches. The LPL recognised all trade union tickets and was recruiting in the Arsenal and other factories as well as on the wharf side.[15] Assisted by young militants from the more traditional unions, the LPL branch's helped initiate the movement for independent labour candidates in Woolwich.

In September 1889, following closely on the success of the gasworkers and dockers in the East End, the yard labourers employed at Messrs. Silver's India Rubber, Gutta Percha and Telegraph Works Ltd., Silvertown, situated in North Woolwich, sent in a request that their wages should be raised to a 'tanner' an hour. The managers of the factory at once put up a notice that said that if any man was dissatisfied with the present pay they could go to the cashiers' office at 4.00pm and be paid off. Almost all the yard labourers did so and left work. They were informed they would not be re-employed. Discontent continued to increase until 700 or 800 of the men struck; the works closed altogether on Thursday 19 September, locking out about 2000 employees.[16] Although Silvertown is some five miles from Canning Town and Poplar, the workers of the area were certainly influenced and impressed by what could be gained through trade union militancy. This small group of men and women, stimulated by the example of the dockers among whom they lived, suddenly awoke to the need to fight. It is worth noting that the leaders of the New Unionism were prominent from the beginning of the dispute as were some Radical Liberals and representatives of the Church.

Contrary to expectations the engineers went back on Monday 7 October. One branch of the Woolwich engineers had passed a resolution strongly condemning the action of the executive in deciding to keep the men in. They called on the engineers to 'have self respect and come out'. [17] The executive ignored the Woolwich engineers' protestations. On Monday 9 December about 1000 of the workers drifted back to work, after the three farthings that were withdrawn initially from the yard labourers was reinstated. The rest returned under the threat of a lockout and after instruction from the Strike Committee:[18] After twelve weeks the strike ended on 14 December. This incident was clearly an influential episode in the growth of trade union consciousness and played a part in the development of a programme and agenda for independent labour representation in Woolwich. The Silvertown strike had a wider influence than that of its immediate milieu because a number of workers who lived in the area, trade unionists who worked across the river in Woolwich, must have reported the strike to their branches. For example, Pete Curran regularly spoke at the strike meetings.

The beginning of the Woolwich Labour Party coincides with the re-emergence of socialist influence in Britain and the founding of the Social Democratic Federation in the 1880s.[19] Among the pioneers of this movement was Robert Banner, a Scottish bookbinder and a leading local socialist. He was a member of the cabal that split from the SDF to form the Socialist League in January 1885, and was one of the signatories of its first manifesto. His political colleagues included John Lincoln Mahon, William Morris and Eleanor Marx-Aveling. He spoke at Eleanor Marx's funeral in April 1898.[20] Banner was among the first to start a branch of the Independent Labour Party (ILP) in Woolwich in 1894, and was to remain — until his death in 1910 — along with William Barefoot (secretary of Woolwich Trades Council, and in 1903, secretary of the Woolwich Labour Representative Association), the backbone of the local socialist movement. He was a founder member of the Labour Representative Association, held other positions nationally and locally, and became a local councillor in November 1903.

By 1891, the Woolwich Labour Representative League (WLRL) emerged. It was the result of an initiative by the London Trades Council to put up a candidate in the 1892 London County Council elections. In the same year, Ben Jones was adopted as the parliamentary candidate by the WLRL to run in the next General Election. Jones was the manager of the London Branch of the Co-operative Wholesale Society (in 1896, the Co-operative Congress assembled in the Tabernacle, Beresford Street, Woolwich, under his Presidency),[21] and a keen believer in an alliance between co-operation and trade unionism.[22] He was adopted and supported by the Co-operative Society, the engineers', the gasworkers' unions, and the local Radical Clubs.[23] He stood for the eight-hour day, old age pensions and the democratisation of Parliament. Calling for the eight-hour day, he urged the 'workers themselves to arise, for they had nothing to lose but their fetters'. [24] In 1892, Jones polled 4,100 votes, but Hughes' 5,992 votes gave him a majority of 1,892.[25] He also stood against Hughes in 1895.[26]

The Liberals did not nominate a candidate in either 1892 or 1895.[27] In 1900, Hughes was returned unopposed, as was Beresford in 1902. As Pelling points out, Woolwich was the only 'mixed-class' seat in the southeast London constituencies left uncontested by the Liberals in 1900.[28] This seems to point to the lack of Liberal confidence in its political competence to achieve acceptance by the working-class man, other than through organised labour representation. The problem for the Liberals, especially in Woolwich, was in promoting an ideology that focused attention on working-class representation. The formation of the LRC challenged the Liberal belief that parliament should promote the interests of society rather than those of any section.[29]

The sequence of events in 1892 led to the founding of the Plumstead, Woolwich and Charlton branch of the London Reform Union in 1893,[30] and in 1894 the Woolwich District Trades and Labour Council (WTC) was founded, followed by the ILP. Within a year, the WTC had 3,000 affiliated members, including the two principal Radical Clubs.[31] These developments, and the emergence of growing socialist organisations like the ILP, SDF and the Socialist League, were pivotal to the growth of an independent Labour movement. In addition, the resurgent trade unionism of the late 1880s and early 1890s had a major radicalising influence on the RACS' development in this period, especially around the engineers' eight-hour day campaign (which was achieved in the Arsenal in 1894), and the engineers' lock out 1896-7. This advancement led to closer links between the RACS and the political and trade union organisations in the area.[32] An important factor in this setting was the geographical isolation of the RACS from the North of England co-operative societies. It was distanced from the traditional ideological 'purity' of these organisations, which normally stayed out of Labour politics. In this, it differed sharply with other co-operative societies, as many of its members were active in the movement pressing for independent Labour representation. However, it did not enter into a definite alliance with the Trades Council and its affiliates on a Labour political programme until 1896.[33] The education classes and propaganda work of the co-operative, and the labour movement during the late 1890s was among the influences locally that helped create the demand for independent labour representation and lay the foundation for a trade union-socialist alliance that was to prove decisive.

During this period, the Liberals in the Woolwich district were obviously concerned about their ability to win workingmen to their political cause, because they formed the Progressive Association in 1897 and a New Liberal Association in January 1899.[34] The Progressive Association did not remain long under Liberal influence. The Trades Council and the ILP were concerned about the Association because the Tory Progressives were using the organisation for advertising their own interests, and Banner became district secretary in October 1899.[35] After that, it served as a platform for the growing political strength of organised Labour. It has been said that the Liberals did not oppose Crooks in 1903 because 'he was too involved with the Progressive party in London County Council politics.'[36] The real reason was that the Liberal Party was rotting at its roots in Woolwich.[37]

It is not clear that the ASE moved dramatically towards a belief in independent politics after the great engineering dispute of 1897-8, towards which the RACS donated £500. A national ballot on affiliation to the Labour Representative Committee was held twice as a result of the abysmally low level of participation, although a delegation representing the ASE attended the founding conference in 1900. They joined during 1902-3.[38] Another important factor in the evolution of local political development was a series of lectures by George Bernard Shaw at the Woolwich Radical Club, on industrial history and the economics of socialism. The Woolwich ILP also arranged many lectures and propaganda meetings in the Old Assembly Rooms, Woolwich New Road. Speakers included Keir Hardie, J. Ramsay MacDonald, Bruce Glasier, Philip Snowden, and others who preached the gospel of socialism and independent labour representation.[39]

A central figure in the process of the development of the labour movement was Charles Grinling, a progressive clergyman who arrived in Woolwich in 1889, after several years of social work at Toynbee Hall and in Nottingham. He went on to become secretary of the local Charity Organisation Society, from which he was sacked because of his unorthodox approach. He was a Christian Socialist of a more socialist than Christian variety. Grinling left the church and concentrated on adult education and the local socialist movement. He helped to found the Woolwich branch of the University Extension Association, and served on the RACS education committee between 1895-98. He was also the first editor of *Comradeship*, the local co-operative magazine that was launched in October 1897. This publication was Grinling's most enduring bequest to the society from his spell on the education committee.[40] As well as being an influential new means of contact with the membership, it published wide-ranging discussions on education, social and industrial conditions and social movements. *Comradeship* carried regular news and comment on local political affairs, and stated its aims in the first issue: 'Comradeship is the utterance of Woolwich co-operation. It will seek to unfold the aims and work, the aspirations and daily life of 10,000 men and women from Woolwich, Plumstead, Charlton and Erith ... hold up before them the "love of comrades" which inspired the earlier pioneers of co-operation.'[41] The newspaper conveyed something of the enthusiasm and excitement of those years, when the RACS was part of a progressive new movement for independent politics.

The links between the Poplar Fabians and the Woolwich labour movement were to prove important and influential upon the development of the agitation for independent Labour representation in Woolwich, especially the example of Crooks 'College'. To the Woolwich pioneers of labour representation the 'College' exemplified what could be achieved through a broad alliance of trade union, socialist and progressive organisations. Bob Banner and Fred Hammill had experienced first hand at Crooks 'College' the potential of factory gate meetings, and the impact that regular political meetings could have upon workers that were organised. They began a programme of Arsenal Gate meetings 1896-7, helped by Jim Turnbull, Jim Steer, Harry Snell, and other labour pioneers,[42] by inviting speakers who proclaimed propaganda of an explicit socialist character. The speakers included John Burns, Tom Mann, Ben Tillett, Will Thorne, Andreas Scheu, Herbert Burrows, Edward and Eleanor Marx-Aveling, Harry Quelch and Henry Mayers Hyndman.[43]

It is important to recognise that the close political contacts between the Woolwich trade union and labour movement and the Poplar movement in the late 1890s and the early 1900s, helps explain why Crooks was chosen to stand as a Labour candidate in the 1903 Woolwich by-election. Tom Chambers, LCC member for Woolwich, worked with Crooks on the LCC Woolwich Ferry subcommittee, and thus was party to the Fair Wage Clause. Thus Woolwich activists, such as Chambers, Banner, and Hammill, were well aware of the work that Crooks had done for the benefit of the working-class on the LCC, and the support his reforms were given by the people of Poplar. The Woolwich pioneers recognised that this was due initially to the education classes that were provided by Crooks 'College' and the Fabians for the working people of Poplar, and it was through these classes that the Poplar platform was explained and supported. Thus, the Poplar experience became the precursor for the

Woolwich Arsenal Gate meetings, and the educational classes of the RACS and the ILP.

This relationship between the Poplar and Woolwich working-class movement is a complex story. There is no doubt that a strong network of mutual understanding existed between them, which began in 1889 and continued well after Crooks' election. These contacts between the districts are on record. The South Side Labour Protection League was affiliated to the Poplar Labor League, and the Plumstead Radical Club began subscribing in 1896.[44] In the same year Gilbert Slater (lecturer at Woolwich Polytechnic, and later Principal of Ruskin College), gave a course of lectures 'on the duties of Citizenship, under the auspices of the L. S. B. [London School Board] evening classes', at the Co-operative Institute, Poplar.[45] It is worth remembering that Crooks was a member of the LCC TEB, which had close contact with Woolwich Polytechnic, and therefore it seems most likely that he knew Slater. Another relationship overlooked by historians was the Fabian connection. Hubert Bland, who spoke at the PLEC inaugural meeting (1891), lived in Woolwich, and was a friend of Banner. Therefore, it is most likely that Crooks invited Bland to speak after Banner suggested him. After all, they were Fabians of the same persuasion, believing in an independent Labour party. Furthermore, another Fabian, Fred Butler, who was a Trustee of the Poplar Labor League, and a close friend of Crooks, was his agent and election organiser in the Woolwich by-election.

During July and August 1899, the Trades Council organised public meetings, focusing on 'Trade Unionism its Benefits and Uses' in Beresford Square (outside the No. 1 Arsenal Gate) on Sunday evenings.[46] In 1898, the Woolwich branch of the ILP had begun to publish the *Woolwich and District Labour Notes*, after October 1899 known as *Woolwich and District Labour Journal*. Some dozen issues were published, and then for a time it declined. A joint committee of the ILP and the Trades Council revived it in 1900 under the title *Woolwich Labour Journal*, but after a few editions, the venture petered out. The advent of the Boer War, and the consequent overtime in the Arsenal, left little time for its distribution. That a committee produced the journal was probably a further handicap.[47] Fred Knee, compositor, member of the SDF and secretary of the Workmen's National Housing Council,[48] Edward Pease, secretary of the Fabian Society, Ben Tillett and Keir Hardie were all contributors. Articles by Frederick Engels, which had previously been published in *The Standard*, 'Fair Wage for a Fair Day's Work' and 'The Wages System' were also included.[49] A more successful attempt to launch a Labour journal was made by the Trades Council, and the first issue of the *Borough of Woolwich Labour Journal* was published in October 1901. This continued until September 1904, when it was incorporated into the *Pioneer*, the first edition of which was published on 14 October 1904,[50] William Barefoot becoming the editor. [51]

In February 1900 the formation of the Labour Representation Committee (LRC) in the Memorial Hall, Farringdon Street, London,[52] was to have an impact on independent Labour representation both locally and nationally. Woolwich was the first of the London trade councils and the third nationally to affiliate to the LRC in 1900 with 10,000 members.[53] In the same year, due to the inability of the Woolwich trade union and labour movement to agree on a candidate to contest the parliamentary seat, Colonel Hughes was returned unopposed. In the early days of promoting independent politics local activity was centred upon the Trades Council, who seized their opportunity in a Borough by-election in July 1901 in St Mary's ward, where Colonel Hughes, the local MP and Mayor, was beaten by Edwin Fennel, a local shoemaker and son of a Chartist. This was followed twelve months later by a Progressive and Labour victory for Revd. Jenkins Jones, Unitarian minister, and the first Labour Mayor for Woolwich 1903-5, in St Margaret's ward by-election on 12 July 1902.[54] Woolwich was 'the first town in Great Britain to possess a Labour Mayor elected by a Labour Council'.[55]

After Fennel was elected, the Woolwich and Plumstead Branches of the National Democratic League (NDL) set up an organisation in August 1901, which was to become the local Parliamentary Committee 'to secure for Labour and Democracy a Parliamentary Candidate who would contest the Borough of Woolwich at the next Parliamentary Elections.'[56] With this new impetus, workingmen turned their thoughts to fighting the next parliamentary election. With the committee's support a Conference was held in the Royal Assembly Rooms, Woolwich, on 9 October 1901. Delegates representing local Trade, Labour, and Temperance organisations adopted Frank Hugh O'Donnell, vice-president of the NDL and a former Irish Nationalist MP (1877-1885), as Parliamentary Candidate. When the opportunity arose to contest a by-election on 25 April 1902, the money to finance an election could not be found. [57] Colonel Hughes resigned on health grounds, having secured the consent of Lord Charles Beresford to contest the Woolwich vacancy on behalf of the local Conservative and Unionist Association.

In the Spring of 1902 a joint Registration Committee representing the Woolwich District Trades and Labour Council, the Borough of Woolwich Progressive Association, Woolwich Branch of the Independent Labour Party, and the local Parliamentary Committee was formed to undertake an exhaustive check of the voters' register to achieve the registration of all supporters.[58] Also a Trades Council Registration Committee was appointed in June 1902, 'to secure the registration of every eligible Trade Unionist and reader of the *Labour*

Journal.[59] Work of securing registration of all supporters had never been organised before and it was seen as a significant factor in political organisation if they were to win the Parliamentary seat for Labour. Following their successful work the Joint Registration Committee set up a small committee. The Clarion Club took the place of the Progressive Association, whose rules forbade Parliamentary action.

Charles Grinling addressed the protracted problem of Labour Parliamentary representation and accountability in a letter to the *Labour Journal* on the 30 May 1902. He believed that in future, to avoid factionalism between organisations on whether a candidate is representative, as happened in both 1900 and 1902 when choosing a Parliamentary candidate, it was necessary to put forward a candidate that they were all agreed upon. At the moment: 'The Parliamentary Committee is said to represent some 15 out of the 150 Trades, Friendly, Temperance, and Co-operative organisations of the district'.[60]

> Let them summon a public meeting of all reformers, and let a vote be taken by ballot, and let us all agree to abide by this result. It will then be open for every organisation to bring up its members to the poll. It will be open to reformers who do not belong to any organised body each to make his own voice heard by his single vote as clearly as the voice of any other. It will be simple for the committee of each organisation to express its views to its own members, and to issue a voting card to each. Outside reformers can have voting cards issued on application to the Parliamentary Committee or to the Trades Council, or any organised bodies on making it plain that their claim is *bona-fide*. Let the vote be by ballot.[61]

This procedure to organise democratic representation was pursued, and a Conference was held in the Trinity School Rooms, on 21 November 1902, where delegates representing nearly all the organisations in the Borough unanimously resolved to invite Will Crooks to contest the seat.[62]

Evidence shows that Crooks was not, as Paul Thompson argues, chosen to contest the Woolwich seat 'after prolonged consideration in 1902'. The local trade union and labour movement selected him unanimously, and within three weeks, Crooks' acceptance of the nomination was endorsed. Thompson further argues that Crooks was a 'straight progressive'.[63] If this had been the case, he would have accepted the Vice-Chairmanship of the LCC when it was offered to him, instead of choosing to remain an independent Labour man. This study aims to clarify the confusion surrounding Crooks' candidature.

LABOUR CANDIDATE

Crooks accepted the nomination. The decision was endorsed that he be adopted as the Woolwich Labour parliamentary candidate at a Public Meeting held on 12 December 1902, at the Co-operative Institute, Parson Hill, Woolwich. Grinling chaired the meeting.[64] Crooks' adoption meeting gave an indication of the type of campaign he was to fight. George Bishop, chairman and treasurer of the Free Church Council, proposed Crooks as a man 'who united them all'.[65] Crooks in his acceptance speech contrasted the worker with the university man, saying the former knew much more of human nature. He expressed his pride for the solid achievements of the trade union movement and supported the closure of public houses on Sundays. His speech was such that the organisations affiliated to the parliamentary committee, or at least sympathetic to it, for example, the Free Church Council, Temperance League, and the Irish League, could all find themselves in agreement with something that he said.[66] After the adoption meeting the Woolwich Labour Representative Association (WLRA) was formed. It 'was formed in 1902, with the definite object of winning for Labour a Parliamentary seat which, since the creation of Woolwich Parliamentary Constituency in 1885, had been held by the Conservative Party.' [67]

On 10 and 16 January 1903, the United Society of Coopers' Union and Woolwich Trades Council informed the LRC officially that Crooks had been adopted and asked them to sanction his candidature.[68] It is important to note that after Crooks' adoption the local LRA through the auspices of the Trades Council had agreed with the Coopers' Union that they would be responsible for Crooks' financial maintenance. This arrangement was necessary because of the LRC ruling that only Labour Associations in constituencies not covered by Trade Councils were eligible to affiliate.[69] The Woolwich LRA did not affiliate to the Labour Party until 1917.[70] Thus, the Coopers' Union was indirectly responsible for Crooks' financial support. Fred Butler subsequently became the administrator of the Will Crooks Parliamentary Maintenance Fund. Crooks signed the LRC Constitution on 22 January 1903.[71] Central to the controversy surrounding Crooks' signing of the 1904 Constitution was the financial arrangement between the Coopers' Union and the LRC.

The choice of Crooks by the conference was an astute one. An ardent socialist would have been unlikely to capture the seat. Crooks was ideally suited to bridge the old and new styles of political campaigning, and able to build a coalition and draw upon those voters disillusioned by economic issues, including the Tory working class threatened by the laying off of labour in the Arsenal. Crooks' style of Labourism, an evident moral fervour combined with a practical view of what could be achieved, was to prove an irresistible force in Labour's rise at national level.[72]

On the 11 March Will Crooks was returned to Parliament as the first Labour member for Woolwich and the fourth member of the Parliamentary Labour Representative Committee in the House of Commons. The resignation of Lord Charles Beresford on 18 February 1903, to take command of the Channel Squadron, gave notice of an impending by-election for the Woolwich Constituency.[73] It was the first time in eight years that the seat had been contested. By mid-February Crooks was accepted onto the LRC list. MacDonald wrote to Crooks' union secretary, Isaac Rogers, advising on procedure: 'Be careful not to raise any Liberal or Conservative business at all and do not make Crooks in any way so far as we are concerned a Liberal candidate.'[74]

Possibly unbeknown to MacDonald, Rogers had been an executive member of the Poplar Labor League 1897-8, and was a friend of Crooks, therefore better placed than most to know that Crooks was a Fabian, who split with the Liberals in 1893, and would never promote Tory policies. MacDonald wrote to Rogers because he was concerned that Crooks would be associated with the Liberals given his past membership of the Poplar Liberal and Radical Association, and because of his support for, although he sat on the Labour bench, the Progressives on the London County Council. MacDonald was wary of Crooks because he was seen by him to have no clear political philosophy above his dedication to working-class progress. From the outset, Crooks was tagged as less extreme than the previous Labour candidate, Ben Jones. The *Woolwich Gazette*, a moderate Unionist paper, saw the distinct possibility of some surprise at the next election. The editor, referring to Crooks' many journeys to meetings in Woolwich, commented: 'It is a fact too that ... in previous elections the Radical candidate has been an extremist ... Mr Crooks has received the unanimous support of every Radical, Labour and Trades organisation in the Borough.'[75]

Crooks addressed seven public meetings in all parts of the Borough, one under Temperance auspices, and one with the ILP, before the contest was announced. He concentrated on Arsenal wages, local housing, tariff reform and the 1902 Education Act. As the campaign progressed the working-class nature of Crooks emerged. His was a class-consciousness that appealed as readily to the Tory as to the Liberal working man: 'All the intelligence and patriotism in the country [do] not belong to the upper and middle-classes', he told an Eltham gathering.[76] His public speaking, based on years of addressing dock-gate meetings, was rooted in storytelling and cockney jokes. Frequently, just to illustrate a point, he used stories as parables to win over his audience, and to identify with them he would speak of his own experience of living in poverty and with unemployment. He would go on to assert the rights and dignities of working people.[77]

A delay in the announcement of the parliamentary vacancy was caused by Beresford's visit to the USA. Once he returned, his appointment to the command of the Channel Fleet was made official, and the Woolwich vacancy declared. The hierarchy of the Woolwich Conservatives, Colonel Hughes and his associates, went straight into a private meeting on 18 February with Beresford, and emerged to announce Geoffrey Drage as the Unionist candidate; a 42 year old with every Unionist credential.[78] Life had taken him through Eton, Oxford and around the world. The recommendation of the Woolwich Conservative and Unionist Emergency Committee was unanimously adopted immediately after a private meeting at the Masonic Hall, William Street, Woolwich.[79]

The hasty manner in which Drage was chosen led to a meeting of the Liberal Unionists to discuss attitudes to the election.[80] It was rumoured that Professor William Smith, Liberal Unionist, would emerge as a third candidate.[81] This meeting came about because in May 1902 the Tory caucus system — the Woolwich Conservative and Unionist Party — was split between differing factions, one led by Colonel Hughes. This schism had caused dissent and concern among the faithful because Hughes had been influential in the selection of Drage. Although the Liberal Unionists resolved in favour of Drage, it was not a promising start to the Unionist campaign.

THE 1903 BY-ELECTION

Drage had served as secretary to the Labour Commission (1891-94) and had published several works on labour questions. He had sat as junior member for Derby 1895-1900. Richard Bell, secretary of the Railway Servants, who was a Liberal/LRC candidate, replaced him.[82] Drage hoped that his Derby experience, in addition to his imperial connections, including the chairmanship of the Imperial South African Association, would serve him well in the by-election. He found that his antecedents carried little weight in such a working-class constituency as Woolwich. While advocating a labour register and the fuller use of trade union unemployment benefits, Drage made little attempt to develop a coherent programme in his speeches to the electorate. What he did say was conciliatory. Drage's election material emphasised that his campaign was aimed at the Tory workingman. It was edged in red and emblazoned with 'Vote for the Conservative and Labour Candidate.' In one leaflet addressed to the 'Men of the Arsenal', he states 'do you want to bring back the Liberal party to Office that has **always** meant slack work in the Arsenal. Then vote for Mr

Will Crooks'.[83] Drage declared his main difference with Crooks to be over socialism. He also tried to associate Crooks, who was a Home Ruler, with the Irish Nationalists, a tactic designed to appeal to all those with army connections. Crooks satirised these tactics, saying 'we have made a Tory democratic socialist Radical Labour Candidate come out with a programme that would give Lord Wemyss a paralytic shock.'[84]

He returned to his old theme that a real workingman knew more of the people's problems than any ex-university student. The WLRA issued *A Warning to Woolwich Workmen*: 'Remember! That Mr G. Drage, who now poses as the Champion of Labour, was once the Secretary of Liberty and Property Defence League.'[85] The leaflet accused Drage of representing 'an over-pampered and over-privileged class' thus drawing workingmen's attention to how this 'reactionary body has dealt with legislation that would have been a great boon to the workers'. It concluded that Will Crooks was the sweaters' foe and the workers' friend.[86] The leaflet also pointed out that the Liberty and Property Defence League had voted against the Trade Union Bill, the Cheap Trains Bill and the Workmen's Compensation Act of 1897, Amendment No. 2.

His opponent gave the catchphrase of the election to Crooks when Drage was being quizzed on his record over the Arsenal labourers' wages. Apparently, he had voted against a Liberal move to raise wage rates in 1896. His justification, that began with the statement 'because half a loaf is better than no bread' was lost in the jeering engendered in those opening words.[87] The cartoonist of the *Westminster Gazette* wrote to Charles Grinling, chairman of the Labour Representative Association, asking for two photographs 'and at the same time let me know whether Mr Crooks is tall or short ... the most effective treatment for a cartoon would be to emphasise the difference between the real working man candidate (Crooks) and the sham one (Drage).'[88] Subsequently a cartoon entitled 'On the Woolwich Platform', showing Crooks standing full square on a large loaf and Drage balancing precariously on half a loaf, appeared in the *Westminster Gazette* and was widely distributed.[89]

In the early days of the election campaign Drage found difficulty in securing votes of confidence at his meetings. A boisterous one in the Drill Hall followed the 'half-loaf' meeting, when Drage was forced to abandon part of his speech, and the chairman had to appeal, on Crooks' behalf, for order. The Unionists complained of organised gangs and arranged their meetings as all ticket affairs. These were more orderly, though heckling continued. Compared with Crooks' campaign activities, Drage made few appearances on the platform. During the week before polling day Crooks was attending up to three meetings a day, which always included lunch hour at No 1 Arsenal Gate, besides visits to the Dockyard, and Siemens Brothers. Siemens was a telegraph and electrical engineering factory, based in Charlton, which employed over 2,000 people in 1903.[90]

While Crooks was able to call on a cross-section of well-known speakers to support him on platforms in Woolwich, visiting Unionists were rare. Labour speakers included J.R. MacDonald, secretary of the LRC, George Barnes, secretary of the ASE, Havelock Wilson, secretary of the Seamen's Union, John Burns MP, Sydney Buxton MP and Arthur Henderson, secretary of the Ironfounders. Henderson had received a telegram from his Executive Committee, asking him to go to Woolwich at once.[91] Alex Wilkie, general secretary of the Shipwrights, was not sure whether he would be in London for the election, stating 'but our other representatives would be'. [92] Barefoot wrote to Keir Hardie asking him to 'send a few words of endorsement' to Crooks. In response, Hardie expressed great disappointment that Crooks' election address ignored the ILP and promoted the Radical Clubs and temperance organisations:

> ... you ignore the first organization most responsible for his being in the field — the ILP. I hope you are not ashamed of the movement to thus leave it out of account.... The first danger in connection with his candidature is that your Tory working man may get the impression that it is another Liberal fight ... After all this straightforwardness commends itself in the end and considering all that the ILP has done to make this movement what it is, I regret exceedingly that you should have ignored it as you have done in the campaign thus far.[93]

Hardie's criticism of Crooks' campaign was uncharacteristic. He was usually attuned to local political tactics, and should have realised that the electoral strategy was to play down any socialist connection in order to win over workingmen that had traditionally voted Tory. Furthermore, Hardie's view differed from that of the ILP Council, who, while acknowledging the work of the local branch, gave Crooks' candidature unequivocal support.[94]

The WLRA opened an Election Fund for Crooks in January by appealing for £600.[95] The *Daily News* followed, raising £1,000 within a fortnight.[96] The newspaper also issued five leaflets in support of his campaign while the *Weekly Dispatch* and the London Liberal Federation issued one each. The Federation's was in letterform, 'To the Liberals of London.' It described the Woolwich vacancy as a 'grand opportunity', firstly to inflict a blow on the Unionist Government, secondly to make a point about the proposed abolition of the London School Boards and thirdly 'to show that we are in earnest ... in our desires to see Labour directly and adequately represented in the House of

Commons.'⁹⁷ This support led to Unionist counter-propaganda that sought to implicate Crooks in Liberal activity.

The propaganda work undertaken by Labour was unprecedented in Woolwich, possibly anywhere in the UK. Besides the *Labour Journal* carrying particular arguments and exhortations from December to March, the WLRA printed over thirty different leaflets advertising more than twenty meetings in two months. Of the leaflets, four were produced by the WLRA in conjunction with other bodies, such as the Free Church Council, the Woolwich Tabernacle Total Abstinence Society, the Woolwich Radical Club and the United Irish League. Leaflets put out by the WLRA concentrated on Drage's record, pertinent quotations from his publications, particularly his pamphlet *Old Age Pensions*, and his connections with the Liberty and Property Defence League. A sixteen-page pamphlet *Who is Will Crooks?* by George Haw, and subtitled: 'The Life Story of the Servant of the People', was published and distributed free by the local Association.⁹⁸ Leaflets concentrated on issues like housing reform, old age pensions, industrial accidents, education, rates and the trade depression, all of which reflected the current situation. It contrasted the Taff Vale⁹⁹ decision and the threat to labour combinations with the growth of employers' associations: 'We appeal chiefly to work men, but ... *we address ourselves to all classes in Woolwich* who believe that moral and social benefit can come from wise legislation.' ¹⁰⁰

The result of the by-election on 11 March was a resounding victory for Crooks, who won with a considerable majority. Crooks polled 8,687 votes, and Geoffrey Drage 5,458 votes.¹⁰¹ Crooks returned 64.4 per cent of the poll on an 87.7 per cent turnout.¹⁰² Thus underlining the importance of registration; of targeting Labour promises, turning those promises into votes on the day, and increasing the turnout in Labour's favour. Compared with 1895, Crooks increased the Labour vote by 4,830, and increased the turnout by over eleven per cent.¹⁰³

After the election result, Crooks eventually made his way to Beresford Square. He told the waiting crowd 'Tonight Woolwich has sent a message of love and hope to labour all over the world.'¹⁰⁴ The *Journal*'s report supported this statement, 'Messages received by Will Crooks from such far distant lands as New Zealand and Australia bear testimony to the universal interest created by the victory won for Labour.'¹⁰⁵ On the evening of the election:

> ... it was the grand boast of nearly everyone of the thousands of men who gathered in the square that he had done something towards securing the glorious victory. Each man felt it was his victory. The same responsibility remains to day. The victory of Will Crooks was but the first step in the

march towards full and complete victory. As with the Parliamentary elections so with all future elections, they are soldiers' battles in the great campaign for workers' rights.[106]

Among the numerous letters and telegrams of congratulations that Crooks received was one from Sidney Webb warning him not to over do things:

> My wife and I send our very heartiest congratulations. What a triumph! — and it is all for you personally ... member for Woolwich, with a bigger poll than any other London M.P. But you deserve it all, for the excellence of your administrative work. For heaven's sake don't break down. You have been doing too much for years, and you can't add the House of Commons life, with all its incessant distractions and late hours, with impunity. You <u>must</u> slacken off somewhere.[107]

It seems the Webbs sent this letter of congratulation out of politeness — middle-class etiquette — given their personal grudge against Crooks' attempt to cut the grant of whisky money made to the LSE in 1898. Although the letter does underline the concerns that the trade union and labour movement had for Crooks' health.

By comparison Crooks received a letter of genuine heartfelt cheer from Ben Tillett, who proposed to meet Crooks in the House of Commons Lobby after he took his seat on 16 March:

> I suppose after all the congratulations, a word of good cheer from one of the "old 'uns" will not be out of place. It has done my heart good to know you have won, now it seems we must look after that Wages-fund. My heart gave a leap of joy when I heard your colossal scoring. We are not dead yet. I want to see you take your seat tomorrow, so kindly prepare to see me in the Lobby ... The victory is portentous, boom-clanging the knell of parting power, to the present parliament. Tom Mann, will be glad to hear of triumph. The wife and children shouted a labour-hallelujah for you.[108]

Tillett, Mann, and Crooks were close friends; they had been at the forefront of the New Union and the Poplar agitation since the late 1880s, and organised around Crooks 'College'.

The question that most historians ask is why was Will Crooks elected in a constituency that had consistently returned a Conservative and Unionist MP since its formation in 1885? There are a number of reasons, not least among them being the groundwork put in by the Woolwich and Poplar progressive movement on tariff reform and trade protection, job security, trade union interests, education and religion. The Poplar Labor League endorses this view: 'Woolwich is to be congratulated with *ourselves* [my italics] in the achievement of the result, brought about by the cooperation of all the forces making for progress.'[109] It was obvious to the labour movement that if Crooks were to win Woolwich he would need the support of the worker in the Arsenal, both labourer and skilled artisan.

In 1902, 2,372 workmen had been discharged from the Arsenal. Crooks promised to bring to the attention of the House of Commons the question of Arsenal discharges, also the Arsenal workers' claim to raise the minimum day rate from £1. 1s. He knew how the workers lived and the hopeless task of making both ends meet on one guinea a week. Speaking of his wife he said: 'She was lucky ... if she could make one end meat and the other end bread.'[110] The Arsenal workers took Crooks to their hearts; he was a man of stirring eloquence with a fund of homely humour and wit. Many of them would forego their lunch-break to listen to him speaking at his dinner hour meetings in Beresford Square.[111] Workers, especially those in the Arsenal, felt loyalty towards their respective unions who had endorsed and donated funds towards the election of Crooks. The Labour Representation Committee, an organisation to which the Engineers, Ironfounders and Railway Servants were affiliated, supported his electoral programme.[112] In addition, three branches of the Labour Protection League, branches of the Smiths' and Hammermen, and the Pattern Makers, contributed to the Will Crooks Election Fund established by the Woolwich Labour Representation Association. Altogether 73 organisations contributed £389. 14s. 6p. to the Fund.[113]

Crooks not only helped to politicise the workingmen of Woolwich, but he was also instrumental in providing them with better access to work. He was at the forefront of the campaign to build a tunnel at Blackwall, the opening of which had a significant social and political impact upon the Woolwich district. In addition, while he was Chairman of the LCC Bridges Committee (1899), he oversaw a scheme to provide a foot-tunnel underneath the Thames between Woolwich and Silvertown, which provided an alternative to the Ferry. The foot-tunnel opened in 1902. In addition, it is worth remembering, Crooks was on the LCC Woolwich Ferry subcommittee. Therefore, most workers in Woolwich were well aware that Crooks had influenced improvements in their daily life, whether they had to travel over the river to work, and attend either trade union or political meetings.

Those people unaware of Crooks' dedication to improving the quality of life for the working-class, especially the children of the poor and old age pensioners, were enlightened by the scathing article 'Municipal Socialism', in *The Times*, on 22 September 1902. This article only served to further Crooks' reputation as the servant of the poor, and the workers' friend. The timing of the article — September 1902 — must have helped focus people's minds because the Woolwich labour movement selected Crooks in November to represent them at the next parliamentary election.

Free Trade and Protection was important during the election, the 'half-loaf' episode was evidence of this, and from that moment, the loaf became the feature of the contest. Crooks was opposed to tariffs on imported foodstuffs — import controls would increase the price of wheat, thus bread. Britain had abandoned protection in the 1840s.[114] Geoffrey Drage's past record in Parliament in support of ruling-class ideas, especially those against trade union interests, cost the Unionists the support of the Arsenal workers and other trade union organisations in the constituency. Moreover, in 1902, the government introduced an Education Bill that aimed to abolish the School Boards in favour of a new, more rigid structure of secondary education to which access from elementary schools was to be gained only by scholarships.[115] It was broadly perceived in the labour movement as an attempt to maintain the Church's authority over maintained education, and to exact a block against the improvement of secondary education for working-class children. The *Labour Journal* pointed to: 'School Board education, like the London County Council, has developed into something which its promoters did not altogether intend, and there is a great desire in many quarters to strangle the Democratic infant now fast growing to be a giant.'[116]

Before the by-election the electorate knew where Crooks stood on the 1902 Education Bill, because on 22 February 1902, at a conference organised by the Royal Arsenal Co-operative Society, he spoke against its implementation, describing it as sectarian and increasing the power of local vested interests.[117] A progressive movement against the Bill developed among trade unions, co-operators, and the Free Churches that brought together the local labour movement behind the call for non-sectarian and democratic education.[118] The Bill was seen as undemocratic because it took away the right of election, and of representation, to School Boards from working men. The Conservative and Unionist government had introduced what was a draconian Bill, slighting the educational and religious rights of the working-class. They were not to be trusted and did not represent the workers' interests. On 29 July 1902, the Woolwich Trades and Labour Council sent a petition to the House of Commons against the Government's Education Bill on behalf of its affiliated societies. Lord Charles Beresford, MP, presented it:

"The humble petition of the Trade Unionists of the
Parliamentary Borough of Woolwich
"Showeth:-
"That your petitioners being deeply concerned in the education of the working classes
and of their children, desire to call for the withdrawal of the Education Bill now before
Your Honourable House.[119]

It would be true to say that the national image of Crooks was a confused one. Crooks' manifesto, widely distributed by Barefoot directly to trade unions, was not a socialist one, though Ramsay MacDonald 'swelled into some Woolwich brag', as he negotiated the 1903 electoral pact with the Liberal Chief Whip, Herbert Gladstone. [120]

Attempts by some Liberal papers to portray Crooks as the official Liberal candidate were to confuse trade unionists still further. John Hodge, secretary of the Steelsmelters, and an LRC executive member, needed particular reassurances about Crooks' Labour credentials from MacDonald and Barefoot before sending £25 on behalf of his union.[121] The ILP stated: 'It was on the initiative of our [ILP] branch ... that the machinery was set in motion, which resulted in the selection and final triumph of Mr Crooks.'[122] The *ILP News* pointed out that it was the Liberal press who were responsible for the confusion:

Will Crooks was a Socialist and a thoroughly sturdy Labour man before and during his Woolwich candidature ... no one believes that a Liberal candidate could have obtained the enormous vote which Will Crooks received.... That Liberal workingmen in the mass voted for Will Crooks cannot be doubted any more than that a large portion of Tory workmen voted for him. [123]

In June, Barefoot wrote to MacDonald explaining Crooks had complied with the objects of the Newcastle resolution:

Why so much anxiety about Woolwich ... Crooks as a Labour member is in an absolutely independent position so far as the liberals or tories are concerned ... we were ... in the somewhat unique position of having cleared with the official Liberal before we started the campaign, and at the conference before Crooks was adopted as a candidate it was unanimously decided that whoever was adopted should run as a labour independent of either political party. As a matter of fact the only embarrassment throughout the campaign came from the labour side outside Woolwich, presumably because they took no pains to discover the real facts of the situation.... I fear the misunderstanding ... has arisen owing to the unique position here. There is no Liberal Association; the Radical Clubs are as strongly Labour as the most strenuous among us. They would readily join the LRC if they could. You would not have us deter them from our Association.... My hope is that future labour candidates who are not I.L.Pers (I speak as a member) will not be looked upon with so much suspicion. [124]

In the meantime, Hardie and MacDonald had drawn the conclusion that working-class action without Liberal support was ineffectual. This realisation initiated the long negotiations between MacDonald and Gladstone on an electoral alliance to get some agreement on the allocation of seats.

Although local political configurations differed, David Shackleton had been returned unopposed in the by-election at Clitheroe (Lancashire) in 1902; Crooks won in a straight fight at Woolwich, and Arthur Henderson took a seat from the Liberals in a three-cornered fight at Barnard Castle (Durham) in July 1903.[125] The Liberals must have been impressed. Herbert Gladstone made a secret pact with MacDonald in September 1903. They agreed to give thirty LRC candidates a clear run in designated constituencies, while the LRC would encourage working-class support for the Liberals elsewhere.[126] The chief reason why the MacDonald/Gladstone pact was kept secret was because of the need to implement it with caution in each locality. This was necessary to enable the LRC to retain the allegiance of its left-wing activists who were anti-Liberal in their rhetoric and acutely suspicious of the leadership. Gladstone for his part not only saw Crooks' victory as a boost for the LRC but also as confirming the wisdom of his strategy. He saw the success of Crooks and Arthur Henderson as triumphs for candidates barely distinguishable from orthodox Liberals.[127]

Following the by-election victory, there was little time to relax, for immediately ahead lay the municipal elections. Therefore, it was decided to broaden the remit of the WLRA. On 31 March 1903 it was amended, to secure the representation of Labour on *all* elected bodies. The Trades Council affiliated, and the Progressive Association dissolved, encouraging its members to join the Labour Association.[128] Charles Grinling was instrumental in bringing the local progressives and socialists together to constitute the association. Individual membership, grouped in ward committees, was made the basis of organisation, while the general management and decisions on policy were vested in a General Council, consisting of two delegates from each ward committee and affiliated organisations. The first constitution of the party was framed with these principles in mind. This constitution is still the basis of that governing the party over one hundred years later.

Woolwich was the first Labour party nationally to make individual membership the basis of its effectiveness, and the ward the unit of organisation.[129] The WLRA constitution was adopted by an AGM in May 1904, after the General Council had previously agreed it on 15 June 1903. The importance of individual membership was recognised and this principle became part of the Labour Party's constitution in 1918.[130] The first officers of the WLRA were Charles Grinling, chairman, George Bishop, treasurer, and William Barefoot, secretary. Barefoot was to hold this position, and that of local councillor, from November 1903 until his death in 1941. Offices were opened at 83-85 Powis Street, which served as party headquarters until a lease was taken on the premises at 3 Woolwich New Road in 1905.[131] Not only was the WLRA successful in gaining a majority on the local Council in November 1903 but they also returned two Labour representatives to the LCC in March 1904 and nine to the Board of Guardians in the following month.[132] Woolwich was unique in this period, being the first constituency in the country to be represented by Labour at every level of government, local, regional, and national.[133]

Crooks was the first LRC candidate to win a straight fight against a Conservative in a single seat constituency. Hardie and Bell, for example, were returned in the two seat constituencies of Merthyr Tydfil and Derby respectively in 1900; Shackleton was returned unopposed at Clitheroe in 1902. Therefore, Crooks' victory in Woolwich was the first example of what could be achieved in a Tory stronghold without Liberal opposition. His election victory accelerated the electoral success of Labour, and became pivotal in the electoral pact between MacDonald and Gladstone. Crooks' victory, therefore, should be seen for what it was, the beginning of Labour's rise as an electoral force of political significance. The Woolwich election result marked the beginning of Labour's rise electorally, and had a lasting political resonance on the pattern and style of future elections throughout the country. The advent of Labour threatened the electoral supremacy of both the Liberals and the Conservatives by influencing decisions that sought to change the balance of power within the bounds of national politics. An analysis of the evidence shows that not only was Crooks' contribution significant to the emergence of the LRC, but that he played an important role in the consolidation of the Labour Party after 1906.

Taking into consideration Crooks' dedication to furthering the interest of working people, especially those living in Woolwich, and the reputation he had within the wider labour movement, it was not surprising that he was selected unopposed. Crooks stayed loyal to Woolwich, he remained MP for the constituency throughout his parliamentary career, and was one of the few early Labour MPs to do so.

PART TWO

Labour Pioneer and Member of Parliament 1903-1921

5

MEMBER FOR WOOLWICH

Shortly before the Woolwich by-election a decision was taken by Ramsay MacDonald and Herbert Gladstone, the Liberal Chief Whip (1899-1905), to formulate an electoral arrangement between the LRC and the Liberals.[1] Given this, it would be appropriate to revisit the period of the deliberations between MacDonald and Gladstone to determine how, and why, an electoral understanding came about, and whether the Woolwich triumph was influential to the negotiations between MacDonald and Gladstone, and thus significant to the development of the LRC. At the same time, evidence will be brought to the discussion that has been omitted by historians, evidence based on a letter in the *Labour Leader* from Jim Middleton, assistant secretary of the Labour party, which puts forward an electoral consideration different from the orthodox view that the Liberals made 'concessions' in the accommodation of 1903. This discussion will place Crooks' by-election victory in perspective by exploring the impact of the Woolwich triumph on the negotiations between the Liberals and LRC.

Not since Frank Bealey published his two articles on the electoral arrangements and negotiations between the Liberal Party and the LRC (1956), and Bealey and Pelling discussed the issue in *Labour and Politics 1900-1906* (1958), has the detail of the electoral arrangement been examined.[2] Duncan Tanner in his seminal work *Political change and the Labour Party 1900-1918* refer to the 'negotiations' in passing. They 'have been ably discussed elsewhere', he states.[3] This implies that Bealey and Pelling's research is the definitive work on the subject, and therefore does not merit revisiting. On the contrary, while the internecine polemics of the Liberal Party and the LRC are discussed, and the correspondence in the Gladstone papers between Herbert Gladstone and his private secretary Jesse Herbert are emphasised by Bealey, the research does not elaborate or venture to analyse the detail of the arrangement in the constituencies where Labour men were 'allowed' to have a 'straight fight' with the Tories.

The working-class appeal of the Conservative party, and the electoral failure of the Socialists and Liberals, the Liberals appearing incapable of even denting Tory influence after 1885, formed the political background — Tariff reform being the key issue — of the Gladstone-MacDonald entente of September 1903.[4] What worried the Liberals, and a significant factor in the arrangement with Labour, was that working-class support for the Tories was 'threatening ... "Liberal" areas such as Yorkshire and the North-East.'[5] A further influence to any Liberal/Labour understanding was the independence of the ILP and the LRC, who were more likely to gain Tory working-class support in areas where conservative Liberalism was dominant.[6] Therefore if Labour was given a 'clear run' in these constituencies, not only would they appeal to dissident radical Liberals, but there would be less likelihood of a split vote, which would let in the Unionists.

An accommodation with Labour would not only protect the Liberal left flank against attacks from progressivism, but remove the threat in Liberal strongholds, which according to Tanner, 'was widely regarded as a major influence on the result of the 1906 General Election'.[7] The evidence put forward by Middleton shows that the Liberal 'concessions' of 1903 were primarily an electoral scheme to win Labour support in areas that previously had been unwinnable because of Tory opposition. Middleton points out: 'It is well to remember that in 17 constituencies out of a total 31 in which the Liberals "stood aside" they similarly made way for the Tories in 1900.'[8] In other words, the Liberals gained from the pact. The LRC would contest those seats that the Liberals were unlikely to win, gaining seats from the Tories, and thus increase the prospect of a Liberal majority. Labour in turn would positively support Liberal candidates in areas they were not contesting, which would again favour the Liberals.

It is noteworthy that Jesse Herbert in his correspondence with Gladstone in 1905 considered the Woolwich and Barnard Castle by-elections as Liberal gains.[9] This is not to say that Labour was disadvantaged by the arrangement, quite the opposite, they were in a stronger position not having to fight 31 three-cornered seats. Crooks believed that the Liberals should support Labour representation. Writing in the *Speaker* he said: 'The Labour Party is quite a natural result of the indispensable failure of rich people legislating for the poor ... and the duty of the Liberal Party is to assist into the House of Commons men who know and live the lives of ... the common people.'[10]

On the question of whether Crooks' victory was influential to the negotiations between MacDonald and Gladstone, it is important to note that:

'Events at Woolwich accelerated the proceedings' and that the 'victory was a great fillip to the cause of Labour representation.'[11] MacDonald and Herbert met the day after the election to discuss what arrangements needed to be made enabling MacDonald to see Gladstone.[12] Two days after the election (13 March), Gladstone outlined the proposals put forward by the LRC in a memorandum to the leader of the Liberal Party, Henry Campbell-Bannerman:

> We are ready to do this as an act of friendship and without any stipulation of any kind, because we realise that an accession of strength to Labour representation in the House of Commons is not only required by the country in the interests of Labour but that it would increase progressive forces generally and *the Liberal party as the best available instrument of progress*.[13] (My italics).

Woolwich was greeted by many Liberals as an example of how both parties could benefit from local co-operation between progressive forces.

Both Sir Edward Grey, a Liberal imperialist, and Campbell-Bannerman welcomed the Woolwich victory.[14] Gladstone regarded the LRC as the latest instalment of radicalism (from Chartism onwards) that could be contained naturally and easily within Liberalism. The victory confirmed Keir Hardie's belief that to capture the votes of Tory workingmen, Labour must remain independent of the Liberals in the constituencies.[15] From the above evidence, it can be argued that Crooks' election was significant to the negotiations, and to the subsequent development of the LRC. A unifying and crucial political link between LRC and the Liberals was an agreement over social and progressive reform. They disagreed on so little. They were united in their belief that the destructive strife in the Churches over the Education Act of 1902 should end, and be replaced by a system of non-sectarian education. Both parties were opposed to 'the Taff Vale decision and, from mid-1903 onwards, Chamberlain's Tariff Reform campaign.'[16] The other issues upon which they agreed were Unemployment, Home Rule for Ireland, Old Age Pensions, Parliamentary Reform, and One Man One Vote.

WILL CROOKS' PARLIAMENTARY PLATFORM 1903-1906

The disintegration of the Conservative ministry, especially after Chamberlain resigned in September 1903, seemed to give the Labour group a new lease of life. Its primary function, at this time, had been limited to serving the purpose of propaganda, attempting to correct grievances, and revealing general injustices. 'For the next two years all the forces of opposition, both inside and outside parliament, were in full hue and cry after the Government.'[17] Crooks was an important protagonist in this agitation.

After Crooks' introduction to the Commons by Shackelton and Burns on 16 March 1903,[18] he engrossed himself in the procedures of debate that would enable him to intervene in the interest of working people. Crooks' experience as a Poor Law administrator enabled him to digest difficult legislation, and make informed and telling interventions on behalf of the poor, old age pensioners, underprivileged children, the unemployed, and the low paid. In addition, this administrative work had taught him how to deal with permanent officials, whose unseen power in the affairs of the nation is far greater than the uninitiated suppose. He believed that men were elected to parliament because of their special gifts, even though he thought in some cases money might have had something to do with it. Writing in 1905, Crooks said: 'I went into the House ... not at all with the feeling that I should not be able to hold my own at a pinch if necessity arose ... that a member should really know and understand the subject he might at any time be called upon to speak about.'[19] Hence, Crooks was usually well briefed. On entering the House Crooks undertook the bulk of work pertaining to protesting against wages and conditions of Government workers for the Labour group. He objected, for example, to the discharge of his constituents from Woolwich Arsenal and 'demanded to know on what grounds private manufacturers received Government contracts'. [20]

Crooks' maiden speech on 26 March was on the Army Estimates. This followed a contribution at question time. When he asked William Broderick, the Secretary of War (1900-1903), how many men had been discharged from or were under notice to leave Woolwich since peace (Boer War) was proclaimed, Broderick's reply was that in all 2,375 men had gone or had been given notice to go. Crooks made two speeches in the Army Estimates debate, where the Government was to set aside a sum not exceeding £1,920,000 to defray the charge for the staff in the Engineering Services. In his first speech, he criticised the Government's policy that work had been diminished purposely in government factories to give it to private contractors; an issue he raised repeatedly 1903-1915. Crooks argued that 'when there is to be a division of government work between ordnance factories and private contractors the ordnance factories should be employed to their full-time capacity and only then the surplus given to the contractors.' [21]

His second contribution related to the Government as employers. He believed that the Government should set an example to other employers by paying the best wages with a view of getting in return the best service. Crooks was concerned that low paid workers, especially Government employees, should be allowed to make their representations regarding pay and conditions through their union without the threat of being made redundant. He told Broderick in August: 'If the men and women were dissatisfied they were perfectly free to ventilate their grievances, and to approach the authorities on the matter, and he would take care that they would not be penalised for doing so.' Thus, Crooks in his usual frank manner informed the House that his position would be clear, direct, and unequivocal. Low paid Government workers would be heard, and he would champion their cause. Crooks stood by his word. He advocated a 30s. minimum wage for Government employees during debate in March 1904. Subsequently in 1907, the 30s. minimum became Labour Party policy, due mostly to the advocacy of Will Crooks and the Woolwich Trades Council. [22]

During May 1903, in the debate on the Old Age Pensioners Bill, Crooks stated the difficulty of administering an old age pensions scheme would be no greater than that of administering the present complicated Poor Law system. He further said that those who supported the Bill ought to insist upon 'the Government making some provision for those veterans who had done so much to uphold the commercial supremacy of the country.'[23] Crooks was adamant that old people should be kept as far away as possible from the workhouse. He maintained 'it is both lawful and right to pay pensions through the Poor Law'. To the contention that this practice is only "glorified out-relief," he retorted: 'So are most pensions ... out-relief to the poor is no more degrading than out-relief to the rich.'[24]

After the King's Speech Motion on 19 February 1904, Keir Hardie moved an amendment expressing regret that government advisers had not seen fit to recommend the creation of a Department and Minister for Labour. Crooks seconded the amendment, and spoke of the difference between the worker and the loafer. He declared that, 'he desired work for the worker and not to provide assistance to the loafer.' Under the present workhouse system, with its habitual casuals, it was difficult to compel wasters and tramps to work: 'If the Local Government Board would unite districts and enable Guardians to take land ... something might be done to make useful labourers of them.' [25] The essence of Crooks' argument was that the setting up of a Department of Labour would help guardians and councils to provide work and relief to those men who were most deserving. He wanted the unemployed to be registered officially by local councils. If this system was implemented, Crooks believed, genuine workmen looking for employment would be given priority over the loafer, who sought relief instead of work.

A Licensing Bill was introduced during the session on April 1904, which encouraged the tied at the expense of the free public house, and the payment of compensation to the tied licence-holder. Crooks disapproved and objected to this Bill, speaking in the interests of the 'poor men and barmaids in the tied houses who were the slaves of the brewer, and who when the house was shut up, would find it difficult to turn their hand to anything else'.[26] Crooks said the measure 'ought to called the Brewers' Endowment Bill', because in 90 per cent of cases publicans would not receive compensation because the majority of licence-holders were absentee landlords. Also those publicans who were 'licence-holders were mere tenants at will, and could be turned out at a minute's notice.' He believed that: 'This was a Bill imposed ... by clever people', and the brewers would make 'much out of it and safeguard their interests'.[27]

Crooks was fervently against working people being exploited by the monopoly interests of breweries. On 5 July, when members divided and passed into the lobby to vote after the Prime Minister moved the motion for closure of the Licensing Bill, Crooks declined to move. Corrie Grant, Cramer, Whitley 'and other hon. members endeavoured to persuade him to proceed to the lobby' but he refused, 'declaring in a loud voice, "Somebody must protest.... this is the only way in which one has a chance of bringing before the public the iniquitous act of the Government over this Bill." ' [28] The press took note of Crooks' resistance to the Bill. The *Yorkshire Daily Post*, for example, made the point that Crooks' hostility to the closure had 'not evoked the enthusiasm in the Labour world which presumably he was led to expect, and will possibly be on surer ground to-morrow [12 July] ... on the subject of unemployment.'[29]

However, the protest served its purpose. It served as a reminder to working people that Crooks could be trusted to look after their interests. The implementation of the Licensing Bill would mean that a certain number of public houses would close, job losses would follow, and the unemployed kept at the expense of the ratepayer. Crooks' reputation of representing the concerns of working people was well known. During the progress of the Licensing Bill through parliament, the *Nottingham Daily Express* said: 'Parliament is the place for men who know how to serve their fellows, and the people surely never had a better servant and truer friend than "honest Will Crooks".'[30]

In the House of Commons on 10 August, Crooks made an eloquent appeal on behalf of underfed children attending school. It was a speech made with sympathetic insight, and compassion only gained from harsh experience. 'Dealing with the question ... [Crooks] urged that something should be done in this matter at once, and it should not be put off to next year.' He advocated free school meals for the deserving school children, and that all educational needs 'should be paid for out of the Imperial Exchequer so that they might get rid of all questions of equality in the matter of education of local burdens.' Crooks continued:

They had the same cry every winter - casual employment, sick father, mother broken down in health, children going to school unfed.... Some people would, no doubt, say that the parents could feed their children if they were only more careful, did not drink so much ... But, be that as it might, it had nothing to do with the children, and it was the children that they had got to look after. [31]

He believed that the first principle of education was the question of feeding the children, and that the House should not shirk its responsibility. He saw it as a question of economics.

The State must invest in the health and education of its children if they wanted a healthy and educated workforce in the future. Shortly after Crooks' intervention on behalf of underfed school children, he presented, supported by the Labour Group, the Women's Enfranchise Bill: 'To enable Women to vote at all Parliamentary Elections.'[32] It received a second reading in May 1905, when it fell.[33] By putting forward this Bill, Crooks was honouring a promise he made in his election address.

The reform of feeding pauper school children, first suggested by Crooks, became LRC policy at the beginning of 1905. At the LRC Liverpool conference, a resolution was passed urging Labour members of Parliament to introduce such a Bill.[34] One was introduced in May 1905 by Henderson that would 'have given local authorities permissive powers to feed elementary school children, "unable by reason of lack of food to take full advantage of the education provided for them".'[35] The Bill was withdrawn at the end of the session after its First Reading.

LIBERALISM AND THE FREE TRADE PLATFORM

Amid the hue and cry in the House of Commons, the LRC was often drawn into pursuit and 'sometimes found it difficult to maintain its position of independence',[36] because on a number of issues, such as Chinese labour, unemployment, and Free Trade, their position was often indistinguishable from that of the Liberals. Crooks seemingly exacerbated the problem. He was accused of advocating Liberalism by speaking on Liberal platforms, thus going against the LRC Constitution. It seems that Crook' eclecticism, and his Liberal past, served to incite criticism from the wider Labour movement, who were influenced, in some cases, by Liberal mischief and newspaper reports. MacDonald in a letter to Crooks wrote: 'I am afraid from all I can hear that the way which certain Liberal Associations are abusing the neutrality of the Free Trade platform will get us into trouble and will give our extremists another opportunity of narrowing our Constitution. This will be a fearful misfortune.'[37]

It is evident from these remarks MacDonald was concerned that the Liberals were trying to compromise Crooks and the LRC, and therefore Crooks should be more discerning when selecting which platform to speak on in future. His selection of platform was seen by some as a dereliction of his duty to support the Labour cause.

MacDonald stood by Crooks throughout 1903-5, out of deference to both Crooks and the Woolwich LRA, probably because of their pivotal and political importance in helping to deliver the Lib-Lab pact. MacDonald and Crooks were old friends. Both had been engaged in the early struggles around Labour representation in the East End, and colleagues on the LCC. Crooks campaigned for MacDonald when he stood as ILP candidate for Hackney South, unsuccessfully, in the LCC elections of 1898. These early struggles had taught them both how to deal with adversity, especially with the 'wrecker' mentality of political opponents, including rival factions inside the movement.

Norwich, Devonport, and Bangor

Before the election of Crooks, an amendment to the LRC constitution was put forward at the annual conference at Newcastle in February 1903, because according to the LRC Executive 'the present constitution is worded in such a way as to make its meaning doubtful.'[38] The amendment was deferred until the Bradford conference in 1904 and changed, root and branch, the relationship between the LRC and Labour candidates and MPs. Also of significance was the proposed fund for the maintenance of Labour members in the House of Commons, put forward at Newcastle; payment out of this fund was dependent upon all Labour members and candidates pledging themselves to the new constitution or resigning. On the issue of an independent Labour platform the new constitution was specific, 'to abstain strictly from identifying themselves with or promoting the interests of any section of the Liberal or Conservative parties, and not to oppose any other candidate recognised by this Committee'.[39]

To help understand Crooks' political position it is important to recognise that before Newcastle and Bradford, Crooks signed the old constitution in January 1903, which read quite differently. It called upon him to 'embrace a readiness to co-operate with any party which for the time being may be engaged in promoting legislation in the direct interest of Labour.' This difference of emphasis, its acceptance as a prerequisite to maintenance, especially the insertion 'or resign' would have been an insult to Crooks' political integrity. His reluctance to sign the new constitution may have been determined by the fact that his power base in Woolwich was secure, and he could depend on the local LRA to pay his maintenance. It is notable that neither the Coopers' Union nor the WLRA pressured Crooks to sign. The LRC on the other hand realised that calling for Crooks' resignation would do irreparable damage to the party, and decided to play a long game.

During May, a circular requesting contributions to the Will Crooks Maintenance Fund was made by the WLRA to affiliated organisations of the LRC. This action was questioned by affiliates. Why had Crooks not received adequate assistance from the LRC? Had he signed the constitution? Why had he not signed the new constitution, and 'what reason was given for the Committee's refusal for accepting financial assistance from the L.R.C. when first elected for Woolwich.'[40] The LRC had offered to pay Crooks' extra expenses as a member of the House of Commons, but he declined the offer. 'Many thanks to your EC but I understand from the EC of the Woolwich Labour Representative Association that they will be responsible for the Extra Expenses my membership of the House of Commons entails.'[41] These enquiries disconcerted MacDonald and Pease, who tried even harder to get Crooks to sign the constitution in the hope of avoiding further criticism by those societies affiliated to the LRC. It turned out that the reason for Crooks' reticence about signing the constitution was less sinister than some people read into it, namely political differences with the LRC. It was simply a financial oversight by the Coopers' Society. MacDonald informed Isaac Rogers that Crooks 'was quite willing to receive from his Society a recommendation'[42] to sign the constitution, but Crooks according to Pease 'was not eligible to receive money from the Parliamentary Fund because the Coopers' Society had not paid into it.'[43] This oversight was corrected and Rogers returned the constitution: 'Will Crooks has attached his signature to the form of constitution which I am now returning'. [44]

The behaviour of Richard Bell MP in supporting the Liberals in the House of Commons was according to Bealey and Pelling 'the most compelling factor in favour of the amendment of the constitution of the LRC.'[45] The situation was further aggravated when Bell refused to speak on a Labour platform in support of the LRC candidate George Roberts at the Norwich by-election in January 1904. Crooks stayed away, for what reason is not clear, avoiding any disagreement that might have arisen from his critics. He would have felt uncomfortable speaking against a Liberal who was a supporter of the Trade Union Bill. Bruce Glasier wrote to Hardie: 'Crooks has funked. Snowden before leaving wrote him a strong letter but there is no reply,' and later: 'Crooks finally "cannot come" and sends us no message. Even Richards is trying to hedge!'[46] Bell was not so discerning. He sent a telegram to the Liberal victor that ran: 'Great triumph for progress. Hearty congratulations.'[47] When Bell refused to sign the LRC constitution 1904-5, 'he had to be expelled.'[48]

Similar disquiet, though not leading to expulsion, was experienced when Crooks, Shackelton and Henderson spoke on a Free Trade and Labour Union platform in support of John Benn, at a by-election meeting in Devonport on 14 June 1904.[49] Their conduct nearly split the party, coming as it did in the middle of an attempt to discipline Bell for similar infidelities. Crooks had informed the Woolwich party of his intentions and requested its acceptance. He told them of the invitation 'to speak at Devonport by the Devonport L.R.A., of the Free Trade Union.... It was resolved. That the E. C. has no objection to Mr. Crooks accepting the invitation provided that Messrs. Shackleton & Henderson have the consent of the L.R.C.'[50] There is no record of any response, which suggests MacDonald wanted a quiet end to the matter. Further, it seems Crooks was influenced to appear on the platform because Shackleton and Henderson, Chairman and Treasurer respectively of the LRC, had also consented to speak in support of Benn.

In reply, to a complaint from Will Thorne, Macdonald states, 'as to whether the L.R.C. Sent down Mr. Crooks, Mr. Shackleton, and Mr. Henderson ... the question has never been before them.'[51] Crooks knew that the invitation was genuine; he did not realise that the Liberals were using the neutrality of the Free Trade platform. The LRC Executive finally accepted their explanations and let the episode drop. It is important to note the constitutional procedure of the LRC regarding complaints. They believed it was the 'duty of the body that paid him to deal with it'.[52] In Crooks' case, this did not happen. Even after Barefoot wrote again to MacDonald to inquire whether Shackleton and Henderson 'had permission ... to speak at Devonport at the recent by-election', the LRC did not respond. [53]

Unfounded and irritating complaints continued to plague Crooks and the LRC. For example, a meeting that was addressed by Crooks and Lloyd George at Bangor on 29 September 1904 was reported in the *Liverpool Mercury* to have been held 'under the auspices of the Liberal Association'. According to the report, Crooks had been invited by Bangor Liberal Association to explain the principles of the Labour Party.[54] The Liberal Association out of courtesy invited Lloyd George, MP for the Caenarvon District, which included Bangor.

Sometime later MacDonald received a complaint from the secretary of the Amalgamated Clothlookers and Warehousemen's Association. MacDonald needed to know the exact nature of the meeting from Crooks, enabling him to 'counteract troublesome complaints that were being spread about ... from time to time.'[55] Contrary to the newspaper report Crooks had been invited to address the meeting by the North Wales Quarrymen's Union, who wrote: 'Your attendance would be much appreciated and would also we are convinced greatly aid the cause of progress in the district.'[56] Crooks was angry, he forwarded a copy of the letter to MacDonald, which included the comment: 'I am sick of these folk who ... cry Liberal', and question my *bona fides*.[57] MacDonald replied 'obliged by yours with enclosure. It really shows that somebody should be shot ... let me send a copy of the invitation to the *Labour Leader* ... I find that any correction published in this paper generally gets into the right hands.'[58]

The Norwich, Devonport, and Bangor episodes illustrate how difficult it was for the LRC to maintain a position of independence. The Liberal drift towards reformist politics was not universally popular in the localities. Powerful forces in constituency Liberal executives were opposed to Progressive politics and an alliance with Labour.[59] These Old Liberals, who saw the independence of the Labour party as a threat to its electoral interests, were determined to make trouble for the LRC, and wherever possible make public mischief on the question of LRC independence. Thus, the LRC found it increasingly difficult to counter the intimidation that was designed to attract the conservative working-class into the Liberal orbit. On a number of occasions, MacDonald had to be evasive to fend off complaints about Crooks' behaviour. He told Crooks privately that the Liberals bragged about how easy it was to dupe him into speaking, and to be more careful when accepting invitations in future. Given Crooks' antecedents as a Radical Liberal it must have been difficult for him to keep clear of Liberalism. His weakness was that he was too trusting of those who professed social radicalism, and in turn, they played on his sensibilities as an old fashioned radical.

Among his many duties, Will Crooks played a major part in the development of the local LRA, by placing his services at their disposal, always keeping them in touch with all the important problems of the day, and helping to work for their resolution. Crooks believed that if they were going to do anything about helping the working-class, Labour must stand alone, and not rely either upon the Liberal or Conservative parties.[60] In September 1904, Will Crooks was chosen instead of the King to open the New Town Hall, Woolwich, in January 1906.[61] This honour was bestowed on him to acknowledge the respect Crooks had gained by his selfless representation of the people of Woolwich. His constituents affectionately knew him as the "People's Will," a sentiment that Crooks earned through hard work and personal sacrifice. Because of the work of the WLRA, and the support they received from Crooks, the membership 1903-1905 had increased from 1,954 to 2,500.[62]

In addition to speaking at the Arsenal gate in support of the Trades Council, the ILP, and on numerous trade union platforms, Crooks also held a number of meetings, under the auspices of the WLRA, at ward branches throughout the borough from October 1904 to December 1905.[63] Opening the campaign at the Co-operative Hall in October, Crooks said 'he was glad to be amongst his own again, after a journey of 3000 miles ... addressing all sorts and conditions of men. He was glad to be amongst his own people to answer one or two things that cropped up since he had been away.'[64]

At branch meetings, he spoke against unemployment, Tariff Reform, and the use of Chinese labour in South Africa. These propaganda meetings were organised to counter the arguments for tariff reform and preference duties set out by Joseph Chamberlain. The issues around Tariff Reform had taken on a new lease of life since May 1903, when Joseph Chamberlain 'began his bid for tariff reform'[65] and in September 1904, when he resigned from Balfour's Cabinet to lead the tariff reform campaign. Chamberlain believed 'without preferential duties it would be impossible either to raise the money required for social reform or to lower the rate of unemployment', and unless the question of trade and commerce was resolved, there would be disunity in the Empire.[66] Crooks obviously thought the time was appropriate to put forward the Labour party's position to its members, enabling them to defend the cause of Free Trade, against the arguments of Protectionists and Tariff Reformers.

Crooks deemed that the taxing of unearned income would create jobs, the dredging of rivers, land and marsh reclamation, road building, and other work of benefit to the community. Further, he felt: 'How much good work could be done [at home] if they had the money.'[67] The nationalisation of the canals and railways would enable home manufacturers and producers, co-operative and small enterprises to flourish in the interests of working people, instead of railway companies, providing privileges to foreign interests and 'throttling enterprise' at home.[68] 'While not forgetting the Empire', Crooks wanted, 'a little more of home matters in the next five years than in the past five years.'[69] Although Crooks was an Empire man, he believed in good governance by example, not in the exploitation of people at home to serve colonial interests, and neither should the colonies be exploited to serve the interest of the capitalists in Britain.

It was during this campaign that Crooks was taken ill. He suffered a relapse after his speaking tour in January 1905. He was out of action for five weeks. It was fitting, therefore, that Will Crooks' first public appearance since his enforced absence should coincide with the second anniversary of his parliamentary victory, which was celebrated on 9 March at the Drill Hall, Woolwich. Will Crooks' speech was scathing of a dying administration that was torn between free trade and protection, 'they ought to make up their minds one way or the other. They ought to leave off talking about "loafers and wasters" when we see that lot wasting your time.' We are told they carried the Empire on their backs: 'I have seen a man carrying a sack of coal with greater responsibility.' Crooks talked of how the Liberals and Tories used society and democratic Government for the privileged classes and powerful interests. He said that he hated 'the whole system top to bottom'; it was immoral, oppressive, and corrupt. The sooner they went the better: 'When they had forty or fifty Labour Members in Parliament they could challenge whichever party was in power.'[70] It can be deduced from the tenor of Crooks' speech that he thought a general election was imminent. He believed that it would be fought on the maintenance of free trade, education and constitutional reform, increased working-class representation, and Tory misuse of the 1900 electoral mandate.

In response to Balfour's resignation on 4 December 1905, Campbell-Bannerman formed a Liberal Government, and subsequently dissolved Parliament on 8 January 1906.[71] The response of the LRC to Balfour's resignation was to send circulars to all prospective candidates and local LRCs informing them that speaking arrangements for the general election would be organised centrally by the LRC.[72] The Woolwich Labour movement was also ready, and had been for some time. Organising voters onto the electoral register had begun in mid-August 1905, with Will Crooks addressing a huge crowd of Arsenal workers at a lunch-time meeting in Beresford Square.[73] In addition, William Barefoot had been in place as Crooks' election agent since 11 December.[74]

THE GENERAL ELECTION OF 1906

As soon as the election was declared in January 1906, other LRC candidates inundated Crooks with requests to speak in other constituencies. 'I am being worried to death by candidates who want me to speak', Crooks told MacDonald, 'as you know so much will depend on the Liberty I get from Woolwich.'[75] Again on the same day Crooks wrote, 'all my time outside Woolwich ... is in the hands of the Labour Representative Committee ... who have to arrange where I go if I have any free dates.'[76] MacDonald replied: 'I do not want you to neglect your own constituency and I should advise you to stick to it after a certain date, which you ought to fix, say January 8th, until your fight is over' and if he needed him after that date, he would only be sent to those places 'where a speech from you would really have an effect upon the poll.' [77] MacDonald saw Crooks as an electoral asset, and wanted to protect him from approaches from candidates in hopeless constituencies, when his presence would be better served in winnable seats.

The Woolwich election campaign began when Monday morning dawned on 1 January 1906. Overnight the constituency had been transformed. Election posters appeared on nearly every street corner urging them to

'Vote for Will Crooks.' People saw 'portraits of Will Crooks beaming down upon them hurrying to their daily toil in the Arsenal or workshop.'[78] This was possibly the first time a mass poster campaign of this type was used in any election in the country. The question of when this type of mass poster campaigning began is a subject for historians that would repay investigation. The Pioneer Press obviously made the printing of the posters possible. That night Crooks opened his campaign at the People's Hall, North Woolwich. It was the first meeting of many. He spoke every evening throughout the borough, and held Dinner-Hour Conferences every day in Beresford Square and at the Arsenal Gates.

Crooks spoke out against fiscal reform, which to him meant 'protection to the sweater to the detriment of the poor ... the Fiscal Question has been raised to divert the attention of the electorate from Industrial and Social Reforms.' He strenuously advocated revoking the Ordinance permitting Chinese labour in South Africa, and on the Irish question, he was in 'favour of the largest possible share of self-government being given to Ireland.'[79] His Unionist opponent, Major William Adam, supported the ideas of both Chamberlain and Balfour, and at his first meeting at the Arsenal Middle Gate on 3 January, spoke against Home Rule, and in favour of Tariff Reform, which he said were the 'two main issues before the electors.'[80]

Because polling in the 1906 elections was distributed over two or three weeks,[81] Adam did his best to tie Crooks down by fixing a late polling date on 17 January, thus undermining any considerations the LRC might have of using Crooks to promote support in other constituencies. For example, Philip Snowden telegraphed Middleton from Blackburn: 'Please get down to Woolwich to beg Crooks Committee to let him come here on Saturday afternoon.'[82] MacDonald was already in Woolwich trying to pursued Crooks to speak at Blackburn, and wrote to Snowden stating he was disappointed he did not succeed: 'Nothing would have pleased him [Crooks] better to have a good go once more at his old friend "Jeff" [Drage]. Saturday, however is out of the question ... fixed to open the new Woolwich Town Hall ... he came off with top vote against the King.' According to MacDonald, a more valid reason was that Adam was holding regular meetings at the Arsenal Gate, and Crooks needed to be 'on the spot at the Gates at Midday to nail the many yarns on the counter right away'. If Crooks were not there, even for one day, Adam would be sure to take advantage. In addition, the Conservatives were putting in effective canvassing, and Barefoot was reluctant to let Crooks go, as the Labour canvass looked 'none too satisfactory.'[83] Barefoot need not have worried, the Labour vote held up; proving the 1903 victory was no fluke. Crooks increased the record poll of 1903 by 339 votes, polling 9,026 votes, against 6,914 votes for Adam, a Labour majority of 2,112, on a turnout of 89.2

per cent. It seemed the church vote went to Adam, owing to the controversy over educational training. Nationally the elections were a Liberal landslide, primarily according to Russell 'a Free Trade victory; and there is little doubt that — in the length and breadth of the country — the majority of voters opted for the fiscal *status quo*.' [84] Overall 400 Liberals were returned, 157 Unionists, 83 Irish Nationalists, 29 Labour, and one Independent Labour candidate, J. W. Taylor, (Durham, Chester-Le-Street), who took the Labour whip upon entering Parliament.[85]

In Lancashire, the Liberal/Labour electoral agreement was an important factor. It ran smoothly in twelve constituencies. The LRC contested fourteen seats, and returned twelve candidates, who were given 'clear runs'.[86] However, in Yorkshire, 'such accommodations were neither necessary nor possible', according to David Howell, with the exception of Bradford and Halifax. The LRC ran eight candidates, the Liberals opposed six, and consequently only three were successful, Fred Jowett in Bradford West, J. Parker in Halifax (the only two member borough in the West Riding), and O'Grady in Leeds East.[87] Tanner points out that in Yorkshire 'the Liberals needed to reaffirm their position as the major radical party more urgently here than almost anywhere else.'[88] Taking into account Tanner's analysis of Yorkshire politics, this 'reaffirmation' must have been one of the reasons why the acceptance of a progressive alliance differed so much in the two counties. The strength of conservative institutional Liberalism, plus a weak trade union movement, especially in South Yorkshire and the East Riding, were other significant factors that worked against a progressive alliance in the region. The ILP heartland - the woollen towns of Bradford and Halifax - were an exception to the rule. In Halifax, clearly, an understanding existed; one was possible in Bradford, but even here, the Liberals opposed Jowett.

In Wales, the LRC made little headway against Liberal sectionalism, Nonconformist radicalism, and Welsh nationalism. 'Wales remained sunk in the politics of nostalgia and its Gladstonian past', Morgan argues. They felt indignant about and 'rejected pressure from the central party organisation in London to let in lib-lab or LRC candidates.'[89] The LRC ran three candidates, two were returned, J. Williams in Gower, and Keir Hardie, who was opposed by the Liberals in the dual seat of Merthyr Tydfil. Overall, with the exception of Lancashire, the success of the LRC electoral arrangement with the Liberals was patchy. It proved harder to win the regions over to participate in a political accommodation than originally anticipated by either the LRC or the Liberal leadership. It is important to note that every constituency was contested in the 1906 elections by a Liberal, Labour, or a Free Trade candidate. By contrast, at the 1900 elections the Conservatives were given 159 seats unopposed by the Liberals.[90]

The ideas of socialism, liberalism and radicalism, and collectivism, played their part in developing the character of the Labour Party before the First World War. A contemporary commentator of the Labour Party observed: 'We now have men to represent us who know what it is to *feel* the pinch of poverty and the uncertainty of employment, whose homes for years have had the grim spectre of the rent lord hovering over them if work should fail.' Within this statement lies the central truth of the arrival of the Labour Party. [91]

It is important to note that Arthur Balfour and the Conservatives believed that the Liberal victory did not give them a mandate to change the law. Balfour had lost his Manchester seat in the general election, only to be returned at a by-election in the City of London on 27 February, just after the first session of Parliament began. He told Lord Lansdowne after his return: 'There has certainly never been a period in our history in which the House of Lords will be called upon to play a part at once so important, so delicate, and so difficult.'[92] This ideological position spelt danger for the Liberal legislative agenda, and undermined their authority in the Commons. John Fair argues that a period of continual stress, between the Liberals and Conservatives, lasted until the outbreak of war in 1914.[93] It began with the Education Bill in 1906, and as Dangerfield points out, the Conservatives could only irritate the opposition through words in the Commons: 'they looked to the obedient House of Lords to do all the heavy work. And the Lords began by mutilating Mr Augustine Birrell's Education Bill beyond hope of repair.'[94]

THE ARSENAL DISCHARGE CAMPAIGN

It would be relevant to the following debate, before looking at the Woolwich campaign against the Royal Arsenal discharges, to outline the number of men made redundant 1901-1904; thus putting into political perspective the campaign against the discharges of 1906-7 that was imposed under a new policy by the War Office and Liberal Government.[95] The Murray Committee (1907), reported that the primary function of the Ordnance Factories (OF) was to provide 'reserve productive power capable of being utilised to the full in times of emergency', and its existence supplied the insurance necessary 'against the possible failure of supplies in time of war.'[96] It is important to note that the Royal Arsenal at Woolwich was the chief manufacturer of munitions in the country, and composed of three Ordnance Factories, the Royal Laboratory (RL), the Royal Gun Factory (RGF), and the Royal Carriage Factory (RCF). A Building Works Department and a Central Office in Woolwich supported these.

At the end of the South African War in 1902, the average number of employees in the Arsenal was 20,501. The number discharged by 1904 was 4,653, which left a workforce of 15,848.[97] Will Crooks, in a Parliamentary speech in 1907, gave a truer picture of the situation regarding the discharges in Woolwich between 1901 and 1906. If the men employed in the Arsenal and Woolwich Dockyard are considered together the maximum number was 26,321 in 1901-2. Crooks pointed out that: 'In March, 1906, the number was reduced to 16,704 (a reduction of 9,674), many of those remaining being on short time.'[98] The impact of these continual discharges damaged the local economy. The population of Woolwich in 1904 was approximately 130,000. Of these, there were probably 20,000 men of working age, nearly 16,000 of who worked in the Arsenal. Allowing for fathers and sons, there were possibly 10,000 men who were the breadwinners, or 50 per cent of the working population. Hence the importance of the wage of the Arsenal worker to the well being of the local economy, especially to many shopkeepers and local traders. Crooks explained the basis of the economic problem in his maiden speech in 1903. He believed that the interest of the economy was being sacrificed by the allocation of Government orders, in proportion of two-thirds to private contractors, instead of to national workshops that were only allocated one-third of Government work.

Between January and October 1906, the new Liberal administration discharged 1,586 men,[99] which led Crooks to believe that the Liberal party was going to play into the hands of the contractors regarding Government work, as did the Tories. He had often said that the Liberals were as bad as the Tories, and that they could not be trusted to look after the interests of the working-class. Crooks' knowledge of parliament would have told him that the shareholders and directors of private contracting firms were represented in Conservative and Liberal Cabinets, and throughout both Houses of Parliament. He also knew that the War Office's permanent officials, after retirement, sometimes obtained lucrative appointments on the staff of these private firms, and therefore he was acutely suspicious of the War Office. It seemed to him that the War Office, and not the Government of the day, determined policy around the supply of ordnance. For example, the officials in the Arsenal had slightly increased from 1,676 to 1,689 during 1903-6. At the same time the workers in the Ordnance Factories declined by 1,776. In other words, there were more supervisors to look after fewer workmen.[100]

Will Crooks after his return to public life in March 1906, although he was under the shadow of the Poplar enquiry, was soon at the centre of the agitation against the discharges, helping locally to convene meetings between the Borough Council, the Trades Council, the Labour Protection League, the

RACS, and the trade unions. He supported resolutions to the TUC and the Labour Party from the Woolwich trade union movement, sometimes personally intervening on their behalf. Crooks supported the direct action of the Arsenal workers in their protests by helping to co-ordinate marches, and organised a petition to the King. He organised deputations to Richard Haldane (MP for Haddingtonshire 1885-1911), Secretary of State for War, and persistently pressured him in the Commons on the question of the Woolwich Arsenal discharges, wages, and the minimum level of employment.

Will Crooks had gained the support of the PLP, who lobbied for the setting up of the Henderson Committee (1907), which was eventually appointed to examine whether articles other than munitions could be manufactured in the Woolwich Ordnance Factories.[101] The Member for Woolwich was central to the struggle, showing leadership under pressure, although on three occasions he suffered attacks that caused great physical disability, brought on by overwork. One of these attacks, a recurrence of his confinement of 1904-5, 'floored' him for eight weeks during October and November 1907.[102]

The Sinews of War

After Haldane had stated in the Commons in June 1906, that discharges 'will not exceed 320 men and boys', 650 reductions had taken place between 1 April and 14 July.[103] Because of these continual reductions the Mayor, Dr. Gilbert Slater, supported by Will Crooks, on 9 July, convened a protest meeting in the Town Hall. This course of action was adopted because the Mayor had received representations from 'a large number of men who are affected or likely to be affected by the discharges.'[104] The meeting represented all shades of political opinion. This inclusive approach was to be a characteristic of the discharge campaign, as Crooks' speech points out:

> There could be no difference of opinion as to the feeding of men, women, and children. They might quarrel about methods, but as to the necessity they must all agree ... they should not have the fear of poverty or to be kept in a state of torture and dread as to what was going to happen next. (Hear, hear.) In Woolwich they were labouring under this difficulty. There was only one large employer, all other employers in Woolwich were dependent upon the money earned in the Arsenal to keep them going.[105]

The discharge of Arsenal workers concerned everyone. An attack on the Arsenal was seen as an offensive on the economic wealth and resources of Woolwich.

Crooks urged the people of Woolwich to 'awaken to a sense of their responsibility, by utilising every effort to bring pressure to bear on the Government at a crisis like the present.'[106] Following the Town Hall meeting, Crooks brought the matter of the discharges before the Labour Party, and Messrs. Crooks, T. F. Richards, J. Jenkins, G. Wardle, and C. Duncan were appointed to a subcommittee to investigate the matter and to make representations to the War Secretary. On 9 July, they received a deputation of workmen from the Arsenal in the House of Commons, and after hearing their complaints sought to see Haldane, who was unavailable until a later date. This being the case they addressed a letter to Haldane on 11 July. The letter suggested: 'That short time should be worked, instead of discharging the workman ... Trade Union officers and members of deputations ought be protected, and not specially selected for discharge ... that an inquiry should be instituted by a few Labour members who shall report upon the above.' *The Pioneer* states that Crooks was instrumental in placing on the political agenda the inquiry into Woolwich Arsenal, and the Labour party supported him wholeheartedly in bringing pressure to bear on the Government to accede to this demand.[107]

In response to continued discharges — 669 in the June quarter of 1906 [108] — the Woolwich Borough Council convened a Conference at the Town Hall on 8 November. At this Conference, at which Crooks was present, it was resolved to call for the appointment of a Select Committee to assess the present system of work in the Arsenal. It was also proposed that the Committee should look into whether it was viable to produce implements of peace for Government Departments when men were not required to manufacture munitions.[109] This was possibly the first time that diversification in the armaments industry had been discussed anywhere in the country. A delegation was selected from this Conference to wait upon the Secretary for War, and Crooks was asked 'to introduce such deputation'.[110] This extra-parliamentary agitation coupled with a concerted campaign in the Commons was characteristic of Crooks' political style. It had been successful in the past, especially around the campaign against unemployment in 1904-5. Crooks was not only the driving force behind the discharge campaign, but his contribution was significant in placing before the Government and Parliament the grievances of the Arsenal workers. Two events occurred during November that exemplifies Crooks' pivotal position in the campaign. On 15 November, at the weekly meeting of PLP, the Woolwich Arsenal subcommittee presented a special report that recommended:

> ... that the understanding by which two-thirds of the Government orders go to private contractors should be reconsidered; and that arrangement

should be made whereby locomotive engines for State railways in India and other parts of the British dominions, and heavy motors for military purposes, should be made at Woolwich, so as to ensure that the plant would be fully utilised and fluctuations of employment now so common be minimised.[111]

Following this report a delegation of Labour MPs, led by Keir Hardie, the party Chairman visited Woolwich Arsenal on behalf of the Labour Party on 19 November. The object of the visit was to ascertain what proportion of machinery was lying idle, and how much of it could be put to work in turning out other than war materials. Crooks, in all probability, put forward the idea of a delegation to the Woolwich Arsenal so that the Labour men could see for themselves what conditions were like inside. Because of the visit, Barnes and Henderson prepared a report for the next PLP meeting.

During late November, the deputation appointed by the Woolwich Conference was refused a meeting with Haldane, and Crooks was asked to step in to negotiate a hearing for them. It was felt action should be taken immediately because information had been received that more discharges were to take place: 'Crooks induced Mr. Haldane to give the deputation an interview of ten minutes', on 28 November. Gilbert Slater, who led the deputation, stated that 'the Arsenal must have a second string to its bow, like any other private firm' if discharges were to be stopped. Replying, Haldane said, 'the whole problem was receiving his very earnest consideration', and that he would consider a policy of 'subsidiary manufacture in the Arsenal', In addition, he said that any further discharges would be 'very slight.' Haldane dismissed the idea of a Select Committee.[112] A few days later Haldane informed the House of Commons 'that ... further discharges from the factories will not be more than 150 or 200 men.'[113]

During February 1907, the Government agreed that a Committee should be set up to examine the viability of alternative work in Woolwich Arsenal. It seems that the pressure Crooks applied, with the help of the PLP, and the Woolwich Conference, to get the Government to set up a Committee of Labour MPs, had paid off. Haldane, on 25 February, announced the Government's intention: 'He was prepared to have an investigation, and suggested that hon. members should propose three experts, and the War Office should propose the other three.' The Labour Party selected Arthur Henderson, George Barnes, and Bill Steadman, 'the latter representing the trade union group.'[114] Will Crooks was pleased with this investigation. The remit of the Committee coincided with everything he had been working towards for a long time — a steady number of men working during peacetime in the Arsenal, below which the number would not go.

It should be noted, as George Barnes pointed out in the Commons on 28 March, that the workmen who had been suspended in the Arsenal OFs attended work each day, and were frequently kept without work. When given work the weekly earnings were often below time wages, not a guaranteed day rate. A spokesman for the War Office replied that the men were suspended because of the slackness of work, and therefore they were not entitled to be paid at day rates. He belied the permanent officials' concern towards the reductions by making a statement more typical of a Tory: 'If preferred, the men can be discharged.'[115] Some men were taking home as little as 14s. for a 48 hour week.[116]

The assurance given by Haldane in November 1906 that discharges in future would be 'very slight' proved to be misleading, because in April 1907, he gave notice of a further reduction of 1,200 men. Crooks shed some light on Haldane's conflicting remarks in a statement to the Commons in August. He said: 'Over and over again from information given to himself at Woolwich he was aware that the right hon. Gentleman [Haldane] knew absolutely nothing of the true facts', because his permanent officials were not supplying him with the correct information.[117]

With the agreement of the Arsenal workforce Crooks negotiated with Haldane that the reductions should be delayed and then staggered. If the men agreed to work a five-day week, sixty men would be discharged each week. Crooks believed that if the discharges took place over a period, work might be found for the Arsenal in the meantime, and the number of discharges reduced accordingly. Haldane replied to Crooks' telegram, 'that all discharge notices will not take effect; they are suspended until the end of the month.'[118] Crooks' intervention on behalf of the proposed discharges was important to the people of Woolwich. He had helped lift the gloom and anxiety that hung over the town at the news, and gave the people some hope that the consequent misery could be avoided.[119]

The local trade union and labour movement, upon receipt of the discharge notices, decided that direct action *en masse* was the only way that the Government could be made to reverse its policy. It was felt that although Crooks had done everything possible, 'by personal interview, questions in the House of Commons, and individual persuasion, the result had been only assurances and promises, followed by fresh discharges.' It was decided by the WLRA that the local movement must 'make a strong appeal' to the nation as to the importance of the problem of Arsenal discharges. The appeal must rouse support for the nation's workshop. It should 'be fully employed for the national benefit, that it shall be utilised for the manufacture of the implements of peace as well as the munitions of war.'[120]

The Woolwich Conference met on 19 April 1907, and decided to organise a 'Right to Live March' for 22 April, and march the nine or ten miles from Woolwich to Westminster via New Cross, concluding with a deputation of Arsenal workmen to see the Prime Minister. The organising committee also invited the tradesmen in the town to join the public demonstration, and asked the local clergy and ministers to make Sunday 21 April, "Arsenal Sunday." Ten thousand workmen, women, and children supported the deputation and marched to Westminster.[121] The demonstration had a very considerable effect on the attitude of the Cabinet towards Woolwich. It had been agreed between Crooks and Haldane that the discharges would not exceed sixty a week and 400 fewer discharges would go.[122] 'Crooks had also been informed that the Admiralty had placed an order for heavy guns', and if the order was carried out satisfactorily more orders would be placed with the Arsenal. Haldane had spoken to the Secretary of State for India, 'and the hope is expressed Woolwich may get some orders from the Indian Government.'[123]

It seemed to the Arsenal workers that direct action was the best way to express their indignation at the discharges, and they were worrying the authorities to good effect. However, in the Commons on 29 April the news was not so good. Crooks asked Haldane: 'Has the minimum yet been fixed?' Only to be told: 'I shall have to reduce it still more to get back to the proper minimum.'[124] This announcement only served to stiffen the resolve of the people of Woolwich, who were determined to continue the agitation to stop the discharges. At a conference of the Woolwich committee on 8 May, it was decided to petition the King, and organise another march for 18 May, around the issue: 'A 10,000 Minimum v. Full Employment of the National Workshop.'[125] Crooks told the men to stand shoulder to shoulder, in 'one popular cause ... and the result of the march ... had made such strides as to exceed his wildest dreams.'[126] Crooks was in a position to tell what impact this agitation was having on the Government, and it seems from what he reported it was having a positive effect. Therefore, he saw it as his duty to support the men in their struggle, and positively urged further agitation.

Will Crooks' suspicion that a new policy produced the present series of discharges were justified when the *Report of the Government Factories and Workshops Committee* (Murray Report), was revealed in the Commons on 25 July. The report removed the veil of secrecy from the War Office's policy, and avowed the intention of reducing 'employment in the Arsenal to the lowest possible level.'[127] Presenting the report Haldane stated his intentions. The RCF was to be reduced by 120, the RGF by 420, and the RL by 2,227. The OFs were to be reduced from the April level of 10,767, to a new minimum of 8,000. The total reduction from the number employed in April announced by Haldane was not 1,200 men, but 2,767.

Crooks pointed out that: 'These numbers added to the reduction affected before last April, viz., 9,674, make a total reduction of **12,441** from war strength.'[128] The Government refused, and stifled, any debate on the subject of the discharges with the backing of the Commons. 'Crooks protested ... with the support of Shackelton on behalf of the Labour Party, but the protest was of no avail.' Crooks had always thought that the new policy being carried out was part of a Tory agenda from 1905, when the Murray Committee was appointed, and that the permanent officials in the War Office had decided to continue 'the policy to reduce the Arsenal to "Mr Broderick's minimum of 8,000".'[129]

On the same day, the Henderson Report was presented, no doubt intentionally to try to assuage the Labour Party after the disclosures on the proposed minimum. It found that the machinery at the OFs was capable of manufacturing implements of peace, and 'this additional work, if all given to the Arsenal, would approximately double the present output and amount of employment in the Arsenal.'[130] This was what Crooks had been saying all along. It did not matter how pleased he was with the report's conclusions. Any feeling of delight was overshadowed by the proposed discharges in the Arsenal. Will Crooks harried the Government at every opportunity to discuss the discharges before the end of the session. He was shut out, and not given a chance to discuss Woolwich Arsenal when he tried to intervene in the Army Estimates debate. Crooks protested to the Prime Minister, but Campbell-Bannerman and the Government refused to discuss the issue.[131] Crooks was keenly aware that the Government would use the recess as an excuse for implementing further discharges, and that the permanent officials in the War Office would be free to carry out the 'new minimum' policy unhindered.

The parliamentary recess — August to October — did not obstruct agitation against the proposed minimum. The Woolwich Trades and Labour Council continued to organise large anti-minimum meetings in Beresford Square, not only to demonstrate the strength of the Woolwich workers, but 'bringing home to the people, not only of Woolwich, but of the country, the true position of affairs.'[132] During September, the Trades Council strongly condemned the actions of Haldane for placing orders of munitions with foreign firms, 'while discharges are being made from Woolwich Arsenal', and urged 'the extension of the principle of the Nation's work being done by Direct Labour.' [133]

The pressure of work, including campaigning on behalf of the Arsenal workers, took its toll on Crooks' health during October and November 1907. This attack of physical exhaustion, according to Crooks, was caused by overwork, 'he had started out into the country to do five Labour meetings... developed into thirty-five ... there had been eight meetings in one day'. After this tour of meetings Crooks felt weary and worn out. He said the physical disability that floored him: 'left him quite unable to move' though his brain was active 'to think that some of his efforts had remained to ripen, in however small a way.'[134] This description by Crooks of his confinement helps explains the character of the man, although he lay unable to move he was concerned about what impression his efforts had had on championing the needs of the poor.

The Labour Party was also concerned about Crooks' health. For example, in December 1907, Crooks asked MacDonald if he would be required to speak at the Labour Party Conference at Hull in February 1908.[135] MacDonald replied: 'There is a general feeling that you should take things easier this year and take more care of yourself or you will incur a permanent breakdown, but if you do attend representing the Coopers, I am sure all your friends will be glad if you would take part in the discussion on Unemployment and Old Age Pensions.' MacDonald also thanked Crooks for serving the party 'so well at by-elections during the past twelve months'. [136] It is evident from MacDonald's comments that if Crooks' contribution to the Labour cause was to be of any significance, it was important for him not to over commit himself. It should be noted that during 1903-7, Crooks had fought for and won trade union recognition for the men in the Arsenal. However, mainly due to the Liberal record on discharges, Crooks lost the first election in 1910, largely because of the turnover of votes on the Arsenal discharge question.

THE PROVISION OF SCHOOL MEALS
UNEMPLOYMENT & OLD AGE PENSIONS

In the summer of 1905, Crooks continued where he had left off in August 1904, by pressing the Conservative Government to intervene by giving local authorities and voluntary organisations the powers to undertake the duty of feeding necessitous school children. Crooks felt that if children were compelled to attend school they should be fed 'to enable them to get some benefit from their education'.[137] Will Crooks pointed out to the Commons that he was not just pleading on behalf of poor children, but for all children, including those children whose fathers were out of work. Crooks urged the Government to remove the taint of the Poor Law from these children at once because he wanted boards of guardians to be relieved of the heartbreak and the agonizing experience of administering relief to poor children. Crooks stated that the Government was 'wrong to pretend that there was no precedent for doing this kind of work' because the feeding of children now was the responsibility of the

Home Office.[138] He believed that those parents who refused to maintain their children, and had the means to do so, should be sent to prison.

In 1906, the success of Crooks' agitation in the Commons for the provision of school meals was realised when the Labour Party introduced the Education (Provision of Meals) Bill on 22 February. It was given a second reading without a division. In moving the adoption of the Bill (2 March), W. T. Wilson (Labour MP for Westhoughton), called upon the Government to provide public funds enabling local education authorities to give meals to children who went to school without food.[139] On 21 December 1906, the Bill received Royal Assent. Crooks was pleased with the provisions that were included in the Bill. They were more or less identical with those that he had been arguing for in the Commons for over two years. It is important to note that Crooks believed that if the Government could be persuaded to implement such important social reform, the Bill would introduce a new morality to social legislation, and thus imply the Government accepting responsibility for poverty.

The problem of unemployment as such did not figure significantly in the election campaign, argues Kenneth Brown, because the majority of Liberal candidates made equivocal and ambiguous statements on the subject and those who made any constructive remarks, such as Crooks, supported land reforms.[140] Furthermore, it did not play an important part in the first session of Parliament. 'Labour members were temporarily dissuaded by the promises of the new Government from pressing for an immediate amendment of the Unemployed Workmen Act or for the implementation of their own policy.'[141] Although no detail was given, they were informed that it would be amended later in the session. It was not until the Easter adjournment debate in the House of Commons that the non-appearance of the amended Bill was brought up by Hardie.[142] John Burns, President of the Local Government Board, would not commit a day for its introduction, 'and thereafter the Labour members grew increasingly restive'.[143]

In the Whitsun adjournment debate Crooks stated the Unemployed Workmen Bill in 1905 was a 'capital jumping off ground', an 'excellent starting point'. However, since its implementation he was grieved that it had 'never seemed to get beyond the stage of investigation and inquiry', although the Act was drawn up to try to reduce the growth in the number of unemployed men applying for Poor Law relief. Crooks was of the opinion very little had happened because of the lack of funds, and that 'the way out was to get men on the land'.[144] Although Crooks believed that unemployment legislation based on the LRC Liverpool resolution should take precedence over the amendment of the existing Act, he was essentially eager in the short term for dispensing work for the unemployed by expanding the power of local distress committees and the Poor Law.[145]

Crooks was concerned that since the setting up of distress committees the unemployment situation in Poplar had not changed, and in Woolwich it was decidedly worse, due to the Arsenal discharges.[146] Because of pressure from Crooks and other Labour members, and after they withdrew arguments for an extension to the existing Act, John Burns made a parliamentary grant of £200,000 in July, as a 'recognition of the principle that unemployment relief should be subsidised from national funds';[147] a measure welcomed by Crooks. He said: 'It was absurd to say the Act had done no good; £200,000 had come out of it that very afternoon. Many and many a home had been kept which would have been broken up to-day but for that Act.'[148]

In February 1907, Crooks was concerned that the Government had not referred to unemployment in the King's Speech, and took the opportunity to criticise the LGB for failing to deal with the unemployed. He pressed yet again for the employment of people on the land, 'it was cheaper to do that at once than to keep them on outdoor relief.'[149] John Burns replied, 'that the problem was being dealt with ... by home colonisation, afforestation, and the improvement of hours and wages.'[150] By early 1907, the Labour party had become exasperated with the Government's intransigence over unemployment, and decided to collaborate with the TUC and the General Federation of Trade Unions to produce an unemployment bill of their own. Ramsay MacDonald introduced the Labour party's Unemployed Workmen Bill to the Commons on 9 July 1907.[151] The Bill advanced the idea of setting up a central unemployment committee to undertake a scheme of national work, and the assignment of local commissioners to generate and organise local works. Each local authority should be given the responsibility of finding employment for the registered unemployed in its area, and for such work, they could use rate money to pay them.[152] The essence of the proposition, put forward in clause three, embraced the principle of the right to work:

> Where a workman has registered himself as unemployed it shall be the duty of the local unemployment authority to provide work for him in connection with one or other of the schemes herein-after provided, or otherwise, or failing the provision of work, to provide maintenance should necessity exist for that person and for those depending on that person for the necessities of life.... This Clause is a Right to Work clause and not a Right to Doles clause.[153]

Harris points out that the 'right to work' clause 'was sufficient to alienate most Liberal support.' The Bill did not reach its second reading in 1907. [154]

The 'Right to Work' Bill was reintroduced on 13 March 1908,[155] against a background of depression following a financial crisis and bad harvests in a number of countries, industrial unrest, and rising unemployment at home. 'A significant minority of Liberals and Nationalists supported the Bill, but it was defeated by 267 votes to 118.'[156] The main argument put forward by the Liberals who opposed the Bill was that it would undermine trade unionism and increase unemployment, and that the Government should delay legislation until the Poor Law Commission reported in 1909.[157]

During October the Prime Minister, Herbert Asquith,[158] who had been put under pressure from Arthur Henderson to do something to alleviate unemployment, promised to introduce legislation in the next session for dealing with unemployment on a permanent basis, and reform the Poor Law. Also to deal with the distress that was foreseen in the winter 1908/9, John Burns had conceded to demands that the parliamentary grant to Distress Committees under the Unemployed Workmen Act should be increased to £300,000.[159] Crooks was not satisfied with the Government. He said they 'were going to give them £300,000 to keep them quiet.... It was not money they wanted at the moment, but an organised system which would put the unemployed to work.' He also attacked the Government's proposals for being inadequate. He believed that due to their negligence there was an absence of proper machinery, even for carrying out the powers that already existed to meet the pressing needs of the unemployed during the winter. Crooks continued to press for land reform to resolve the unemployment question, stating that 'if they had a statesman to tackle the land question there would be no unemployed.'[160]

Before Crooks' election to the House of Commons, he had advocated that the Government should find the money to pay old age pensions out of the exchequer, and not be dependent upon the ratepayer to meet the bill by paying pensions through the Poor Law. Crooks continued to endorse this position at every opportunity after his election to parliament. He began this agitation in May 1903, for those forgotten veterans of industry who had done as much to create the wealth of the nation, as had the Army and Navy to defend it. Crooks said the question of old age pensions was 'very near his heart. It had caused him more trouble than anything else in his life.'[161] Hansard records that every time old age pensions were discussed in the Commons 1903-8, Will Crooks played an important part in the deliberations.[162] He believed that by paying old age pensions it would remove old men from the competition for employment, who were solely employed because they were cheap, and give younger men a better opportunity of finding work. Further, he believed: 'The House of

Commons was created for the express purpose, and for no other purpose, of adjusting social inequalities', therefore it was the duty of Parliament to pay old people a pension, and stop recruiting them into the workhouse.[163]

By July 1908, an Old Age Pensions Bill had been passed by Parliament. It was a non-contributory pension for the very poor, very old and the very respectable. The Bill gave a 5s. a week pension at the age of 70, to those with an income of less than £26 per annum provided that they had not received poor relief after 1 January 1908. Other qualifications of payment included having not been imprisoned in the previous ten years for any offence, including drunkenness, and not being guilty of 'habitual failure to work according to his ability, opportunity, or need for his own maintenance or that of his own legal relatives.' After much parliamentary disquiet the pauper disqualification was removed in 1911.[164] There was nothing degrading about old age pensions, said Crooks 'except when they get down to 5s. a week.... What could he [workman] do with it?' He attacked the Government for always finding fault with the workingman for not being thrifty. Crooks' riposte to that disclaimer had always been 'if a man is foolish enough to get old, and then if he has not been artful enough to get rich, you have no right to punish him.'

Crooks believed that no man should sit in parliament in judgement of the poor, without first having served ten years 'as a Poor Law guardian. He would then know something about human nature.' Crooks considered then perhaps they would not question the workman's thrift. During the third reading of the Bill, he lectured the Commons on family economics. Crooks asked how children could be expected to look after their parents' needs when they found it difficult to look after their own: 'what I want to do, and I am sure we shall do by this Bill, is to enable children to keep their parents and give them what they cannot buy, a little love and sympathy.'[165]

Although Crooks was pleased that the Government, at last, was deemed responsible for paying old age pensions out of the Exchequer, he was critical of the Bill for not going far enough, especially the financial clause and the inclusion of the qualifications that did nothing to alleviate poverty. As was the case with the Unemployed Workmen Act of 1905, Crooks believed it was better to have legislation on the statute book, because it could be revisited and amended at a future date. When debating the reform of social policy he was also of the opinion that the setting of a precedent was always useful.

6

ROLE IN PARLIAMENT AND THE GENERAL ELECTIONS OF 1910

After the victory of 1906, the Liberals had reached their nadir by the winter of 1908/9. The Liberal administration had estranged omnipotent interests by their attempts at reform; a House of Lords that was intent on mutilating its legislation confronted it. The country was in the grip of a deepening trade recession, and by-elections were running strongly against the Liberals. In the nine months January-September 1908, the Liberals lost seven by-elections.[1] However, what caused the greatest unease for the Government, as the by-elections indicated, was that prevailing economic conditions favoured the Unionists and their tariff propaganda.[2] In the hope of restoring the initiative, the Liberal Government embarked on a radical budget of social and fiscal reform. The Liberal *Review of Reviews* said in summing up Government policy in February 1909:

> If we can reform the Poor Law, maintain the Navy, carry a democratic Budget, safeguard Free Trade and keep the Jingoes out of office, we shall have done enough for glory, even if on all other questions we have to bow the neck before the Balfourian yoke.[3]

Against press warnings that a Government could not survive by finance alone, Lloyd George was about to prove otherwise, and at the same time steal the clothes of the 'socialists'.

Throughout the winter, an unexampled depression of trade and unemployment coincided with the Government's slump in its electoral fortunes. In the summer of 1908, unemployment grew month by month, 'while the average for 1908 — 7. 8 per cent — was worst than for any year since the depression of the mid-1880s.'[4] This severe downturn in the economic cycle meant that there was, according to the *Pioneer*, 'not less than one million unemployed men, not less than three million persons in dire distress from unemployment' nationally. The unemployed and distressed 'have been left to the tender mercies of the Local Government Board, and the Local

Government Board has dealt with them in the spirit of its callous and cynical tradition.'5 This predictable and indifferent response to the general distress by John Burns and the LGB, led to demonstrations in Trafalgar Square and the West End of London in February 1909. Also, the Right to Work Committee organised a great demonstration of 6000 wives of unemployed men on 16 February to coincide with the opening of Parliament.6 The Government's inappropriate measures for dealing with unemployment also resulted in hostile criticism from the PLP. For example, in the House of Commons on 17 February, Will Crooks charged Burns and the LGB with incompetence in his reply to the King's Speech Motion.

Parliament 1909
At the opening of Parliament, the Labour Party protested strongly against the Government's legislative measures to deal with unemployment. The proposals in the King's Speech caused great disappointment among Labour members, given the promise of the Prime Minister in October 1908, to deal with the root causes of unemployment. The Labour Party's response was to force the Government's hand on the question. They demonstrated this by moving an Amendment to the Address:

> we humbly desire to express our regret that, in view of the serious distress arising from the lack of work, the proposals for legislation which your Majesty's Advisers have thought fit to recommend are altogether inadequate for dealing effectively either with the root causes or the evils arising out of Unemployment.7

Moving the Amendment, George Barnes said that he would not sit day after day, 'and see matters of comparative insignificance and trifles take up the time of the House.' He continued, compared with the need to tackle the problem of unemployment, everything else 'sank into absolute insignificance', even housing the people.8 It was felt by the Labour Party that the Government instead of offering effective legislation on social reform, had embarked upon a programme that made 'reactionaries and Tariff Reformers chuckle with unholy glee',9 especially those in the House of Lords.

John Burns responded. He spoke for fifty minutes in defence of the Government's position. Burns, as usual, preached the morality of the necessity for thrift and temperance among trade unionists, and said that poor men should seek the shelter of the casual ward in the workhouse. Crooks was angry, but calm, towards Burns' contemptuous attitude towards the poor working man: 'He and I have been lifelong teetotallers, yet we still knew what it was like to go hungry, and to walk about the streets of London on the uppers of our boots. There is no use preaching thrift on nothing', Crooks retorted. He also took Burns to task for suggesting 'the casual ward for decent, respectable, hard working people.' He reminded the House, that Poplar had provided the poor with food and shelter, only to be 'told that we were creating pauperism and promoting thriftlessness'. Crooks reminded Burns of Asquith's promise, 'and how are you going to deal with it? You are simply going to leave it alone.... we are ridiculed in a fifty minutes speech and told Town Planning is going to do something'. He accused Burns of offering: 'Absolutely nothing', to resolve the unemployment problem. Also we were being told, said Crooks, that Labour Exchanges will solve the unemployment problem: 'The right hon. Gentleman knows perfectly well that they will do nothing of the kind.'[10]

Crooks' knowledge and understanding of the Poor Law and unemployment must have been disquieting for John Burns, a man full of his own self-importance. Crooks' speech was from a man who knew his brief, who knew the Poor Law inside out. He did not need to be lectured on the needs of the poor. Crooks harassed and tormented Burns on his incompetence in finding and creating work for the unemployed: 'Turn your attention to the land', was Crooks' advice. He was his usual unequivocal self in conclusion: 'I shall as long as God gives me power to think and act, denounce this or any other Government that neglects its duty to starving men, women and children.'[11] He criticised the King's Speech for being 'all window dressing', and believed that the Liberal legislative programme lacked substance.[12]

In the Commons on 16 March, Reginald McKenna, First Lord of the Admiralty, and Asquith presented the Naval Estimates for 1909-10. They both spoke openly, and disclosed their anxiety over evidence that suggested a rapid increase in German naval construction. The Government's response to this threat was that four battleships (Dreadnoughts) should be laid down immediately. And that 'the Government be empowered, with Parliament's concurrence, to lay down four more' if thought necessary in the current financial year. McKenna and Asquith's alarmist speeches had the desired effect on the Commons. A majority of MPs accepted the proposed increases.[13]

In February, the Labour Party announced it would oppose any increase in the naval estimates.[14] Will Crooks rebelled and voted in support of the Government. He was not alone. J. H. Jenkins, President of the Cardiff Shipbuilding Society, and Labour MP for the dockyard constituency of Chatham, and Alex Wilkie, Dundee based Secretary of the Shipwrights Union, also defied the Labour party whip.[15] What 'obviously weighed most heavily on the consciences' of both Crooks and Jenkins, was the problem of unemployment in the dockyard and the Arsenal. Jenkins and Wilkie were also officials of trade unions, whose members depended upon the production of war materials for their livelihood.[16] It is important to recognise Crooks' position, when the question of armaments came up against wider international and socialist feelings. He had to be aware of local constituency opinion, and answer to trade union pressure, especially from the Arsenal workers. In this context, Crooks recognised that it was due to his constituents' loyalty that he was elected to Parliament in the first place. The needs of the workers, for him, were above party politics. Thus, looking after his constituents' interests was always his primary concern. Furthermore, the War Office's attitude towards the Arsenal workers in the past must have influenced Crooks' decision to vote the way he did. Haldane, during the 1907 Arsenal discharges campaign, had repeatedly dismissed pressure from Crooks, explaining that the Arsenal discharges 'were the outcome of general reductions in naval and military expenditure.' Haldane's replies to Crooks' questions were hardly designed to win him over to the cause of arms limitation.[17] For him armament reductions meant further Arsenal discharges, and unemployment in Woolwich.

Between March and July, Crooks pressed both McKenna and Haldane on numerous occasions at question time, regarding the Arsenal and the manufacture of battleship gun mountings to no avail.[18] On every occasion that Crooks broached the question, he received the same reply. The manufacture of hydraulic gun mountings at the Arsenal would not be a viable concern because special plant would have to be installed in the gun shops. According to McKenna private firms were to be given the contracts because 'before beginning the manufacture of hydraulic gun-mountings at Woolwich special plant would have to be installed.'[19] And further, according to both McKenna and Haldane private firms were to be given the contracts, because the Government must have the contractors to fall back upon in times of emergency, and unless they subsidised them in times of peace they would not oblige in times of war. Much to Crooks' annoyance, during this period the Government continued suspensions among the workforce in the Arsenal gun shops, arguing that this was due to the lack of work.

The policy of the Government convinced Crooks that the need of national defence was the source of private profit. He believed the manufacture of war materials was a matter of national interest, and not of private enterprise. This meant that Crooks could both argue for armaments, and attack the Government. Crooks was further induced to believe, after his experience with the War Office in 1907, that there should be a searching enquiry into the whole question of the relationship of the Admiralty, the Army Council, and the War Office with wealthy and powerful firms that were engaged in the manufacture of armaments. The feeling within the Labour movement was that these close ties between private contractor and Government ministries were dangerous. It spelt danger to the nation in times of peril. Millions of pounds were being paid from the national exchequer to private firms, which compromised national security, when this money could be better spent investing in the efficiency of the national ordnance factories in readiness for the emergency of war.[20]

THE 'PEOPLE'S BUDGET'

Neal Blewett argues in his book, *The Peers, The Parties, and the People*, that Lloyd George's Budget was designed by him to 'recapture the working-class electorate', and 'stop the electoral rot'.[21] In May 1908, Lloyd George had written of his Budget plans in a letter to his brother: 'It is time we did something that appealed straight to the people — it will, I think, help to stop the electoral rot, and that is most necessary.'[22] Thus in a four hour speech to the House of Commons on 29 April 1909, Lloyd George presented his Budget as a political instrument for reviving the Liberal Party.[23] It was a Budget that aimed a blow at the rich, especially the Lords. It attacked the landlords, a duty on undeveloped land, 'a duty on coal and mineral royalties and a reversion on the termination of leases. To these he added, by way of revenge', for the Lords' emasculation of the Licensing Bills of 1908, 'tremendous duties on the liquor trade; and, as an appeal to socialist opinion, a super-tax on all incomes over £5,000 a year.'[24] Some historians maintain the Budget was designed as a provocative and deliberate trap for the Lords' power of veto. George Dangerfield claims that it was. John Grigg states that 'at least two of Lloyd George's biographers implied the same.[25] On the other hand Roy Jenkins suggests that Lloyd George's 'primary aim was to circumvent the veto rather than destroy it'. Blewett argues that it was 'most unlikely that the Cabinet intended to provoke a decisive conflict with the Lords over the Budget'.[26] Whatever the intention of Lloyd George the Budget induced 'one of the fiercest parliamentary struggles in recent British history.'[27] It provoked attacks from the House of Lords supported by Tariff Reformers in the Commons. They saw it as financially reckless, and committed themselves to fight it without quarter.

The Labour Party received the Budget warmly but with qualified support. Three months before, MacDonald had moved a resolution at a special conference on taxation held by the Labour Party. The motion called for a 'super-tax on large incomes, special taxes on state-conferred monopolies, increased estate and legacy duties and a really substantial beginning with the taxation of land values.'[28] William Barefoot, who had just been elected to the National Executive Committee stated, 'they had only taken up this subject because it afforded the means for social reform until the country was ripe for Socialism.'[29] It seems that the motion was devised to pressure the Government into introducing a progressive system of taxation. MacDonald felt, now that Lloyd George had introduced a package of reforms that could be supported by the Labour Party, that they had no option but to back him as strongly as possible. 'Of the Budget as a whole, I say "Bravo",' he wrote shortly after its introduction. 'I am going to support it through thick and thin.' MacDonald's enthusiasm did not wane. Early in the summer he wrote: 'Mr Lloyd George's Budget classified property into individual and social incomes into earned and unearned, and follows more closely the theoretical contentions of Socialism and sound economics than any previous Budget had done.'[30]

Will Crooks also welcomed the Budget. He believed if anything should be taxed it should be land values, and mining royalties, not food. At a meeting in January, Will Crooks spoke on land values. He instanced the case of the Blackwall Tunnel, and said, 'that before the tunnel was made land was selling at £3 an acre down there. As soon as the hole was through the land went up to £200. Who made the value? Not the owner; but the working men who paid the cost of the tunnel.'[31] It was the workingman who created the wealth not the landlord. Clearly, the taxing of land values gave Crooks great satisfaction, but not so much as the Government's proposal in the Budget Scheme of a Development and Road Improvement Funds Bill. This was a scheme to deal with the problem of unemployment similar to that which Crooks had been urging Governments to introduce since the 1890s. It was also similar to the 'Right to Work' scheme put forward by the Labour Party in 1908. In his Parliamentary Report to the Labour Party in 1910, Henderson wrote:

> The [Development] Bill was in two parts, the more important part being that in which £2,000,000, extending over a period of four years, was to be devoted to schemes of afforestation and the promotion of agriculture and dairy farming. Commissioners were appointed by the Bill to consider the suitability or otherwise of the schemes submitted to them, and one important Amendment the Party secured enables the Commissioners themselves to frame schemes. There is no doubt that the possibilities under the Bill are very wide, and, incidentally, could be productive of much good in dealing with the question of Unemployment, for in the operation of the Bill due regard has been given to fluctuations of ordinary employment.[32]

Will Crooks saw the Budget as a struggle between Free Fooders and Tariff Reformers. He believed that if anything should be taxed it should be land values, and mining royalties, not food. Crooks told a meeting in October 1904: 'They had won Woolwich for the kitchen table, and if they put a tax on corn and gave preference to the Colonies it meant a higher price for the loaf.'[33] He was referring to the 'full-loaf' platform of 1903 that had played a crucial part in his election victory. It is worth remembering that the Woolwich electoral victory and tariff reform was of primary significance to the Lib-Lab pact.

As early as June 1909, Crooks thought that the Government would call a general election eventually on the Budget issue. For example, in response to a letter from the Plumstead Conservative and Unionist Association, he wrote that he intended to support the Budget 'in every way I can ... I will fight your party ... to the bitter end when the next election comes. The people will ... be asked to decide whether they are for placing the burden of taxation upon those best able to bear it, or whether the food of the poor is to be taxed so that the rich may become richer and the poor poorer.'[34] He saw the Lords' veto question as a smoke screen, arguing that the real issue was still Tariff Reform. The Tories preferred a system of taxation by means of a reform of the tariff, which included a tax on the food of the people, and were willing to bring the Government down so that the opinion of the country could be sought. The Lords finally rejected the Finance Bill on 30 November. This breach of the Constitution and the usurpation of the rights of the Commons made a general election in January inevitable.[35]

On 30 April, the day after the Budget was presented, John Hodge proposed the Second Reading of the Labour Party's Unemployed Workmen Bill (The Bill had been re-drafted in detail in consideration of the publication of the Poor Law Commission's Minority Report on 17 February). It is not clear whether Crooks had a hand in drawing up the Bill. Since he had contributed in the past it can be assumed, he was consulted. It was not the details of the Bill on which the Commons was asked to affirm, but the principle 'that *there must be provision by the community itself* against the waste, misery and degradation caused by unemployment.'[36] On this question, the Labour Party was adamant, nothing short of a national organisation would suffice to co-ordinate the public works that were necessary to deal with the problem. The *Clarion* claimed that the Bill's purpose had been merely to expose the reality and magnitude of the problem.'[37] It was defeated: Ayes 115, Noes 228.[38]

Will Crooks, among others, believed that the reason why many Liberals did not vote for the Labour Bill was because it was introduced the day after the Budget. In the *Pioneer* he wrote, 'many a Liberal was comforted with the belief that he need not vote for the Right to Work Bill, seeing what provisions had been made in the Budget.'[39] He continued in a philosophical vein:

> I was asked what I thought of the opposition of people who ought to be entirely in sympathy with us, but who never lose a chance of speaking against us in the House or out of it — I observed. These people are useful fertilisers for the growth of the Labour movement; they are not always pleasant, but very necessary. These attacks have never done us any harm, but a great deal of good ... So on the whole, I don't think we have much to complain about, even if they don't love us very much.[40]

This statement illustrates Crooks' optimism that however difficult it was to argue for the needs of the unemployed, opposition served ultimately to undermine the very arguments against those needs being addressed.

Crooks was among those who felt that the Government had conceded the 'Right to Work' demand in the Development Bill and the proposed unemployment insurance. Similarly, when Churchill introduced the Labour Exchanges Bill in May, John Clynes claimed that it was really part of the 'right to work' bill.[41] Unemployment insurance, state contributions to such a fund were equivalent to the Labour Party's demand for state maintenance.[42] This confirmation of Labour party policy indicates how difficult it was for Labour members to respond to Liberal initiatives. The Labour party's reactions to Liberal reforms were ambivalent, a combination of welcome hostility. Churchill told the Commons on 19 May that the success of the unemployment insurance scheme depended on the setting up of Labour Exchanges. 'And money had to be raised — which meant that the ... 1909 Budget had to be passed before progress could be made with the introduction of insurance.'[43] By the end of March 1911, Lloyd George had still not settled the fundamentals of the insurance measure.[44] Will Crooks believed, as he told Burns in February, that Labour Exchanges would not by themselves solve the unemployment problem. He thought that for a national scheme of Labour Exchanges to succeed, they should be an integral part of administering the organisation of labour. Crooks summed up his past frustrations on the second reading of the Labour Exchanges Bill on 16 June, when he said: 'The fact is these Exchanges are going to begin where we ought to have begun 20 years ago.'[45] He probably thought better late than never.

Tour of the Colonies

Will Crooks had been planning a tour of the colonies starting in September, since May 1909, when he was advised by his doctor to take a long sea trip to regain his health. Crooks planned to be away for three or four months, first visiting Canada, and afterwards Australia, 'from which place he has several long standing invitations'.[46] He had discussed his itinerary with Keir Hardie, who had been in Canada in 1908, and was the guest speaker at the Canadian Trades and Labour Congress held in Halifax, Nova Scotia. A return ticket to sail around the world was arranged for Crooks and his wife Elizabeth to travel as the guest of Baron Strathcona, Canadian High Commissioner for London (1896-1914), on the Canadian-Pacific Railway (CPR). Strathcona was also a Director of the CPR. Crooks was to recall later, 'his personal character had prepared the way for him so that he found free passes almost over all the railway systems' of Canada and Australia: 'But he paid his way in all cases except where he received the free passes that he had mentioned.'[47]

Crooks was often asked why did he go away? He replied: 'I am naturally an optimist, but I found myself so run down through my work generally, that I could not give a civil answer to poor persons, and I found that if I did not get a good rest I should permanently break down.'[48] All Crooks' friends and colleagues were concerned about his health and were glad he had decided to take a break. Since his breakdown in 1905, even after MacDonald had told him to take it easy for the sake of the cause, Will had continued to ignore advice about overdoing things. This included attending the House of Commons against doctor's orders. His constituents were loath to see their member leave them even for a short period. A letter from one of them in the *Pioneer* typifies their feelings toward Crooks: 'We are loath to part with you, our champion, but stern necessity compels ... We sincerely hope that you will return as a giant refreshed, to renew the fight, for you know you have a reputation to keep up — and that will take some doing.'[49] This letter exemplifies how his constituents saw Crooks. He was not just their MP, but also a dear friend who was sympathetic to their needs and fought for their needs and rights regardless of personal sacrifice.

Just before Will and Elizabeth departed on their trip there was a huge gathering: 'Poplar's Farewell to Mr. and Mrs. Crooks', on 2 September, at Poplar Town Hall. The meeting was organised by Poplar Council, the churches and the trade union and labour movement of the district. Messages wishing Will and Elizabeth a happy trip were received from a number of Labour MPs, including Keir Hardie, MacDonald, Henderson, and Clynes. MacDonald wrote: 'It is the special duty of Labour men to make a supreme effort to see the working of Labour parties outside their own country.' Hardie writing along similar lines said that such visits helped the Labour movement of the world to foster closer relationships, 'and thereby to hasten the advent of Socialism and universal brotherhood.' The Chairman of the meeting, Cllr. A. H. Darley, spoke of Crooks' antecedents, and his contribution towards making Poplar a better place to live in: 'Since we took Crooks from the bench twenty years ago to represent us Poplar has set the pace... The greatest piece of work Crooks ever did was to humanise the Poor Law institutions of the country. In paying a generous tribute to his good friend, Pete Curran, who was also on the platform — made a significant statement that puts Will Crooks into political context: 'Whenever the interests of Labour are at stake in Parliament there is Will Crooks ... In every industrial centre throughout this country the name of Crooks is a household word.' This statement by Curran shows how important Crooks was to the Labour movement, and how necessary it was for Crooks to take a rest if he was to continue the good work.[50]

On 10 September, Will Crooks, Elizabeth and their niece, sailed from Liverpool, arriving in Quebec on the 17th.[51] They were met at the dockside by two members of the Quebec Parliament, the Hon. C. Devlin MP, Minister for Works and Fisheries, and W. R. Trotter MP, the British Canadian delegate for Labour. Trotter had been a fraternal delegate to the Labour party conference earlier in 1909. He possibly organised the reciprocal visit, through Hardie, for Crooks to speak at the 25th Annual Convention of the Canadian Trades and Labor Congress on 20 September. On being introduced to the Convention by A. Verville, President of the Congress, Crooks spoke about the dignity of the workman, 'that a workman is sometimes heard to say: "I am only a poor workman." For God's sake, don't apologize for that', said Mr. Crooks, 'let the fellow who doesn't work do that.'[52] On 22 September, Crooks met Sir H.

Pellitier, Governor of the Province, for informal talks at Spencer Wood. Crooks said of the visit: 'The papers are all very kind, and at Quebec the [Congress] delegates fairly took us off our feet by presenting us with a silver tea service.'[53]

In late September, Crooks visited Montreal and Ottawa. Whilst in Ottawa he had informal discussions with the Canadian Prime Minister, Sir Wilfred Laurier (1896-1911), McKenzie King, the Minister for Labour, his deputy Mr Acland, and a son of the old war correspondent, Charles Williams. Crooks then continued on to Winnipeg, where he addressed a mass meeting organised by the Winnipeg Labour Council, and a meeting organised by the CPR engineers at the 'Congregational Chapel, the largest in Winnipeg.'[54] The next stop was Toronto, where he states: 'We had a great Labour meeting in the Labour Temple, Toronto... under the auspices of the Trades and Labour Council.'[55] Whilst in Toronto he was also invited to speak at a luncheon organised by the Canadian Club, and at the Knox Presbyterian College's graduate convention. Crooks was possibly in Winnipeg between 24-25; Toronto 27-29 September, before travelling to Vancouver, and sailing for Brisbane, Australia, at the beginning of October. Crooks was met at Brisbane by the Australian Prime Minister, and then travelled on to Sydney, where the local Trades Council entertained him. Will and Elizabeth then visited Melbourne, Adelaide, and New Zealand.[56]

Owing to the expectation of a General election — Parliament was prorogued on 3 December — Will and Elizabeth Crooks who were in New Zealand at the end of November, curtailed their tour and sailed for home. They sailed on the *Orsova*, an Orient mail boat from Melbourne, Australia, as far as Naples, then travelled overland, reaching Woolwich on the eve of the election on 16 January. The journey home took over six weeks. Will and Elizabeth received a tumultuous welcome from an estimated crowd of 100,000 people who lined the streets of Woolwich. The *Pioneer* reported their welcome: 'The oldest inhabitant is unable to recall anything in its history [Woolwich] that approached the demonstration ... A remark frequently heard ... was that "one would think that the King and Queen were coming to Woolwich".' [57]

During December, while Crooks was travelling home, the House of Lords upheld the Osborne judgement, which ruled against unions' spending money for political purposes. The judgement in December, by the House of Lords, made unlawful any political action whatsoever by trade unions. It was aimed specifically at the payment of salaries and election expenses of Labour MPs. This ruling had obvious repercussions for the Labour Party regarding the payment of the political levy by trade unions. But McKibbin argues that this ruling was not reversed, 'partly through the intransigence of the Labour party, until 1913.'[58] In the elections of 1910, the judgement had limited impact upon the trade union rank and file because according to Blewett, 'a significant minority viewed with antipathy the efforts at reversal.'[59] Also, for many in the

Labour movement the Osborne judgement was seen as a minor issue associated with the House of Lords constitutional question.

THE GENERAL ELECTIONS OF 1910

The first election campaign of 1910 was the longest in modern British history. It was an eight-week campaign that saw 400 Liberal seats (seats they had gained in 1906), being reduced to 275, just two more than the Conservatives, who gained 116 seats with an average swing of 4.3 per cent. The Irish Nationalists and the Labour Party held the balance of power with eighty-two and forty seats respectively. The pre-dissolution position of Labour was forty-five seats that included the miner's representatives whose union, the Miners' Federation of Great Britain, had joined the Labour Party in 1909. Of this number, Labour lost seven and gained two seats, losing five to the Conservatives, and Jarrow and Colne Valley to the Liberals[60] In contesting seventy-eight seats in the election, the Labour Party suffered a drubbing, especially in three-cornered contests. They came bottom of the poll in 'twenty of the twenty-four seats where Labour opposed Liberal candidates'.[61] The Liberal Party saw this expansion as aggression. Blewett argues: 'Their [Liberal] policy was one of containment — to confine Labour to the seats won in 1906.'[62] This containment policy of the Liberals was obviously pursued with success, and was an important factor in Labour's dismal results. Thus as McKibbin argues: 'From Labour's point of view ... the Party's position seemed, rather, one of humiliating dependence.'[63]

The main reason why the Labour Party's results in the election were so poor was because their distinctive identity was undermined. Instead of the election being fought on social and industrial platforms, the constitutional issue was top of the agenda. As far as the House of Lords was concerned, Labour's position was quite clear. It ought to be abolished.[64] Although after Christmas, the constitution was of secondary concern to that of the Budget, the Labour Party found it difficult to respond, 'as many voters were susceptible to the argument that the Budget was the first instalment of Socialism.' The *Daily Express* declared in early December the issue 'is, and must be the Socialism of the Budget ... or Tariff Reform.'[65] In the New Year the Conservatives managed to press fiscal alternatives to the Budget, and 'Tariff Reform began to replace the House of Lords in the forefront of the electoral debate.'[66] On the question of Tariff Reform, John Grigg asks why was it that people apparently voted against themselves 'in the struggle of "peers versus people"?' He argues that while the Unionists gained from the recent economic downturn that made many voters take a more doubtful view of Free Trade than in 1906, despite a perceptible revival in trade since 1907, and a less cynical view of Tariff Reform, 'those who had voted for sound finance were unlikely to feel much enthusiasm for the Lloyd George Budget.'[67]

The pledge of a Home Rule Bill for Ireland in the next parliament, given by Asquith at the Albert Hall on 10 December, was a significant difference between 1906 and 1910. It was a gift to the Unionists argues Grigg, 'because opinion in Great Britain remained as strongly pro-Unionist, in that sense, as it had ever been.'[68] The resurrection of the issue of Home Rule, which had remained dormant since 1893, obviously antagonised pro-Unionist feelings, thus costing the Liberals votes. The spectre of Home Rule was to haunt the Liberal Government from the outset, especially as the Irish Nationalists held the balance of power in the House of Commons.

J. T. Macpherson, MP for Preston, opened the Woolwich Labour election campaign on 15 December at High-street LCC School, Woolwich. Two great meetings 'Will Crooks for Woolwich' were held at the Town Hall, Woolwich, on New Year's Day and on 6 January 1910, and daily dinner-hour meetings in Beresford-square followed. They were held 7-16 January. Other meetings were organised throughout the borough, which drew large crowds in support of Crooks. These meetings were organised by the local Trade Union and Labour movement, the Free Church Council, the United Irish League, and other societies representing the temperance and progressive movement in the district. Margaret Bondfield, in the absence of Crooks, 'bore much of the brunt of the fight'.[69] She spoke at numerous meetings, including those at the Arsenal Gate. The Tory candidate was Major William Adam, who had opposed Crooks in 1906.

At the meeting on New Year's Day, Crooks' friend Arthur Henderson, Chairman of the PLP (1908-10), opened his remarks by recalling the 1903 election, which 'succeeded', according to him, 'in achieving one of the greatest victories ever associated with political history'. On the question of Tariff Reform, Henderson restated similar arguments put forward by Macpherson at the December meeting. He believed that if the 'noble lords and capitalists' succeed in getting Tariff Reform, they will not do any 'different in the future from what they have done in the past', wages would remain stationary while prices go up.[70] Crooks agreed Tariff Reform would mean dearer food, but he differed from Henderson over wages, believing that although wages would seem stationary, in real terms they would be lower. An increase in the cost of living would not be offset by an increase in wages or pensions. Henderson's speech was designed to win the support of the Woolwich working-class, especially the Arsenal worker, on the bread and butter issues of the election. These were the issues on which Crooks had concentrated, especially since 1903. Macpherson and Henderson explained that a vote for the Tories was a vote for the Lords and Tariff Reform. The Lords attacked the Budget because it undermined the landed class interests through taxation. The Unionists believed in keeping the burden of taxation upon the working-class by removing it from the luxuries of the rich, and imposing it upon the food of the poor.

Crooks' contribution to the struggle of Home Rule for Ireland, even in his absence, was recognised by the Central Executive of the United Irish League, who pledged in their Manifesto 'to support, work for, and do all in our power to return' Will Crooks on 17 January. For example, Daniel Crilly, General Secretary of the United Irish League, who spoke at the Henderson meeting, argued that the English should join forces with the Irish in their common struggle against the Lords, and appealed to his fellow-countrymen to vote solidly for Will Crooks. At the meeting on 6 January — that was held under the auspices of the Irish League — Crooks' credentials towards the Irish and John Higgins, secretary of the Woolwich United Irish League, who proposed a resolution pledging support for Crooks, commended the progressive cause. Higgins said, 'Will Crooks ... has always proved himself a true friend of Ireland, a pioneer of Freedom, and champion of the poor ... Ireland had no better friend than Will Crooks.' The principal speaker at this meeting was Swift McNeill MP, of the Irish National Party.[71]

It is important to note that Crooks had worked throughout his political life for Irish Home Rule; supporting Gladstone's attempt in 1886, campaigned for 'home rule all round' in the LCC elections of 1892, and supported Gladstone's Second Home Rule Bill in 1893. Crooks had further pledged himself to Irish self-government in his election manifestos of 1903 and 1906. He had supported the cause of Irish self-determination for over thirty-five years, and it was in recognition of this that he had won the hearts and minds of all like thinking Irish people. Their gratitude manifested itself through the representatives of the United Irish League and the Irish National Party, who campaigned for Crooks during the election.

The Conservatives during the campaign took advantage of Crooks' absence by scandalising his name, denigrating his representation of the Arsenal workers, and manufactured a series of 'scares' in the closing days of the election campaign. Obviously inspired by *The Standard's* posters at newsagents that 'Crookism meant more Arsenal Discharges' the Tories spread rumours that discharges were being held back until after the election. They distributed thousands of leaflets the following day giving extracts of the newspaper story, calling on electors to vote for Adam. 'The Tory Club was placarded with a poster stating that a vote for Will Crooks meant another march to London.' The *Pioneer* commented, stating that this series of 'unscrupulous attacks' was no coincidence, because they 'followed each other in such orderly sequence'.[72] This scaremongering obviously affected the result because a great number of Arsenal men voted for the Tory candidate. The result was Adam, 8775 votes, Crooks, 8420 votes, a Tory majority of 295 votes. The swing from Labour to Conservative was 7.5 per cent, the turnout 92.4 per cent.[73]

After the election Crooks received numerous messages of condolence, including a letter from his friend, Sydney Buxton (Post Master General), which summed up the general feeling of incredulity at Crooks' defeat: 'I was awfully disappointed at your defeat. It was disgusting. I fear ... Mrs Crooks will feel it most. Better luck next time.'[74] If Crooks was devastated, which he must have been, he did not show it. It was the first time Crooks had been defeated in any election, and as such, it was a new experience for him. He put on a brave face, and although he seemed uncomplaining in defeat, he must have felt that his life's work of dealing with the needs of the working-class had suffered a severe blow.

On 27 January, Crooks whilst speaking at the Plumstead Radical Club said that the election was a temporary setback to the cause of Labour principles, and: 'No man was worth being called a citizen unless he was prepared to face defeat for his principles.'[75] We need not be ashamed of defeat, Crooks told the audience at his first public meeting in early February: 'Who wants to win a fight like that? Not Will Crooks ... nor his friends. They are welcome to their victory - their dirt, their filth, their lies — every one of them.' Crooks warned the Tories of his intent, that 'the fight is but begun. It is not ended. The setback is so small as to be hardly noticeable.' He continued by saying that the Government 'had got to settle the question of the Lords' right away. The Government must not give way to anything. It was going to be a fight to the finish, 'and the people shall have the last word.'[76] It seems from the last remark that Crooks' disappointment was tempered by his uncanny foresight that there would be soon another election. Little did he know that there would be an election in December 1910. Among the tributes paid to Crooks' work was a commemorative medal: 'Will Crooks, Champion of the Poor', presented to him by the Browning Settlement.[77]

The vote of the Arsenal men was the deciding factor in the Crooks' election defeat because of the turnover of votes on the Arsenal discharge question. A turnover of 150 votes would have beaten the Tory candidate. The Tories took advantage of the Liberal record on discharges and played on the fears of the Arsenal workmen losing their livelihood. Another significant factor was the absence of Crooks. His magnetism would have won the waverers over. Crooks would have been merciless with the Tories for playing politics with the bread and butter of the Arsenal workers, and would have attacked the Tory scaremongers outside the Arsenal gate, spiking their arguments on the spot.[78] Will Crooks was not the only casualty in a constituency with a large number of Government employees. In the dockyard seats Labour lost Chatham to the Conservatives, and the Liberals lost both Portsmouth and Devonport, namely due according to Grigg, to the 'fear of ... alarmism over relative naval strengths.'[79]

The Months in Between

Contrary to expectations Crooks did not contest the LCC elections in March. Before leaving on a speaking tour he had told his supporters at the Poplar meeting in September 1909, 'that there had never been an election so important as next March.... It is the fight for the children ... If God spares me ... I am coming back for that fight.'[80] Crooks' decision not to contest his seat on the LCC was obviously made with regard to his election defeat at Woolwich. It was the first time in twenty-four years (since his election as a Poplar Trustee in 1886) that the opportunity had arisen that he would be free from the commitments of public life. It would therefore enable him to fulfil a greater number of platform engagements without having to juggle his diary around public duties. A further consideration that influenced Crooks' decision was that his revived health, due to his world tour, would be further improved by freedom from civic life. Also, as Crooks was essentially a home-loving man he could now count on having 'an evening free or a week-end to call his own'.[81]

Between elections, Will Crooks did not receive financial assistance from the Labour Party, but received money as a paid Trustee of a Society. Evidence shows that this was possibly the Liverpool Victoria Friendly Society. This Society was subject to a bank conversion bid in 1907, and because Crooks would not let his name go forward in support of this bid, it is most likely that the Society rewarded him with a Trusteeship.[82] In the ten months between the elections of 1910, Crooks took the opportunity to undertake a speaking tour throughout the country. He spoke on local and national Labour party platforms, to organisations affiliated to the WLRA, and at religious and temperance meetings. For example, in April Crooks addressed the annual meetings of both the British Women's Temperance Association and the Woolwich Brotherhood, held at Eltham and Woolwich Tabernacle respectively. Crooks' theme at both meetings was: 'Lead us not into temptation.' He said it meant for him, 'that those who were strong enough to resist temptation [drink] had to help their weaker brother to resist it' for the sake of the children, that we might give them the opportunity 'to lead a clean life'. Crooks believed that giving children a good home life, thus a good domestic education, and free schooling, was the moral imperative of all adults. He often said 'Parliament can make laws, but cannot make good men and women.' Crooks maintained men and women had an obligation to do good, to set an example, for the sake of the children.[83]

On 12 April at a specially convened conference, attended by sixty-eight delegates representing local labour organisations, at the WLRA Offices, Will Crooks was unanimously re-selected as the prospective Labour candidate for the district. In May, the Fabian Society approached the WLRA about taking over Crooks' candidature from the Coopers Union, which according to Pease 'only nominally financed it'. The officers of the Party decided to accept the Fabian offer of half or £500, whichever was the greater, towards any election expenses that Crooks' campaign would incur at the next Parliamentary election.[84] On the eve of the death of King Edward VII (6 May), Crooks was invited to speak at the Browning Settlement, Wandsworth, during Labour

Week.⁸⁵ The death of King Edward VII delayed the constitutional conflict between the Houses of Commons and Lords over the Parliamentary Bill — that had been introduced by Asquith on 14 April — for six months.

Throughout the summer months Crooks was busy attending local labour and church meetings. At the beginning of August he supported the Woolwich Labour Party's registration campaign. Crooks urged upon all qualified men how important it was to register their vote because Labour men had 'practically a double fight to wage', the plural vote of the property owner and the vote of the Tory working man.⁸⁶ During October, a rumour in the London press that Crooks would be contesting South Shields on behalf of the Labour Party proved unfounded. The *Pioneer* commented 'all the rumours that are current must be regarded as so much political kite-flying.'⁸⁷ The press, especially the 'yellow press', had always been politically mischievous towards Crooks. In this case, they sought to create confusion among the Woolwich electorate by undermining Crooks' candidature, and by so doing, lend support to the Unionist cause. The Tories/Unionists wanted Crooks to contest a constituency other than Woolwich, because they saw his candidature as an obvious threat to regaining the seat in a future election.

Between the elections of 1910, the Parliamentary Session was an exhausting and barren period for the Liberal Government. Asquith described 1910 'as an *annus mirabilis* in British politics', and Peter Rowland agreed, 'his claim can hardly be denied.'⁸⁸ The fate of the Budget, according to Blewett, was left 'in the hands of the Irish', who desired from the Liberals a compromise on the whisky duty. The Irish saw this as a bargaining-ploy to coerce the Government into embracing a robust anti Lord's policy that would practically pave the way for Irish Home Rule. John Redmond, leader of the Irish Nationalists, threatened by a revolt within the ranks of his own party over the Budget, was forced to take a firm line with the Government. He threatened 'No Veto, No Budget'. Blewett argues that Redmond was possibly bluffing.⁸⁹ Bluffing or not, in return for guarantees from Asquith of a 'veto' Bill becoming law during the Session, Redmond supported the Budget. Although, claims John Fair: 'That such a bargain was ever transacted, either orally or in writing, has never been proved.'⁹⁰

The most likely reason that finally prompted the Cabinet to take a decision on guarantees was the threat by Lloyd George on 13 April to 'leave the Cabinet'.⁹¹ This seems more plausible given that the statement was made the day before Asquith introduced his three veto resolutions that were the basis of the Parliament Bill. These were: 'To abolish by statute the Lords veto on Money Bills; to restrict by statute the Lord's veto on legislation, so if a Bill was passed by the Commons in three consecutive sessions, it should become law ... to limit the duration of Parliament to five years.'⁹² The following day Asquith warned the Lords:

If the Lords fail to accept our policy, or decline to consider it as it is formally presented to the House, we shall feel it our duty immediately to tender advice to the Crown as to the steps which have to be taken if that policy is to receive statutory effect in this Parliament ... Let me add this, that in no case will we recommend a dissolution except under such circumstances as will secure that in the new Parliament the judgement of the people as expressed at the election will be carried into law.[93]

In other words if the Lords refused to pass the Parliamentary Bill the Government would ask for the King to use his prerogative, and give guarantees that if the electorate gave the Government a workable majority he would increase the number of Liberal peers in the Lords, thus enabling the Parliament Bill to be passed. Subsequently with the support of the Irish Nationalists the Budget went through both Houses and onto the Statute Book on 29 April — exactly twelve months to the day since its introduction in 1909.

Following the death of Edward VII, a party truce was declared between the Liberals and Tories. This would provide a breathing space for George V succession, and would hopefully help settle the constitutional problem through conciliatory means. The Unionists were obviously worried. For them the removal of the Lords veto meant that the way would be open for the Government to carry through Irish Home Rule. On 17 June a Constitutional Conference was convened between the Liberals and Unionists in the hope, argues Blewett 'of averting, or at least delaying, the second election... All it did was delay for five months the second election.' The situation when the Conference broke down on 10 November, 'was as before.'[94] After the Lords had rejected the Parliament Bill for a second time on 21 November, Parliament was prorogued and dissolved a week later.

THE SECOND ELECTION OF 1910

The December election in comparison with that of January was considerably shorter. The Woolwich campaign lasted only fifteen days, from 21 November to 6 December. The Woolwich campaign began with Will Crooks speaking to a crowded meeting at the Town Hall on 21 November. He said that he was not in the 'slightest degree dismayed' that he had lost ten months ago: 'I was simply let loose to spread the gospel of industrialism and the need for Labour Representation throughout the Kingdom.' Crooks claimed he was not defeated, just that the victory was 'put off a bit.' His theme throughout the election campaign was that this was a 'soldiers' fight, not an officers' battle', a reference to Major Adam, the Conservative candidate. 'I am a humble private in the industrial army ... I am a mere standard-bearer in the army', he said. Crooks then reminded the meeting that Tariff Reform had not gone away, and that the Tories still believed: 'Half a loaf was better than no bread ... You remember (the 'half a loaf' slogan used by the Unionist candidate, Geoffrey

Drage, in the 1903 by-election campaign), I am going to take good care you don't forget it.' Crooks told the meeting not to believe the 'other side' that said he was 'played out.' Continuing, he said: 'Bill is not played out ... You can take my word for it — as I have lived, so shall I die — a servant of the people.'[95]

In his election address, Crooks asked for the electorate's confidence. He stated that his position had not changed on Adult Suffrage, or Temperance. On the question of the Osborne judgement, Crooks pledged to 'drive home on every occasion the absolute necessity for its reversal'. On the subject of industrial matters, Crooks said he would persist in pressing for direct labour and the 30s minimum for 'all Government employees'. The address continues: 'Reason and justice for Ireland is beginning to assert itself', and he would continue to support the cause of Home Rule, 'which I have supported for so many years, in and out of Parliament.' In conclusion, Crooks thanked the people of Woolwich for the opportunity to 'show England that the last election was not the well-considered verdict of the voters of Woolwich.' The cause of the people is my cause: 'I leave the result in your hands.'[96]

During the campaign, the Labour Party focused on exposing the record of Major Adam. The *Pioneer* pointed out that Adam 'had been the champion of the officers in Parliament', and was absent fifty-four times out of 159 divisions during the last Parliament.[97] It is important to note that at the end of the last Parliamentary session (1909), Crooks 'secured a promise from the Government that big-gun mountings should be made in the Arsenal.' During Crooks' absence from Parliament in 1910, the orders went to private contractors, due in no small measure to Major Adam and the Tory party who promoted private enterprise, and opposed State support for the Arsenal.[98] It was therefore vitally important, given the significance of the Arsenal vote in the election, for the Labour campaign to expose Adam, and point out that whilst in Parliament he had not represented the interests of his constituents, especially the Arsenal workers.

Will Crooks' position on the veto of the Lords had not changed. He had told a gathering of the WLRA in August that there was only one kind of veto he believed in, 'and that was to finish the House of Lords right off.' Crooks told them that he would believe in the abolition of the veto when it happened: 'Politicians at election times made all sorts of promises.' The Liberals, for example, had been given the opportunity to abolish the Lords in 1907, and 'they opposed the proposal.'[99] Crooks implying, why should we trust them now. He believed the House of Lords to be a mockery, 'and so undemocratic, that Labour had no use for it.' Crooks continued to attack the House of Lords at the beginning of the campaign. He said at the Town Hall: 'Labour is the Nation ... I say to the House of Lords ... Who is going to deny the nation the right to govern itself in its own way? Only you?' Crooks believed the people, with the support of the Labour Party, could govern themselves better without the interference of the Lords. [100]

The election campaign meetings throughout the borough were 'crowded out', whether they were held in Silvertown, North Woolwich, Eltham, Plumstead, or Woolwich itself. Crooks said it was a pity that Woolwich did not possess a building big enough to hold public meetings of the Labour Party. Frequently there were more people outside the meeting halls than the buildings could accommodate before the doors opened: as usual regular dinner-hour meetings were held in Beresford square. The *Pioneer*, reporting on the meetings held in the square, said: 'Never have there been such crowds as have greeted Will Crooks daily.' At the first dinner-hour meeting on 28 November, Crooks said that the election was not about Will Crooks against Major Adam: 'It is the People against the Peers.' He said that he was ready to deal with 'our opponents drastically. I have got the gloves off ... They hit me when I was away, and I am hitting back now.'[101] On 6 December Crooks hit the Tories where it hurt most, at the ballot box. He won the Woolwich seat back for Labour, overturning Adam's majority in the January election of 295 votes. Crooks polled 8,252 votes, against Adam 8,016; Crooks' majority was 236 votes, a swing to Labour of 3.2 per cent. The turnout was 87.8 per cent.[102]

The significant factors in Crooks' victory were his presence, his dignity, past parliamentary record, and the turnover of the Arsenal vote. According to Crooks, Major Adam was disappointed because he had declined four safe seats that were offered to him. He claimed that Adam wanted him to go to give Adam himself a chance. Crooks stayed to fight Woolwich because he wanted to avenge his defeat in January. Crooks said: 'They [Tories] are always waiting until people are absent, and then attacking them. I am here to reply.' Throughout the campaign, the Tories planted and paid hecklers to interrupt Crooks at Labour meetings. On 30 November, Crooks told a meeting at Plumstead Baths Hall that: 'I have private information that the opposition has come to the conclusion that the only way to prevent Crooks from being returned is to interrupt him, so he shall not be heard.' This tactic of the Tories backfired, because Crooks used hecklers to good effect in his speeches to illustrate a point aimed at lampooning the Tories and the House of Lords. At a meeting in Beresford square the following day, Crooks said he had proof the 'Tories pay for interrupters.'[103]

At every meeting, Crooks exposed and condemned Adam's Parliamentary record, drawing comparisons with his own.[104] With regard to workers rights — Crook's record spanned more than twenty years. He had always advocated, and never missed an opportunity of demanding a fair share of Government work 'for the London riverside workers.' For example, Crooks had always supported the demands of various unions and societies — Shipwrights, Boilermakers, Caulkers, ASE, and Gasworkers — for the continuation of shipbuilding on the Thames. It is important to note, as Crooks pointed out himself, that he not only represented the men with the vote, but also those that were not enfranchised, irrespective of their politics. Crooks was seen as an exemplary constituency MP because he represented the needs of working-class families, especially those who wanted help and support in times of adversity. It was well known among his constituents that within a few weeks of his election in 1903, he obtained compensation for the widows of the workers killed in the Lyddite Explosion at the Arsenal. Crooks said that: 'The widows got their compensation in a lump sum, instead of having it doled out to them in the shape of a pension.'[105]

Also it was directly due to Crooks' persistence and intervention that the Liberal Government set up a Special Committee in 1907, alleviating much suffering amongst the Arsenal workers and their families. Subsequently the Henderson Committee's recommendations were implemented and the Arsenal minimum was raised from 7,000 to 8,400. Moreover, said Crooks, altogether 'over 12,000 men are kept on in the Arsenal instead of the strength being put at a figure that the Tories desired'.[106] It is important to recognise that to win the Arsenal vote a significant part of Crooks' campaign had to focus on the conditions of work in the Arsenal. Some people may have complained that he was spending too much time talking about Arsenal affairs, but Crooks knew the importance of pressing home his parliamentary record, as opposed to that of Adam, in supporting the biggest employer in Woolwich. This strategy combined with a programme of widespread canvassing organised by the local Labour party returned Will Crooks to Parliament.

Overall the election results were not unlike those of January, but as Rowland argues, the Liberal 'Government was now immeasurably more secure than in January 1910, and occupied, paradoxically, a far stronger position than in 1906.' The Liberals lost three seats, being returned with 272 seats, equal with the Unionists.[107] The Labour and Nationalist vote increased very slightly. They were returned with forty-two and eighty-four seats respectively, each gaining two seats. The Labour party gained five seats in Sunderland, Bromley and Bow, Fife, Whitehaven, Woolwich, and lost three seats in straight fights with the Tories in Newton, St. Helens, and Wigan. In Fife, W. Adamson won against Liberal opposition, and in the two-seat constituency of Sunderland, F. W. Goldstone won with Liberal support.[108] In the January election Labour put up seventy-eight candidates, in December it was reduced to a more exiguous fifty-six. The Liberals once again were dependent on Labour and Nationalist support for a working majority. This troubled the Tories greatly because they knew that in return for helping the Liberals to deliver the Parliament Bill, the Nationalists would expect something to be done on the question of Home Rule. The Tories were justified in being worried, because it had become increasingly clear that the removal of the Lords veto would make Home Rule inevitable. The political conflict over Home Rule would continue between the Liberals and Tories until the outbreak of the Great War.

Although the Unionist vote remained the same, the election took its toll. Blewett argues it was the Unionists 'hope to impair ... sufficiently to thwart the Government's constitutional designs',[109] and undermine the Liberal majority at the election. That a reduction in the Liberal majority did not materialise was to prove a gamble in the dark for the Unionists. They had now been defeated in three elections in less than five years, primarily because the issue of Tariff Reform had fallen on stony ground, being rejected by the majority of the working-class three times, and also because their constitutional reforms had been discarded by the electorate, who preferred democratic governance to hereditary dominance.

Blewett further argues that by 1910, formal Lib-Labism had been eclipsed, and the line between the Labour and Liberal parties was now more clearly defined. The Liberals saw Labour expansion as a threat, deciding on a policy of containment to confine Labour to seats won in 1906, including the seats held by the miners. It was across this line that the Liberal Party did not want Labour to sanction further intrusion. They made it clear they would not permit any further expansion.[110] In a letter to Liberal candidates, Pease (Liberal Chief Whip) wrote 'if an aggressive attitude was persisted in by the Labour Party, Labour could not expect official Liberalism to stand on one side and remain unnominated.'[111]

In January, Labour proposed to put forward 103 candidates, but because of MacDonald's powers of persuasion, they put forward a shorter list of candidates in order not to antagonise the Liberals. It was due to the threat of Liberal retaliation that the Labour Party sacrificed its electoral independence in 1910. It was felt that it would cost Labour votes if the party were seen breaching the electoral 'arrangement' between themselves and the Liberals. MacDonald was aware of the position. He told his executive 'as soon as the Lords became an issue three-cornered fights were "foredoomed".'[112] Although Labour was dependent on Liberal electoral strategy, the *Clarion* warned Labour candidates that 'to confine their campaign to the great constitutional crisis would be madness. The great constitutional crisis is *not* the important thing for us.'[113] To give prominence to the Lords was to endanger Labour's distinctive programme, its social and industrial objects.

In this period, being tied to political liberalism was clearly a problem for the Labour Party. They had to appease left activists in the Party, appeal to the conservative working-class to vote on an independent programme, and at the same time not risk the Liberal majority. Blewett contends that the *Clarion* was right to remind Labour candidates to put forward the Labour Party position on social, economic, and industrial issues.[114] In this way, the party would satisfy its supporters, remain independent, and fulfil its electoral obligations to the Liberals.

The relationship between the Liberal and Labour parties was not enthusiastic despite the MacDonald-Gladstone 'arrangement' during the elections, but it was adhered to although arguably neither side were happy with it. After 1910, especially at local level, 'many local associations could not accept their permanence', and even Pease and Asquith did not feel obligated to support any attachment to the Labour Party.[115] While it was the distinctive social, economic, and industrial issues of the Labour Party that Will Crooks sought to promulgate, his primary concern was towards serving the interests of the working people, especially those of the disenfranchised working-class poor of Poplar and Woolwich. Above all, he had no time for empty promises that would be detrimental to the livelihood of the working-class, as his attack on the LGB for its incompetence over unemployment shows. It was part of Crooks' nature to articulate the needs of the poor and vulnerable in society. This irresistible calling drove him on, and inspired his work. The suffering of working people inspired him to put together and introduce his Labour Disputes Bill in 1911, and intervene in defence of the dockers and their families in 1912.

This unselfish quality underpinned every moment of Crooks' political life, and goes a long way towards explaining his world outlook. Illustrative of this is the period after the January elections of 1910, when he could have put his feet up and convalesced. Instead, he chose to go on a speaking tour throughout the country to educate the workers on why they should embrace the Labour cause. Throughout this period, Crooks demonstrated that his Woolwich constituents came first every time, even if it meant going against the Labour Whip. His defence of work for the Arsenal over the issue of the naval estimates 1909-10 is symbolic of this. He voted with the Government, and rebelled against the Labour Party. Thus, Crooks saw his main role in Parliament as protecting Arsenal jobs, and its corollary, the social and economic interests of Woolwich.

7

RETURNS TO THE PARLIAMENTARY FRAY

On Will Crooks' return to Parliament in 1911 – Parliament assembling on 6 February — he started as he left off, agitating for work in the Arsenal by persistently harrying Haldane and McKenna, both in the Commons and at the War Office. He concentrated on issues relating to Arsenal wages, pensions, gun mountings, the OF minimum, and working conditions in Government Ordnance Factories and establishments generally. Since the Government appropriated most of allocated parliamentary time up until Easter, Crooks was limited to questions on supply — the Army/Navy Estimates — and the introduction of the Labour Party's motion on the Minimum Wage in April. The main business for the Government was the re-introduction of the Parliamentary Bill, and a new bill on National Insurance. It was intended that both bills should pass through the House by early May. On the thorny issue of Home Rule, the Liberals decided that it would be presented in 1912, giving them time for it 'to be knocked into shape' during the summer recess.[1] In May, Lloyd George introduced his National Insurance Bill. The long awaited Payment of Members was introduced in August. Although Crooks did not participate in the debate on either of these issues, it is necessary to the discussion to look at his position on them, thus enabling a better understanding of the man. In September, Crooks introduced his Labour Disputes Bill.

On 9 February, Richard Haldane received a deputation from the TUC on the issue of the 30s. minimum for Government workers in the London district, 'abolition of piece-work amongst explosive workers in Woolwich Arsenal, and a substitution of a day work rate of 36s'. In reply, Haldane informed them that the Government proposed increasing the Army Estimates in March, and although he could not promise a 30s. minimum, 'it meant an increase in the minimum rates for labourers in Government establishments from April 1st, 1911.' Further, he said he hoped Labour MPs would support the Estimates in the Commons.[2] During the debate on the Army Estimates on 14 March, Crooks exposed the War Department's reluctance to employ men at the

Arsenal in times of peace, and castigated the officials at the War Office for always giving evasive answers to questions. He said that the Treasury saved money in 1909-10 because the War Department returned £250,000; while at the time it was laying off men in the Arsenal, and not transferring them to other Departments who were craving for men. Although 'in the immediate neighbourhood the contractor was working overtime doing the very work your own Department ought to have been doing.' Regarding the officials, Crooks said: 'They say, "It is not my fault." "If I had my way"... and of course, you raise the matter in the House, and it will receive the same consideration as every question you raise. "It shall have the attention of my Department".' He concluded by asking when the Government was going to 'alter this state of things', or would it be the same old story of giving work to the contractor? [3]

After revealing to the House of Commons his feelings on how the War Office evaded questions, Crooks spoke along similar lines at the annual dinner of the ASE Club and Institute, Woolwich, on 24 March. He disclosed that in the previous week 'he had very serious thoughts of giving up Parliament altogether', because he was tired and weary of Ministers' broken promises in relation to the Arsenal. He felt he was there to represent the people: 'Beyond that Parliament meant nothing to him.'[4] Crooks had served the interests of the Arsenal workers and the people of Woolwich for seven years, with most of the time being spent at the War Office, or asking questions related to the Arsenal in the Commons. As he said himself in the House most of the questions were avoided. He was played off against one Department and another, and this behaviour by them had precipitated Crooks' thoughts of resigning. However, these dark thoughts soon passed and he was back urging trade unionists and Labour men to support the people's cause.

THE MINIMUM WAGE AND INDUSTRIAL RELATIONS

In the House of Commons on 26 April, Will Crooks moved the Labour Party's Motion on the Minimum Wage, which according to press reports 'caused both great Parliamentary parties to gasp with horror and indignation.' He moved:

> That the right of every family in the country to an income sufficient to enable it to maintain its members in decency and comfort should be recognized; and this House is therefore of the opinion that a general minimum wage of 30s. per week for every adult worker should be established by law, and also declares that the Government should set an example by adopting this standard in it own workshops.[5]

The Liberal and Tory feelings of 'indignation' were because in order to increase wages they would have to cut profits. This was an anathema in a House of Commons composed largely of capitalists.

The motion stood no chance of acceptance from the beginning. Crooks knew this. But it was the dissemination of the principle to a wider audience, through the press, that was important to him and the Labour Party. The use of Parliament in this sense was important to the Labour Party. It allowed for a wider distribution on the issues of policy, and kept supporters informed of the party's position.

In moving the motion Crooks said: 'I make bold to assert this is the most important proposal that has ever been made in this House, certainly in my lifetime.' This may have sounded like a grandiose statement, but Crooks believed that the health and well being of the poor came before anything else, even before 'the defence of the Empire, represented by "Dreadnoughts" and armaments'. He said 'the greatest and most important thing' for him was the children, "the children of to-day being the men and women of to-morrow".' Crooks pointed out that a legal minimum wage would protect the workers from the unscrupulous employer, who used the workingman 'for what can be made out of him.' Crooks said he was pleading for the independence of the breadwinner to give them a 'choice between bread or no bread at all.' It was a national travesty, Crooks said, that people were better off in the workhouse than they were trying to earn a living outside. He was of the opinion that 30s. a week was a miserable wage, but believed that it was a start to improving the workers' lot, and would help overcome the pinch of poverty that was always upon them.[6]

Crooks used the opportunity afforded him by the Commons to attack Tariff Reform and its supporters, who believed it was a panacea for all ills. And yet he said, 'in the same breath he will say that he desires to find work for the men at home ... As a friend of mine said, "It will find work, Bill; looking for it." ' Crooks concluded by saying it was the responsibility of the Government to look after men, women, and children 'whom the country can not do without ... it ought not to be afraid of spending a few thousand pounds in keeping them in decency and comfort ... The Government should begin to-morrow.'[7] The motion fell; it was talked out by Sir F. Banbury, the MP for the City of London. Crooks introduced a similar motion on behalf of the Labour Party in April 1913, only this time it was talked out by a Liberal Member, the Parliamentary Secretary to the Board of Trade, J. M. Robertson.

The debate on the Minimum Wage had the desired effect outside Parliament that Crooks and the Labour Party were seeking. It was taken up and discussed in the press. Most of the Unionist press was hostile towards it, maintaining that it was another hopeless socialist scheme doomed to failure. The *Daily Mail* went so far as to say Crooks' adoption of a 30s. minimum was a 'skinflint policy'. It believed that: 'If the House of Commons can give everyone 30s a week, it can also presumably give them 60s.'[8] The tactics and strategy of the Labour Party on this issue were correct. The party knew that the motion would fail, but if a member of Crooks' reputation moved the resolution, the press would report it, thus educating a broader section of the public as to the party's position on the question of a 30s. minimum wage per week for all adults.

Will Crooks' introduction of the Minimum Wage did not go unrecognised by the Labour Party, because the next day three Labour MPs supported him on the platform at the Radical Club, Plumstead. They were Arthur Henderson, George Roberts, and William Harvey; Henderson and Roberts were members of the NEC. It was a demonstration of solidarity in support of Crooks to show how much the party recognised his tireless and unstinting work for the cause of Labour. Also, without doubt, the party was concerned about Crooks' frame of mind, which had led him to give serious thought to resigning his seat the previous month. It was unlike the Crooks they knew, since it was out of character. He was not someone who would throw in the towel when faced with adversity. Crooks would always fight back even if the odds were stacked against him. Hence, the physical and moral support afforded him by the Labour Party. Other matters may have influenced his deliberations, but other than the extant record, any supposition would be mere conjecture. That the party owed a debt of gratitude to Crooks' pioneering work was clear in Henderson's speech:

> They [the LRC MPs] went from one end of the country to the other, and in the educational work that was done there was no greater factor than they possessed in the striking personality of the member for Woolwich ... They had had many opportunities of learning that the educational work then done was done effectively, with the result that they...had the satisfaction of seeing a highly organized Labour Party in Parliament.[9]

Crooks and Henderson had been friends since they were both elected within five months of each other in 1903. If anyone knew Crooks' antecedents Henderson did. It is obvious from Henderson's remarks that Crooks' contribution to the trade union and labour movement was held to be of *great* significance to the development of the Labour Party

A short time after the new Parliament assembled, Asquith introduced the First Reading of the Parliament Bill in the same form as it was presented in 1910. The Bill did not leave the Commons until 15 May, only to be returned by the Lords in mid-July heavily amended. Following the Lords' rejection, the House of Commons met on 24 July to hear Asquith respond on the issue of the veto amendments. When he started to speak on the introduction to the motion – 'Parliament Bill: Consideration of Lords' amendments', scenes of absolute mayhem, instigated by the Tories, met him. Frank Dilnot, parliamentary correspondent of the *Daily Mail*, described the scene as 'the greatest parliamentary scene I have witnessed.... The state of the House may be imagined when I say that the great resonate cockney voice of Mr Will Crooks was immediately drowned out when he got up to put a point of order to the Speaker.'[10] The Commons was in uproar. The Opposition, led by Lord Hugh Cecil was determined to shout down Asquith - shouting: 'Traitor, traitor, traitor!... Where is Redmond?... He [Asquith] has degraded Parliament!'[11] For three-quarters of an hour, Asquith was derided, insulted, and reviled. Dangerfield notes: 'Indeed, it was Will Crooks ... who struck the first blow for decency. He sat near enough to Lord Hugh to be heard. "Many a man", he shouted, "has been certified for less than half of what the noble lord has done this afternoon." '[12]

The Unionists were trying to stop the inevitable, the passing of a bill which would stop them controlling future Liberal legislation, especially Home Rule. The Tory rebels, the champions of hereditary government, were seen by many as noble hooligans who 'had done no good either to themselves or the cause they were promoting.'[13] The Parliament Bill received the Royal Assent on 18 August.

The National Insurance Bill was introduced to the House of Commons on 4 May. After a tortuous journey through Parliament it received the Royal Assent in late December. The Insurance Bill was a combination of schemes: unemployment insurance, which was compulsory to some trades (especially those prone to cyclical unemployment such as the building industry), sickness and maternity benefit, and 'finally a right to sanatorium treatment for tuberculosis'.[14] The Labour Party was divided on this issue, but in spite of this, they managed to get important Amendments incorporated into the Bill. When the bill was introduced, Will Crooks saw it as a distinct step towards the Government recognising its duties towards the weak and poor. He reserved judgment on its wider implications, especially upon the issue of workers' wages, until after the party's amendments were accepted.

In welcoming the final outcome, Crooks said of the Act to the Arsenal workers, 'for the first time in history' working people were going to get money they 'never had before ... They were going to come under a national scheme, and the War Office ... [and] Treasury would have to pay ... for everyone of them.' Crooks also must have been quietly pleased that at last Trade Unions would be recognised in the bill, because under the Act each union had the option of becoming an approved Society.[15]

During August, the House of Commons resolved to pay members £400 per annum. Labour MPs welcomed this. They would not have to rely on payment out of the Labour Party's Parliamentary fund. The payment of members came at an opportune time for the party because the political fund had been depleted by the restriction on the unions by the Osborne judgement. The payment, which the Labour Party had been pushing for since the Liberals came into office, could be seen as a sop to Labour for being patient and not pushing too hard on the repeal of the judgment. One of the clauses of the Act was the payment of Returning Officers at elections, something, for which Crooks had been agitating since the 1890s. It would, he believed, get rid of the taint of any political corruption at elections, and protect the electorate by underlining the Government's legal obligations to it.

THE LABOUR UNREST: 1911-1913

The main reason behind the industrial unrest between 1911-14 was that since 1905 the cost of living had far out stripped the increase in real wages. This together with the growing strength of the trade union movement, [16] the blatant display of affluence by the rich, and improved communications — which made for better national co-ordination of news — were contributory factors to this period of unrest. Henry Pelling points to the difference between the 'new unionism' of 1889-91, and the labour unrest; new unionism was mainly a peaceful protest against unemployment, while the labour unrest involved bitter strikes over wages. Pelling further states, 'there were ... some remarkable parallels in the early development of the movement in 1911 with that of 1889. In both cases, the Seamen's Union had a role in triggering off the unrest among the dockers.'[17]

The bitter conflict of 1911-13 was seen by G.D.H. Cole as a reaction against the failure of orthodox trade unionism and modern parliamentarism to secure for the working-class an improvement in the standard of living.[18] Aggressive industrial action on the docks and railways began with what Bob Holton calls 'the second main phase of "labour unrest" June and September 1911', the earlier phase being the Miners' Strike in the South Wales coalfields between September 1910 and August 1911. This dispute centred on grievances over wages and conditions.[19] As this period of labour unrest has been widely discussed by other historians, including the explosive rise of Syndicalism, the main focus of the following dialogue concentrates on the involvement of Will Crooks, who took a more pragmatic view than most on labour unrest.[20]

Will Crooks' Labour Disputes Bill was published at the end of August and it was introduced to the House of Commons in early September 1911. The idea of drafting the Bill had occurred to him during his tour of Canada two years previously. The Canadian Industrial Disputes Investigation Act of 1907 had left an impression upon Crooks that was to prove significant in influencing his trade union outlook of how to deal with industrial disputes at home.[21] The main proposal in Crooks' Bill was that when workmen and employers were in dispute they should call on an independent arbitrator – the Board of Trade – to conciliate and try to settle the grievance. If the dispute was not settled to the men's or employers' liking then a lockout or a strike could take place.

On publication, the Bill was received, according to Crooks with a 'tremendous amount of criticism, more or less just', he confessed. He went on to explain that the reason behind introducing this Bill 'had been to help the women and children ... They might ... call that "sloppy sentimentality".... [But] hear me first: Condemn me afterwards.' Crooks believed that in strike situations it was the weak and the vulnerable that suffered — especially poor women and children. He said that it was a 'fact that Labour representation all over the country has brought about a revolution in the condition of the poor in the land', and it was the introduction of this Bill that would protect these gains. In other words, needless disputes could have been settled by arbitration, and have been avoided, thus saving the poor old man or woman from the workhouse, who had been brought down because of a strike or lockout. [22]

The TUC Annual Conference on 19 September censured Crooks for his action of introducing a Bill into the House of Commons to establish Industrial Conciliation before submitting it to the trade union movement or the Labour Party:

> ... we desire to make it clear that we will by every means in our power to resist every attempt to prevent or hinder the right of the workers to strike at any time when they consider such action necessary in defence or furtherance of their rights. [23]

W. Marsland (Cotton Spinners), seconding the motion, said: 'The Bill Mr Crooks has introduced takes away in great measure the right of workmen to strike.'[24]

This was not the case. Crooks was careful to retain and safeguard the workers' right to strike. This part of his Bill was overlooked, or conveniently ignored, by some of his colleagues in the labour movement, especially members of the TUC. It seems the hostile reaction to Crooks' Bill at the TUC was aimed to tarnish his reputation, and label him a reactionary, which he was not. Although Crooks attended the Newcastle Congress, he left two days before the motion was tabled; he had not been given notice that his Bill would be discussed. This action of the Congress infuriated him. 'It must be unprecedented', he said, 'for a Labour man to be censured and his work condemned by a Labour Congress in his absence, without even giving him notification of such a proposal.' [25] On the subject of submitting his Bill to the Labour Party before it was introduced, he hit back: 'My answer to that is that there is no rule or understanding that such a course must be adopted.'[26]

Ramsay MacDonald took a similar view to Crooks on the issue of strikes, and their impact on the wider community. For example, he told the House of Commons in February 1912: 'We are too fond of imagining there are two sides only to a dispute ... there is the side of the general community; and the general community has no business to allow capital and labour, fighting their battles themselves, to elbow them out of consideration.'[27] Within this speech lies the Parliamentary Labour Party's dilemma, of being seen to serve both national and trade union interests at the same time.

In February, a miners' national strike for a minimum wage began. It continued until April. A district minimum wage was achieved after the Liberal Government rushed a Bill through Parliament; after the settlement of the miners' strike, there followed widespread unrest in the transport industry. The most important event occurred in May, on the Port of London waterfront. The main cause of the stoppage was the refusal of the men to work with non-unionists, after the transport employers insisted that they do so. By taking this action, the employers breached agreements made in August 1911, with the Amalgamated Society of Watermen and Lightermen, and the National Transport Workers' Federation (NTWF).[28] In response to the NTWF call for a general strike in the port on 23 May, the stevedores and dockers came out the next day.[29] Bob Holton points out that: 'Episodes of violent conflict between strikers, blacklegs and police were ... somewhat more widespread in 1912 than on the earlier more peaceable occasion[s],' in 1889 and 1911. 'Significant numbers on both sides [strikers and blacklegs] carried revolvers.'[30] It was this violence which prompted Crooks to speak out in support of the dockers in the House of Commons on 12 June, in the debate on the protection of workmen from intimidation by the police and employers.

During this debate, Crooks accused the employers of being intimidatory, by bringing in 'shiploads' of blackleg labour to break the strike. The Government was no better, he said, they just stood by and watched as strikers' wives and families were being starved into submission, 'to satisfy what?' To satisfy the dividends of the employer, as opposed to the economic needs of the worker. Crooks began his censure of the Government's complicity in the employers' action by saying:

> You are trying your best to prove that we are the only people guilty of intimidation and assault, but what is going on at the moment? You have convoys conveyed along the road by police. Is that not intimidation to anybody at all? Is that not intimidating men who are trying to save their souls? Is it not intimidation for you to introduce men to take the bread out of their mouths?[31]

Crooks was indignant at the employers' intransigent attitude. He pointed out that the money they spent on breaking the strike could be better spent on settling it. They were bent on smashing the unions. The employers were using the police to bludgeon the strikers back to work, and compromise was not part of their agenda. [32]

At the end of June, Crooks intervened on the strikers' behalf. He interviewed Lord Devonport, the chairman of the Port of London Authority: 'He declined to see the dockers.' Most probably Crooks' friend, Ben Tillett, the dockers' leader, had invited him to mediate on the dockers' behalf, otherwise Crooks would not have met Devonport without being asked to do so.

The other employers also refused to meet with either the NTWF or the Lightermen and Bargemen's Union. Crooks told the Commons on 1 July that all he wanted was to bring 'the masters and men together ... You ask us to go on indefinitely, you are asking men to go on starving their wives and families'.[33] This episode illustrates not only Crooks' commitment to conciliation, but also his support for the use of strike action in the face of ruthless employers. He wholeheartedly backed the dockers but tried to mediate on their behalf for the sake of their starving families. The strike was called off on 27 July because there were no funds left in the union coffers, and 'further resistance only meant meaningless suffering.' Some of the men stayed out, and did not resume work until mid-August because the employers had made no provision to reinstate the strikers.[34]

Also in 1913, the Trade Union Act reversed Lord Halbury's judgement in the Osborne case. Trade Unions were once more permitted 'to engage in any lawful purposes that their members desired ... made subject to any objecting member being enabled to withhold that part of his contribution applicable to political purposes.'[35] It is important to note the strength of the opposition by union members to paying the political levy; forty per cent of those who voted opposed their union having a political fund, and thus affiliating to the Labour Party.[36] This rejection by a minority of trade unionists seems to point to their distrust of the party, especially over their seeming compliance with the Liberals over labour unrest.

Empire Tour and Arsenal Strike 1913-14

Between July and November 1913, Will Crooks went abroad as a delegate of the Parliamentary Empire Association that visited Canada, Australia, and South Africa. Lord Alfred Emmott, Under Secretary of State for the Colonies (1911-14), led the delegation: Crooks was the only Labour Member of a party of thirteen Parliamentarians. It is significant to the discussion that two events took place in the summer of 1911. The Empire Parliamentary Association was formed, with Crooks as a founder member, and the British, Australian, and South African Labour Parties agreed to set up an International Secretariat. At a special conference, organised by the British Labour Party in July, the Labour Parties agreed: 'That an interchange of visits between members of the Labour Parties in the Parliament at home and in the Dominions is desirable and should be arranged ... to consider ... The utilisation of the delegations for enlightening public opinion and demonstrating the solidarity of the Labour Movements in the Empire.'[37] Thus the Empire Tour afforded the PLP the opportunity to fulfil its obligations as joint signatory to the July agreement.

It is important to note that Arthur Henderson had joined the Fabians shortly after replacing MacDonald as secretary of the Labour Party in January 1912. Although Henderson would have been a pivotal figure in Crooks' selection, his motivation was possibly borne out of both altruism and self-interest. He saw the choice of Crooks as an opportunity to endorse his Fabian credentials. It seems that Crooks' successful visit to the colonies in 1909, as a guest of the Canadian and Australian trade union and labour movement, influenced the decision of the Labour Party. In addition, that Crooks was already a member of the Empire Association must have been crucial to his selection. The Labour Party at this time had shed its image as a pressure group, and needed to impress upon the Empire its Parliamentary credentials. By choosing Crooks, who was looked upon as a friend of the Empire, the party felt he was just the person to pioneer links with the colonies. At Plumstead in 1912, Henderson had praised Crooks' qualities as a pioneer of the PLP. Tom Fox, Harry Orbell, and MacDonald, respectively Chairman, Vice-Chairman, and Treasurer of the Labour Party, would have supported Henderson's preference.

Harry Orbell would not have needed persuading about Crooks' qualities. He and Crooks had been friends and comrades since the 1880s, working side by side in supporting the interests of London dockers and their families. Keir Hardie, MacDonald, Clynes, Hodge, Wardle, Anderson, and Roberts, who were all members of the Labour Party NEC, had all worked with Crooks at one time or another, and knew the calibre and worth of the man. It was a sign of the esteem Crooks' friends had for him — his unselfish contribution of placing the cause of Labour above all else in life — that he was chosen to carry the greetings and goodwill from the British Labour Party to comrades overseas. They knew they could depend upon Crooks to help strengthen the growing solidarity of Labour on the Empire Tour, and carry out Labour's foreign policy. The basic principle of which was that 'the Labour Party would do its best to keep the British workers in friendship and goodwill with all their comrades in other lands.'[38] MacDonald, Henderson, and other members of the Labour Party also went on world tours to study social and constitutional issues. For example, Australia was seen as a laboratory for the introduction of welfare measures. On the Empire Tour, Will Crooks visited Canada, the Fijian Islands, Australia, New Zealand, and South Africa. The schedule was strenuous and tiring; for example, while in Australia the party travelled 6,000 miles in one month.

In July 1914, the Royal Arsenal at Woolwich went on strike during the escalating tension in the Balkans. Due to the grave developments in Europe, the Government took this dispute very seriously indeed and needed to deal with it quickly, as the Arsenal was at the heart of Government attempts to rearm. The resolution of the dispute became a priority. Thus, it was brought to an end in six days after Crooks requested Asquith to set up an inquiry, which would resolve the matter.

The strike began on Friday 3 July, when an engineer, John Entwistle, was sacked for following District ASE instructions to boycott a 'blacked' area. He had refused to erect machinery on a concrete base in the Royal Carriage Department (RCD), an area deemed laid by blackleg labour. These events happened in the morning. In the afternoon the ASE engineers in the RCD went on strike in support of Entwistle's action, and against any victimisation that management might impose upon him. On Saturday morning, all the Arsenal engineers were called out, and the unskilled workers joined in. On Monday, the Labour Protection League and the Workers Union called for indefinite strike action. As a result, all classes of worker were out by Monday. The workers – 11,000 in number – had 'joined in a general withholding of labour to enforce the rights of Trade Unionism', which was according to the *Pioneer* unprecedented: 'FIRST GREAT "ALL GRADES" CONFLICT IN THE ORDNANCE FACTORIES.'[39] On the surface, the dispute seemed to be over Entwistle's sacking, but trouble had been brewing in the Arsenal since 1912. The strike was the outcome of a deep-seated dissatisfaction with the management of the establishment, especially over the employment of private building contractors — a triennial contract for jobbing work made in 1912 and running until 1915 — who used blackleg labour. The management were warned of the consequences but chose to ignore them.[40]

Within three working days of the outbreak of the dispute, it was brought to the notice of the House of Commons. On 6 July Will Crooks asked Asquith: 'Whether he can make any statement to the House with regard to the progress of the dispute at Woolwich Arsenal.' Asquith replied: 'The Government are fully alive to the importance of what is occurring and are taking such steps as are necessary ... I hope to do so [make a statement] tomorrow.' Crooks then asked the Prime Minister if he would see him 'personally, presently and talk it over?' Asquith answered: 'Yes, Sir, certainly.' The following day Asquith made a statement to the Commons that the Government was going to set up a Court of Enquiry 'consisting of five persons', two representative trade unionists, two representative employers, 'with Sir George Askwith as chairman.' Asquith further said that the men could return to work, and that particular work which the dispute was about 'should be in abeyance pending the Report of Inquiry.' The men returned to work on 9 July. [41]

It is not possible to determine what private conversation took place between Crooks and Asquith, but it is obvious from the outcome that due to Crooks' intervention the dispute was settled swiftly and amicably in the men's favour. The Strike Committee recognised the importance of Crooks' personal talks with Asquith, and thanked him; 'thanks and appreciation of the valuable services rendered in the House of Commons'.[42] The Askwith Inquiry cleared Entwistle completely of any wrongdoing.

The Arsenal strike cannot be seen as part of the labour unrest. It was an organised and disciplined dispute, where the rank and file trade union members followed instructions from their union officials. This was not the case in the general unrest when ordinary members dictated the agenda, and demoted their trade union leaders to mere onlookers. The strike was more likely to have been timed to coincide with the Government's concerns over the European crisis. This being the case the Arsenal shop stewards probably took advantage of the situation, and played on the Government's vulnerability to the military interest.

RETURNS TO THE QUESTION OF THE POOR
AND EDUCATION 1912-14

It is possibly because most historians have tended to concentrate upon the wider issues during 1911-14, such as the Labour unrest, and the Home Rule Crisis, that the contributions of people such as Crooks have been overlooked. Political historians have rigorously examined the leading politicians of this period, and only seem to mention Crooks in passing. This is probably the reason why there is no record that gives an insight into Crooks' attitude towards the Liberal leadership. He was not seen as important. This omission impairs an understanding of the nature of social radicalism, an ideological stance, to which Crooks, and other Labour and Radical Liberal MPs, such as Sir Charles Dilke adhered.[43] Throughout Crooks' Parliamentary career the majority of his contributions were based around the inextricable link of unemployment, low pay, poverty, and education. He returned to these subjects repeatedly, reiterating his disdain, lampooning the Government, especially the LGB, for their incompetence and ineptness for not dealing with them. Crooks believed that social reform should be seen to work. It was not enough just to legislate; adequate funding should be provided that would underwrite their successful implementation. Further, he was of the opinion that Poor Law reform was not the platform of any one party. It was the duty of all Members to relieve poverty.

During March 1912, in the Vote on Account of Poor Law Administration debate, Crooks said that 'it does not matter what happens in debate in this house. The wicked part of it is that we get up and state our case and find fault with the right hon. Gentleman [John Burns] and his Administration; we devote ourselves to criticising him, and he gets up and punches us back again, but the poor get no better off.' He felt the whole House should give up its time completely, for a month or so, 'to discuss all the intricacies of the present administration of the Poor Law as it stands'. This would not be too much to ask, to help the children of the nation, who would be after all the 'administrators and governors of a great Empire to-morrow'. Crooks repeated his concern that the LGB only acted when a man was down: 'My idea would be to save the man from getting down there. That would be a new reading of the Poor Law and of the whole system of Poor Law administration'. In conclusion, Crooks said: 'I hope I may live to see the day the House will thoroughly overhaul the administration of the Poor Law from top to bottom, and that, like Oliver Twist, it will be a memory.' [44]

Crooks was of the opinion that if the House discussed the detail of the Poor Law the debate would serve as an educative tool, and Members would be more inclined to see the issue of social reform from a more holistic perspective. It was only then, he believed, that MPs would think twice before espousing single-issue politics. Crooks emphasised that it was imperative that Members understand that a change in the Poor Law would help improve the living conditions of the poor, especially the children. It was an invidious Poor Law system, which by its very nature affected the social condition of education, and unemployment. He said: 'It is no wonder that a man like myself hates a system that treats little children so.' [45]

The indelible experience of the Workhouse in 1861 was fundamental in shaping Crooks' determination to champion the cause of poor children. They were always of primary concern in his deliberations on the administration of the Poor Law, and education. For example, during the Education (Provision of Meals) Bill in November 1912, Crooks continued to argue that the children were an asset to the nation, and should not be punished 'for the sins of their parents'. He said the argument against supplying meals for the children was that 'the father will get drunk with the money that should have bought that meal. Feed the children first ... and punish the parents afterwards.' Crooks castigated MPs for their ambivalent attitude towards the feeding of children. They may be 'exceedingly sympathetic, but it is wonderful the number of bleeding hearts there are in this House at election times.' Crooks went on to inform the House that he believed many local authorities were 'anxious to feed the children'. He blamed hon. Members — because they could not be made to do anything — for not resolving to feed necessitous children. The problem for Crooks and other social radicals was that whenever the issue of social reform was raised in the House the temperance question always bedevilled debate. On the question of Poor Law reform, unemployment, education, and pensions, the Tories persistently used the drink question to block the progress of a Bill. This prompted Crooks, in the education debate, to state that no doubt we shall 'have the old argument about the lack of parental control'. [46]

In 1914, after returning from the Empire Tour, Crooks' contributions, especially in the debates on education and the Poor Law, exemplify his radical overview and pragmatic approach to questions around social reform, thus helping give an insight into his philosophy. In the debates on the Education (Administrative Provision) Bill, and Local Government Supply, in March and June respectively, Crooks makes clear the fundamental interrelationship between poverty, education, and low pay. In his speech on educational provision, Crooks returned to the complaint he made in 1912, that of the vacillating attitude of some Members when it came to making important decisions. He said:

> What one cannot quite understand is the fact that everybody gets up and praises the Bill and says we are all human beings, and all the rest of it, and then launches off into reasons why they cannot do anything. They speak of parental control and parental responsibility, while at the same time the poor children are going without food, which is the most important thing. [47]

Crooks was scathing, turning his scorn on the LGB administration for not responding to cases of distress promptly. He ridiculed the Poor Law Order that said that 'you may not feed a person except in cases of sudden and urgent necessity'. He said: 'You cannot starve suddenly. You gradually get into that condition, but when you are starving it is very urgent.' Crooks returned to this Order, and what he considered a lack of intelligence in some Departments of the LGB, in the June debate on Supply.

Crooks, while reminding the House about parental control, and the frequently heard excuses for not feeding the children, said 'there is also parental opportunity', the opportunity to work. 'I am talking of the enormous number of casual labourers whose wages are very uncertain', who receive 'from half-a-crown to 10s. a week'. How can you preach thrift to that man? He said. In other words, Crooks was stating that you cannot expect a man who lives from day to day to keep a roof over his head, to prioritise his children's educational needs. That is why the government should act, and respond positively by feeding the school children of the poor. [48]

In June, Crooks returned to the subject of casual labour in the debate on Supply. He complained about a Report of the LGB which had never been discussed in the House; a Report that stated it was advantageous to certain districts to have a 'reservoir of casual labour'. When the Report was before the House, Crooks had tried to get a discussion started. He stated: 'The person who remains in the reservoir for the convenience of the person who requires casual labour wants feeding'. It was dismissed with the rejoinder: 'It is no part of our duty [LBG] to adjust social inequalities.' Crooks was infuriated; he said: 'Just think of that from an intelligent Department! What does Parliament exist for? What is it created for? The fact is that we are attempting to adjust social inequalities ... it does hit me on the raw sometimes when I have to face statements like that'. [49] As far as Crooks was concerned the LGB should give relief that was adequate to meet the multifarious needs of the poor. Instead, it had been shown that individual Departmental Orders conflicted on the issue of poverty relief. They were insensitive to how poverty issues impacted on unemployment, education, and low pay. This lack of administrative co-ordination by the LGB, according to Crooks, was to blame for the social inequalities that were his duty to correct.

HOME RULE 1912-14

Although Crooks supported Home Rule in the House of Commons, his main contribution to the debate was concentrated on educating the English working-class on the need for its implementation. It is therefore proposed to look at his involvement at the local and constituency level, especially in Woolwich, where in May 1914, W. A. Redmond MP, the son of John Redmond, spoke in honour of Crooks' work for the Irish cause.

In 1912, the third and final Home Rule Bill twice passed the House of Commons, but both times, it was defeated in the House of Lords. Protestant Ulster, under the leadership of Edward Carson, Unionist for Dublin University (1892-1918), prepared to resist its incorporation into a self-governing Ireland. A solemn oath of covenant was sworn to resist Home Rule, signed by Carson and other leaders in Belfast in September 1912 and afterward by thousands of Ulstermen. Early in that year, he recruited a private Ulster army that openly drilled for fighting in the event that the Home Rule Bill was enacted. On 6 April 1914, the Home Rule Bill of 1912 passed the Commons for the third time which, according to the Parliament Act of 1911, made ratification by the House of Lords unnecessary.[50] In preparation for a full-scale civil war, Carson successfully organised the landing of a large supply of weapons from Germany at Larne, County Antrim, on the night of 24/25 April 1914. [51]

A civil war in Ireland (between Irish Nationalists in the South and Unionists in the North) seemed imminent. The British Government, however, began to make concessions to the Northern Irish, and in July 1914, Carson agreed to Home Rule for Ireland apart from Ulster (effected in 1921). The Bill became law on 18 September, but was deemed inoperative for the duration of World War I.

In 1913 and 1914, the WLRA organised a series of Home Rule meetings supported by local Labour councillors, the United Irish League, and the Irish National Party. Daniel Crilly of the United Irish League, who spoke at a dinner-hour meeting in Beresford Square, in June 1913, thanked the people of Woolwich 'for the way they helped the cause', of Home Rule. The next speaker, O'Malley, Nationalist MP, declared amid laughter and applause:

> ... all this talk about "Ulster will fight,"... and the threat of civil war, "dying in the last ditch"... and so on, was all bunkum. All this agitation had been organised not on behalf of the Ulstermen, but in the interests of Toryism in England ... The Tories were desirous of getting back to power again, with the object of defeating Home Rule, and restoring the power of the House of Lords. That was the real meaning of the Ulster agitation.[52]

Will Crooks was of the same mind with regard to the Tories. He was of the opinion that on the issue of Home Rule, they were eager to undermine the will of the people. For example, Bonar Law and Lord Lansdowne had been pressing King George V to use his prerogative and force dissolution in 1914.[53]

On 25 May 1914, the United Irish League organised a Home Rule meeting at the Town Hall, Woolwich; at this meeting, Crooks shared the platform with W. A. Redmond MP, and E. Kelly MP, both representatives of the Irish National Party. In his opening remarks Redmond said:

> ... he could truthfully say that there was no other constituency throughout the length and breadth of Great Britain which he had more pleasure in visiting than the constituency represented by the long-tried, trustworthy friend and brother of the Irish people, Mr. Will Crooks ... who did not require any recommendation from him to the Irish people of Woolwich ... Mr. Crooks was no fair-weather friend of Ireland: in season and out of season he had upon the platform and in the House of Commons, championed that great democratic cause, which with his loyal assistance, was about to culminate in a complete and final triumph.[54]

Crooks' response was to congratulate the Home Rule movement, saying that they should also congratulate themselves on their achievement after twenty-five years. 'Yet amidst all their own troubles, the Irish members had found time to champion the cause of the English workers', especially on the issue of the minimum wage for Government workers, he said. Another example, Crooks told the meeting, that it was due to the Irish members that flogging in the British Navy was raised, and eventually abolished. Continuing, Crooks pointed out that, 'over and over again the English had been under an obligation to the Irish members.' Crooks also reiterated his strongly held belief that, 'the Irish workers' question was an English workers' question.'[55]

On 18 September when the Home Rule received Royal Assent, and Parliament prorogued, there was according to Alexander Mackintosh such a breach of etiquette: 'Never seen before in my time', as a journalist. 'Patriotic emotion broke conventional bound when the House, led by Will Crooks ... sang the National Anthem.'[56] Hansard records: 'Mr. Will Crooks: Would it be in order to sing "God Save the King"? In response, all the Members present joined in singing the National Anthem, the occupants of the Press and other galleries standing. Mr. Crooks: "God Save Ireland." Mr. John Redmond: "And God Save England, too."'[57] It would be an understatement to say Crooks was happy with the outcome on the Home Rule Bill. He believed that if the working-class in this country had fought half as hard as the Irish had done over the right to self-determination, they would have swept away monopoly and privilege years ago.

Further unrest, at times violent, surrounded the 'Votes for Women' campaign 1909-1914. It reached a high point when in 1912, the National Union of Women's Suffrage Societies made an historic alliance with the Labour Party, which according to Jill Liddington 'brought about for the first time in English history the great weight of the trade union movement ... behind the demand for women's political rights'.[58] Subsequently, in recognition of this alliance, the 1913 Labour Party conference declared that it would oppose any franchise bill in Parliament that did not include women: 'It [called] upon the Party in Parliament to oppose any Franchise Bill in which women are not included.'[59] This resolution was supported by TUC later in the year. Crooks endorsed the Labour Party's position, he had supported the idea of Adult suffrage all his political life; he believed women should be given the vote on the same terms as men. For example, Crooks spoke at the Adult Suffrage Demonstration held at the Albert Hall, London, on the eve of the opening of the 1912 Parliament (18 February), it was organised by the Labour Party NEC in cooperation with the ILP, and the Fabian Society. The meeting was presided over by Ramsay MacDonald, and the other speakers were Arthur Henderson, Keir Hardie, Mary Macarthur, and Charlotte Despard. The demonstration demanded 'a genuine measure of Adult Suffrage, conferring full rights of citizenship on all men and women.'[60]

In the early 1900s amongst some socialists and trade unionists, there was a genuine fear that limited suffrage for women would enfranchise those with property and strengthen support for the Conservatives and Liberals at the expense of Labour, just as the Labour Party was beginning to build an independent electoral base. This led many to support 'adult suffrage' in opposition to 'women's suffrage'. Many women, particularly members of the middle class, saw limited suffrage as an important step in the struggle to win the vote. This led to the founding by Emmeline Pankhurst of the Suffragette movement, the Women's Social and Political Union (WSPU) in 1903. Some supporters of women's suffrage were totally opposed to the idea that initially only certain categories of women should be given the vote. They formed the

Adult Suffrage Society in 1905. Its first President was Margaret Bondfield, who had worked closely with Crooks in both Poplar and Woolwich. Crooks and members of the Society believed that a limited franchise would disadvantage the working class and feared that it might act as a barrier against the granting of adult suffrage. Later in the first general election of 1910, when Crooks was abroad, Bondfield campaigned on his behalf. In the 1911 elections, she was selected by the WLRA to represent Woolwich on the LCC.[61] The Woolwich Labour Party was one of the first – if not the first – to declare in favour of women's enfranchisement. In 1904, three women were elected to the local board of guardians on a Labour ticket.[62]

By 1908, most MPs, including most of the Cabinet, openly supported women's suffrage except Asquith, who had declared his opposition to women's suffrage. The anti-suffrage line of Asquith, according to Mary Davis, 'induced [the WSPU] into launching, in 1909, a campaign of direct action which involved window breaking and, later, more serious acts of criminal damage to public and private property, courting the arrest and imprisonment of the perpetrators.'[63] The campaign for women's suffrage was bogged down by politics. After 1910, the government was faced by other crises, especially trouble in Ireland, and many MPs thought there were more important things to worry about. Many Irish MPs voted against female suffrage because they wanted more time for the Irish Question. The Suffragettes' reaction was to increase the violence. They burned down churches and bombed Lloyd George's house. When arrested, they went on Hunger Strike. And once you have Suffragettes smashing windows, and burning down churches and attacking works of art, a great mass of society had a very negative view of them, which is, perhaps, not surprising. The contribution of women towards the 1914-18 War effort, especially in the munitions factories, did more to advance women's suffrage.

What did Will Crooks think about the direct action of the Suffragettes, and why did he support the adult suffrage platform? Law breaking activities to further political ends upset Crooks. Extra-parliamentary agitation, demonstrations, rallies, marches, and petitions, combined with lobbying the House of Commons, were for him the best way to air grievances. The Arsenal discharge campaigns of 1907-8, and the Minimum Wage campaigns of 1911-12, are examples of Crooks' approach. Crooks' view on women's suffrage was underpinned by his Mazzinian radicalism and Christian values. Man and Woman were equally sacred:

> Consider Women ... as the partner and companion, not merely of your joys and sorrows, but of your thoughts, your aspirations, your studies, and your endeavours after social amelioration. Consider her your Equal in your civil and political life.... Parents, sisters, brothers, wives, and children, be they all to you as branches springing from the same stem.[64]

He believed that the cause of progress had nothing to fear from electoral reform that encompassed adult suffrage. At the centre of Crooks' worldview was his belief in the sanctity of the family, especially women and children. He said, it seemed 'absurd ... to hesitate to give women the right of the citizen', after all we entrust them as teachers and mothers. [65]

Will Crooks' contribution towards the development of the Labour Party was important in this period, and it was recognised by his colleagues. For example, the day after he introduced the Minimum Wage, three Labour MPs, two of them NEC members, came to support him on the platform in Woolwich. Henderson's remarks about Crooks' contribution to the cause of Labour were testimony to the esteem in which he was held. In addition, in recognition of his work the Labour Party selected Crooks to represent them on the Parliamentary Empire tour of 1913. Such an accolade was not given lightly. It had to be earned. Although Will Crooks was held in high regard by his contemporaries, including his political opponents, historians have not told his story.

According to the record, Crooks was a very important member of the party, a more important figure than previously thought. Why then, given his record of tireless support for the movement throughout his life, is it that historians — with the exception of George Haw's biography in 1916 — have failed to recognise Crooks' significant contribution to the Labour cause in any way? Was it because historians were influenced by Paul Thompson's erroneous description of Crooks 'as a prematurely decrepit father figure ... hardly the statesman Woolwich deserved'?[66] This statement was hardly conducive to invite further investigation. Not withstanding Thompson's fallacious remarks, Woolwich did not need a statesman; it needed a conscientious MP such as Crooks, who would represent the needs of the working-class.

8

WAR AND PEACE

It is important to recognise that the historiography of this period has focused mainly upon political questions that arose in relation to the impact of the Great War on Britain, and the experiences of a society that was unprepared for this conflict. There have been many historical studies of the circumstances surrounding the outbreak of the War and the formation of Coalition Government — led by Asquith — plus many examinations of the socio-economic impact of the war itself. These include numerous biographies of Asquith, Lloyd George, Bonar Law, and Kitchener, leading politicians who held high office 1914-1918. Historians have examined the relationship between Government, the Labour Party, and the Trade Union movement, but in the wider context of their contribution to the war effort.[1] Only a few, notably Peter Stansky, have specifically focused on the Labour Party during this period.[2]

Stansky has argued that the pressures and experiences of wartime had a great effect on the party, and that it was during this period Labour came of age. Labour demonstrated 'its ability to participate in Government'; it needed to prove it was competent in 'playing a responsible role in governing the country'.[3] Will Crooks, along with a majority of Labour MPs, was convinced 'that under the circumstances it was impossible for this country to have remained neutral'.[4] It was this attitude, which embraced old-fashioned Labour patriotism that was fundamental in determining Crooks' contribution to the war effort. An adherence to patriotism, demonstrated by a right-wing Trade Union offensive in 1917, together with the new party constitution of 1918, played an important part in the evolution of the Labour Party. By then Labour had matured and become a 'full-fledged party', according to Stansky.[5] These changes played a significant part in determining whether the party was competent to govern, and led to the first Labour Government in 1924. This was the end championed by Will Crooks throughout his political life. Crooks, it will be argued, was a more important figure in these developments than previously thought by historians. For example, he was a central figure in the 'Shell Scandal' of 1915, which, it will be argued, was a contributive factor in the downfall of the Liberal Government, providing Labour with the opportunity to serve in Coalition.

It is of particular note that during this period there are no significant local studies which discuss in detail the important contributions of individual MPs such as Crooks, and the relationship between a sitting backbencher and his constituents. For example, George Haw in concluding his biography of Crooks in 1916, states the parliamentary session of 1914-15 'invites suppression', and further comments: 'The subsequent political events of 1916 are not entertaining',[6] which does nothing to help investigate Crooks' parliamentary career in this period. One of the aims this book is to rectify the above omissions, and at the same time chronicle Crooks' twilight years 1917-1921; a period of his life not previously examined.

RECRUITMENT AND PATRIOTISM

On 5 August, the day after the declaration of war, Ramsay MacDonald resigned as Chairman of the PLP, in effect party leader, because a majority of MPs, including Crooks, rejected his proposal that they should abstain in voting for £100 million war credits. MacDonald opposed Britain's entry into the war, believing that it was the duty of the Labour movement 'to secure peace at the earliest possible moment'.[7] The great majority who refused to abstain saw this as sitting on the fence. Most Labour members supported the Government, and were for winning the war. C. P. Scott wrote in his diary, 'Ramsay MacDonald's leadership is in very serious danger. A considerable number of men including Crooks Roberts Hodge Walsh etc. are in favour of absolute support for the Government.'[8] All of them, unlike MacDonald, were trade unionists, and workingmen by origin. The fact that Hodge and Roberts were also National Executive Committee (NEC) members of the party shows how untenable MacDonald's position really was. Arthur Henderson succeeded MacDonald as Parliamentary Chairman.

At the end of August, a Parliamentary Recruitment Committee (PRC) was set up. Asquith invited Henderson and the Labour Party to 'join their forces to the other two parties to secure a common purpose'.[9] A majority of the NEC endorsed the party's involvement, and they agreed to place the party organisation, both locally and nationally, at the PRC's disposal. At the same meeting the NEC decided to engage in an electoral truce with the Liberals and Unionists, and not contest vacancies that arose throughout the duration of the war.[10] The purpose of the Recruitment Committee was to appeal to political associations 'throughout the country to give general assistance to the work of [voluntary] recruitment', and call upon Peers and MPs to speak at public meetings to promote recruitment. [11] On 11 September at a 'Call to

Arms' meeting at London Opera House, Crooks shared the platform with Winston Churchill (Liberal) and F. E. Smith (Conservative) at the 'first joint meeting of senior members of the three political Parties.' All MPs received a letter at the beginning of October from the PRC requesting assistance in the campaign. [12]

Unlike the Boer War, when Crooks supported the pro-Boers because he thought their liberty was in danger, his support for the Great War was unequivocal. It was being fought, he believed, in defence of individual liberty, 'an inherited liberty won for them on many bloody fields by their forefathers.' Crooks said: 'It is the war of the people, fighting for their liberty and for the protection of their wives and children.' Anything that 'touched the home affected them deeply', and must be defended. Crooks often said that the war was against the Kaiser, and not against the German people, and however long it lasts 'they were going to fight to the finish.'[13] For Crooks, home-life was central to his idea of Empire, and his love for King and Country defined his patriotism, which often passed into deferential conservatism. This old fashioned patriotism was shaped by nineteenth century Radical attitudes to war and peace, and continued to inform Radical Liberalism and Labourism. These antecedents describe Crooks' patriotism throughout the war, and help define his attitude towards his constituents.

In March 1915, the Government sought a voluntary agreement with the trade unions to relax demarcations, and regulations between trades, enabling the utilisation of semi-skilled or unskilled labour, thus resolving the problem of non-union and unskilled labour in a rapidly increasing munitions industry.[14] The unions saw this dilution as a means of undermining trade union conditions and principles. It would lead to industrial conscription, which eventually 'will bring the whole male working-class population under the military control of the ruling classes'.[15] Crooks shared the concerns expressed by the unions. He saw dilution as conscript labour, and believed that it was the government's intent to bully the working-class into accepting it. At the Conference on 17 March, Lloyd George sought to allay these strongly held fears, 'and promised safeguards both as to the limitation of employers' profits and as to the restoration after the War of any Trade Union regulations abrogated during the war period which the Unions might subsequently desire to retain.'[16] To accelerate the output of munitions and equipment of war it was agreed that:

> During the war period there shall in no case be any stoppage of work upon munitions and equipments of war or other work required for a satisfactory completion of the War.... Any departure during the War from the practice ruling in our workshops, shipyards, and other industries prior to the War, shall only be for the period of the War.[17]

The Joint Committee on Labour Problems after the War welcomed the clause on the restoration of trade union rights, '... these form the first substantial guarantee afforded to Labour.'[18] However, others in the Labour Party, notably Snowden, saw it as part of a long conspiracy leading towards industrial conscription.[19]

THE GREAT SHELL SCANDAL
MINISTRY OF MUNITIONS AND COALITION

During May, the Government through the intransigence of the Ordnance Department (War Office), and despite having made an agreement with the trade unions to increase the production of munitions, suffered the embarrassment of a 'Shell Scandal'; a shortage of munitions manufacture, which went much further than the shortage of skilled labour. A number of historians have debated the issue; some seeing it, notably R. J. Q. Adams, as less significant in the downfall of the Liberal Government as the political crisis which led to the resignation of the First Sea Lord, Admiral John Fisher, from the Admiralty. However, Adams does contend: 'It too [shell scandal], had a part in the political drama which brought to life both the Coalition Ministry and the Ministry of Munitions.'[20] Chris Wrigley, on the other hand, has argued that 'the shell scandal ... was a major factor in causing the downfall of the purely Liberal Government and in precipitating the creation of the Ministry of Munitions.'[21] Perhaps the most compelling argument is that posited by Trevor Wilson, quoting from the Asquith Papers, 'in which he [Asquith] gave the shell shortage equal weight with the Fisher resignation.'[22]

Notwithstanding the debate around the 'Shell Scandal', historians have neglected to focus specifically on the episode itself, particularly, the pivotal role played by Crooks, who made public the deplorable conduct of officials at the War Office towards Woolwich Arsenal. He was not happy that Arsenal workers were on short-time waiting for work, while at the same time private contractors were working overtime. The official history of the Ministry of Munitions, with the obvious intention of hiding the facts, does not reflect any shortcomings in the supply of munitions in the Royal Ordnance Factories. It states: 'Immediately on the declaration of war, expansion took place in *all* [my italics] the Royal Ordnance Factories by employing additional staff to work the shops to full capacity.'[23]

On the issue of munitions, C. P. Scott wrote in May: 'The Government had failed most frightfully and discreditably in the matter of munitions ... the matter was so vital that no government which neglected to make itself thoroughly informed as to the facts could be absolved from grave responsibility.'[24] Cameron Hazelehurst goes further, partly blaming unselective recruitment and the War Office: 'The War Offices contracts system,' he writes, 'was partly to blame, as was the reckless over commitment of the armaments firms to production targets which they were incapable of reaching.'[25] These two interpretations of events help explain Crooks' strongly held assertion that the War Office was chiefly to blame for the munitions shortage, and that the Government had a responsibility to keep itself up to date with the production of munitions.

Crooks believed that the present munitions crisis, especially the shortage of skilled labour in Woolwich Arsenal, was a consequence of the Government and War Office policies of 1907, when they introduced an 8,000 minimum on the recommendation of the Murray Report.[26] The assumption was that the Arsenal could expand to full capacity to meet the demands of war:

> The existence of the Ordnance Factories is part of the necessary insurance of the nation against the possible failure of supplies in time of war, and their primary function is to provide a reserve of productive power capable of being utilised in the full in times of emergency.[27]

Crooks and the local trade union and labour movement saw this reduction in the Arsenal's manpower as a blatant wrecking manoeuvre to impose sanctions on national workshops in the interests of private enterprise. Consequently, 'the bottom dog suffers,' alleged Crooks, to satisfy 'the demands of the dividend mongers', thus meeting party exigencies.[28] Later in July 1914, Barefoot wrote: 'I am no Jeremiah ... but I make bold to assert that a rude shock is waiting for the "powers that be" who place their faith on the findings of the Murray Commission.'[29] This warning proved prophetic — it was born out by the 'Shell Crisis'.

The May crisis predated Fisher's resignation. The signs that something was wrong in the supply of munitions began in March, when the *Pioneer* revealed that the Royal Gun Factory was waiting for work. Orders had been 'taken from the R. G. F. and placed with a firm that had no experience in the manufacture of armaments.'[30] This behaviour by the Armaments Ring in the War Office did nothing to support the appeal from the Secretary of State for War (Lord Kitchener), who told munitions workers that their services are indispensable to the State and the prosecution of the war. Crooks, speaking in the Commons, pounced upon this point, seizing the opportunity to support the Arsenal's case, to expose the conspiracy of private interests in the War Office and the shortcomings of the Murray Report:

> ... the men in the forges in the Royal Gun Foundry, Woolwich, are complaining that, notwithstanding the appeal of the Secretary of State for War for men to do their best, they have insufficient work given them to keep the press of the department at work for more than half

the time it might be ... recently an order was given for fifteen breech-loader inner A-tube guns, and that the billets were received, but only seven were forged, the remainder being sent out to be manufactured; that of another order of thirty breech-loader guns only fifteen were forged; that of another order of twenty-one guns only five were forged.[31]

Sixty per cent of the Arsenal's allocated work was being redirected to private companies.

The Financial Secretary to the War Office, H. T. Baker, in reply to Crooks' complaint, was disingenuous, and further helped fuel the accusation of a conspiracy by his Ministry. He explained that 'special work of the big forging press has not been increased by the War, but the forges themselves have been fully occupied up to the present [which was not the case] ... heavy forge work is slackening off.' Baker did not address the question of work being directed away from the Arsenal. His excuse was that some Admiralty orders were 'subsequently withdrawn or cancelled.'[32] Crooks saw the Minister's reply as another cover up by the Government.

In the House of Commons, for three months Crooks continued to complain, without an official explanation about the slackness of work in the Arsenal. In June, even the *Daily News* pressed for an explanation: 'For three months since the facts first came to light, Mr Crooks has steadily kept the facts before responsible officials.'[33] Crooks was obviously annoyed by the contemptuous manner in which the Government had treated the Arsenal question, and clearly felt frustrated and compromised; he was unable to fulfil his obligations to his constituents and carry out the job he was elected to do. Crooks explained the situation to them a week later in the *Pioneer*: 'Woolwich could do more work.' In this article, Crooks defended the Arsenal worker against slanders that they were not giving of their best, and questioned the Government's mysterious policy of the diversion of work. He was of the opinion that the root cause of the problem was private profit. 'I do not suppose', Crooks wrote, 'that even in times like these the armament making firms are positively refusing to make a profit upon work they are doing for the State.'[34]

After the war, the *Pioneer* summed up the situation: 'These firms ... working for private profit, and not for national service, did magnificently — for the shareholders. Taxpayers' money, loan money, flowed in rivers, and Big Business was on the alert to scoop it up.'[35] Without doubt, for Crooks, the workers' interest came first every time. He 'was quite serious about this'; he told a meeting of the Woolwich Workers' Union, 'because the welfare of the workers was his life's object. He looked on the working people of this country as his sons and brothers, and it was a beautiful thing to do, the least he could do for them, even though it cost him his life to do it.'[36] Evidence shows, if the Liberal Government thought Crooks' revelations about private munitions contracts would go away, they were mistaken.

Munitions supply, and the Fisher resignation, helped to make the idea of a Coalition — which was announced in the Commons on 19 May — publicly acceptable. Also, it created an 'atmosphere agreeable to the new Ministry of Munitions [founded 26 May] and its first chief, Lloyd George.'[37] It can be argued that Crooks' persistence on the supply of war materials helped bring about the establishment of the Ministry of Munitions, and contributed to the demise of the Liberal Government. The historiography of the period has neglected to record Crooks' involvement. It does not reveal his contribution, especially in relation to the setting up of the Ministry of Munitions, which was more significant than previously thought.

The challenge for the new Ministry was formidable. There was a need to establish the nation's wherewithal of the essentials needed to turn out munitions: 'machinery, raw materials and labour', in other words, how to remedy the armaments shortage. The War Office was suspicious and uncooperative: 'the War Office officials were unwilling to release sufficient powers to the Ministry.' For example, controls over the Arsenal and the Inspection Department at Woolwich were to remain for 'the present' with the War Office and no date for the transfer of authority was agreed.[38] Could it be that the officials were unwilling to relinquish benefits made from diverting work away from the Arsenal to the private contractor? It seems that Crooks' accusations that officials connived with the private sector was not without justification. The complete transfer of the Royal Arsenal to the Ministry did not take place until late 1915.

During June, a Munitions of War Bill came before the House of Commons. The object was to authorise the Ministry, and provide it with adequate powers. On the motion for the second reading, Will Crooks and Philip Snowden both spoke of the sinister aspects of the provisions relating to the labour question. Snowden used the expression 'forced labour', and Crooks 'conscript labour' to describe the intent behind the implementation of the Bill. 'It is a long time since I addressed this House' (two years); Crooks said, and he felt 'compelled to do so now'. He accused the Government of abusing and bullying the working-class to 'in a word, get conscript labour, when what the workers of the country want is guidance ... My country is in danger, and there is sufficient loyal, patriotic spirit to meet that danger in the workshop as in the field.' Crooks could not resist a loaded comment aimed at the lack of work in the Arsenal. 'I know perfectly well that the man who can finish the War is the man who does not get the job:

> What the working men of this country whom you are trying to coerce think to-day is that some people are on the make. I really think they are

on the make ... It is all very well for us to make speeches about loyalty and patriotism, but, as the working man frequently says, It is all very well telling me to be a patriot, but that is no earthly reason why you should rob my wife and family.[39]

In response, Sir J. Simon, the Government spokesman, said: 'There is no intention of using the Bill to secure by a side wind what the Bill does not plainly say.'[40]

Subsequently the Labour Party welcomed the Munitions of War Act: 'At no other time in the history of Trade Unionism in this country have Trade Unions been taken so much into the confidence of the Government and of those responsible for carrying on of affairs.'[41] Will Crooks' position on patriotism, the working-class, and production was quite clear. He believed real and true patriotism had to come from the workers every time; what did the contractor care about patriotism, or Government employees, or the country for that matter? Crooks believed all they cared about was making a profit. Speaking to the Woolwich Labour Institute in 1914, he had outlined the duty of the working-class. He said the 'workers had a duty to see that the wrongs from which people suffered were put right ... they had to seize it as a sacred obligation.' If they did not 'they committed a crime against their own class, and against common humanity.'[42] In this statement lies the essence of Crooks' political work, to deal with the sufferings of the working-class. He believed that it was a sacrosanct responsibility to represent the working-class, no matter what the cost.

During July, both Snowden and Crooks continued to complain that the Arsenal was still waiting for work. The scandal surrounding the Gun Factory continued. For example, work on 18-pounder field guns had entirely ceased, and the '4,000 ton press had only been worked on odd jobs since war began.'[43] The RGF had been idle on a number of occasions since Crooks brought it to the Government's notice in April, and since then the state of affairs had grown decidedly worse. On 1 July, during questions to Jack Tennant, Under Secretary of State for War, Snowden asked: 'Is it not a fact' that 97 per cent of munitions contracts were going to private firms and only 3 per cent to the Arsenal? Crooks pointed out that things had not changed since he complained in April regarding supply. He asked if Tennant was aware 'that the orders were actually placed [with the Arsenal], and the materials for [their] execution ...were in the department, but were transferred to a private firm of contractors, and your own men were kept idle?' Mr Tennant: 'No, Sir, I am not aware of it.'[44] In other words, the Under Secretary of State for War did not know what was going on in the War Office. Dr. Addison, Parliamentary Secretary of Ministry of Munitions, later endorsed the allegations by Crooks that the War Office was manipulating contracts, being obstructive, and secretive. Addison complained about the lack of consultation by the War Office with the Ministry of Munitions over orders, '... we have now found that Woolwich itself is giving orders to outside firms without consulting us. The situation is impossible, if we are to be responsible for supply.'[45] During the debate on the Second Reading of the Munitions of War Bill — which took place the same evening (1 July) — Crooks said, in a strongly worded speech:

> I have been in mortal terror as to the condition of things.... As to the output of the Arsenal, I declare now, for the first time in the House, that you might increase ... output by one-third. How is it that the superintendent of the Arsenal ... has to beg and pray for orders? When you talked the other day about commandeering works, and of making work compulsory, it seemed to me that you have the best object lesson at the Arsenal. You have got 40,000 men there at work, or rather more or less at work, but you may have 140,000 and still be unable, if you do not work the place and the machinery properly, to increase the output. What is wanted is not an ornament or a superior person, but a practical man.[46]

Crooks believed that in 1914-15 people in the Government had the chance to destroy the power of German militarism and neglected it. This lack of attention to supply men who were fighting in the trenches was, he said, 'not war, it is murder'. [47] He was also of the opinion that the manufacture of munitions by private firms almost lost the war, prolonged it, and added tremendously to its cost in blood and money. The Munitions of War Bill received Royal Assent on 9 July 1915.

It was without doubt due to Crooks' strenuous efforts, with the support of the *Pioneer* and Labour Party, which resulted in the London daily press being awakened to the fact that men engaged on war work of vital importance were on short time. At last, the Government had taken notice of the scandalous behaviour within the War Office. In his diary, Addison was quite clear on the issue: 'After a long discussion ... it was agreed ... to take over the Ordnance Factories, lock, stock, and barrel', from the War Office. 'It is the only thing to do'; 'L.G. has definitely decided that we must take the whole Factory [Woolwich Arsenal] over.' On the day that the War Office finally accepted the transfer (23 August), Addison and Lloyd George visited the Arsenal, possibly to meet with Crooks, to discuss the issue.[48] Although there is no extant record, the fact they were visiting a member's constituency, and the given protocol, it would be not be unreasonable to assume that they did meet. Will Crooks' confrontation with the authorities again demonstrate the pressure that a backbench MP could exert on Government.

The 'Shell Scandal' graphically illustrated the point that if Ministers wanted to quell any disquiet in the Arsenal, they had to deal with Crooks and the ASE; such was their authority on matters concerning the Arsenal. Equally, Crooks felt it his duty to represent the citizens of Woolwich the best and only way he knew, by campaigning assiduously, representing all grades of the working population, on wages, bonuses, and conditions of work. He repeatedly lobbied on issues that concerned his constituents on the floor of the House, and spread the gospel of fair play in the press whenever the opportunity arose. Crooks defended the civic rights of the people of the town. He kept abreast of what was going on in the locality, even when he was away. He kept in touch through the columns of the *Pioneer*, and constantly updated people upon his parliamentary activities. It was common knowledge that if a constituent had a problem, however unimportant it seemed, you could depend on Crooks to provide the answer. His surgery door never closed. When he was not available, Barefoot kept a note of his appointments. Crooks was a vigilant servant; he was approachable, down to earth, never aloof, and always available to serve the needs of the people of Woolwich. He exemplified a first-class backbench constituency MP. According to Barefoot, the secret of Crooks' power went beyond 'more than a Member of Parliament…[he] was a guide, counsellor and friend.' People knew that 'this end of town' was safe in the hands of the Gov'nor — Will Crooks.[49]

AT THE FRONT

Will Crooks' visit to France, for two weeks at the end of July 1915, gives an insight into what encouraged him to undertake a great recruiting campaign, which was not unanimously approved by his followers. It was an exhaustive campaign; Crooks travelled over 50,000 miles in fifteen months, sometimes speaking at thirty meetings and travelling over eight hundred miles a week. This extra-parliamentary work was organised by Barefoot, thus enabling Crooks to carry out his public duties, whether lobbying the Commons, or speaking at a function in Woolwich. It was a formidable enterprise, and it undermined his health, and helped to hasten his death.

The trip to France demonstrates that Crooks had a personal relationship with his constituents that went much further than just being their MP. This discussion of his trip, together with his subsequent tour of Tyneside munitions and shipbuilding firms, is based on articles, letters, reports, and Crooks' recollections, published (July-November) in the *Pioneer*. During his two weeks at the front Crooks visited twenty-six camps and held twenty-two 'family gatherings', as he called them. At the first meeting 'he opened his remarks by saying he hoped they were not expecting a speech, adding, "speeches are made up for people who don't know you." ' He knew most of the soldiers there, and they knew him. Crooks spent over two hours speaking to the men. On his return, Crooks said his first impression had been of finding 'a small Woolwich Arsenal in France.' For example, in the Ordnance Workshops where 750 men worked, most were Crooks' constituents, Woolwich men. He went on to recall: 'Many of the faces of the men and their names were also familiar.' On a visit to the Mechanical Transport Camp, where 1,700 London men worked, Crooks said, 'I must have known 500 or 600 personally.' In a letter to Barefoot, he wrote: 'I have simply met thousands of Woolwich men, both at the Camp and Ordnance Workshops.'[50] Over 11,000 men from the Arsenal were serving with the Army, either as engineers or combatants.

The men that Crooks met from Woolwich asked after the welfare of their wives and families at home. Subsequently, on his return, he delivered numerous messages, and made a number of personal calls, carrying out promises he had made to individual men, and acting as messenger and postman. This deed in itself is evidence that an extraordinary relationship existed between them. It exemplifies the trust and respect the people of Woolwich had for Crooks, and Crooks for them. It would have been most unlikely that Crooks would not have supported the war given the circumstances. Woolwich was economically dependent upon the wages earned in the Arsenal. The production of war materials was imperative if the town was to survive the War. Furthermore, it was a barrack town where fathers and mothers, wives and sweethearts, had someone serving in the Armed forces. The efficient supply of munitions was for Crooks a matter of life or death. It was more than a personal crusade; it was part of his duty to serve the people. His outspoken support for the war effort, more work for the Arsenal, and the recruitment campaign, was for him the best way to serve his country and constituents. For Crooks, campaigning on these issues meant shortening the conflict, and handing 'down to our children who come after us as free a country and as great a love of liberty as we ourselves enjoy.'[51]

The anxiety felt among the soldiers about the supply of munitions was the most important message that Crooks brought back from France. It was the message: 'Don't betray the men in the trenches,' that Crooks took to the shipyards and munitions factories of the North-East of England on his return. Crooks 'held 36 big recruiting meetings, on the Tyne, the Tees and the Clyde in 28 days.' He delivered 'rousing addresses' at two meetings on Tyneside on 10 August, one at the Walker naval construction yard of Armstrong Whitworth & Co., and the other at Walker shipyard. On the following day, Crooks addressed 3,000 men at the North-Eastern Engineering Works, Wallsend. In mid-August, he journeyed south to Cowes on the Isle of Wight, where he emphasised hard work and liberty. Crooks said it was a family war, a war they 'had to win. It was victory or absolute ruin and slavery.'[52]

At the end of September, Kitchener met a deputation from the Labour Party's Recruiting Committee urging them to join with the PRC and form a Joint Recruiting Committee. Kitchener 'called upon them to mount an intensive recruitment campaign' based upon special recruitment rallies and public meetings organised by the trade union and labour movement. The Joint Committee began work in October.[53] This reorganisation did not make any difference to Crooks' contribution. He was in Lancashire, urging eligible men that it was their obligation to enlist. In November at the Coliseum, he spoke at one of the largest recruiting meetings held in London. Whilst speaking in support of those who had put on khaki and blue, Crooks said, 'the day of public meetings seemed to be over',[54] possibly referring to the implementation of 'compulsive voluntarism', the so-called 'Derby Scheme.'[55]

This Scheme emanated from a tactical decision by Asquith (5 October) to appoint Lord Derby as Director of Recruiting. The reason for the plan was primarily a final attempt to head off the conscriptionist lobby in Cabinet, and in both Houses of Parliament. The House of Lords had made it clear that to extend the life of the House of Commons — which was due to end in January 1916 — would depend on conscription being acted upon at the same time. Although the 'Derby Scheme' was not designed as a move towards conscription, it was viewed as such, possibly because Derby was an unashamed conscriptionist. For three months, it served to put off compulsory military service.

Meanwhile, during the first six months of 1915, 'while the negotiations and conferences ... which led up to the Munitions Act, were in progress, the process of 'dilution', that is, of the extended employment of less skilled men and women on munitions work', was increasingly being extended under the provisions of the Treasury Agreement.[56] This was not the case in Woolwich Arsenal, where the ASE was in the unique position of being able to control dilution. Therefore, the introduction of women did not take place until November.[57] Another reason for the delay in introducing women workers into the Arsenal was the fact that workshops, toilet, and canteen facilities required building to accommodate them.

The influence of the Arsenal ASE was considerable. They had 'worked with the government's Advisory Committee on Wages' since 1909. The secretary was an Arsenal worker, and the Labour Party secretary and Arsenal engineer, William Barefoot, was the chairman. 'One former Arsenal [worker, and] ASE member', George Barnes, 'was in the War Cabinet, another worked in the Ministry of Munitions and a third', J. T. Brownlie, 'was President of the Amalgamated Society of Engineers.'[58] And there was their friend Will Crooks. The relationship between Crooks and the Arsenal Shop Stewards was one based on comradeship and mutual respect. Crooks did not interfere on the issue of dilution. He saw it as an internal trade union matter, something in which he should not get involved. His trade union background (fifty years) informed him of the practice that you do not interfere in union matters that do not concern you. Often when faced with difficulties, the Arsenal unions would call upon Crooks' inside knowledge, particularly whom to go and see, and to assist in putting wage and bonus demands to the Munitions Ministry. For example, in September Crooks helped organise a deputation by the United Trade Union Conference, comprised of twenty-two Woolwich trade unions, to Lloyd George with regard to a four shilling per week war rise in wages.[59]

It is of significance that Jack Mills, chairman of the Arsenal Joint Shop Stewards Committee, and Barefoot, staunch allies, regularly discussed Arsenal affairs with Crooks. Also, it is important to understand the powerful influence that William Barefoot had upon the trade union and labour movement in Woolwich, and thus, the contribution he made towards making Crooks a successful constituency MP. Deborah Thom notes the crucial link between Mills and Barefoot. The local Labour Party and Trades Council 'were linked to the Royal Arsenal Shop Stewards Committee through Barefoot', who was secretary of both and editor of the *Pioneer*. Further, Barefoot wrote the 'Arsenal and Labour Notes' column in the newspaper under the pen name 'Freelance'. [60] Barefoot had also been Crooks' agent since 1905. Job states that because of the 'powerful advocacy' of the *Pioneer* (in support of the Woolwich trade union and labour movement), it 'was threatened with suppression under the Defence of the Realm Acts [DORA] on several occasions.'[61]

THE RT. HON. WILL CROOKS MP

In December 1915, Asquith informed Crooks that 'I have pleasure in proposing, with the King's approval, that you should be sworn a Member of His Majesty's Most Honourable Privy Council at the New Year.' Subsequently Crooks was named a Privy Councillor in the New Year's Honours List (4 January), and was sworn 'by His Majesty's command' to the Privy Council, 'and took his place on the Board' on 27 January 1916.[62] The newspapers, except the *Pioneer*, which was noticeably silent, congratulated Crooks. The illustrated press depicted him on the doorstep of his home, in shirtsleeves, shaking hands with well wishers. The *Kentish Independent* said of Crooks: 'He ... remains — just natural.... the Woolwich member is the personification of the spirit which animates the working classes of the country today.' The *Pioneer*, even though it had reported Crooks' recruitment campaign, could not be seen to support Crooks, who was honoured for his services to the State, because most of the local Labour movement opposed Crooks' support for the Military Service Act, which was at that time before Parliament. Their behaviour towards Crooks was ambivalent. In January, the Trades Council called upon him to oppose the Military Service Act, and the WLRA condemned him for supporting the Bill. Notwithstanding these criticisms, in June, Crooks was re-elected Chairman of the WLRA, a position he had held since 1911.[63]

In spite of the 'Derby Scheme' having produced nearly 3,000,000 volunteers for the Army, 'preparations were soon in full swing for the first compulsory Military Service Act, which became law on 27 January 1916, the same day as the Munitions of War (Amendment) Act.'[64] The Munitions of War (Amendment) Act extended dilution, the engineers receiving a guarantee that dilutees would not be used to break the power of trade unions.[65] While the Military Service Act called for the compulsory enlistment of unmarried British males aged between eighteen and forty-one, this compulsion was extended to married men in May.[66] This Bill, before passing through Parliament, received a mixed reception by the trade union and labour movement.

On 6 January, the TUC held a Special Congress at Westminster Hall, to 'reaffirm the Bristol Congress [1915] resolution against Compulsory Military Service'. Its deliberations were ambiguous. On the one hand, it called for Labour members to vote upon the Bill 'as they individually think fit', and on the other, an amendment instructed 'Labour members to vote against'. The same night, Henderson, Brace, and Roberts withdrew from the Coalition Government.[67] The Labour Party's position was just as unclear. It was 'quite astounding', according to Chris Wrigley, that the Labour leaders were able to 'reconcile the irreconcilable to their own satisfaction'. The Parliamentary Party decided to oppose the Bill, 'but individual members should be free to vote for it'. On 11 January, fourteen Labour members voted for it, including Crooks, and eleven against. The following day the Labour men withdrew their resignations after Asquith had assured them: 'I am not in favour of compulsion in regard to any industrial work; I see no reason for it. As far as I am concerned I shall resist it to the last.' At the Bristol Labour Party Conference on 26 January, the party 'absurdly opposed the Bill yet approved the Labour men remaining in office.'[68]

By comparison, the Woolwich Trades Council and the WLRA were unequivocal about where they stood on the Conscription Bill. For example, before the Bill became law the Trades Council urged Crooks to oppose it:

> ... we are strongly inclined to regard the attempt to enforce Conscription as a conspiracy on the part of the capitalist and governing classes to cripple Trade Unionism and permanently enslave the working classes.... We call upon Mr Will Crooks ... to oppose the Conscription Bill in the House of Commons and to vote against any suggested compromise with the Conscriptionist Party'.[69]

After the Military Service Bill was passed, the WLRA condemned Crooks for voting for it 'in opposition to the views expressed by organised Labour'.[70]

This resolution was more an indication of local feeling, hardly a reflection of the facts, considering that the wider trade union and labour movement could not make up its mind one way or another on whether to support the Bill or not. Crooks' response to this condemnation was robust. The PLP had left him free to vote with his conscience, thus given the situation he had voted for the Bill in the national interest — it was the patriotic thing to do — not out of spite for the wishes of the local movement. Much to their annoyance, Crooks proved to be his own man when it came down to the use of conscription as a way towards winning the War. Crooks believed that the only way to achieve peace was to beat Germany, and the advent of conscription was the means to this end. He was not alone in believing this; other PLP members took a similar view, including Henderson.

On 22 January, two days after the WRLA General Council had condemned his actions, Will Crooks made his first speech as a Privy Councillor at the Drill Hall, Woolwich, in support of a grand recruiting concert organised under the auspices of the YMCA. That Crooks could have been so bold as to make a statement in support of conscription, and in Woolwich of all places, rankled with party members. Later, William Barefoot, reflecting upon Crooks' political style, gives an insight into what it was about him that exasperated his friends and opponents alike: 'Will Crooks was a tactician with methods so unique that they cut across all orthodox rules and tenets, and his originality and versatility frequently discomfited his opponents and sometimes his friends.'[71] It is of particular note that the difference of opinion between Crooks and the local party over conscription did not reach the public domain. The WLRA's condemnation of Crooks' behaviour was strictly a private issue between him and the party. To divulge publicly any rift between them would have been foolish. It would have served to stimulate accusations from their political opponents, the Tories and Unionists, that the local Labour Association was unpatriotic. The General Council's disquiet over Crooks' conduct is recorded in the Minutes of the WRLA, an examination of local newspapers shows that the story never leaked out, due without doubt to deft handling by Barefoot.

In exchange for Trade Union co-operation over dilution, the Government through the Munitions of War (Amendment) Act gave explicit assurances that the Ministry of Munitions would fix wage rates for both women and boys; 'that use would be made of the powers to fix rates of wages taken under the amending Bill.'[72] Thom points out that: 'The introduction of women workers in the Arsenal, although relatively easy, did not coincide with the acceptance of dilution', and that 'as late as May 1916 there were as many boys as women throughout the Arsenal'; women constituted only 13 ½ per cent of a total workforce that had grown to 59,900; by December 1917 it was 72,700.[73] Sir Vincent Raven, Chief Superintendent of the Ordnance Factory (CSOF), who took over from Donaldson in October 1915, ignoring outside criticism, was convinced that the introduction of women into the Arsenal must be taken delicately. As a result, women were admitted late and slowly.[74] In May 1916, the question 'with regard to the housing and the welfare outside the factories of large numbers of women workers engaged in munitions and other industries in the Woolwich area', became the responsibility of Will Crooks and Lord Henry Bentinck MP.[75]

During May, the Woolwich Advisory Committee on Women's Employment was established by the Board of Trade (BOT), 'acting in consultation with the Home Office and the Ministry of Munitions'; Crooks was appointed Chairman, and Bentinck vice-chairman. 'The primary functions of the committee ... [were to] advise and assist the Board of Trade with regard to the extension of women's employment in the industrial occupations in the district.' On 17 May, at the committee's first meeting, lodgings for women munition workers were discussed, and a public appeal to local householders to offer lodgings was launched. Regarding women's welfare the committee aimed to deal with 'the urgent question of the care of the children of married women workers.'[76] It was a good decision by the BOT to appoint Crooks to head the committee because not only was he the constituency MP, but he had a personal interest regarding the welfare of women working in the munitions industry. Crooks' nieces worked at a munitions factory in his constituency, Brunner Mond & Co., at Silvertown, North Woolwich. In addition, in recognition of his work, Crooks became a Trustee of the National Federation of Women Workers (NFWW) at its Biennial Delegate Conference on 6 May 1916.[77] It is likely that Margaret Bondfield, who was not only assistant secretary of the NFWW, but was also an appointee to the Woolwich Advisory Committee, and a good friend of Crooks, put his name forward.

Further Controversy
Meanwhile, on 10 May, Crooks spoke with William Hughes, the Labour Prime Minister of Australia, at the inaugural public meeting of the British Workers' National League (BWNL) at the Queen's Hall, London.[78] The BWNL shortened its name to the British Workers' League (BWL) in March 1917. Chris Wrigley argues that the BWL 'was very much' the creature of the Unionists. The League was established, according to Douglas, as a pro-war counterpoise to the ILP, which took a more or less pacifist line within the Labour Party.[79] It was a 'patriotic labour' organisation, set up argues Stubbs, as 'one of Lord Milner's few attempts to transform his views on Empire and Socialism into practice through a political movement.' Milner's

'socialism', states Stubbs, 'was a paternal interest in the wellbeing of the masses who were essential to the strength of the nation and thus to the strength of the Empire which was an extension of the nation.'[80] Milner was responsible in helping to raise financial support for the BWL, offering £5,000 himself.[81]

It is unclear why Crooks, Vice President of the BWL, joined what was a violently anti-German organisation. It was clearly a strategic mistake. It seems that old-fashioned elements within his Mazzinianian religiosity, especially that of duty, converged with the Milnerite social imperialist programme of the BWL. On the other hand, perhaps the League's objects on Empire, educational reform, and free democratic government appealed to Crooks' eclectic nature. The objects were:

> The establishment on a DEMOCRATIC BASIS OF DEFENCES ADEQUATE TO THE EMPIRE'S SECURITY, by the recognition of every citizen's duty to defend the life of the State... EDUCATIONAL REFORM on a national scale to secure technical efficiency combined with more democratic general access to knowledge... The realisation of FREE DEMOCRATIC GOVERNMENT based on Universal Adult Suffrage, instead of the actual Government by caucus and money power.[82]

Later Will Crooks was put under pressure to resign from the BWL when it became apparent that they were to field candidates in opposition to the Labour Party, particularly in Labour constituencies held by anti-war MPs. The Miners' Federation brought that the BWL were using names of certain Labour Members in this connection to the attention of the Labour Party NEC. When Crooks, who was without doubt a Labour man, was asked by the NEC to resign in December 1917, along with William Abrahams and Robert Tootill, he did.[83] The local party meeting in June 1918 raised the question of Crooks' connection with the BWL. Barefoot 'explained that Mr Crooks was no longer a vice-president of the League and had no connection with it in any way.'[84] In December 1916, John Hodge (Labour MP for Gorton), President of the BWL, became the first Minister of Labour in the Lloyd George Coalition.

It should be noted that the setting up of a Minister for Labour was something that Crooks and Hardie had argued in favour of twelve years before in an amendment to the King's Speech in February 1904. Arthur Henderson became Minister without Portfolio and Member of a War Cabinet of five, a position he held until August 1917, when he resigned over the issue of the Stockholm Peace Conference. George Barnes was appointed to the newly created Pensions Ministry. Three other Labour MPs, William Brace, George Roberts, and James Parker also joined the Coalition at the invitation of Lloyd George, as Under Secretary for Home Affairs, Parliamentary Secretary to the Board of Trade, and Junior Lord of the Treasury repectively.[85]

On the question of whether the Labour Party should participate in the Coalition — possibly the most difficult and serious decision that the Party had had to face 'in the whole of its existence'[86] — Crooks was open and frank. He was of the opinion that Labour men should be associated with the new administration, exemplifying to the electorate that Labour was capable, and had the ability to participate in Government, thus helping to prosecute the war effort. On this issue, Crooks once again differed from the local party, who deeply regretted the 'decision of the PLP to allow some of its members to accept office in the new Government ... and expresses its conviction that a policy of strict independence of the other political parties should be adhered to.'[87] Crooks was opposed to these sentiments, considering them misplaced and parochial. He was staunch in his belief that participation in Lloyd George's Coalition would benefit Labour's electoral claims in the future. He agreed with the majority of the PLP, they met on 7 December to discuss the issue, who thought that the opportunity of joining the Coalition administration should not be ignored. It would serve both the 'national interests and the possibility of Labour securing a greater opportunity to mould policy and exercise executive authority in important administrative positions.'[88] Crooks' opinion was to be tested in the 'coupon election' of 1918, when yet again, he sided with the PLP.

Meanwhile, throughout 1916, Crooks continued to represent the concerns of workers, soldiers, children of the poor, and old age pensioners in the House of Commons. He asked numerous questions relating to government workers: housing, air raids and compensation, holidays, holiday pay, and war bonuses; questions about the States' responsibility towards wounded and disabled soldiers, soldiers' pensions, and the Poor Law. Although most of Crooks' time was taken up with constituency affairs, he still felt that it was his responsibility and duty to concern himself with the welfare of children of the poor, and their treatment by the Local Government Board.

Life's Work Impeded

Although Crooks had a strong constitution, there was a limit to what he could endure physically. He had so overtaxed himself in the service of the State and his constituents that early in November Crooks was taken ill in the House of Commons. He was rushed home and seen by his local doctor, who admitted him to Poplar Hospital with a serious internal problem, which later required an operation. Anxiety for Crooks' well-being was universal. For example, in a telegram the King sent his regrets on hearing of the illness and wished him a speedy recovery.[89] Crooks was in hospital for eight weeks. He was held in such high regard in both communities, Poplar and Woolwich that the local newspapers, the *East End News* and the *Pioneer*, carried weekly bulletins on his progress.

On 19 January in Crooks' constituency, just after his discharge from hospital and return home to Gough Street, there was a great explosion at Brunner Mond & Co., a TNT purification factory in Silvertown, North Woolwich. According to Frank Sainsbury, 'it was probably the worst disaster at home during the first World War'. [90] Sixty-nine people were killed, fourteen of them children. The explosion, a detonation of eighty-three tons of TNT, 'razed to the ground every building within 400 yards and flying molten metal set the two flour mills alight on the ... Royal Victoria Dock'.[91] 'The sound of the explosion was heard as far away as Norfolk and Cambridge and even at one point on the South Coast.'[92] and windows were blown out as far away as Whitechapel; wild rumours were in circulation that a German spy was responsible. Following the disaster, Lloyd George and his wife visited the site of the explosion and the hospital where Crooks had recently received treatment. 'Informed of his departure, they drove at once ... to where Mr. Crooks lived,' arriving in time for Sunday tea (24 January).[93] Lloyd George, besides trusting Crooks' judgement, was well aware that Crooks' knowledge and interest in everything that affected the life of people in the East End was incontestable. The Prime Minister knew that by visiting Crooks he would get straight and honest answers to his questions. He would get an objective view of events, and thus be able to access the emergency needs of the local communities affected by the disaster. Crooks convalesced in Bournemouth and returned to his parliamentary duties on 7 March, five months after he was taken ill. In June, when he was beginning to recover his health 'he witnessed the dreadful results of a German bomb falling on a school in Poplar. The terrible scene, in which eighteen little children were killed, appeared to shatter his nerves, and he ... never recovered.'[94] The tragedy happened on the morning of 13th June — it was the first daylight raid on London by German Gotha Bombers — while Will was standing on the corner not far from Upper North Street talking. Will Crooks, who narrowly escaped with his life, describes the disaster:

> I was standing in a street not far from my house [Gough Street] ... with a detective friend of mine. Suddenly there was a crash – then another, and a third. Three bombs had fallen within 30 yards of us. Flat on my face on the ground I went. It was the safest thing to do. There was not time to reach any shelter, for I didn't know when another bomb might come, or when shrapnel from one of own guns might hit me.... One of the bombs had struck a school [Upper North Street]. Right through every floor it went, to the bottom, not exploding until it reached the infants' department. There it killed and injured a number of innocent

little ones.... some of the tiny tots fared badly. One child had its foot blown off, another its leg.... When I recovered from my own shock I mingled with the mothers who had rushed to the school to see how their children had fared. There were some ghastly sights. Portions of nine boys and girls were brought out. All that was left of one was covered by the card which tells the school routine for the day.[95]

The *Daily Sketch* reported that agonised parents made enquiries at the school and Poplar Hospital about their children, 'but in many cases, owing to the nature of the injuries, identification was impossible', such was the devastation.[96]

After the bombing Crooks disagreed with the sentiments expressed by some people, especially the mothers of killed and injured children, who demanded reprisals. He said he would not condone 'the harming of anybody's child, not even a German's ... although I have narrowly escaped being killed myself in the latest raid.'[97] In other words, for Crooks, although the bombing of the school had been a harrowing experience, it had not changed his love for children, irrespective of their nationality; their welfare meant more than anything to him, even his own life. In response to the demand for reprisals, Crooks said: 'Do you want us to sink as low as the Germans?'[98] He believed woman and children should not be made the pawns of war: 'One thing I would do. Fight them – fairly, but with all our power, and make all fight who can ... I missed speaking in the House of Commons ... last week, but on Friday [15th] I'll speak. By the living God who made me, I will.'[99]

This speech was the first that Crooks had delivered to the House of Commons for twelve months; it proved to be his last. Speaking in the debate on the Military Services (Conventions with Allied States) Bill, Crooks blamed the anti-war opposition in the House of Commons for encouraging the Germans to bomb our cities. Obviously still suffering from the effects of the bombing two days before, he was scathing in his criticism of the opposition:

> I have had a painful experience. This very day I have attended a coroner's inquiry on 17 little children, 15 of whom were less than five years old. Is that war? Did we begin to wage war on children and women? Who has encouraged them [Germany] to go on? Why, the opposition in this House. Every word that they have uttered against the war has been translated to mean we are weak, whereas we have never been stronger. [100]

Crooks was unbending in his conviction that division over the war was a weakness that served to encouraged the Germans to believe: 'Keep on a little longer, and we have the British beaten.'

In the enduring struggle to regain his health Crooks 'for a long time was able to carry out a restricted programme of Parliamentary and other public work', especially that of representing Woolwich in the House of Commons.[101] It is important, in the context of the life of Will Crooks, that the bombing of the school should be seen as a crucial and significant event. The sight of children's mangled and mutilated bodies had a traumatic and debilitating effect upon his health, it broke him mentally and physically; he was never the same again.

'THE DOG THAT DIDN'T BARK'

At the end of 1916, according to A. J. P. Taylor: 'The Labour Party was pushed into independence, willy-nilly, by the changed political circumstances which followed Lloyd George's seizure of power,'[102] and after Henderson's resignation from the Government in August 1917. Henderson believed that Labour's independence was not safe while it remained in the Coalition. An independent Labour Party also meant the end of the progressive alliance with the Liberal Party — who were split. The NEC felt that in the circumstances Liberal seats should be contested, as they would be 'less effective opponents even in their traditional heartlands by the end of the war'.[103] The introduction of the Representation of the People Act, which included important boundary revisions, and the proposal to extend the franchise to women, plus the Russian Revolution were other significant factors, which led to the new Constitution of 1918.[104] Ross McKibbin claims that: 'Fear of Bolshevism and the extreme left throughout Europe was almost certainly a preliminary to the new constitution, and international developments were the occasion for its drafting; it was ... written immediately upon Henderson's resignation.' Between September 1917 and January 1918, Henderson worked on and prepared the Party's reorganisational document, and 'paraded it before the movement' on a speaking tour throughout the country.[105]

Crooks, a close friend of Henderson, played a significant part in paving the way towards the Woolwich Labour Movement accepting the reorganisation. Henderson realised that not only the unions but also the rank and file must be consulted, and won over to the idea of change. He needed to see whether the new policies would be acceptable. It was to this end that Henderson turned to Crooks, who was seen as an 'elder statesman' of the Labour Party by the working-class. He was aware Crooks was close to the thinking of the rank and file, and they would listen to him out of respect for his sincerity. Thus, Henderson needed to enlist Crooks' support, as he would add legitimacy and help push the reforms through. But first

Crooks' opinion needed to be sought about the proposed new constitution. Henderson need not have worried. Crooks was aware that if the Labour Party was to consolidate on its pre-war base it needed to take advantage of Liberal weaknesses and the proposed franchise extension. As Tanner points out, in order to consolidate its electoral position Labour had to 'realise its pre-war potential in Tory areas where the Liberals had hitherto held sway as the second party despite their intrinsic weakness. Labour had not overcome its problems or realised its potential in many Tory areas by 1918.'[106] Crooks recognised this, believing that Labour's electoral limitations could be improved and strengthened through collectivism. It was with this imperative in mind that Crooks and Barefoot invited Henderson to put the case before the Woolwich trade union and Labour movement at a Special Conference on Labour Party Reorganisation. When opening the Conference, which was convened at the local party offices on 10 January, Crooks said that:

> the conference was the most important in the history of the local Labour Movement. We were on the eve of a revolution and Mr Arthur Henderson, Secretary of the Labour Party, was present to explain the proposed changes in the constitution of the Party made with the object of enabling the workers to take advantage of the present situation.[107]

Henderson explained to the conference the reasons that led the NEC to re-draft the constitution. He stated that since its foundation the Party had been organised 'on lines of federation of national unions, and showed how political, social and industrial evolution demanded a broadening of the constitution of the Party'.

Henderson also drew the conference's attention to the Representation of the People Act, which would enfranchise at least eight million new electors, four million of whom would be women; this 'made changes in the constitution imperative.' The 'most important proposed changes' therefore would be individual membership, enabling these women to join the Party – 'The majority of women enfranchised would be married women ineligible for membership of a trade union.'[108] 'As a notion, individual membership was not new', it had been one of the main objects written into the WLRA's Constitution in 1903, and the NEC 'had attempted unsuccessfully to introduce it in 1912.'[109]

When Crooks claimed: 'We were on the eve of a revolution', he was not just talking about the new constitution, but also about the new Representation Bill, and what was planned for Woolwich. The boundary changes and the increase in the franchise meant splitting the constituency into two parliamentary seats, Woolwich East and Woolwich West, with approximately 30,000 electors each. This being the case the local party needed to be strengthened, 'both by branch affiliations and individual membership, so that both seats could be won for Labour.' Jack Mills grasped the moment, and moved the following resolution at the Special Conference:

> In view of the importance of the second Parliamentary seat for Woolwich being contested by a Labour candidate, the Woolwich Labour Party be requested to convene at an early date a conference, as provided by the Party's Constitution, for the purpose of adopting a *second* [My italics] Labour candidate.[110]

The resolution was passed unanimously. It implied that the local party would not be seeking to replace Will Crooks – irrespective of their concerns for his health, he would be contesting Woolwich West at the next general election. This episode exemplifies the respect that the local party had for Crooks; they were ready to support and stand by him. Barefoot summed up local feelings towards Crooks thus, 'his connection with us has endeared him to us all, and we pray that he will be given renewed health and strength to continue to carry the banner of Labour in the strenuous days that are to come.'[111] The new Constitution of the Labour Party was adopted at an adjourned conference in February 1918.

It is appropriate to the discussion of the 1918 Constitution to note the historiography debate surrounding the approval of clause IV, and what importance, if any, was given to it. For example, Ross McKibbin writes: 'It is easy to be over-impressed with the socialist objective and to be unconcerned with the corpus of the 1918 constitution, whose uncharacteristic adornment clause IV was. That constitution embodied not an ideology but a system by which power in the Labour Party was distributed.'[112] The trade unions were more interested in that part of the proposed programme that dealt with Labour's problems after the war, that part that said something about the relationship with the State — the control and nationalisation of industry.[113] Ralf Miliband argues in his book *Parliamentary Socialism* 'that clause IV was the figleaf of Labourism, the first of a number of reformist treacheries.'[114]

At the WLP General Council in March, Will Crooks and Alexander Cameron were nominated as Parliamentary candidates for East Woolwich and West Woolwich respectively. A selection conference was called for April; local trade unions and progressive organisations were invited to attend and make nominations.[115] Cameron, who was well known throughout the trade union and Labour movement, was Assistant General Secretary of the Carpenters and Joiners Union, and a member of the Labour Party National Executive.[116]

Over one hundred delegates representing fifty-four organisations attended the Selection Conference, which took place on the 16 April at the local Party offices, Woolwich New Road. The WLP Executive Committee endorsed the decision in May. In June, Crooks relinquished the chairmanship of the WLP for health reasons. On his retirement he was elected the first President of the WLP, an honour bestowed upon him in recognition of the service he had given to the constituency party.

THE 'COUPON' ELECTION OF 1918

In June, the Labour Party Conference endorsed the NEC decision to end the political truce with the Liberal and Conservative parties, 'wherein it was agreed that in the event of any Parliamentary vacancies occurring [during the war] there should be no contested elections.' The party saw this as an essential prerequisite, coupled with constitutional change, towards political autonomy, and electoral independence. These changes were seen as fundamental if the party was to contest an election within the proposed new franchise arrangements, and be prepared for an election that was just round the corner; the statutory term of parliament had overrun by three years.

These developments in the party's outlook meant, argues McKibbin, that by 'the end of 1918 the Labour Party was 'independent' at last, and could look to the future free from old traditions and allegiances', and also free itself from embarrassing 'disputes about how 'independence' might be won.'[117] With these changes Labour managed to liberate itself from its association with the Liberals, and thus unfettered, it could appeal to the working-class in its own right during the election of 1918 on an anti-Coalition and collectivist platform. At the June Conference, Arthur Henderson announced that over three hundred candidates 'were either adopted or were in the process of adoption to contest seats on behalf of Labour at the next Parliamentary Election.'[118] It was with such an eventuality in mind that the WLP put in place Crooks and Cameron.

To the outsider the decision by the Woolwich Labour movement in April to put Crooks and Cameron in place may have seemed premature, especially while the country was still at war. The reasoning behind the pronouncement was that it would enable the WLP and its affiliates to concentrate on introducing Cameron, supported by Crooks, at public meetings and rallies in the new constituency of West Woolwich, which was predominantly middle-class. As early as July, unbeknown to his political opponents, Lloyd George, with the support of F. E. Guest, chief Coalition Liberal whip, 'was making preparations for a Coalition election.... regarding an "agreed programme", "jointly signed" ', by Bonar Law and the Conservatives, war or no war.[119] This agreement formed the basis of the 'coupon' election of 1918, which was called twenty-four hours after the armistice with Germany on 12 November. It was 'an election', according to Trevor Wilson, 'whose "khaki," almost "jingo," atmosphere pointed clearly to a Conservative victory.'[120]

In the election Crooks was unopposed, spending his time supporting Cameron's campaign in West Woolwich. Crooks was not awarded the 'coupon'. 'The "coupon" — so dubbed by Asquith in the jargon of wartime rationing — was a device employed by the Coalition leaders', namely Lloyd George and Bonar Law, 'to indicate which candidates they wanted elected', and as such, 'the Coupon was an almost certain passport to the House of Commons.'[121] Although Crooks was not awarded the 'coupon', it seems that if a candidate had opposed him, the government leaders would have supported Crooks. This assumption is based on the fact that although Crooks, likewise Clynes, and Thomas, had gone with the Labour party into opposition, 'the government leaders preferred to reward their [Clynes, and Thomas] wartime services by not supporting candidates against them.'[122] In this sense the same criterion was germane to Crooks' position. The Coalition leadership's decision not to oppose Crooks in East Woolwich proved to be a politically astute manoeuvre. It enabled the Conservative party to concentrate its campaign on winning the West Woolwich seat, and return Sir Kingsley Wood, the Coalition candidate.

During the four-week campaign, the Conservatives tried everything to undermine Cameron's antecedents. They even went so far as to send a circular round Woolwich stating that Crooks was a friend of the Coalition candidate Howard Kingsley Wood, and that Crooks hoped the electors would support him. 'I don't hope anything of the kind,' Crooks told a meeting held in North Woolwich, 'I am here to support Alec Cameron.'[123] It was during this campaign that Crooks was only able to speak for a minute or two; a sign that he had started to lose his power of speech. Cameron duly lost the election; the Coalition won a big majority — 5,260 votes.[124]

The turnout in the election, which was low, went against Labour, and played into the hands of the Coalition. The Coalition Unionists and Coalition Liberals returned 309 and 133 members respectively. The independent Liberals were routed - only twenty-six were returned. Despite the Liberal low poll, Labour won only fifteen constituencies in three-cornered contests. Overall it increased its members from forty-two to fifty-seven (sixty-one took the Parliamentary Whip), 'all but one of whom had been put forward by a trade union.' Ross McKibbin points out that most of the party leaders were defeated — Henderson, MacDonald, Snowden, Anderson, and Jowett. All except Henderson were members of the ILP, and held anti-war sentiments. It was the case that: 'Successful Labour candidates rode the unions to parliament.'[125] Crooks held the view that the Coalition Government was not such a 'dreadful thing.' He felt it was a pity that the party should separate from the Coalition. Crooks said that until Labour 'has a reasonable chance of coming into power as a party, [it] should seize every opportunity to direct and control.' Despite his opinion, unlike George Barnes – who joined the 'patriotic labour' National Democratic Party – Crooks was unwilling to give up his Labour roots and join the Coalition.[126]

THE TWILIGHT YEARS: POPLAR'S FAREWELL

The last two years of Crooks' parliamentary life was a sad period for his friends and comrades, who as time progressed, were ever concerned for his health. They had to watch him struggle to carry out his parliamentary work as he slowly deteriorated. Crooks, as described by Barefoot, became by 1920, 'a spectacle of almost majestic senility — bodily shrunken and emasculated, but spiritually untrammelled and unfettered, always looking forward to the day', when he could take up his work again unhindered by physical disability, 'work that he had reluctantly' to lay aside in 1921.[126]

In January, with Parliament scheduled to meet on 11 February, Crooks assured a gathering of the local party that irrespective of any impediment he would remain vigilant to the needs of Labour. Crooks said that he regretted he had lost his voice that night, and that 'he would not fail to make his voice heard in the House of Commons in defence of the rights of Labour ... Personally,' he said, 'although he was not as strong as he could wish, he assured them there was life in the old dog yet.'[127] He remained true to his promise, asking numerous questions in the House in relation to the needs of his constituents; questions around the issue of soldiers' leave and army pay, discharges of Arsenal men and women, Arsenal wages and conditions, munitions, demobilisation, state pensions, Government housing, Woolwich Dockyard, and Government contracts.[128] Throughout 1919, it seems Crooks did not suffer any prolonged periods of ill health, except in September, when he was able to take advantage of the parliamentary recess and take a much-needed rest on an Essex farm.[129] In October, his brother Robert died – which must have been another jolt to his already frail physical condition.

The following year he was so unwell that he was unable to continue his parliamentary duties, and he resigned in February 1921. In 1920 he was too ill to attend functions in his constituency. For example, it was said at a meeting held to celebrate the achievements of the Shop Stewards Committee: 'To have dragged Mr. Crooks there that night would have put an extra strain upon him which was uncalled for, although he was always ready and willing to attend at either Woolwich or Westminster on their behalf.'[130] This meeting took place in early January; the guest speakers were Tom Mann and George Lansbury. Therefore, it can be assumed that Crooks' health had taken a decided turn for the worse over the Christmas break 1919.

In April 1920, Jack Mills, who had been chairman of the Arsenal Joint Shop Stewards' Committee, was elected MP for Dartford, with a massive Labour majority.[131] Mills' election was significant in that Crooks may have contemplated resigning earlier than he did. Mills took upon himself a share of Crooks' parliamentary work, especially that pertaining to the Arsenal, and helped relieve him of what had otherwise become an arduous task. However, this merely put off the inevitable. Between July and November, Crooks only attended the House of Commons on seven occasions, attending just to ask questions on Woolwich Arsenal. There is no record of him having passed through the lobby during this period.[132] His last appearance in the House of Commons was on 16 November, when he asked a question on the proposed Arsenal discharges.[133] It was an appropriate swan song; he had dealt with the subject of Arsenal discharges in his maiden speech seventeen years before. It was a subject he had returned to time and time again over the years. Crooks announced his resignation on 7 February 1921.[134] The WLP General Council received with regret his resignation:

> No words of ours can express the regret shared; we are sure by all members of the Party — with which the retirement of Mr. Crooks was received. For twenty years he has been one of us and a great unifying influence in our local movement. His great gifts were ever at the service of the common people. *No constituency was ever better served by its member* [My italics], as is testified by political friend and opponent alike. His retirement is a loss to the Movement which it can ill afford. [135]

This statement is another example of the esteem that the local party had for their member, and underlines one of the main reasons – his unifying influence — why they stood by Crooks whatever his health. It was not a token gesture; the statement expressed the party's feelings towards a man who had given the best years of his political life serving them. Upon Crooks' retirement from Parliament, Arthur Henderson set up a Testimonial Fund. It was given 'cordial endorsement' by Balfour, Asquith, and Lloyd George, the three Prime Ministers who held office during Crooks' parliamentary life. Henderson is on record as saying the reason for setting up the Fund was to enable people to contribute towards Crooks' financial maintenance because 'his withdrawal from Parliament involves the loss of his main source of income.'[136] Charles Bowerman, secretary of the TUC, was treasurer to the Fund. The local party also set up a Testimonial Fund.

Following the resignation of Will Crooks, the WLP met to consider a proposal put forward by the NEC, who 'were of the opinion that the opportunity should be used to secure the return to Parliament of Mr.

Ramsey MacDonald.' The WLP unanimously adopted the recommendation, 'and the necessary steps taken to secure Mr. MacDonald's return.' Will Crooks sent a message of support: 'MacDonald should have the solid support of the whole of Labour. He is the Labour candidate, and we want him in.'[137] According to Harry Snell, it was an election of 'unexampled orgy of violence and slander. A more discreditable election never took place in any community…. the constituency went patriotically mad and dirty. Labour women were assaulted, MacDonald was stoned, execrated, and defeated.'[138] In his diary, MacDonald noted 'the filth used was absolutely disgusting.'[139] On polling day (3 March) Captain Robert Gee V.C, the Coalition candidate, 'was returned with 13,724 votes to MacDonald's 13,041.'[140] In November 1922, Harry Snell recaptured the East Woolwich seat for Labour.

In March, soon after the Woolwich by-election, Crooks was removed from his home, at his own request, to Poplar Hospital, Whitechapel. His physical condition grew decidedly weaker throughout April and May. Finally, after slipping into unconsciousness, Will Crooks passed away peacefully on 5 June.[141] The national press was filled with a chorus of encomiums the following day: 'The Best Loved Man in Great Britain', *Evening News Correspondent*: 'The Best Type of English Artisan', *Star*: 'A Man of the People', *Daily News*: 'A Romance of Noble Character', *Daily Telegraph*: 'The Voice of the People', *Daily Chronicle*: 'Life's Work Well Done', *Daily Herald*.[142] Among the innumerable letters and telegrams of sympathy received by Elizabeth Crooks were those from the King and Queen, and the Prime Minister, David Lloyd George. Crooks' funeral, according to W. H. Green, the Mayor of Deptford, 'was one of the most remarkable and extraordinary gatherings he had ever seen in his life.'[143]

On the day of Crooks' funeral (10 July), all traffic was held up on the main roads of Poplar, and the side streets were blocked with mourners. Thousands of East Enders lined the thoroughfares; 'all flags on public buildings and in the Docks were at half-mast', shops were decked 'out in black emblems of mourning', and all the schools of Poplar and the district were closed, enabling children to attend Will Crooks' funeral. 'The suggestion that Will Crooks should be buried in Westminster Abbey found no local support'. The feeling was that Crooks was born, married, lived, and died in Poplar, therefore he should be buried in the Borough, according to his wishes.[144] The pall-bearers included his friends Fred Butler, Arthur Henderson, Charles Bowerman, William Barefoot, and Frank Jackman, chairman of the Woolwich Trades Council, who between them represented both the national and local trade union and Labour movement. It was fitting testimony of how the movement felt about the loss of Will Crooks. He was buried at Bow Cemetery, next to his old comrade Harry Orbell, on whose grave Crooks unveiled a memorial in 1914.[145]

Legacy and Evaluation

It is important to recognise that Crooks' early political career in Poplar and Woolwich tells us significant details about the early Labour movement. In the Poplar militant agitation 1891-93, he saw the importance of bringing progressive forces together in the campaign for independent Labour representation, and the development of New Unionism. Crooks demonstrated how trade unions that were linked and organised around a Labour association could benefit the cause of a progressive platform. Crooks led the campaign to overturn Liberal political hegemony in Poplar, and with the WLRA helped challenge and end Tory domination in Woolwich. The link between the industrial and political wings of labourism became a dominant organisational force in the development of the LRC and subsequently the Labour Party, and Crooks helped pioneer the Labour movement's adherence to this strategy. Historians have failed to recognise that Crooks was central to the development of the LRC and the consolidation of the Labour Party. They have usually depicted him as a background, shadowy figure. Evidence shows this was not the case. That the party owed a debt of gratitude to Crooks' pioneering work was made clear by Arthur Henderson, when he told a meeting of the WLRA that in the educational work done by the LRC, there 'was no *greater factor* [my italics] than they possessed in the striking personality of the member for Woolwich.'

Crooks' achievements were significant, and the legacy of his life's work extensive. Among Crooks' early legacies was his contribution towards alleviating the debilitating effect of the Poor Law upon the poor throughout the country. After his election, along with George Lansbury, to the Poplar Guardians in 1893, the reforms implemented by them to improve conditions within the Poplar Poor Law Union became a model among other Poor Law authorities throughout the country. The Poplar example was one frequently recommended by the President of the Local Government Board. In addition, Crooks and other Labour members oversaw the founding of the LCC Works Department in 1893. Throughout the country, councils followed the example of the LCC and set up works departments. Thus, the employment of direct labour by borough and county councils became widespread in the late nineteenth and early twentieth century.

Crooks saw that unemployment and low pay were a major cause of poverty, hence his emphasis upon the issues surrounding unemployment and the minimum wage. He believed that the Government of the day should be made responsible for poverty, and played a significant role in placing unemployment and low pay before the House of Commons. The Unemployed Workmen Act of 1905 and the implementation of the minimum wage are testimony to Crooks' early insight into industrial relations. Also of significance were his contributions in the creation of

Labour Exchanges to deal with the unemployed, and the payment of old age pensions to workingmen. Crooks played a leading role in calling for Government intervention in the feeding of schoolchildren. He spoke in support of a Bill that provided for the feeding of necessitous school children. It was eventually passed in December 1906. After 1945, with the onset of the Welfare State, free school milk and a national network of school meals provision came into being; a measure Crooks had campaigned for since the 1890s. The provision of school meals highlighted for Crooks the relationship between poverty, low pay, unemployment, education and poor housing conditions, which he believed were all contributory and important factors in determining poverty.

The main reason why historians have failed to see Will Crooks as a leading Labour figure is that he has been incorrectly placed. Historians have moved his political surroundings, making him the councillor for Woolwich, thus obscuring his fundamental nature as a social radical and Labour man from Poplar. This misunderstanding has led to a view that Crooks was too parochial, too narrow. His contribution to the Labour movement has been devalued because he was seen as an unimportant figure not worthy of serious research. This study has shown that Crooks was an important Labour figure, and that his experiences in both Poplar and Woolwich influenced his judgement on the wider issues of unemployment, low pay and poverty. Crooks' local knowledge of the needs and interests of his constituents informed his national outlook. Thus, he was able to make better assessments because of his strengths as a local MP.

'The first characteristic of Mr. Crooks, which must strike anyone who has ever had to do with him, even for ten minutes', according to G. K. Chesterton, 'is this immense fact of the absolute and isolated genuineness of his connection with the working classes ... he expresses the claims of the populace.... He is the journeyman genius.'[146] His early experiences of unemployment and poverty put him in a unique position. Crooks was respected by the working-class throughout the country because of his genuine rough-and-ready speeches. Not only did he speak their language, but also he spoke from bitter experience. He understood the needs of working people, whether they were miners in Wales, shipbuilders in the North East, quarrymen in Cornwall, or dockworkers on the Thames. Crooks was a national figure, who by example and sacrifice put the cause of Labour above all else. The inscription on his gravestone sums up Crooks' life: 'He lived and died a servant of the People.' [147]

REFERENCE AND NOTES

INTRODUCTION

1. *Pioneer and Labour Journal*, 27 March 1914. The Weekly newspaper of the Woolwich Labour Representation Association/Labour Party 1904-1926, microfilm at Greenwich Heritage Centre (GHC), Artillery Square, Royal Arsenal, Woolwich, London, (henceforth *Pioneer*). The LRC/Labour Party correspondence is at the Labour History Archive & Study Centre, Manchester (LHASC), unless stated otherwise.
2. W. Kent, *John Burns, Labour's Lost Leader*, 1950; K. D. Brown *John Burns*, 1977; W. Stewart, *The Life of J. Keir Hardie*, 1921; C. Benn, *Keir Hardie*, 1992; H. Hessell Tiltman, *James Ramsay MacDonald*, 1929; D. Marquand, *Ramsay MacDonald*, 1977; R. Postgate, *The Life of George Lansbury*; J. Shepherd, *George Lansbury, At the Heart of Old Labour*, 2002; D. Torr, *Tom Mann and His Times*, vol. 1, *1856-1890*, 1956.
3. S. Pennybacker, *A Vision for London 1889-1914*, 1995, p.128; Brown, *Burns*, p. 65.
4. For a discussion on this tradition see T. Rothstein, *From Chartism to Labourism*, 1983. Also E. P. Thomson, 'Homage to Tom Maguire', in A. Briggs and J. Saville (eds.), *Essays in Labour History*, 1960, pp. 276-316, especially pp. 281-2, 288, for the links between old Chartists and Liberal and Labour politics; E. G. Biagini and A. J. Reid (ed.), *Currents of radicalism: Popular radicalism, organized labour and party politics in Britain 1850-1914*, 1991, p. 5.
5. J. Ramsay MacDonald, *Labour and Empire*, 1907, p. 14.
6. W. Crooks, 'Piety in the Home', in *Labour and Religion*, 1910, p. 63, HD7791, Trades Union Congress Collection at London Metropolitan University, (TUC/LMU). It is unclear which book Crooks was referring to, because research shows that a life of Mazzini was not published until 1872 – Charles Stubbs, *Joseph Mazzini: his life, writings and political principles*. The reference that fits 'more than sixty years ago' is An *Essay on the Duties of Man Addressed to Workingmen*, written in 1844, which was later published in 1875, as 'The Duties of Man', in A. E. Venturi, *Joseph Mazzini: A Memoir*. Mazzini's, *The Duties of Man*, was translated from Italian in 1862. 'The work was interrupted ... and was left untouched until 1858, when it was concluded in the *Pensiero ed Azione.—Translators's Note*', p. 6.
7. Stubbs, *Mazzini*, p. 199.
8. Venturi, *A Memoir*, p. 280.
9. J. Maccunn, *Six Radical Thinkers: Bentham, J. S. Mill, Cobden, Carlyle, Mazzini, T.H. Green*, 1964, p. 191.
10. Quoted from *The Times*, 29 June 1922, in D. Smith, *Mazzini*, 1994, p. 221.
11. Maccum, *Six Radical Thinkers*, pp. 185-6.

12. Quoted from the *Slaithwaite Guardian*, 19 February 1904, in D. Clark, *Colne Valley: Radicalism to Socialism*, 1981, p. 146.
13. *Pioneer*, 11 September 1908.
14. G. Haw, *The Life Story of Will Crooks*, 1917, p. 270. I am indebted to Len Byott (Crooks' great-grandson) for drawing my attention to this quote, and for discussing the significance of Mazzini in relation to Crooks' religious radicalism.
15. I am grateful to Jeff Williams for these insights into the formative years of his great-grandfather.
16. E. R. Pease, *History of the Fabian Society*, 1916, p. 155.
17. L. J. Satre, *Thomas Burt, Miners' MP*, 1837-1922, 1999, p. 2.
18. Haw, *From Workhouse to Westminster: The Life Story of Will Crooks*, 1907, and *Life Story*;
19. J. Shepherd, *George Lansbury*, 2002, pp. 51-67;
    N. Branson, *George Lansbury and the Councillors' Revolt: Poplarism 1919-1925*, 1979.
20. P. Tyler, 'Will Crooks and the Origins of Independent Labour Representation in Poplar, 1888-1892', in *Working Class Movement Library Bulletin*, 10, 2000, pp. 13-18.
21. See M. Mansfield, 'Flying to the Moon: reconsidering the British labour exchange system in the early twentieth century', in *Labour History Review*, 66.1, Spring 2001, pp. 24-40.
22. J. Harris, *William Beveridge: a biography*, 1977, p. 93.
23. K. Laybourn, 'Recent Writing on the History of the ILP, 1893-1932', in D. James, T. Jowitt and K. Laybourn (eds.), *The Centennial History of the Independent Labour Party*, 1992, pp. 317-336, p. 320.
24. J. F. B. Firth and E. R. Simpson, *London Government under the Local Government Act*, 1888; J. Lloyd, *London Municipal Government: History of a Great Reform 1880-1888*, 1910; A. G. Gardiner, *John Benn and the Progressive Movement*, 1925; J. Davis, *Reforming London*, 1988; A. Saint, (ed.), *Politics and the People of London*, 1989; S. D. Pennybacker, *A Vision for London 1889-1914*, 1995.
25. Haw, *Workhouse*, p. 220.
26. See for example K. Laybourn, *The Rise of Labour*, 1988, p. 18; E. P. Thompson, Homage', p. 306.
27. *Pioneer*, 'Pen Pictures of Woolwich Worthies', 20 November 1908.
28. Haw, *Workhouse*, p. 279.
29. Ibid.
30. *Pioneer*, 'A Speech in the House of Commons', 11 August 1911.
31. Ibid., 10 June 1921.
32. *Municipal Journal*, special issue, June 1897; Haw, *Workhouse*, pp.103-4.
33. Haw, *Workhouse*, p. 221.
34. Parl. Deb. 4th series, vol. 130, col. 451 (19 February 1904).
35. *Labour Party Annual Report 1917*, 'Parliamentary Report', p. 43.

1
WILL CROOKS OF POPLAR

1. F. Bedarida, 'Urban Growth and Social Structure in Nineteenth Century Poplar', *The London Journal*, vol 1, 1975, pp. 159-188, p. 159, 165,
2. London County Council, *Census of London 1901*, LCC Publication No.627, 1903.
3. C. Booth, *Life and Labour of the People of London*, First Series, Poverty 1, 1902, p. 64.
4. Bedarida, *Urban Growth*, p. 177. Also G. Rose, 'Locality, Politics and Culture: Poplar in the 1920s', *Society and Space*, 1988, pp. 151-168.

5. Bedarida, *Urban Growth*, p.178.
6. W. Lax, *Lax of Poplar*, 1927, pp.54-5.
7. See LCC *Census 1901*, p. 11. Also Parliamentary Paper Cd. 3240/1906, *Report to the President of the Local Government Board on the Poplar Union*, by J. S. Davy, pp. 7, 36-7, hereafter *Report on the Poplar Union*, (THLHL).
8. C. Booth, *Labour and Life of London: East London*, 1889, Table XIV, pp. 86-7.
9. Ibid. See analysis of "Great Poverty" and "Poverty", p. 147.
10. B. Tillett, *The Dock Labourers' Bitter Cry, An Address by a Docker*, 1889, p.5, MSS. 74/4/1, Modern Records Centre, Warwick University, Coventry, (MRC).
11. G. Haw, *Workhouse*, 1908, p.4. The account that follows is based mainly on this source and Will Crooks essay, 'My Early Struggles' in *Great Thoughts*, 24 February 1917, pp.250-51, and his reminiscences in the *Woolwich Pioneer*. I am particularly indebted to Ray Jefferd, Crooks' great-grandson, and family historian, who on many occasions discussed and helped me clarify important events in Crooks' early life.
12. Haw, *Workhouse*, pp. 6-7.
13. *Pioneer*, 11 August 1911.
14. H. Moncrieff, *Roots of Labour*, 1990, p.10; Crooks, *Struggles*, p. 250.
15. Crooks, *Struggles*, p. 250.
16. *Pioneer*, 20 November 1908.
17. Ibid.
18. Haw, *Workhouse*, p. 36.
19. Ibid., p. 37
20. Crooks, *Struggles*, p. 250
21. Haw, *Workhouse*, p. 44.
22. A Stafford, *A Match to Fire the Thames*, 1961, p. 47.
23. *Pioneer*, 11 February 1921.
24. Haw, *Workhouse*, p. 46.
25. Crooks, *Struggles*, p. 250; also see Haw, *Workhouse*, chapter VI.
26. Ibid.
27. Tom Mann and Ben Tillett, *The "New" Trades Unionism*, 1890, p. 14-15, MSS. 74/4/1/2, (MRC).
28. For a detailed view of the Liberal split, see D Judd, *Radical Joe*, 1977, pp. 121-147.
29. Sydney Buxton's majority in 1886 was 78, compared with that of Henry Green the Liberal Candidate in 1885, who was returned with a majority of 1,977. In 1885, Green secured over 65 per cent of the vote, and in 1886 Buxton only managed over 50 per cent, F. W. S. Craig, *British Parliamentary Election Results*, 1974, p. 54.
30. *East End News*, 9 July 1886. This newspaper and other local records are used extensively throughout this period, and are held at THLHL.
31. G. D. H. Cole and R. Postgate, *The Common People*, 1946, p. 413.
32. G. Stedman Jones, *Outcast London*, 1971, pp. 296, 302-3. Stedman Jones source is from A. C. Pigou (ed.), *Memorials of Alfred Marshall*, 1925, p. 273.
33. N. Thompson, *Political Economy and the Labour Party*, 1996, p. ix.
34. E. Hopkins, *Working-Class Self-Help in Nineteenth-century England*, 1995, p. 141.
35. P. Thompson, *Socialists, Liberals and Labour: The Struggle for London*, 1967, p. 25.
36. *East End News*, 28 May 1887.
37. J. Adderley, *In Slums and Society*, 1916, p. 199, 208.
38. J. Mazzini, *An Essay On the Duties of Man: Addressed to Workingmen*, 1898, p. 145.

39. C. Cook and J. Stevenson, *Modern British History 1714-1987*, 1988, pp. 21, 149.
40. L. Barrow and I. Bullock, *Democratic Ideas and the British Labour Movement 1880-1914*, 1996, p. 2.
41. *Morning Leader*, 15 November 1904.
42. *Survey of London*, 1994, vol. XLIV, p. 592.
43. Bedarida, *Urban Growth*, pp. 186-7.
44. Haw, *Workhouse*, pp. 64-5.
45. *East End News*, 9 October 1888.
46. Ibid., 18 December 1888.
47. Ibid., 22 January 1889.
48. Ibid., 1 February 1889.
49. H. A. Clegg, A. Fox, and A. F. Thompson, *The History of British Trade Unions since 1889*, vol..1, 1964; K. Coates and T. Topham, *The Making of the Labour Movement*, 1994; Kapp, *Eleanor*; J. Lovall, *Stevedores and Dockers*, 1969, and A. L. Morton & G. Tate, *The British Labour Movement*, 1956.
50. *East End News*, 20 August 1889.
51. Morton & Tate, *Labour Movement*, p. 191.
52. Haw, *Workhouse*, p. 67-69.
53. *Amalgamated Toolmaker – Monthly Record*, 'Character Sketch: Will Crooks', p. 5, HD6661 M5 191, (TUC/LMU). I am indebted to Brigit Collins for this reference.
54. *Royal Commission on Labour*, Cd 6078, vol. V, 1892, Q. 4925-38; quoted in Clegg, Fox and Thompson, *British Trade Unions*, vol. I, pp. 73-74.
55. Clegg, Fox and Thompson, *British Trade Unions*, pp. 77-82.
56. J. Saville, 'Trade Unions and Free Labour: The Background to the Taff Vale Decision', in A. Briggs and J. Saville (eds.), *Essays in Labour History*, 1967, pp. 317-350, p, 317.
57. J. Belcham, *Industrialization and the Working Class*, 1991, p. 236.
58. *East End News*, 20 May 1890.
59. J. Gillespie, 'Municipalism, Monopoly and Management: The Demise of 'Socialism in One County', 1918-1933', in A. Saint (ed.), *Politics and the People of London*, 1989, pp. 103-125, p. 104.
60. Clark, *Colne Valley*, p. 2.
61. B. Lancaster, *Radicalism, Cooperation and Socialism: Leicester working-class politics 1860-1906*, 1987, p. 112.
62. Stafford, *A Match*, p. 48.
63. Fabian Society Membership File, (BLPES).
64. *East End News*, 4 April 1893.
65. P. Adelman, *Radicalism*, p. 132.
66. Crooks replaced T. J. Davies on 26 February 1891, London Trades Council Minute Book 6, 3 January 1889 - 2 April 1891 (TUC/LMU).
67. J. Jacobs, *London Trades Council 1860-1950*, 1950, p. 72.
68. J. Hinton, *Labour and Socialism, A History of the British Labour Movement 1867-1974*, 1983, pp. 54-55.
69. Ibid., p. 55.
70. E. J. Howarth and M. Wilson, *West Ham*, 1907, pp. 149-52.
71. J. Shepherd, 'Labour and parliament: the Lib.-Labs. as the first working-class MPs. 1885-1906', in Biagini and Reid, *Currents of Radicalism*, 1991, pp. 187- 213, p. 188.
72. A. K. Russell, *Liberal Landslide*, 1973, p. 37.
73. *East End News*, 3 April 1891.
74. Cole and Postgate, *Common People*, p. 423.

75. Fabian Society Membership File (BLPES).
76. J. Morley, *Life of Gladstone*, 1903, vol. III, p. 462.
77. Adelman, *Radicalism*, p. 129.
78. *East End News,* 16 October 1891. The Poplar Group consisted of nine constituencies: (Whitechapel, S.W. Bethnal Green, N.E. Bethnal Green, Bow and Bromley, Mile End, Stepney, St. George's, Limehouse, and Poplar); and the Hackney Group comprising eight constituencies (Central Hackney, South Hackney, Haggerston, Hoxton, N. West Ham, S. West Ham, Walthamstow, and Epping).
79. H. Pelling, *Social Geography of British Elections,* 1967, Table 3, p. 43.
80. D. Tanner, 'Ideological debate in Edwardian labour politics: radicalism, Revisionism and socialism', in Biagini and Reid, *Currents of Radicalism,* 1991, pp. 271-293, p. 273.
81. *East End News*, 13 November 1891.
82. H. Bland, 'The Outlook', in *Fabian Essays in Socialism,* G.B. Shaw (ed.), 1889, p. 262. For his career see *Dictionary of Labour Biography,* vol. 5, pp. 25-9.
83. Crooks to Pease, 11 December 1891, Fabian Society correspondence A7/1, f 60.
84. *East End News,* 1, 8 January 1892.
85. Haw, *Workhouse*, pp. 75-6. Among the subscribers to the Wages Fund were the Amalgamated Society of Engineers, the Stevedores' Labour Protection League, the London Saddle and Harness Makers' Society, the Postmen's Federation, the London Carmen's Trade Union, the Friendly Society of Ironfounders, the Municipal Employees' Association, and the Amalgamated Society of Railway Servants, Ibid., p. 78.
86. *East End News,* 8 January 1892.
87. Ibid.
88. Ibid., 5 February 1892.
89. Ibid.
90. A. J. Reid, 'Old Unionism reconsidered: the radicalism of Robert Knight, 1880-1914', in Biagini and Reid, *Currents of Radicalism,* pp. 214-243, p. 242.
91. *East End News,* 5 April 1892.
92. Ibid. It should be pointed out that the London programme of the progressives foreshadows Fabian involvement in Municipal politics. The basis of the measures of the Local Government Bill of 1888 was in a resolution moved by Prof. James Stuart MP, seconded by George Howell, and supported by James Firth, at the London Liberal and Radical Union in 1888. *East End News,* 24 February 1893.
93. Ibid.
94. Alf Graham to *East End News*, 30 March 1893, in *East End News,* 4, 7 April 1893.
95. Cook and Stevenson, *Modern British History*, p. 74.
96. E. Hobsbawm, 'The Fabians Reconsidered', *Labouring Men,* 1967, p. 251, 235, 253. For another revisionist view: A. McBrier, *Fabian socialism and English politics,* 1962.
97. R. J. Harrison, *The Life and Times of Sidney and Beatrice Webb 1858-1905: The Formative Years,* 2000, p. 308.
98. M. Bevir, 'Fabian Permeation and Independent Labour, *The History Journal,* 39, 1, 1996, pp. 179-196, pp. 179-8, also see note 1. p. 179. I am indebted to Professor Bevir for helping me locate this article.
99. *East End News,* 5 April 1892.
100. Ibid.
101. Ibid.
102. Ibid.
103. Adelman, *Radicalism*, p. 10.
104. Fabian Tract No. 104, October 1900, p. 4.
105. *East End News,* 6 May 1892.

106. D. Howell, *British Workers and the Independent Labour Party 1888-1906*, 1983, pp. 254-55. The ILP inaugural conference was held in Bradford, 14-16 January 1893, Ibid. Appendix 1.
107. *East End News*, 17 March 1893. Those attending the meeting included, Jack Helps, Ben Tillett, Bob Banner, Will Crooks, Harry Kaye and Will Thorne.
108. Howell, *British Workers*, p. 258.
109. The draft manifesto included: 'The abolition of plural voting ... Reform of the Poor Law ... to further legislation, without delay in favour of equalization of rates throughout London.... Classification of the Indoor Poor.... Trade Union Wages and Hours. All work to be carried out by the Board without the intervention of the contractor.... Adequate pensions for the worthy poor in lieu of the present Poor Law relief. Sick and Maimed not to be Pauperised.... All children left in the care of the Board.... shall be trained in special institutions (*i.e.,* the cottage home system) or boarded out in the country and sent to efficient public schools. The Board to make every endeavor to find temporary and honorable employment.' *East End News,* 24 February 1893.
110. Ibid., *East End News,* Abrahams, (Amalgamated Society of Carpenters and Joiners), A. Mercer, (LCC, Seamen and Firemen's Union), Rickcard, (Engine Drivers and Firemen's Union), S. Simms (Amalgamated Stevedores' Labour Protection League), Frank Thurston, general secretary, (Engine Drivers' and Firemens' Union). Thurston became President of the League in 1896. Poplar Labor League, *Fourth Annual Report & Statement of Accounts,* 1896, p. 9.
111. *East End News,* 10 March 1893.
112. Ibid.
113. Ibid. Jack Helps (Dockers' Union) seconded, and Will Thorne (general secretary, Gasworkers' Union), A. Humphrey (general secretary, Navvies' Union), and W. Godfrey (Executive Committee Dockers' Union), supported the resolution.
114. Ibid.
115. Ibid., 14 March 1893.
116. Ibid.
117. Ibid., 17 March 1893.
118. Ibid.
119. Ibid., 21 March 1893.
120. Ibid.
121. Ibid., 28 April 1893.
122. Ibid.
123. Howell, *British Workers,* p. 363.
124. J. Lawrence, 'Popular politics and the limitations of party: Wolverhampton 1867-1900', in Biagini & Reid, *Currents in Radicalism,* pp. 65-85, p. 85.

2
GUARDIAN OF THE POOR

1. J. Davis, 'The Progressive Council, 1889-1907', in A. Saint (ed.), *Politics and the People of London,* 1989, pp.27-48, p. 27.
2. J. Davis, *Reforming London: The London Government Problem 1855-1900,* 1988. p. 31.
3. S. Pennybacker, 'The millennium by return of post', in D. Feldman and G. Stedman Jones (eds.), *Metropolitan: London,* 1989, pp. 129-162, p. 130.
4. Davis, 'Progressive Council', p. 27.
5. Davis, *Reforming,* p. 115.
6. London Liberal and Radical Union, *Second Annual Report* 1888-9, p. 2 (BLPES).

REFERENCES AND NOTES   231

7. *East End News*, 9 October 1888.
8. Haw, *Workhouse*, pp. 92-3; Davis, 'Progressive Council', p. 35.
9. London County Council, *Minutes of Proceedings*, 25 March 1898, p. 416, (hereafter *LCC Minutes*).
10. Vestry of the Parish of All Saints, Poplar Minute Book 1888 - 1903, p. 23, (THLHL).
11. *East End News*, 13 August 1889.
12. Fabian Society: election leaflets of candidates for the London County Council election of 1892, Coll. Misc. 0839, (BLPES).
13. Trustees of the Parish of All Saints, Poplar, Minute Book 1889-93, 12 March 1890, p. 42, POP 85 (THLHL), hereafter Trustee Minutes.
14. *East End News*, 6 January 1891.
15. Ibid.
16. Trustee Minutes, 1 January 1891, p. 124.
17. *East End News*, 3 February 1891.
18. Trustee Minutes, 29 January 1891, pp. 125-33; *East End News*, 3 February 1891.
19. Ibid., 16 December 1891, pp. 224-229. The Special Committee of the Trustees who looked into this were, W. Bineham, Chairman of Special Committee, I. Sinclair, John Gibbon, Will Crooks, F. Kidd, William Turiff - members, and John Waters, Hon. Secretary of the Trustees; Report, *East End News*, 22 December 1891.
20. *East End News*, 22 December 1891.
21. LCC Election Address, 1892, Fabian Society, Coll., Misc. 0839, (BLPES).
22. Poplar Labor League, *Annual Report 1896*, p. 8.
23. Ibid.
24. Ibid., Annual Reports, 1896-1906.
25. Fabian Tracts 30-37. For a complete list of Fabian publications, 1884-1915, see E Pease, History of the Fabian Society, 1916, Appendix IV, pp. 273-280; M. Cole, The Story of Fabian Socialism, 1961, pp. 18-19; Fabian Tract 26, Questions for London County Councillors, Fabian Society, Coll., Misc. 0839, (BLPES).
26. LCC Election Address, 1892; *Illustrated London News*, 23 February 1892
27. *East End News*, 8 March 1892.
28. G. L. Bernstein, *Liberalism and Liberal Politics in Edwardian England*, 1986, p. 71.
29. Ibid.
30. C. Wrigley, 'Liberals and the Desire for Working-Class Representatives in Battersea, 1886-1922', in K. D. Brown, *Essays in Anti-Labour History*, 1974, pp. 126-158, p. 133.
31. A.G. Gardiner, *John Benn and the Progressive Movement*, 1925, p. 148.
32. Ibid., pp. 147, 151-2.
33. G. Clifton, 'Members and Officers of the LCC, 1889-1965', in Saint, *Politics*, pp. 1-26, Table 1, p. 3.
34. Davis, 'Progressive Council', p. 44.
35 Quoted in Gardiner, *John Benn*, p. 151.
36 *Reviews of Reviews*, vol.V, 1892, p. 328.
37. Besides Will Crooks and Ben Tillett the other Fabians elected to the Council were Sidney Webb for Deptford, Frank Smith for North Lambeth, William Steadman for Stepney, Fred Henderson for Clapham, and F.C. Baum for North Kensington. See A. M. McBriar, *Fabian Socialism and English Politics 1884-1918*, 1962, p. 198.
38. *LCC Minutes*, 22 March 1892, pp. 227-234.
39. P. Thompson, *Socialists*, p. 223.
40. Crooks to MacDonald, 1 February 1898, NRO 30/69/1142, (National Records Office).
41. *LCC Minutes*, 22 March 1892, p. 241.

42. Presented Papers to the Bridges Committee, 20 February 1889, LCC/MIN/1284, London Metropolitan Archive (LMA).
43. Report, *East End News*, 19 March 1889.
44. Ibid., 25 March 1889.
45. *LCC Minutes*, 19 March 1889, p. 60.
46. Report, *East End News*, 22 March 1889.
47. Ibid.
48. Ibid.
49. *East End News*, 22 March 1889. Charles Ritchie was Conservative MP for Tower Hamlets 1874-1888, Tower Hamlets (St George's) 1885-1892, and Croydon 1895-1905. He was President of the Local Government Board, August 1886-August 1892: President of the Board of Trade, June 1895-November 1900: Secretary for Home Affairs 1900-August 1902, and Chancellor of the Exchequer 1902-October 1903. He resigned in 1903 on the tariff reform issue.
50. *LCC Minutes*, 25 March 1889, p. 93.
51. Report of Bridges Committee to LCC, *LCC Minutes*, 18 June 1889, p. 432.
52. Report, *East End News*, 21 June 1889.
53. *LCC Minutes*, 24 February 1891.
54. The tender was accepted 3 November 1891, *LCC Minutes*, vol. II, p. 1091; the Solicitor was instructed to settle the contract, Bridges Committee Minute Book, 12 November 1891, LCC/MIN/1273, p. 286 (LMA); the contract was sealed 24 November, *LCC Minutes*, vol. II, p. 1176.
55. McBriar, *Fabian Socialism*, p. 245, fn. 4.
56. Pennybacker, *A Vision*, 1995, p. 12.
57. Brown, *John Burns*, p. 77.
58. Bridges Committee Minute Book, 11 February 1892, p.444, LCC/MIN/1273, London Metropolitan Archive (LMA).
59. Ibid. 1 April 1892, p. 529. Other members of the Woolwich Ferry Subcommittee were Richard Grosvenor, Chairman, who was also Chairman of the Bridges Committee, and Tom Chambers, an elected Alderman, who stood as a Woolwich Labour Representative League candidate for the LCC in 1892, and was defeated. J. Attfield, *With Light of Knowledge*, 1981, p. 20. The other Fabian councillor on the Bridges Committee was Bill Steadman (Stepney), Secretary of the Bargebuilders' Union.
60. Amalgamated Engine and Cranedrivers' Union, 6d. an hour; United Plumbers' Union, 10d; Amalgamated Society of Chippers, Drillers and Navvies, 9d; Operative Bricklayers, 9d; Amalgamated Society of Carpenters and Joiners, 9d; United Smiths' and Hammermen, 6d. Bridge Committee Minute Book, 27 April 1892, LCC/MIN/1273, p. 556, (LMA).
61. Haw, *Workhouse*, p. 86. The minutes of the first Labour Bench meeting, according to Haw, were in the possession of Will Crooks; possibly stolen along with other correspondence from his grandson in Cornwall.
62. Ibid., p. 87.
63. *LCC Minutes*, 3 May 1892, p. 394.
64. Report, *Daily Chronicle*, quoted in Haw, *Workhouse*, pp. 88-9.
65. *LCC Minutes*, 31 May 1892, p. 492.
66. Report of Special Committee on Fair Wages, *LCC Minutes*, 26 July 1892, p. 756.
67. Adjourned Report, *LCC Minutes*, 16 December 1892, pp. 1225-32.
68. Poplar Labor League, *Annual Report 1897*, p. 5.
69. Ibid.
70. McBriar, *Fabian Socialism*, p. 226.
71. *LCC Minutes*, 28 May 1893, p. 356.

72. McBriar, *Fabian Socialism*, p. 226.
73. *LCC Minutes*, 21 March 1899, p. 397.
74. *Municipal Journal*, special issue, June 1897; Haw, *Workhouse*, pp. 103-4.
75. Will Crooks, *Dictionary of National Biography*, 1968, 7th Series, p. 138.
76. Pennybacker, *A Vision*, 1995, pp. 11-12.
77. Brown, *John Burns*, 1977, p. 66.
78. E. Hobsbawn, *Worlds of Labour*, 1984, pp. 162-3.
79. Clifton, 'Members and Officers', p. 3.
80. Pennybacker, *A Vision*, 1995, p. 115-6.
81. Davis, 'Progressive Council', p. 47.
82. *East End News*, 6 March 1895.
83. *LCC Minutes*, 1895-1902.
84. Ibid., 13 November 1894, vol. II, p. 1150.
85. Ibid., 30 July 1895, p. 771.
86. *East End News*, 10 August 1895.
87. *LCC Minutes*, 3 May 1898, p. 495.
88. *East End News*, 20 April 1900.
89. *LCC Minutes*, 23 July 1901, vol. II, p. 1024
90. *East End News*, 2 September 1902.
91. Ibid; *LCC Minutes*, 21 October 1902, vol. II, p. 1504.
92. *East End News*, 30 August 1902.
93. Ibid, 2 September 1902.
94. Haw, *Workhouse*, p. 98.
95. TEB Minute Book, 8 May 1893, p. 4, TEB/4, (LMA).
96. TEB/5, 19 March 1894, pp. 160-1; TEB/6, 25 March 1895, p. 86.
97. A. Saint, 'Technical Education and the Early LCC', in *Politics*, p.77.
98. Domestic Economy Subcommittee Agenda, 6 May 1896, p. 2, TEB/57.
99. Scholarships Subcommittee Agenda's, TEB/58, passim.
100. George Ford to the Science, Art and Technical Subcommittee (SA&T), 16, 22 January, 6 October 1896, SA&T Minute Book, 28 October 1896, TEB/ 46.
101. SA&T Agenda 'Technical Institute for Poplar', 5 April 1897, p. 19, TEB/1.
102. Report of the Technical Education Board, 15 May 1899, *LCC Minutes*, 27 June 1899, vol. II, pp. 940-1.
103. Poplar Labor League, *Annual Report 1898*, p. 6.
104. *LCC Minutes*, 10 April 1900, pp. 574-5.
105. Ibid., 23 July 1901, vol. II, pp. 1028-9.
106. *Municipal Journal*, 26 January 1906.
107. *Morning Leader*, 15 November 1904.
108. Haw, *Workhouse*, p. 105. The record shows he was elected to the LCC on 5 March 1892, *East End News*, 8 March 1892. Crooks and Lansbury attended their first meeting of the Poplar Guardians on 3 May 1892; Poplar Union of Poor Law Guardians, Minute Book, vol. XII, p.103 (LMA).
109. *Transcript of the Shorthand Notes taken at the Enquiry ordered by the Local Government Board into the Administration of the Poor Law in the Poplar Union, Cd. 3274/1906*, p. 278, hereafter *Shorthand Notes*, (THLHL).
110. C. Tagg and L. Glenister, *London Laws and Byelaws*, 1907, p. 898. See voters' list precepts 5 and 6, for ten pounds and household qualifications.
111. B. Horman, *Good Old George*, 1990, p.46; Haw, *Workhouse*, p. 106.
112. Lansbury, *My Life*, 1928, p. 134.
113. *Shorthand Notes*, p. 279

114. Haw, *Workhouse*, p. 144.
115. Ibid., Quoted, p. 148.
116. Ibid., p. 112.
117. *Shorthand Notes*, p. 279.
118. Haw, *Workhouse*, p. 112.
119. Ibid., pp. 72-3.
120. *Shorthand Notes*, vol. 2, p. 280.
121. Lansbury, *Life*, p. 136.
122. Haw, *Workhouse*, p.108.
123. G. Lansbury, *Looking Backwards and Forwards*, 1935, p. 201.
124. Poplar Union of Poor Law Guardians, Minute Book, vol. XL, 2 May, 1894, p. 60, (hereafter PU Minute Book), LMA.
125. Ibid., p. 66, 30 May, 85.
126. Ibid., 3 October, p.205, 12 December, pp. 270-1.
127. Ibid., 1, March, p, 25, 21 March, p. 17, 21.
128. Ibid., vol. XLI, 1895, pp. 1, 3.
129. Ibid., 1 July 1897, p. 104.
130. Ibid., vol. XLIV, 2 November 1898, p. 381.
131. Ibid., vol. XLII, 27 June 1896, p. 112.
132. Ibid., 22 August, p. 165.
133. Ibid., 1 January 1896, p. 8.
134. Ibid., 29 January, p. 35.
135. Ibid., 11 March, p. 69.
136. Local Government Board to Poplar Union, PU Minute Book, 5 January, vol. XLIII, 13 January 1897, p. 11.
137. W. Mornington and F. V. Lampard, *Our London Poor Law Schools*, 1898, p. 40.
138. Lansbury, *My Life*, p. 150.
139. PU Minute Book, 21 April 1897, p. 102.
140. Metropolitan Asylum Board Minute Book, May 1898-9, vol. 32, p. 115. Hereafter *MAB Minutes*, (LMA); Poplar Labor League, *Annual Report*, 1899, p. 11; Haw, *Workhouse*, p. 130.
141. *MAB Minutes*, vol. 32, pp. 124, 125, 129-31.
142. LCC, Industrial and Reform Schools (I&RS) Committee Minutes, 20 March 1901, p. 57, LCC/MIN/8096. In 1898, the boys in its care were given free admission from the LCC's industrial schools to the trade classes at Battersea, Woolwich, and Clerkenwell Polytechnic's, I&RS Minutes, 19 December 1898, pp.353-4, LCC/MIN/8094, (LMA).
143. Children's Committee Minute Book (CC. Minutes), 23 May 1898, vol.1, p. 229, MAB/425; *MAB Minutes*, 25 June 1904, vol. 38, p. 357.
144. The Guardians in the Metropolis deemed such accommodation as unsatisfactory. In the twelve months October 1896-7, 'between 3000 and 3550 cases were sent from the police courts to the workhouses...during any one week in the care of the guardians [there] was nearly 300', CC. Minutes, 11 July 1898, p. 261.
145. Quoted in Haw, *Workhouse*, p. 136.
146. CC. Minutes, 9 23 January 1899, vol. 2, pp. 7-8, 19; 25 March, 17 April 1899, pp. 64, 74, MAB/455.
147. Haw, *Workhouse*, pp. 136-7.
148. CC. Minutes, 29 May 1899, pp. 87-8, 26 June 1899, pp. 138, 165. Crooks was elected Chairman of the Special Purposes Subcommittee, and the Camberwell Green Subcommittee in June 1899, CC. Minutes, 26 June 1899, pp. 110, 112, MAB/455.
149. *LCC Electoral Address 1892*.
150. Quoted in Poplar Labor League, *Annual Reports, 1898, 1899*, p. 11.

REFERENCES AND NOTES 235

151. J. Harris, *Unemployment and Politics*, 1972, p. 193.
152. *Report on the Poplar Union*, p. 5.
153. R. Postgate, *George Lansbury*, 1940, p. 77.
154. *Report on the Poplar Union*, p. 1.
155. *Pioneer*, 15 June 1906.
156. Shepherd, *George Lansbury*, Oxford, p. 63
157. For his evidence to the Poplar Enquiry, see *Shorthand Notes*, vol. 2, pp. 277-413.
158. N and J. Mackenzie (eds.), *The Diary of Beatrice Webb 1892-1905*, vol. II, 15 June 1903, 1983, p. 285
159. J Beveridge, *An Epic of Clare Market*, 1960, p. 41.
160. Mackenzie, *Diary*, vol. II, 14 October 1905, p. 354
161. ———— *Diary 1905-1924*, vol. III, 19 March 1906, 1984, pp. 33-4
162. Ibid., p. 64.
163. Shepherd, *George Lansbury*, p. 67.
164. PU Minute Book, vol. LIV, 1906/7, 3 April 1907, p. 655.
165. Haw, *Workhouse*, p. 279.
166. Ibid., p. 280.
167. J. Belcham, *Industrialisation*, p. 213; Haw, *Workhouse*, pp. 280-1.
168. Woolwich Labour Representation Association, Executive Report and Statement of Accounts for the year 1907, *Annual Report*, May 1908, p.2.
169. Haw, *Workhouse*, p. 280.
170. Lansbury Press cuttings (2), f. 303, (BLPES); Haw, *Workhouse*, p. 285.
171. Haw, *Workhouse*, p. 289.

3
UNEMPLOYMENT AND THE POOR LAW

1. *Report on the Poplar Union*, p. 8.
2. *Royal Commission on Labour: Minority Report* 1893-4, by William Abraham MP (Mabon), Micheal Austin MP, James Mawdsley MP, and Tom Mann, p. 22.
3. *Royal Commission on the Poor Laws and the Relief of Distress*, Vol. XIX, Cd. 4795/1909. *Report on the Effects of Employment or Assistance given to the Unemployed since 1886 as a Means of Relieving Distress outside the Poor Law*, by Cyril Jackson and the Rev. J. C. Pringle, p. 655, (henceforth Jackson and Pringle).
4. Ibid.
5. P. A. Ryan, 'Poplarism' 1894-1930, in Pat Thane, *The Origins of British Social Policy*, 1978, pp. 56-83, p. 57.
6. Haw, *Workhouse*, p. 220.
7. Ibid., p. 223.
8. *East End News*, 12 February 1904.
9. F. Bedarida, 'Urban Growth', p. 172.
10. Stedman-Jones, *Outcast London*, p. 48; Bedarida, 'Urban Growth', p. 177.
11. *Times Weekly*, 16 February 1895.
12. Haw, *Workhouse*, pp. 219-40.
13. P. A. Ryan, 'Poplarism', pp. 57-58; B. Keith-Lucas, 'Poplarism', in *Public Law*, 1962 (Spring), pp. 52-80.
14. Harris, *Unemployment and Politics*, 1972, *passim*.
15. J. Chamberlain, *Pauperism and Distress*: Circular Letter to Boards of Guardians, 15 March 1886, in W. Chance, *The Better Administration of the Poor Law*, 1895, Appendix J, pp. 242-3;

J. T. Dodd, *The Unemployed and the Powers of the Guardians of the Poor*, Appendix, Circular, 15 March 1886, 1903, pp. 15-19.
16. Poplar Labour Electoral Committee, *Annual Report*, 1892, p. 5.
17. Ibid., pp. 5-6.
18. London Trades Council, *Annual Report*, 1892, p. 7, (TUC/LMU).
19. *East End News*, 1 November 1892.
20. Ibid., 4 November 1892.
21. Ibid.
22. Harris, *Unemployment*, p. 81.
23. *East End News*, 18 November 1892.
24. Ibid.
25. Ibid.
26. Ibid.
27. Ibid.
28. Ibid., 2 December 1892.
29. Jackson and Pringle, p. 648.
30. Board of Trade Labour Department, *Report on Agencies and Methods for Dealing with the Unemployed*, 1893, Municipal Relief Work: Particulars of work provided during the winter 1892-3, Poplar Local Board, p. 191.
31. *East End News*, 2 December 1892.
32. London Trades Council Minute Book No. 8, (28 July 1892 - 7 June 1894), 20 October 1892, (TUC/LMU).
33. The Mansion House Conference on the Condition of the Unemployed, *Report 1892-3*, p. 3, in *Unemployed, Reports, Pamphlets*, University of London (UL).
34. Ibid., pp. 6-7.
35. John Burns, *The Unemployed*, Fabian Tract No. 47, November 1893, p. 4.
36. Ibid. pp. 4-5.
37. Haw, *Workhouse*, p. 223.
38. Jackson and Pringle, p. 648; Haw, *Workhouse*, p. 224.
39. Revd. Arthur Chandler to the *East End News*, 24 March 1893.
40. Ryan, 'Poplarism', p. 60.
41. Haw, *Workhouse*, pp. 223-4.
42. *East End News*, 24 March 1893.
43. Jackson and Pringle, p. 648.
44. *East End News*, 24 March 1893.
45. See: 'The Radical Split', chapter 1, pp. 37-39.
46. Haw, *Workhouse*, p. 220.
47. *East End News*, 5 September 1893.
48. Haw, *Workhouse*, p. 221.
49. Jackson and Pringle, p. 648; Haw, *Workhouse*, pp. 224-5; Ryan, 'Poplarism', p. 61.
50. 'Mr. Will Crooks Talks: His Panacea for the Unemployed Trouble', *East End News*, 15 November 1902
51. *East End News*, 24 November 1894.
52. *East End Advertiser*, 19 January 1895.
53. Ibid., 26 January, 9, 15, 16 February, 13 March, 1895.
54. Ibid., 15 February, 13 March 1895.
55. W. Beveridge, 'Emergency Funds for the Relief of the Unemployed: A Note on their Historical Development', *The Clare Market Review*, May 1906, p. 74.
56. Ryan, 'Poplarism', p. 61; *East End News*, 27 March 1895.
57. Evidence of Crooks, *Shorthand Notes*, vol. 2, p. 331.

58. See Crooks 'emphatic protest against 300 or 400 being allowed to Intimidate the members of the Board.' Report, *East End News*, 16 March 1895; Hammond's statement to the Dock Gate meeting, *East End News*, 27 March 1895.
59. J. R. Clynes, 'The Rt. Hon. Will Crooks', a biographical sketch in H. Tracy, *The British Labour Party*, vol. III, 1948, p. 286.
60. Poplar Union Minute Book, 27 February, 22 May, 3 July, 14 August, 1895, pp. 66, 161, 208, 246, 1 January 1896, p. 7, London Metropolitan Archive (LMA).
61. R. Price, *An Imperial War and the British Working Class*, 1972, pp. 212, 214.
62. Board of Trade, Seventeenth abstract of labour statistics, (Cd. 7733), *British Parliamentary Papers*, 61 (1914-16), p. 322, quoted in K. D. Brown, *Labour and Unemployment 1900-1914*, 1971, Table 1, p.190. It should be noted that these figures were compiled from percentages of all trade unions making returns
63. E. Halevy, *Imperialism and the Rise of Labour*, 1929, p. 332-3, n5.
64. Report of unemployed meeting at Bow, *East End News*, 13 January 1903.
65. Harris, *Unemployment*, pp. 146, 148-149.
66. *East End News*, 15 November 1902.
67. Ibid.
68. Harris, *Unemployment*, p. 282.
69. *Eastern Post*, 3 November 1900.
70. Poplar Council Minute Book, 1901, pp. 2-3, (THLHL).
71. *The Times*, 22 September 1902.
72. *East End News*, 4 October 1902.
73. Crooks, 'Municipal Socialism', *East End News*, 4 October 1902. Report of the Poplar Guardians meeting on 17 December in the *East London Advertiser*, 20 December 1902. The number of inmates was 1315. At the same time people receiving out-door relief increased from 6291 in November 1901, to 7003 in November 1902, *East End News*, 19 December 1902, 4 November 1904.
74. Jackson and Pringle, pp. 649-50.
75. *East London Advertiser*, 20 December 1902; *East End News*, 19 December 1902.
76. *East End News*, 23 December 1902. Work would be given to married men with families, and a residential qualification of four months would be insisted upon. The scheme in hand would cost the Borough Council £20,000; it was reported the Council could not get the money to work with unless the Government provided special funds, *East End News*, 19 December 1902.
77. Jackson and Pringle, p. 650; Will Crooks, George Lansbury, A. Lusty (secretary of the Trades Council), and W. G. Martley (secretary of the Poplar COS), were appointed to the Executive Committee, *East End News*, 23 December 1902.
78. *Report of Poplar Labour Colony*, 'The men thus employed were paid from the fund at the rate of 15s. per week, and those selected being married men, their families were at the same time relieved in their homes in the Borough', pp. 9-10. The Borough Council's annual report shows that the total number of unemployed registered in Poplar, Bromley, and Bow was 4,460, of these 2,457 were employed, Jackson and Pringle, p 650; London County Council, *Report of the Conference on the Lack of Employment in London*, November 1903, p. 7; Beveridge, Unemployment Collection, Coll. B, vol. IX, f. 4, Hereafter Coll. B, (BLPES).
79. LCC. *Conference Report*, Beveridge, Coll., B, vol. IX, f. 4, p. 3.
80. John McDougall was Vice-Chairman of the Council during Will Crooks' mayoralty, November 1901 - November 1902.
81. Crooks moved and McDougall seconded an amendment, which became the substantive motion. 'That all administrative authorities in London were invited to appoint representatives to attend a Conference "to consider the present lack of employment, and

to make representations thereon to the Secretary of State for the Home Department and the President of the Local Government Board; and if necessary, to call a further Conference of all public bodies throughout the United Kingdom with a view of approaching His Majesty's Government and urging upon them the necessity of a national scheme for dealing with the problem." ' LCC *Minutes*, 16 December 1902, pp. 1974-75.

82. LCC. *Conference Report: Minutes of Proceedings*, 13 February 1903, Beveridge, Coll., B, vol. IX, f. 4, p. 10.
83. Ibid., p. 11
84. Ibid., pp. 3, 12, 13. Also elected were, T. Bryan (Mayor, Southwark Council); Rev. H. Curtis (Wandsworth & Clapham Guardians); W. Eickoff (Bethnal Green Guardians); Alfred Foster (Chairman, Camberwell Guardians); D. Hennessey (St. Pancras Council); Thomas Nunn (Hampstead Guardians); James Tasker (St. George's Guardians); Edward Tomkins (Islington Guardians); W. H. Wetenhall (St. Pancras Guardians), and T. White (Lewisham Council).
85. LCC. *Conference Report*, Beveridge, Coll., B, vol. IX, f. 4, p. 3.
86. *Report of the Poplar Labour Colony*, p10; Harris, *Unemployment*, p. 140.
87. PU Minute Book, 25 November 1903, p. 320.
88. *Report on Poplar Labour Colony*, October 1904, p. 12.
89. PU Minute Book, 30 March 1904, pp. 511-12, 15 June 1904, p. 92, 27 July 1904, p. 173.
90. Haw, *Workhouse*, p. 266.
91. Lansbury, *My Life*, 1928, p. 145.
92. Mansion House Committee on the Unemployed, *Abstract of the Report of the Executive Committee*, 1903-4, Burns Trade Union Collection, L139 (41). 35, (UL); W. H. Beveridge, *Unemployment: A Problem of Industry*, 1909 and 1930, pp. 159-60; Harris, *Unemployment*, p. 151.
93. Harris, *Unemployment*, p. 152. For Percy Alden see W. Crooks, *Mr. Percy Alden. M.A.: His Public and Civic Life*, 1904, London School of Economics Pamphlet Collection, CT/B15. Alden was 'Honorary Secretary of the National Unemployment Committee, and was chiefly instrumental in organising the great National Conference at the Guildhall on this important question', p. 9. Alden became Labour MP for Tottenham in 1906.
94. Jackson and Pringle, p. 651. The example has been calculated on the assumption that each family received 14s. 6, and 'seventy-men received 6d. each a week' for sixteen weeks.
95. Ibid., p. 650.
96. Brown, *Labour and Unemployment*, Table 1, p.190; F. Bealey, 'Keir Hardie and the Labour Group – II', *Parliamentary Affairs*, 10, 1956-7, p.225.
97. M. Crick, *The History of the Social Democratic Federation*, 1994, p. 174.
98. Harris, *Unemployment*, p. 152; Brown, *Labour and Unemployment*, p. 50.
99. See for example, Report of the Poplar Conference of Metropolitan Authorities, 11 February 1904, in the *East End News*, 12 February 1904.
100. Haw, *Workhouse*, p.232.
101. *Parliamentary Papers, Royal Commission on the Poor Law and Relief of Distress*, Appendix 8, Minutes of Evidence, Cd. 5066/1910, p. 69.
102. *Parliamentary Papers, Royal Commission on the Poor Law and Relief of Distress*, vol.. XXXVII, Cd. 4499/1909, *Report* by Russell Wakefield, Francis Chandler, George Lansbury, and Sidney Webb, p. 1113.
103. K. D. Brown, 'Conflict in Early British Welfare Policy: The Case of the Unemployed Workmen's Bill of 1905', *Journal of Modern History*, 43, 1971, pp. 613-29, p. 617.
104. *Labour Leader*, 14 October 1904.
105. Harris, *Unemployment*, p 153.
106. Conference Report, 'Important Proposal by the President', *The Local Government Journal*, 15 October 1904, p. 584.

REFERENCES AND NOTES 239

107. Ibid.
108. Ibid.
109. Harris, *Unemployment*, p. 154.
110. Report of the Central Executive Committee, *London Unemployment Fund 1904-5*, Beveridge, Coll. B, vol. VIII, f. 1; *London Unemployment Fund 1904-5*, part II. - Official Documents, &c. (a) "Mr. Long's Scheme", pp.115-120; W. Beveridge, *A Problem*, 1909, pp. 160-90.
111. Conference Report, 'Important Proposal', p. 584.
112. *East End News*, 18 October 1904.
113. Ibid., 7 April 1905.
114. Jackson and Pringle, p. 652
115. Haw, *Workhouse*, p. 237.
116. Ibid; *East End News*, 18 November 1904.
117. *East End News*, 18 November 1904. Under Article 10 the Guardians were able to grant relief temporarily to men in urgent need, and report from week to week to the Local Government Board.
118. *East End News*, 15 November 1904.
119. London Unemployed Fund, *Report of Central Executive Committee*, 1904-5, Beveridge, Coll., B, vol. VIII, f. 1, p. 110.
120. Ibid., p. 61. Also see H. E. Sturge, 'Hollesley Bay', *The Toynbee Record*, March 1908, pp. 76-79, and J. Gunning, *Hollesley Bay: Farm Colony Experiment*, (pamphlet), 1907, Beveridge Coll., B, vol. III, f. 21.
121. Balfour to Crooks, 28 November 1904, *East End News*, 2 December 1904.
122. Crooks to Balfour, 30 November 1904, *East End News*, 2 December 1904.
123. Ibid., 2 December 1904.
124. Long to Balfour, 6 December 1904, Balfour Papers, Add. MSS 49776, f. 38-39, British Library (BL). Evidently Balfour kept Longs suggestion of an inquiry to himself because a Royal Commission was set up as part of the 1905 Unemployment Bill. See Brown, *Labour and Unemployment*, 1971, p. 627.
125. Balfour to Long, 23 December 1904, Balfour Papers, Add. MSS. 49776, ff. 40-41.
126. K. D. Brown, Conflict, p. 617.
127. Haw, *Workhouse*, p. 212-3, 242.
128. MacDonald to Crooks, 20 December 1904, LRC, 18/46.
129. Crooks to MacDonald, 21 December 1904, LRC, 18/47.
130. Curran to Middleton, n.d., LRC, 19/52.
131. Clynes to Middleton, 3 January 1905, LRC, 19/55.
132. Shackleton to Middleton, 2 January 1905, LRC, 19/51.
133. Middleton to Crooks, 31 December 1904, LRC, 19/45.
134. Crooks to Middleton, 1 January 1905, LRC, 19/48.
135. Stephenson to MacDonald, 4 January 1905, LRC., 19/57.
136. Special Conference on Unemployment, *LRC Annual Report*, 25 January 1905, Appendix 1, p. 68. Will Crooks moved Resolution III. 'That this Conference considers that the policy of the Labour Party in Parliament relating to unemployment, should be to secure fuller powers for the Local Authorities to acquire the use of land; to re-organise the local administrative machinery for dealing with poverty and unemployment; to bring pressure on the Government to put the recommendations of the Afforestation committee into effect, and to undertake forthwith, through the Board of Trade, the reclamation of the foreshores, and to create a Labour Ministry'.
137. Brown, *Unemployment*, p. 46.
138. *Pioneer*, 10 February 1905.

139. *East End News*, 14 March 1905.
140. Long to Provis (Permanent Secretary of the LGB), 14 March 1905, Long Papers, Add. MSS., 62409, vol. VII, f. 4, (BL).
141. Quoted in Brown, *Labour and Unemployment*, p. 47.
142. Parl. Deb. (4th series) vol. 145, col. 460 (18 April 1905).
143. Brown, Conflict, p. 623.
144. Parl. Deb. (4th series) vol. 145, col. 461 (18 April 1905).
145. Crooks, 'Parliament as I see it', *Pioneer*, 21 April 1905.
146. Haw, *Workhouse*, p. 207, 219.
147. Brown, 'Conflict', p. 622, 625.
148. Brown, *Labour and Unemployment*, p. 52.
149. Ibid.
150. Ibid., pp. 52-3.
151. Parl. Deb. 4th series, vol. 147, cols. 1115-6 (20 June 1905).
152. Ibid., cols. 1190, 1194.
153. Ibid., cols. 1195-1198.
154. Ibid., col. 1127.
155. Ibid., vol. 151, col. 273 (4 August 1905).
156. *Pioneer*, 21 July 1905.
157. Quoted in Brown, Conflict, p. 625.
158. *Pioneer*, 7 July 1905. Akers Douglas, Secretary of State for the Home Department, introduced the Alien's Bill on 18 April 1905. It dealt with regulations restricting the 'admission of aliens into this country'; to put in place machinery for the control of 'undesirable aliens', to expel undesirable aliens convicted of criminal offences, and those 'wandering without means of subsistence or has been living under unsanitary conditions due to overcrowding.' Parl Deb. 4th series, vol. 145, cols. 464-68, (18 April 1905).
159. *Pioneer*, 7 July 1905.
160. Ibid., 21 July 1905.
161. Brown, 'Conflict', p. 625.
162. Ibid., p. 625.
163. *East End News*, 11 July 1905.
164. Ibid., 21 July 1905.
165. Ibid.
166. Ibid.
167. *Pioneer*, 7 July 1905.
168. Crooks, 'Parliament as I see it', *Pioneer*, 21 July 1905.
169. Brown, 'Conflict', p. 626.
170. Brown, *Labour and Unemployment*, p. 59.
171. Ibid., p. 60.
172. Ibid.
173. Parl. Deb. 4th series, vol. 151, col. 429 (7 August 1905).
174. *Daily News*, 5 August 1905.
175. Crooks to MacDonald, 14 August 1905, LRC. 35/73.
176. Crooks, *An Address on the Unemployment Problem*, 20 November 1905, p. 1, HD5/D26, LSE Pamphlet Collection.
177. Harris, *Unemployment*, p. 169. The LGB nominated MacDonald, and LCC nominated Williams Benn and Steadman, ibid., p. 170n. The minutes and reports of the CUB are in Beveridge MSS. (Coll B), vols. ix, xi-xiii, xviii-xx.
178. W. Beveridge, *Power and Influence*, 1953, p. 39.

REFERENCES AND NOTES 241

179. Harris, *Unemployment*, pp. 165-6. Also see Balfour to Poplar Borough Council, 20 October 1905, Lansbury Papers, vol. II, f. 178.
180. *Pioneer*, 10 November 1905.
181. *Daily News*, 10 October 1905; *East End News*, 31 October 1905; Harris, *Unemployment*, p. 165.
182. *The Evening Post*, 6 November 1905; for a detailed discussion see newspaper cuttings in Lansbury Papers, vol. II., ff. 128-145, 230.
183. Harris, *Unemployment*, p. 166.
184. Haw, *Workhouse*, p. 251.
185. C. Merion, *East End News*, 1983, (n.d.).

4
WOOLWICH AND INDEPENDENT LABOUR REPRESENTATION

1. W. Harry, *The Royal Arsenal Woolwich*, (n.d.), p.1.
2. *The Royal Arsenal: Historical Background*, 1991, (n.p.), GHC.
3. *Kellys Directory of Woolwich*, 1902, p. 60. Population 1891 - Woolwich Union (Parish's of Eltham, Plumstead and Woolwich), 98,418, *Victoria County History*, pp. 367-9.
4. Quoted in R. Rhodes, *An Arsenal for Labour*, 1998. p. 68.
5. Howell, *British Workers*, p. 264.
6. O. Hogg, *The Royal Arsenal, Its Background, Origin and Subsequent History*, vol. 2, Appendix X, 1963, pp. 1289-90.
7. Ibid.
8. *Census of England and Wales*, 1891, 1901; W. Page (ed.), *The Victoria History of the County of Kent*, 1936, vol. 3, pp. 367-70; *Statistical Abstracts for London*, 1897; LCC *London Statistics*, vol. X, 1899-1900, pp. 236, 244, 260, 324, based on the annual population estimates of the Registrar General, April 1898/9.
9. C. Booth, *Life and Labour of the People of London*, Third Series, vol.5, 1902, p. 135.
10. See J. Attfield, *With Light of Knowledge*, 1981, chapters 2-3 for a detailed discussion of the Arsenal co-operators, education and social change in Woolwich.
11. For the political programme of Woolwich Radical Club, see *Kentish Independent*, 10 and 31 January 1885.
12. Gasworkers' and General Labourers' Union, Cashbook, July 1889. Working Class History Library, Salford (WCHL).
13. W. Thorne, *My Life's Battles*, 1925, p. 92. Curran was victimised in a dispute in the Arsenal over an alteration of working conditions and became an official of the Gasworkers' Union.
14. *The Star*, 27 August 1889.
15. Clegg, Fox and Thompson, *British Trade Unions*, vol. I, p. 61.
16. *Stratford Express*, 21 September 1889. The following account is derived almost entirely from the contemporary local press held at Stratford Reference Library and Kapp, *Eleanor*, pp. 359-60.
17. Ibid., 12 October 1889.
18. Ibid., 11 December 1889.
19. E. P. Thompson, *William Morris: Romantic to Revolutionary*, 1955, p. 298.
20. Ibid. p. 359. Banner was one of the signatories of its first manifesto. His political colleagues included John Lincoln Mahon, William Morris and Eleanor Marx-Aveling. He spoke at Eleanor Marx's funeral in April 1898. E. Kapp, *Eleanor*, p. 70.

21. *Woolwich Co-operative Congress*, 1896, p. 7; Jones was also an Executive member of the London Liberal and Radical Union, *Annual Report*, 1892, p. 17, (BLPES). Also, see the entry for Jones in J. M. Bellamy and J. Saville, (eds.) *Dictionary of Labour Biography*, vol. 1, 1976, pp. 197-9.
22. Attfield, *With Light*, p.20.
23. Benjamin Jones, *The Next Parliamentary Election: A Labour Representative for Woolwich: Report of the Meeting at the Assembly Rooms...: address, etc.* Labour Representative League, March 25, 1892, pp. 1-55, pp. 11-13. Pamphlets Collection (BLPES), JF2 (42S)/C13, SPECIAL. It should be noted that P. Thompson's reference to this article in *Socialists*, p. 252, fn. 2, is incorrect. There is no trace of this document in the Woolwich Public Library, or in the Greenwich Libraries/Greenwich Heritage Centre catalogues..
24. *Woolwich Gazette*, 31 May 1892.
25. Ibid., 24 May 1892.
26. Election Analyses 1889-1919 (GHC).
27. *Kentish Independent*, 12 July 1895.
28. H. Pelling, *Social Geography of British Elections 1885-1910*, 1967, pp. 37, 40.
29. *Leeds Mercury*, 25 October 1900, quoted in Bernstein, *Liberalism*, p. 66.
30. London Reform Union, Plumstead, Woolwich and Charlton Branch, *First Annual Report 1892/93*, p. 27. A Progressive Association was formed in 1897, and it seems the Reform Union merged the following year as the Progressives subscribed to the London Reform Union, see Annual Report 1899, p. 12, (BLPES). It did not remain long under Liberal influence; Robert Banner became its secretary in 1899. *Woolwich and District Labour Journal*, November 1899 (GHC), henceforth *Labour Journal*
31. P. Thompson, *Socialists*, p. 252. The Woolwich ILP branch was formed in October 1894, 'with over one hundred members ...G. Gunning ... acting as secretary.' *Labour Leader*, 20 October 1894. I must thank Dr. Alan Clinton, whose notes on the Woolwich Labour movement helped clarify a number of issues.
32. Attfield, *With Light*, p. 11.
33. Ibid., p. 20.
34. *Kentish Independent*, 16 January 1899.
35. *Labour Journal*, November 1899, p. 3.
36. F. Bealey, 'The Electoral Arrangement Between the Labour Representation Committee and the Liberal Party', *Journal of Modern History*, 1956, p. 366.
37. P. Thompson, *Socialists*, p. 95.
38. Labour Representation Committee (LRC), *Annual Report*, 1900, p.4; LRC. *Annual Report*, 1903, they paid a subscription fee of £45.0.0 for 84, 000 members, p. 8. Also see H. Pelling, *A Short History of the Labour Party*, 1961, p. 12.
39. Barefoot, *25 Years*, 1928, pp. 11-13.
40. Ibid., p.13.
41. *Comradeship*, No. 1, October 1897, p. 1.
42. Ibid., p. 9.
43. H. Snell, *Men, Movements and Myself*, 1936, p. 80. Snell was MP for Woolwich in 1922, became a Peer and Parliamentary Under-Secretary for India in 1931.
44. Poplar Labor League, *Annual Report*, 27 May 1896, p. 12.
45. Ibid., p. 5; Attfield, *With Light*, p. 13.
46. *Woolwich and District Labour Notes*, August 1899.
47. Barefoot, *25 Years*, p. 15.
48. P. Thompson, 'Liberals, Radicals and Labour in London 1880-1900', *Past and Present*, 1963, p. 63; The Workmen's National Housing Council was founded September 1898. It was backed by the London Trades Council and the powerful London Society of Compositors.

Labour Notes, February 1899, p. 2. Knee was a delegate the LRC, LRC *Annual Report*, 1900, p. 3.
49. *Labour Notes*, July, August 1899.
50. When the journal resumed publication in 1901, it was published by the Woolwich and District Trades Council, with no official ILP involvement, *Bulletin of the Society for the Study of Labour History*, No 28, Spring 1974, p. 37.
51. Woolwich Labour Representative Association (WLRA), *Annual Report*, 1904, p. 7.
52. LRC *Annual Report 1900*, p. 1.
53. LRC *Annual Report 1901*, p. 7. Leeds and Leicester Trade Councils were first and second respectively.
54. *Labour Journal*, July 1902, p. 8; also see 'Woolwich Worthies', *Pioneer*, 1909 (n.p.).
55. *Pioneer*, November 1903, p. 1.
56. Plumstead Radical Club, Report of the Educational Council for the Half-Year Ending 31 December 1901, *Labour Journal*, March 1902, p. 12.
57. *Kentish Independent*, 25 April 1902.
58. WLRA, *Executive Report and Balance Sheet*, 1903, pp. 3-4, presented to members 1 May 1904. Also, see *Labour Journal*, July 1902, p. 7.
59. *Labour Journal*, June 1902, p. 4.
60. Ibid., p. 16.
61. Ibid.
62. P. Thompson, *Socialists*, p. 255.
63. *Labour Journal*, December, p.4.
64. Barefoot, *25 Years*, p. 11. For an account of Crooks' life, see the entry by David Martin in Bellamy and Saville, *Dictionary*, pp. 107-112.
65. *Woolwich Gazette*, 19 December 1902.
66. Ibid.
67. *Pioneer*, 24 June 1921, p. 7; not as R. McKibbin claims, 'the Woolwich Labour Representation Association was founded only after Will Crooks' election as M.P. for Woolwich in 1903.' *The Evolution of the Labour Party 1910-1924*, 1974, p. 8.
68. Rogers to MacDonald, 10 January 1903, LRC. 6/97; Barefoot to Macdonald, 16 January 1903, LRC. 6/98. Also see LRC Circular, March 1903, LRC. Misc. 1/94/3.
69. Ben Tillett tried to delete this ruling at the Liverpool Conference, *LRC Annual Report 1905*, pp. 43-4. It received 43 votes, against 197.
70. *Labour Party Annual Report*, 1917, p. 79.
71. LRC. Misc. 1/18.
72. R. Eatwell, 'The History of the Woolwich Labour Party,' p.9, (n.d.). An introduction to the Woolwich Labour Party Records deposited at GHC.
73. *Woolwich Gazette*, 23 February 1903.
74. MacDonald to Rogers, 23 January 1903, LRC Correspondence.
75. *Woolwich Gazette*, 16 January 1903.
76. Ibid.
77. Martin, *Dictionary*, p. 108.
78. *Kentish Independent*, 20 February 1903.
79. Ibid.
80. *Daily News*, 28 February 1903.
81. *Morning Leader*, 28 February 1903.
82. LRC *Annual Report 1902*, p. 10.
83. Scrapbook of Election material 1903-31, (GHC).
84. *Woolwich Gazette*, 27 February 1903.
85. Scrapbook.

86. Ibid.
87. *Woolwich Gazette*, 6 March 1903.
88. Gould to Grinling, 3 March 1903, Grinling Collection, (GHC).
89. *Westminster Gazette*, 6 March 1903.
90. J. D. Scott, *Siemens Brothers 1858-1958*, 1958, p. 266.
91. Henderson to MacDonald, LRC. Correspondence 7/215 (GHC).
92. Wilkie to MacDonald, LRC. Correspondence 7/425 (GHC).
93. Barefoot to Hardie, 23 February 1903; Hardie to Barefoot, 25 February 1903, the Francis Johnson Correspondence, ILP 4, 1903/16, 1903/20, (BLPES).
94. *ILP Annual Report*, April 1903, p. 4.
95. Barefoot to Trade Union secretaries, 20 January 1903, Scrapbook, (GHC).
96. The proprietor of the *Daily News* was George Cadbury who also supported the ILP financially. It is thought that he may have contributed towards Keir Hardie's election expenses, and therefore his victory at Merthyr in 1900, C. Benn, *Keir Hardie*, 1992, pp. 162-3.
97. W. H. Dickinson and J. Benn, *The Labour Candidate for Woolwich*, London Liberal Federation leaflet, (n.d.), (GHC).
98. Haw contributed to the columns of the *Daily News,* and *Clarion. Labour Journal*, April 1903, p. 8.
99. In the case of Taff Vale, a strike against the Taff Vale Railway Company was sanctioned by the Amalgamated Society of Railway Servants (ASRS) and opposed in the courts by the company manager Ammon Beasley. The Taff Vale case continued after the strike had ended, with the Law Lords under Lord Halsbury granting the injunction against the ASRS to stop picketing, and making the funds of the union liable to damages amounting to £23,000. See Amalgamated Society of Railway Servants, *Reports and Proceedings*, 1901 and 1902, MSS.127/AS/1/1/27-8, (MRC).
100. LRC to the *Electors of Woolwich*, (n.d.), (GHC).
101. 1903 Election Results (GHC).
102. Eatwell, *History*, p. 8.
103. *Woolwich Electoral Register 1902-3*.
104. *Woolwich Gazette*, 13 March 1903.
105. *Labour Journal*, April 1903, p.8.
106. Ibid., July 1903. p.8.
107. Webb to Crooks, 12 March 1903, Crooks Papers.
108. Tillett to Crooks, 15 March 1903, Crooks Papers
109. Poplar Labor League, *Annual Report 1903*, p. 3.
110. Quoted in R. B. Stucke, (ed.), *Fifty Years of the Woolwich Labour Party*, 1953, p. 9.
111. Ibid.
112. *LRC Annual Report 1903*, pp.5-7.
113. LRA, *Executive Report and Balance Sheet*, 1903, p.13.
114. D. Judd, *Radical Joe*, p. 243.
115. See B. Simon, *Education and the Labour Movement, 1870-1920*, 1965, chap.7.
116. *Labour Journal*, January 1902, p. 7.
117. Attfield, *With Light*, p. 24.
118. Ibid.
119. *Labour Journal*, August 1902, p.14.
120. Herbert, quoted in F. Bealey and H. Pelling, *Labour and Politics 1900-1906: A History of the Labour Representation Committee*, 1958, p. 146.
121. Hodge to MacDonald and Barefoot, 12 March 1903, LRC. Correspondence 7/376/1/2 (GHC).

122. *ILP Annual Report*, April 1903, p.4.
123. *ILP News*, March 1903, p.2.
124. Barefoot to MacDonald, 7 June 1903, LRC. 9/468, (NMLH). The Newcastle resolution states '... that all Candidates recommended under L.R.C. auspices must appear before their various constituencies under the title of Labour Candidates only'. LRC *Annual Report*, February 1903, p. 32, Crooks and Barefoot were both delegates, pp. 4, 7.
125. P. Adelman, *The Rise of the Labour Party 1880-1945*, 1986, p.34.
126. Bealey and Pelling, *Labour and Politics*, p. 146; Also see Jesse Herbert's memorandum to Gladstone, 6 September 1903, quoted in G. L. Bernstein, *Liberalism and Liberal Politics in Edwardian England*, 1986, p. 66.
127. K. D. Brown, *The First Labour Party 1906-1914*, 1986, p. 200.
128. *The Pioneer*, 24 June 1921, p.7.
129. McKibbin states, 'by 1909 there were no less than 3000 associate members...', *Evolution*, p. 8.
130. WLRA, *Report of the First Annual Business Meeting*, 19 May 1904, p. 7; Barefoot, *25 Years*, p. 13; Stucke, *50 Years*, p. 12. A sub-committee of the Executive of the Association met to draft the constitution before placing it before the General Council see Minute Book, 21 April 1903, (GHC). At the 1918 National Labour Party Conference the party's constitution was amended to allow the representation of individual membership, Labour Party *Annual Report*, 1918, p. 82; In 1903 the membership of the LRA was 1,954 and fifty years later it had risen to 9,761, Stucke, *50 Years*, Appendix VII, p. 82.
131. Stucke, *50 Years*, p. 11.
132. Jefferson, *Woolwich*, p. 51.
133. Eatwell, *History*, p. 9.

5
MEMBER FOR WOOLWICH

1. For a detailed discussion of the MacDonald-Gladstone Entente, see Bealey and Pelling, *Labour and Politics*, pp. 125-159.
2. F. Bealey, 'The Electoral Arrangement Between the Labour Party Representation Committee and the Liberal Party', *Journal of Modern History*, 1956, pp. 353-373; 'Negotiations Between the Liberal Party and the Labour Representation Committee before the General Election of 1906', *Bulletin of the Institute of Historical Research*, November 1956, pp. 261-274. It is important to note that Bealey's references to the Gladstone papers have changed. This collection was recatalogued in 1957. Thus, the correspondence between Herbert and Gladstone cited by Bealey is now to be found in Add. MSS. 46017-46026, British Library (BL).
3. D. Tanner, *Political change and the Labour Party 1900-1918*, 1990, p. 22.
4. Ibid., p. 21.
5. For the ILPs 'Tory' support even in 'Liberal' areas, especially in Yorkshire, see Howell, *British Workers*, pp. 174-203.
6. Tanner, *Political Change*, p. 23.
7. Ibid.
8. *Labour Leader*, 14 September 1906.
9. Herbert to Gladstone, 28 October 1905, Herbert Gladstone papers, Add. MSS. 46026, f. 170. (BL).
10. *The Speaker*, 12 September 1903.
11. Bealey and Pelling, *Labour and Politics*, pp. 146-7; Bealey, Electoral Arrangement, p. 366.

12. Herbert to Gladstone, 12 March 1903, Add. MSS. 46025, ff. 139-42. The negotiations of necessity were kept secret, so that the socialists in the LRC would not become belligerent and oppose the arrangement.
13. Memo from Gladstone, undoubtedly for Campbell-Bannerman, 13 March 1903, Add. MSS. 46025, ff. 7-9.
14. Bealey, Electoral Arrangement, p. 367.
15. See Crooks and Woolwich workingmen, *Labour Leader*, 21 March 1903.
16. Ibid.
17. Bealey and Pelling, *Labour and Politics*, p. 205.
18. Crooks to MacDonald, 12 March 1903, LRC. 7/143.
19. W. Crooks, 'A Parliamentary Survey', *Pioneer*, 13 October 1905.
20. F. Bealey, 'Keir Hardie and the Labour Group – II', *Parliamentary Affairs*, 10, 1956-7, p. 223.
21. Parl. Deb. 4th series, vol. 120, col. 300, (26 March 1903).
22. *Labour Journal*, August 1903, p. 12. The 30s. Minimum Wage will be discussed around the issue of Arsenal discharge campaigns of 1907.
23. Parl. Deb. 4th series, vol. 122, cols. 1570-1, (22 May 1903).
24. Haw, *Workhouse*, pp. 176-77.
25. Parl Deb. 4th series, vol. 130, col. 451, (19 February 1904).
26. *Labour Journal*, July 1904, p. 5.
27. Parl. Deb. 4th series, vol. 130, cols. 972-976, (10 May 1904).
28. *East End News*, 8 July 1904.
29. *Yorkshire Daily Post*, 11 July 1904.
30. *Nottingham Daily Express*, 28 May 1904.
31. Parl. Deb. 4th series, vol. 140, cols. 81-84, (10 August 1904).
32. Ibid., col. 562 (15 August 1904).
33. Ibid., vol. 146, col. 236 (12 May 1905).
34. LRC *Annual Report*, 26 January 190-5, pp. 69-71.
35. Bealey, Hardie, p. 226.
36. Bealey and Pelling, *Labour and Politics*, p. 205.
37. MacDonald to Crooks, 10 July 1905, LRC. 24/283.
38. LRC *Annual Report*, 1903, p 15.
39. Ibid., 1904, p. 46.
40. Clark to MacDonald, 25 May 1904, LRC. 15/66. J. W. Clark was general secretary of the Scientific Instrument Makers' Trade Society.
41. Crooks to MacDonald, 31 March 1903, LRC. 7/44.
42. MacDonald to Rogers, 6 July 1904, LRC. 16/34.
43. Pease to MacDonald, 20 May 1904, LRC. 14/258.
44. Rogers to MacDonald, 20 July 1904, LRC. Misc. 1/19/1. The Constitution as revised at Bradford, with 'or resign'deleted, LRC. Misc. 1/19/3.
45. Bealey and Pelling, *Labour and Politics*, p. 193.
46. Glasier to Hardie, 6, 12 January 1904, GP/1/1/697 and 696, Glasier Papers, Liverpool University. Tom Richards, secretary of the South Wales Miners, won West Monmouth in March 1904 on a Labour ticket, which was not officially sanctioned by the LRC because the Miners were not affiliated to the Committee. Richards supported the Liberal whip until 1906.
47. *Labour Leader*, 30 January 1904.
48. H. Pelling, *The Origins of the Labour Party*, 1954, p. 239.
49. *The Western Daily Mercury*, 16 June 1904.
50. WLRA Executive Minutes, 13 June 1904, (GHC).

REFERENCES AND NOTES 247

51. MacDonald to Thorne, 16 June 1904, JF2 (425) C26, Pamphlet Collection, (BLPES).
52. See ruling of the Chairman, John Hodge, regarding constitutional procedure in Bell's case. LRC *Annual Report*, 1904, p. 43.
53. Barefoot to MacDonald, 5 July 1904. LRC. 15/88.
54. *Liverpool Mercury*, 2 October 1904.
55. MacDonald to Crooks, 6 December 1904, LRC. 17/104
56. Daniel to Crooks, 13 September 1904, LRC. 17/103.
57. Crooks to MacDonald, 6 December 1904, LRC. 17/102.
58. MacDonald to Crooks, 7 December 1904, LRC. 17/105..
59. Tanner, *Political Change*, p. 42.
60. WLRA Executive Minutes, 19 September 1904.
61. Barefoot, *25 Years*, p. 64.
62. The Woolwich Borough Council consisted of eleven wards. The political composition 1903-6, *Labour Journal*, November 1903, p. 14. Hence: Dockyard (3 seats - 3 Lab.), St. Mary's (3 seats - 3 Lab.), River (6 seats - 1 Lab.), St. Georges (3 seats - 1 Lab.), Burrage (3 seats - 3 Lab.), Herbert (3 seats - 2 Lab), Glyndon (3 seats - 3 Lab.), St Margeret's (3 seats - 3 Lab.), Central (3 seats - 3 Lab.), St. Nicholas (3 seats - 3 Lab.), Eltham (3 seats - 0 Lab). In all 25 Labour, 8 Moderates, 3 Independents.
63 *Pioneer* 17 December 1905.
64. *Pioneer*, 14 October 1904.
65. Judd, *Radical Joe*, p. 245.
66. A. K. Russell, *Liberal Landslide: The General Election of 1906*, 1973, p. 28.
67. *Pioneer*, 4 November 1904.
68. Ibid.
69. Ibid., 14 October 1904.
70. Ibid. 16 March 1905.
71. J. Wilson, *A life of Sir Henry Campbell - Bannerman*, 1973, pp. 406, 473.
72. Hodge to MacDonald, 7 December 1905, LRC. 29/474.
73. *Pioneer*, 18 August, 1905
74. WLRA Executive Minutes, 11 December 1905.
75. Crooks to MacDonald, 18 December 1905, LRC. 28/60.
76. Crooks to MacDonald, 18 December 1905, LRC. 29/470.
77. MacDonald to Crooks, 19 December 1905, LRC. 28/61.
77. *Pioneer*, 5 January 1906.
79. Election Address, *Pioneer*, 29 December 1905.
80. *Pioneer*, 5 January 1906.
81. After the Representation of the People Act of 1918, it was confined to a single day.
82. Snowden to Middleton, 9 January 1906, LRC. 29/436.
83. MacDonald to Snowden, 9 January 1906, LRC. 29/400.
84. Russell, *Liberal Landslide*, p. 172.
85. F. W. S. Craig, *British Parliamentary Election Results 1885-1918*, 1974, Table 3, p. 581.
86. Ibid., pp. 310-332. W. T. Wilson, Westhoughton; Philip Snowden, Blackburn R.Clynes, Manchester, North-East; James Seddon, Newton; John Hodge, Gorton; T. Glover, St. Helens; J. T. Macpherson, Preston; G. D. Kelly, Manchester South-West; A. H. Gill, Bolton; C. Duncan, Barrow-in-Furness; David Shackelton, Clitheroe; S. Walsh, Ince.
87. Howell, *British Workers*, p. 203.
88. Tanner, *Political Change*, p. 249.
89. K. O. Morgan, 'The New Liberalism and the Challenge of Labour: The Welsh Experience, 1885-1929', in D. Brown, (ed.), *Essays in Anti-Labour History*, pp. 159-182, pp. 163, 168.

90. *Daily News,* 1 January 1906.
91. Cited in David. E. Martin, 'The Instruments of the People'?: The Parliamentary Labour Party in 1906, in David. E. Martin and David Rubenstein (eds.), *Ideology and the Labour Movement,* 1979, pp. 125-146, p. 142.
92. Balfour to Lansdowne, 13 April 1906, Lord Newton, in *Lord Lansdowne, A Biography,* 1929, p. 354.
93. J. Fair, *British Interparty Conferences: A Study of the Procedure of Conciliation in British Politics 1867-1921,* 1980, p. 60
94. G. Dangerfield, *The Strange Death of Liberal England,* 1935, (1997), p. 25.
95. The discussion that follows is based on the *Pioneer,* Parl. Deb., and *Parliamentary Papers.* George Haw did not chronicle Crooks' involvement in the Arsenal discharge campaign in either of his two books: *Workhouse* or *Life.*
96. *Report of the Government Factories and Workshops Committee,* 1907, Cd. 3626, p. 8. The Committee was appointed by Hugh Arnold Foster, Secretary of State for War, on 23 March 1905.
97. War Office figures, 17 April 1907, in the *Pioneer,* 19 April 1907.
98. Parl. Deb. 4th series, vol. 179, col. 1647, (15 August 1907).
99. Ibid., vol. 164, cols. 733-4, (8 November 1906).
100. *Pioneer,* 19 April 1907. The officials were employed in the Central Office and Building works Department. The number employed in these Departments was compared with the discharges that had taken place in the RCD, RGF, and the RL.
101. *Report of the Conference appointed to Examine the Shops and Machinery at Woolwich Arsenal, other than the Danger Buildings and Torpedo Factory, in order to consider whether any article not now made in the Ordinance Factories can appropriately be made there with this Machinery,* 1907, Cd. 3514, (hereafter *Henderson Report).*
102. *Pioneer,* 29 November 1907.
103. Ibid., 27 July 1906; Haldane, Parl. Deb. 4th series, vol. 159, col. 923, (27 June 1906).
104. *Pioneer,* 6 July 1906.
105. Ibid., 13 July 1906.
106. Ibid.
107. Ibid.
108. Parl. Deb. 4th series, vol. 180, col. 1649, (15 August 1907).
109. *Pioneer,* 9 November 1906.
110. *Henderson Report,* p. 78.
111. *Pioneer,* 23 November 1906.
112. Ibid. For a report of the deputation see the *Henderson Report,* Appendix XII, pp. 80-2.
113. *Pioneer,* 16 August 1907.
114. Ibid. 1 March 1907,
115. Ibid., 29 March 1907.
116. Ibid., 5 April 1907.
117. Parl. Deb. 4th series, vol. 180, col. 1649, (15 August 1907)
118. *Pioneer,* 12, 26 April 1907.
119. Ibid., 12 April 1907.
120. Ibid., 19 April 1907.
121. Ibid., 26 April 1907.
122. Ibid., 3 May 1903.
123. Ibid., 26 April 1907.
124. Parl. Deb. 4th series, vol. 173, cols. 526-7, (29 April 1907).
125. *Pioneer,* 10, 18 May 1907.

REFERENCES AND NOTES 249

126. Ibid., 3 May 1907.
127. Ibid., 16 August 1907.
128. See the history of the Arsenal discharges: 'Manifesto by the Woolwich Trades and Labour Council', in the *Pioneer,* 16 August 1907. The Manifesto was circulated to every local LRC, trade union, and trades council in the country.
129. *Pioneer,* 19 July 1907.
130. Ibid., 16 August 1907.
131. Ibid., 2 August 1907.
132. Ibid., 23 August 1907.
133. Woolwich Trades Council, Minutes 12 September 1907, (GHC).
134. *Pioneer,* 29 November 1907.
135. Crooks to MacDonald, 6 December 1907, LP. GC/22/104.
136. MacDonald to Crooks, 8 January 1908, LP. GC/22/105.
137. Parl. Deb. 4th series, vol. 140, col. 84, (10 August 1904).
138. Ibid., vol. 143, col. 1256, (27 March 1905).
139. Ibid., vol. 152, cols. 1390-1394, (2 March 1906).
140. Brown, *Labour and Unemployment,* p. 72.
141. Harris, *Unemployment,* p. 238.
142. Parl. Deb. (4th series, vol. 155, cols. 1364-5, (15 April 1906).
143. Harris, *Unemployment,* p. 239.
144. Parl. Deb. 4th series, vol. 158, cols. 462-466, (30 May 1906).
145. Harris, *Unemployment,* p. 235.
146. In Poplar, the number of applications received by the distress committee for relief was 1,951, or 11. 4 per cent of the population. In Woolwich, it was 1,805, or 14. 3 per cent of the population, there were 3,038 or 24 per cent, being dependents. *Unemployed Workmen Act of 1905: Returns Relating to Proceedings of Distress Committees up to the 31 March 1906,* Beveridge Coll. B, vol. XIV, (1), p. 3.
147. Harris, *Unemployment,* p. 239.
148. Parl. Deb. 4th series, vol. 161, col. 441, (19 July 1906).
149. Ibid., vol. 169, col. 951, (20 February 1907).
150. Harris, *Unemployment,* p. 240.
151. Parl. Deb. 4th series, vol. 177, cols. 1446-8, (9 July 1907).
152. Brown, *Labour and Unemployment,* p. 83.
153. J. R. MacDonald, *The New Unemployment Bill of the Labour Party,* June 1907, pp. 6-7.
154. Harris, *Unemployment,* p. 243.
155. Parl. Deb. 4th series, vol. 186, cols. 15-16, (13 March 1908).
156. Harris, *Unemployment,* p. 244.
157. Parl. Deb. (4th series) vol. 186, cols. 28-49, (13 March 1908).
158. On 5 April 1908, Campbell-Bannerman resigned due to ill health. Asquith became Prime Minister, David Lloyd George, Chancellor of the Exchequer, and Winston Churchill, President of the Board of Trade.
159. Parl. Deb. 4th series, vol. 194, col. 1662, (26 October 1908); Harris, *Unemployment,* p. 275.
160. Ibid., vol. 194, cols. 1656-1662, (26 October 1908).
161. Ibid., vol. 174, col. 517, (10 May 1907).
162. Ibid. vols. 122-193, passim.
163. Ibid., vol. 174, cols. 518-20, (10 May 1907).
164. P. Thane, 'Non-Contributory Verses Insurance Pensions 1878-1908' in P. Thane (ed.), *The Origins of British Social Policy,* 1978, pp, 84-106, pp. 103-4.
165. Parl. Deb. 4th series, vol. 192, cols. 193-7, (9 July 1908).

6
ROLE IN PARLIAMENT AND THE GENERAL ELECTIONS OF 1910

1. N. Blewett, *The Peers, The Parties and the People: The British General Elections of 1910*, 1972, p. 45, 47.
2. Camberwell, Shoreditch, Manchester (North West), Newcastle-upon-Tyne, Ashburton, Ross on Wye, and Pudsey. See *Craig, British Parliamentary Election Results 1885-1918*, 1974, *passim*.
3. Blewett, *Peers*, cited, p. 53.
4. Ibid. pp. 46, 50.
5. *Pioneer* 12 February 1909
6. Ibid.
7. *Labour Party Annual Report*, 1910, p. 17.
8. Ibid.
9. *Pioneer*, 19 February 1909.
10. Ibid.
11. *Hansard*, 5th series, vol. 1, cols. 149-152, (17 February 1909).
12. Ibid., cols. 154-5.
13. *Pioneer*, 19 February 1909.
14. Blewett, *Peers*, p. 52.
15. D. J. Newton, *British Labour, European Socialism and the Struggle for Peace 1889-1914*, 1985, pp. 184-5.
16. Ibid.
17. Ibid. p. 186
18. *Hansard*, 5th series, vol. 2, cols. 1050-51, 1071-72, 1913, 1929; vol. 8, cols 1355-56; vol. 9, cols. 643-44.
19. 'Labour in Parliament', *Pioneer*, 2 April 1909.
20. *Labour Leader*, 19 February 1909.
21. Blewett, *Peers*, p. 69.
22. Ibid., cited, p. 68.
23. For Lloyd George's Budget Statement see *Hansard*, 5th series, vol. 4, cols. 472-548.
24. Dangerfield, *Strange Death*, p. 30; for a more detailed account see R. Ensor, *England 1870-1914*, 1936, p. 414.
25. J. Grigg, *Lloyd George: The Peoples Champion 1902-1911*, 1978, p. 179.
26. R. Jenkins, *Balfour's Poodle*, p. 41; Blewett, Peers, p. 54.
27. D. Marquand, *Ramsay MacDonald*, 1977, p. 116.
28. Report of Special Session, *Labour Party Annual Conference Report*, 1909, pp. 102-112.
29. *Pioneer*, 12 March 1909.
30. Cited in Marquand, *Ramsay MacDonald*, p. 116.
31. *Pioneer*, 15 January 1909.
32. *Labour Party Annual Report*, 1910, p. 22.
33. *Pioneer*, 18 June 1909. At the Annual Meeting of the Woolwich Labour Representation Association on 15 June at the Carmel Chapel, Woolwich, Crooks said 'he did not think they would have an election yet; for the fact was that there was a deficiency of £16 millions to make up, and he did not think that the Tories would undertake the job.'
34. Ibid., Crooks to Hinkling.
35. Ensor, *England*, p. 417.

36. *Pioneer*, 30 April 1909.
37. Cited in K. D. Brown, *Labour and Unemployment*, p. 116.
38. *Hansard*, 5th series, vol. 4, cols. 633-38 (30 April).
39. 'Labour in Parliament', *Pioneer*, 7 May 1909.
40. Ibid.
41. *Labour Leader*, 4 June 1909; Brown, *Labour*, p. 123.
42. *Labour Party Annual Conference Report*, 1909, p. 93.
43. J. Harris, *Unemployment*, p. 316.
44. L. Masterman, *C. F. G. Masterman*, 1939, p. 179.
45. *Hansard*, 5th series, vol. 6, col. 1060.
46. *Pioneer*, 21 May 1909.
47. Ibid., 7 October 1910.
48. Ibid. 10 December 1910.
49. 'An Open Letter to Will Crooks, M. P., L.C.C.' in the *Pioneer*, 10 September 1909.
50. Ibid., 10 September 1909.
51. *Shipping Gazettee & Lloyd's List*, 11, 17 September 1909. The details of the tour were compiled using Crooks' diary, and articles on his travel lectures in *Pioneer*, 8, 29 October 1909, 1, 8 July, 7 October, 2, 29 December 1910. I am indebted to Michael MacDonald of the Canadian National Archive, and Don Carter of the National Library of Canada for conducting a search of Will Crooks' Canadian Trip.
52. *Report of Proceedings of the Twenty-Fifth Annual Convention of the Trades and Labor Congress of Canada*, 1909, p. 4 (National Library of Canada).
53. Crooks to Barefoot, *Pioneer*, 8 October 1909.
54. Ibid., 2 December 1910.
55. Ibid., 1 July 1910.
56. Ibid., 2 December 1910.
57. Ibid., 26 November, 21 January 1909
58. R. I. McKibbin, 'James Ramsay MacDonald and the Problem of the Independence of the Labour Party, 1910-1914', *Journal of Modern History*, vol. 42, 2, 1970, pp. 216-35, p. 217. For a statement of the case see W. V. Osborne, *My Case. The causes and effects of the Osborne judgment*, 1910, and his *Trade Union Funds and Party Politics*, 1910; R. Storey (ed.), *The Osborne Case Papers and Other Records of the Amalgamated Society of Railway Servants,* Occasional Publications No. 4, University of Warwick, 1979, especially ASRS, Reports and Proceedings..., 1907-11, MSS. 127/AS/1/1/37-41; Labour *Party Annual Conference Report*, 1910, Appendix 1, pp. 101-10. For adiscussion see, Keir Hardie, *The Party Pledge and the Osborne Judgment*, 1911; S and B. Webb, *The History of Trade Unionism 1660-1920*, 1920, pp. 608-34; F. Bealey and H.Pelling, *Labour and Politics*, pp. 134-42, and 186-97.
59. Blewett, *Peers*, p. 124.
60. For details of the seats lost to the Conservatives: Preston, Sunderland, Chatham, Woolwich, and Manchester (South West), see Craig, *Parliamentary*, pp. 172, 197, 94, 60, and 153 respectively. Pete Curran lost Jarrow by 67 votes; he died within a few weeks of his defeat on 14 February 1910. Tom Summerbell who lost Sunderland also died shortly after the election on 10 February. *Labour Party Annual Conference Report*, 1910, Appendices, 1V, V, pp. 114-5.
61. McKibbin, MacDonald, p. 218, fn. 9.
62. Blewett, *Peers*, p. 234.
63. McKibbin, 'James Ramsay MacDonald', p. 219.
64. Speaking to an Amendment on the House of Lords in 1907 Henderson moved it should be abolished, *Labour Party Annual Report*, 1908, p. 46. Also, the Labour

Party at its Conference in 1908, resolved that the House of Lords 'is a hindrance to national progress and ought to abolished', ibid. p. 68. In 1910, when the Government introduced the Veto of the House of Lords the Labour Party tabled an Amendment, part of which called for the abolition of the House of Lords, Ibid., 1911, p. 30.

65. Cited in Blewett, *Peers*, p. 107.
66. Ibid. p. 105.
67. Grigg, 1902-1911, pp. 240-1
68. Ibid. p. 241.
69. M. Hamilton, Margaret Bondfield, 1924, pp. 77-78. Margaret Bondfield was assistant secretary of the Shop Assistants' Union (1898-1908). She was Labour MP for Northampton 1923-1924, and Wallsend 1926-1931, and was Parliamentary Secretary to the Minister of Labour January-November 1924, and Minister of Labour (the first woman Cabinet Minister) June 1929-August 1931.
70. *Pioneer*, 7 January 1910.
71. Ibid.
72. Ibid., 18 February 1910.
73. Craig, *Parliamentary*, p. 60
74. Buxton to Crooks, 18 January 1910. Sue Spear, Crooks Papers.
75. Ibid. 28 January 1910.
76. Ibid. 4 February 1910.
77. Dated 31 January 1910, in the possession of Len Byott, (Will Crooks great-grandson) Culbokie, Black Isle, Ross-shire.
78. MacDonald had written to Snowden in the 1906 election that: 'Crooks needed to be on the spot at the Gates...nail the many yarns on the counter right away...If Crooks was not there, even for one day, Adam would be sure to take advantage.' MacDonald to Snowden, 9 January 1906, LRC. 29/400.
79. Grigg, *1902-1911*, p. 241
80. *Pioneer*, 10 September 1909.
81. Haw, Workhouse, p. 257.
82. *Pioneer*, 8 September 1911. For the controversy surrounding conversion, see the correspondence between W. J. Burns, District Manager of the Planet Friendly Assurance Collecting Society, MacDonald, and Crooks, 7-15 March 1907, LPGC. 13/143-147.
83. *Pioneer*, 4 April, 6 May 1910.
84. Fabian Society Correspondence, B3/3, f. 2, 12 May 1910, f. 3 n.d. (BLPES); Edward R. Pease, *The History of the Fabian Society*, 1916, p. 155. Pease was still a Trustee of the Labour Party's Parliamentary Fund in 1910.
85. See Will Crooks' speech on 'Piety at Home', in *Labour and Religion*, 1910, pp. 56-66.
86. *Pioneer*, 12 August 1910.
87. *Pioneer*, 14 October 1910.
88. Peter Rowland, *The Last Liberal Governments: The Promised Land 1905-1910*, 1968, p. 331.
89. Blewett, *Peers*, p. 146.
90. Fair, *Interparty Conferences*, p. 81.
91. Cited, ibid. p. 82.
92. Dangerfield, *Strange Death*, p. 36.
93. *Hansard*, 5th series, vol. 16, col. 1548.
94. Blewett, *Peers*, p. 165.
95. *Pioneer*, 25 November 1910.

96. Ibid.
97. Ibid., 2 December 1910.
98. Ibid.
99. Ibid., 5 August 1910.
100. Ibid., 25 November 1910.
101. Ibid., 2 December 1910.
102. Craig, *Parliamentary*, p. 60.
103. *Pioneer*, 2 December 1910.
104. Ibid., 2, 9 December 1910.
105. Ibid., 2 December 1910.
106. Ibid.
107. Peter Rowland, *The Last Liberal Governments:: Unfinished Business 1911-1914*, 1971, p. 1. 'In April...an election court reversed the decision at Exeter, where a Liberal candidate had supposedly been elected...and declared that the Unionist candidate had been elected by one vote...' Strictly speaking, therefore, only 271 Liberals were elected in December 1910', Ibid. f.n; Craig, *Parliamentary*, p. 109.
108. Craig, *Parliamentary*, pp. 51, 60, 177, 197, 208, 209, 323, 540.
109. Blewett, *Peers*, p. 195-6.
110. Blewett, *Peers*, p. 234.
111. Cited in McKibbin, *Evolution*, p. 52.
112. McKibbin, MacDonald, p. 218.
113. Cited in Blewett, *Peers*, p. 236.
114. Ibid.
115. McKibbin, *Evolution*, p. 53.

7
RETURNS TO THE PARLIAMENTARY FRAY

1. Rowland, *1911-1914*, p. 12.
2. *Pioneer*, 10 February 1911.
3. *Hansard*, 5th series, vol. 22, cols. 2161-2168 (14 March 1911).
4. *Pioneer*, 31 March 1911.
5. *Hansard*, 5th series, vol. 24, cols. 1881-2, (26 April 1911); *Pioneer*, 26 May 1911; *Labour Party Annual Report 1912*, pp. 24-5; The resolution for a 30s Minimum Wage for Government workers was initially put to Annual Conference in 1908 by Frank Jackman, Chairman of the Woolwich Trades Council - it subsequently became party policy. See *Labour Party Annual Report 1908*, p. 77. The Woolwich Trades Council discussed the resolution in October 1907, Woolwich Trades Council, Minutes 24 October 1907, WLP 42, 1906-1910 (GHC).
6. *Hansard*, ibid.
7. Ibid.
8. *Pioneer*, 5 May 1911.
9. Ibid., 28 April 1911.
10. Frank Dilnot, 'The Old Order Changeth', in C. Silvester, *The Literary Companion to Parliament*, 1996, pp. 228-230, p. 229.
11. Ibid., pp. 229-30.
12. Dangerfield, *Strange Death*, p. 57.
13. Ibid., p. 58.
14. Rowland, *1911-1914*, pp. 32-3

15. *Pioneer*, 18 August 1911. For a full discussion on the National Insurance Bill of 1911, see W. J. Braithwaite, *Lloyd George's Ambulance Wagon*, 1957, *passim*.
16. Trade Union membership grew by 60 per cent between 1911-1914, the main increases of over 300 per cent was in unions connected with transport. See Henry Pelling, *Popular Politics and Society in Late Victorian England*, 1968, pp. 149-51.
17. Ibid., p. 51.
18. G. D. H. Cole, *Short History of the British Working Class Movement*, vol. III, 1927, p. 70.
19. B. Holton, *British Syndicalism 1900-1914*, 1976, p. 89.
20. Philip Snowden, *Socialism and Syndicalism*, 1911; Graham Taylor, 'The English Railway Strike and its Revolutionary Bearings', an address to the City Club of Chicago, in the *City Club Bulletin*, October 1911, vol. IV, No. 19; William Anderson, *What Means this Labour Unrest?* 1912; W. P. Ryan, *The Labour Revolt and Larkinism*, 1913; G. D. H. Cole, *Short History*; Donna Torr, *Tom Mann*, 1936; Tom Brown, *Trade Unions or Syndicalism*, 1943; G. D. H. Cole and Raymond Postgate, *The Common People 1746-1946*, 1946; John Lovell, *Stevedores and Dockers*, 1969, chap. 7; James Hinton, *Labour and Socialism 1867-1974*, 1983, chap. 5; Holton, *British Sydicalism*; Chushichi Tsuzuki, *Tom Mann 1856-1941*, 1991, chap. 8; Ken Coates and Tony Topham, *The Making of the Labour Movement*, 1994, Part II, pp. 422-511. For details of Tom Mann's books and articles, see Richard Storey (ed.), *Tom Mann: A Bibliography*, 1993.
21. The Act called upon employee and employer, where conflict occurs between them, to notify the Labour Department, who is bound to call an enquiry into the dispute 'within fifteen days. The master must lock out his men, and the men must not strike' until the inquiry has been published. *Pioneer*, 29 October 1909.
22. *Pioneer*, 20 October 1911.
23. TUC *Annual Conference Report*, 1911, p. 229
24. Ibid., p. 300.
25. *Pioneer*, 15 September 1911.
26. Ibid., 22 September 1911.
27. Quoted in Marquand, *MacDonald*, p. 146.
28. For the causes of the dispute see the *Report upon the Present Disputes affecting Transport Workers in the Port of London and on the Medway, together with the Minutes of the Evidence of the Inquiry*, May 1912, Cd. 6229, p. 3. Also, see Harry Gosling's, President of the NTWF, evidence to the inquiry on 24 May, pp. 8-49.
29. Lovell, *Stevedores*, p. 197. For a discussion on the foundation of the NTWF, see Coates and Topham, *The Making*, Part I, pp, 328-331, 341-2, 344.
30. Holton, *British Syndicalism*, p. 123.
31. *Hansard*, 5th series, vol. 39, col. 958, (12 June 1912); *Pioneer*, 14 June 1912.
32. *Hansard*, 5th series, vol. 40, cols. 45-48, (1 July 1912).
33. Ibid., cols. 892-894.
34. Lovell, *Stevedores*, p. 201.
35. S & B Webb, *Trade Unionism*, p. 687.
36. *Labour Party Annual Report*, 1914, Appendix V, p. 137; Tanner, *Political Change*, Table 11. 1, p. 322.
37. Ibid., *1912*, pp. 12-13.
38. Ibid., p. 99.
39. *Pioneer*, 21 November 1913.
40. Ibid., 10 July 1914; John Harkis, 'Industry and Politics in an Armaments Town', (Thames Polytechnic, MA. CNNA, 1991).

41. *Hansard*, 5th series, vol. 64, cols. 829, 887-88, (6, 7 July 1914).
42. Thomas to Crooks, 9 July 1914, in the *Pioneer*, 24 July 1914.
43. For an overview of Dilkes' contribution towards improving the condition of the working-class, see Roy Jenkins, *Sir Charles Dilke*, 1958, especially pp. 388-407.
44. *Hansard*, 5th series, vol. 35, cols. 846-51, (11 March 1912).
45. Ibid., col. 848.
46. Ibid., vol. 44, cols. 84-5, (10 November 1912).
47. Ibid., vol. 60, col. 776, (27 March 1914).
48. Ibid., cols. 777-8.
49. Ibid., vol. 63, cols. 1359-64, (18 June 1914).
50. Fair, *Conferences*, p. 112.
51. C. P. Scott, Diary 26 April 1914, 'Dillon called ... We spoke of the landing of arms and other illegalities in Ulster the previous day', in Wilson, *Political Diaries*, p. 84.
52. *Pioneer*, 18 July 1913.
53. Fair, *Conferences*, pp. 104-5. Also see Memo to Birrell, 24 July 1913, p. 317n.
54. *Pioneer*, 1 May 1914.
55. Ibid.
56. Quoted in Sylvester, *Parliament*, p. 252.
57. *Hansard*, 5th series, vol. 66, cols. 1019-20, (18 September 1914).
58. Quoted in Davis, Mary: *Sylvia Pankhurst: A Life in Radical Politics*, 1999, p. 20.
59. *Labour Party Conference 1913*, p. 87.
60. Ibid., p. 16.
61. WLRA, *Executive Report and Balance Sheet*, 1912, p. 3, presented to members 5 May 1913.
62. Ibid., 1904, p. 5, presented 6 June 1905.
63. Davis, *Sylvia Pankhurst*, p. 31.
64. J. Mazzini, *On the Duties of Man*, 1862, pp. 102, 106.
65. Haw, *Workhouse*, p. 206.
66. Thompson, *Socialists*, p. 255.

8
WAR AND PEACE

1. For example, G. D. H. Cole, *Labour in Wartime*, 1915, and *Trade Unionism and Munitions*, 1916; C. Wrigley, *David Lloyd George and the British Labour Movement*, 1976, and *Lloyd George and the Challenge of Labour*, 1990; R. J. Q. Adams, *Arms and the Wizard*, 1978. For socialist ideas and politics in Britain between 1914-18, see J. M. Winter, *Socialism and the Challenge of War*, 1974. Also relevant to this period is Ross McKibbin's study of the Labour Party, *Evolution*, especially chapter V, 'War and the New Social Order', pp. 88-111.
2. P. Stansky (ed.), *The Left and War*, 1969.
3. Ibid., p. 13
4. Parliamentary Party Report, 1914, *Labour Party Annual Report 1916*, p. 51
5. Stansky, *The Left*, p. 13. The seeming paradoxical position between a right-wing shift and the socialist constitution of 1918 will be discussed later in the chapter.
6. Haw, *Life*, pp. 317, 323
7. Marquand, *MacDonald*, p. 168
8. Mair to Scott, 4 August (1914), Wilson, *Political Diaries*, p. 99.
9. Asquith to Henderson, 28 August 1914, *Labour Party Annual Report*, 1916, pp. 4.
10. Ibid, Executive Committee, pp. 4-5

11. Parliamentary Recruitment General Purposes Committee, Minutes, 31 August 1914, MSS. 54192 A, f. 6 (BL.).
12. M. Gilbert, *Winston S. Churchill*, vol. III, 1914-16, 1971, p. 75; MSS. 54192A, f.8, (BL).
13. *Pioneer*, 12 February, 13 August 1914.
14. C. J. Wrigley, *Lloyd George*, 1976, pp. 91-93. For a discussion on the negotiations between the Government and the Trade Unions, see the Treasury Agreement 17-19 March, and the Supplementary Treasury Agreement 25 March, Cole, *Trade Unionism*, pp. 69-75.
15. *Pioneer*, 18 June 1915; Wrigley, *Lloyd George*, p. 95.
16. Cole, *Trade Unionism*, p. 71.
17. Ibid. pp. 72-3. For details of these conferences consult: Conference agreement between the Government and the ASE on means of increasing output, March 1915, MUN 5/10/180/42; Minutes of Treasury conference with delegates of ASE, 25 March 1915, MUN 5/9/180/10; Minutes of conference between Government and ASE, 25 March 1915, MUN 5/10/180/18 (NRO).
18. Joint Committee on Labour Problems after the War, *The Restoration of Trade Union Customs After The War*, 1916, p. 3, HD4. 801.42, Pamphlet Collection (BLPES).
19. P. Snowden, *Labour in Chains: The Peril of Industrial Conscription*, 1916, p.2, HD4. D33 (BLPES).
20. R. J. Q. Adams, *Wizard*, 1978, p. 31.
21. Wrigley, *Lloyd George*, p, 110. For an inside view of the great shell scandal and the subsequent political crisis see the *War Memoirs of David Lloyd George*, vol. I, 1938, pp. 112-42.
22. T. Wilson, *The Downfall of the Liberal Party 1914-1935*, 1966, p. 54. For a study of events in May 1915, consult S. E. Koss, 'The Destruction of Britain's Last Liberal Government', *Journal of Modern History*, vol. 11, No. 2 (June 1968), pp. 257-77; C. Hazelhurst discusses the Koss thesis, in *Politicians at War*, 1971, pp. 235-260.
23. *History of the Ministry of Munitions* (HMM), vol. VIII, Part 1, p. 24.
24. C. P. Scott to L. T. Hobhouse, 23 May 1915, Wilson, *Political Diaries*, p. 124.
25. Hazelhurst, *Politicians*, p. 197.
26. See Arsenal discharges, Chapter 5.
27. *Murray Report*, p. 8.
28. *Pioneer*, 13 June 1913, 27 March 1914.
29. Ibid. 31 July 1914.
30. Ibid. 2 April 1915.
31. *Hansard*, 5th series, vol. 71, col. 850 (29 April 1915).
32. Ibid.
33. *Daily News*, 29 June 1915.
34. *Pioneer*, 7 May 1915, and see 'The Case of Woolwich Against the Armaments Ring', July 1922.
35. Ibid. 14 May 1915.
36. Ibid. 21 May 1915.
37. Adams, *Wizard*, p. 35.
38. Ibid. pp. 39, 41.
39. *Hansard*, 5th series, vol. 72, cols. 110-113 (7 June 1915).
40. *Pioneer*, 11 June 1915.
41. Parliamentary Report 1915, *Labour Party Annual Report* 1916, p. 56.
42. *Pioneer*, 27 March 1914.
43. S. Pankhurst, *The Home Front*, 1932, p. 211.

44. *Hansard*, 5th series, vol. 72, col. 1922 (1 July 1915).
45. Addison: Diary, 4 August 1915, *Four and Half Years*, vol. 1, 1934, p. 116.
46. *Hansard*, 5th series, vol. 72, cols. 2097-98 (1 July 1915).
47. Ibid. col. 2098.
48. Addison: Diary, 30 July, 4, 23 August 1915, *Four and a Half*, pp. 115-6, 121.
49. In 'The Secrets of his Power', Barefoot refers to Crooks as the Gov'nor, *Pioneer*, 10 June 1921
50. *Pioneer*, 23 July, 6 August 1915.
51. Ibid. 6 August 1915.
52. Ibid. 13, 27 August 1915.
53. R. J. Q. Adams and P. P. Poirier, *The Conscription Controversy in Great Britain 1900-18*, 1987, p. 270, n. 4. The Labour Party Recruiting Committee included representatives of the Labour Party, the TUC Parliamentary Committee, and the General Federation of Trade Unions and the Trade Union Congress. H. Gosling, C. W. Bowerman, W. A. Appleton, W. Sanders, G. Wardle, J. Hodge, and J. O'Grady represented Labour interests on the Joint Committee at one time or another between October 1915 – July 1916. Minutes of Joint Recruiting Committee, MSS. 54192B, 11 October 1915 – 20 July 1916, (British Library).
54. *Pioneer*, 29 October, 19 November 1915.
55. Under the 'Derby Scheme', munition workers were asked to attest; but the calling up of men who were required for work at home was prevented by a double procedure. Lists of 'starred' and 'reserved' occupations were drawn up, and men working in these were not liable to be called up. For a discussion of the Derby Scheme, see Adams and Poirier 'Lord Derby Shows the Way', *Conscription*, pp. 119-143.
56. Cole, *Trade Unionism*, p. 83.
57. 'In the Arsenal, dilution was controlled by the shop stewards. In each group of shops a representative of the men, guided by the shop stewards' executive committee, was present to consult with management, and only if all conditions were fulfilled and dilution unavoidable was permission given.' C. Job, *London's Arsenal*, 1945, p. 11.
58. D. Weinbren, 'From gun carriage to railway carriage': the fight for peace work at Woolwich Arsenal 1919-22', *Labour History Review*, vol. 63.3, winter 1998, pp. 277-297. p. 283.
59. *Pioneer*, 24 September 1915. The deputation included the ASE, Workers' Union, Building Trades Union, Gasworkers' Union, Electrical Trades Union, Labour Protection League, and the National Union of Clerks
60. D. Thom, 'The Ideology of Woman's Work 1914-1924, with special reference to the NFWW and other trade unions', PhD thesis (Greenwich University, 1982), pp. 212-13.
61. Job, *Arsenal*, p. 9.
62. Asquith to Crooks, 17 December 1915; Crooks' Privy Seal, 27 January 1916. Both in the possession of Sue Spear, Mylor Bridge, Falmouth, Cornwall.
63. *Pioneer*, 7 January 1916; WLRA General Council Minutes, 9 June 1916, Minute Book WLP. 1910-17 (GHC).
64. Cole, *Trade Unionism*, p. 106
65. *Pioneer*, 7 January 1916.
66. *Hansard*, 5th series, vol. 82, col. 2345 (26 May 1916).
67. *Pioneer*, 7 January 1916.
68. Wrigley, *Lloyd George*, p. 167.

69. *Pioneer*, 7 January 1916
70. WLRA General Council (GC) Minutes, 20 January 1916, Minute Book WLP. 1910-17.
71. *Pioneer*, 10 June 1921.
72. Cole, *Trade Unionism*, pp. 100-1.
73. D. Thom, 'Women Munition Workers in the Woolwich Arsenal', p. 44, MA. thesis (Greenwich, 1970); Hogg, *The Royal Arsenal*, vol. 2, Appendix X, p. 1290.
74. *HMM*, vol. v, Part 2, pp. 16-17.
75. *Pioneer*, 2 June 1916.
76. Ibid.
77. National Federation of Women Workers, *Biennial Delegate Conference*, 6 May 1916, HD 607a, 1916 (TUCLMU). George Barnes was also nominated a Trustee.
78. J. O. Stubbs, 'Lord Milner and patriotic labour 1914-1918', *English Historical Review*, 87, 4, (1972), pp. 717-54, p. 730.
79. C. Wrigley, *Lloyd George and the Challenge of Labour*, 1990, p7; R. Douglas, 'The National Democratic Party and the British Workers League', *Historical Journal*, xv, 3 (1972), pp. 533-552, p. 534. I am indebted to Stephen Bird for suggesting this article, and to Simon Burgess for the search.
80. Stubbs, Lord Milner, p. 717. For a discussion on Lord Milner, his doctrine and his school, see V. Halperin, *Lord Milner and the Empire*, 1952, chap. V, pp. 177-220. 'Milner had a Liberal past as a writer for the *Pall Mall Gazette*, and as a Liberal candidate in 1885', for Middlesex, Harrow. S. MacCoby, *English Radicalism 1886-1914*, 1953, p. 172n.
81. C. Wrigley, 'In Excess Of Their Patriotism: The National Party and Threats of Subversion', in C. Wrigley (ed.), *Warfare, Diplomacy and Politics*, 1986, pp. 93-119, p. 98; Douglas, National Democratic Party, p. 535.
82. *Objects of the British Workers' National League*, May 1917 (?), War Collection, Hoover Institute of War, Peace, and Revolution, Stanford University, California, USA.
83. *Labour Party Annual Report 1918*, p. 35.
84. WLP GC Minutes, 21 June 1918, Minute Book 1917-23, WLP. 41.1, p. 88.
85. Stansky, *The Left*, p. 173.
86. Ibid.
87. WLRA GC Minutes, 8 December 1916, Minute Book WLP. 1910-17.
88. *Labour Party Annual Report 1917*, p. 43; 'The joint conference [7 December] of the Executive and the Parliamentary Party was held in the House of Commons...under the presidency of Mr. George J. Wardle, M.P., the Chairman of both bodies', Stansky, *The Left*, p. 173.
89. *East End News*, 7 June 1921; Lord Stanfordham — Crooks, *Pioneer*, 17 November 1916.
90. F. Sainsbury, 'The Silvertown Explosion', *Newham History Society Occasional Papers*, No. 2, November 1988, pp. 25-44, p. 25, (Stratford Library).
91. W. Ramsey, *The End East then and Now*, 1997, p. 90. For documents of the Silvertown explosion, see H. Bloch and G. Hill (ed.), *The Silvertown Explosion: First Hand Accounts and Reports 1917*, 1997, (THLHL).
92. Sainbury, Silvertown, p. 30.
93. *East End News*, 26 January 1917.
94. *Pioneer*, 18 February 1921.
95. *Daily Sketch*, 14 June 1917. For the Raid of the 13 June, see F. Morison, *War on the Great Cities*, 1937, pp. 120-7. In the City of London and the East End the casualty list was 97 killed, 439 injured.

96. *Daily Sketch*, 14 June 1917.
97. Ibid.
98. *Daily Graphic*, 9 July 1917.
99. *Daily Sketch*, 14 June 1917.
100. *Pioneer*, 'Parliamentary Dairy', 22 June 1917.
101. Ibid., 22 June 1917, 11 February 1921.
102. A. J. P. Taylor, 'The Great War — The Triumph of E. D. Morel (II)', in Stansky, *The Left*, pp. 306-13.
103. Tanner, *Political Change*, pp. 396, 384. The Woolwich Labour Party (it changed its name in June 1917) were of the opinion that: 'Henderson was dismissed from the Cabinet because he refused to mislead the Labour Party Conference as to the attitude of the Russian Govt. towards the proposed International Conference... In view of this treatment...the Labour Party can do better work for the Country if it is not represented in the Cabinet, we ask the Party to consider the question of withdrawing its representatives from the Government.' WLP GC Minutes, 7 September 1917, WLP. 1917-1923, 41. 1, p. 47.
104. Tanner, *Political Change*, p. 395.
105. McKibbin, *Evolution*, p. 92, 101.
106. Tanner, *Political Change*, p. 399.
107. Minutes of the Special Conference, 10 January 1918, WLP. 1917-23, 41.1, p. 69. One hundred and sixteen delegates representing sixty organisations attended the Conference.
108. Ibid.
109. McKibbin, *Evolution*, pp. 94-5.
110. Minutes of the Special Conference, 10 January 1918, WLP. Minute Book 1917-1923, 41.1, p. 69.
111. *Pioneer*, 19 April 1918.
112. McKibbin, *Evolution*, p. 91.
113. *Labour Party Annual Conference*, 1917, pp. 116-17, 123.
114. R Milliband, *Parliamentary Socialism*, 1964, pp. 60-2.
115. WLP GC Minutes, 15 March 1918, WLP. Minute Book 1917-1923, 41.1, p. 77.
116. *Pioneer*, 19 April 1918.
117. *Labour Party Annual Report*, June 1918, p. 6; Mckibbin, *Evolution*, p. 111.
118. *Pioneer*, 22 June 1918.
119. T. Wilson, 'The Coupon and the British General Election of 1918', *Journal of Modern History*, xxxvi 36, 1964, pp. 28-42, p. 35; *The Downfall*, p. 142.
120. Wilson, 'The Coupon', p. 39.
121. Ibid. pp. 29-30.
122. Wilson, *The Downfall*, Appendix 1B, p. 158. There were nine other unopposed Labour candidates: Watts Morgan (Rhonnda East), W. Abraham (Rhonnda West), F. Hall (Normanton), Vernon Hartshorn (Ogmore Vale), T. Richards (Ebbw Vale), W. Brace (Abertillery), J. O'Grady (Leeds, S. E.), J. W. Taylor (Chester-le-Street), and J. R. Clynes (Manchester, Platting). *Labour Party Annual Report*, 1919, Appendix VI, p. 187.
123. *Pioneer*, 6 December 1918.
124. *Pioneer*, 3 January 1919.
125. A. J. P. Taylor, *English History 1914-1945*, 1975, p. 128; McKibbin, *Evolution*, p. 111, 'twenty-five M.P.s came from the Miners' Federation alone.' For favourable Labour

electoral performances in the 1918 election, see Tanner, *Political Change*, Appendix 6, pp. 466-69.
126. *Pioneer*, 3, 10 January 1919.
127. Ibid. 17 January 1919.
128. *Hansard*, (5th series), vols. 112-122, *passim*.
129. *Pioneer*, 5 September 1919.
130. Ibid. 9 January 1920.
131. Ibid. 16 April 1920. The Labour majority over the Coalition was 9,389 votes. Compared with the general election of 1918, the Labour vote had 'increased by 7,104, and the Government majority of 9,120 had been converted into a minority of 9,048.'
132. *Hansard*, 5th edition, vols. 131-134, *passim*.
133. Ibid. vol. 134, cols. 1877-78 (16 November 1921).
134. *Pioneer*, 11 February 1921.
135. WLP *Annual Report*, 1920, p.7, WLP. 40.2.
136. *Pioneer*, 18 January 1921.
137. Ibid. 11, 18 February 1921.
138. H..Snell, *Men, Movements*, pp. 204-5.
139. Quoted in Marquand, *MacDonald*, p. 275.
140. Ibid.
141. *East End News*, 7 June 1921; *Pioneer*, 10 June 1921.
142. *Pioneer*, 10 June 1921.
143. Ibid. 17 June 1921.
144. *East End News*, and the *Pioneer*, 10 July 1921; *Pathe News*, 8 July 1921, video copy in the possession of GHC and the author.
145. Harry Orbell was national organiser of the Dockworkers' Union from 1889 to 1914.
146. Haw, *Life*, pp. xvii, xviii.
147. Part of epitaph on Crook' gravestone.

BIBLIOGRAPHY

MANUSCRIPT COLLECTIONS

AT BANCROFT LOCAL HISTORY LIBRARY, TOWER HAMLETS
Poplar Labor League, *Annual Reports,* (1896-1904).
Vestry of the Parish of All - Saints, Poplar, Minute Book, (1888-1903).
Poplar Borough Council, Minute Book, (1900-1).

AT THE BRITISH LIBRARY OF POLITICAL AND ECONOMIC SCIENCE
The Fabian Society Papers.
Francis Johnson Collection. Including the Independent Labour Party Collection, and the National Administrative Council Minutes and Letter Files.
George Lansbury Papers.
William Beveridge Papers, (Collection B, Unemployment).
————— Munitions Collection.
A. G. Gardiner Collection.
J. Ramsey MacDonald Papers.
Passfield Papers.

AT THE GREENWICH HERITAGE CENTER, ROYAL ARSENAL, WOOLWICH
Royal Arsenal Co-operative Society, archive
Comradeship, (1897-1954).
Co-operative Society, *Annual Congress Reports,* (1896-1903).
Royal Arsenal Co-operative Society: Political Purposes Committee Minutes, (1876-1985).
————— Letter Books, [5], Declaration Books, (1872-8).
————— Education Committee (c1898-1919).
Woolwich Labour Representative Association/Labour Party archive
Charles Grinling Collection.
Correspondence from Labour Party Central Office, (1903-10).
Election Analysis, (1889-1910).
Letter Book of William Barefoot, Secretary, WLRA, (1903).
Scrapbook of Elections, (1903-31).
Woolwich and District Labour Notes, (1898-9).
Woolwich Labour Journal, (1901-4).

Woolwich Labour Pioneer, (1904-21).
Woolwich Labour Representative Association/Woolwich Labour Party, Minute Books, various (1903-1917/1917-1923).
Woolwich & District Trades & Labour Council: Minute Books, (1904-16). (Complete deposits are in the Board of Trade archives at the National Record Office (NRO), Kew. Some Annual Reports in the TUC Collection, (London Metropolitan University).

AT THE HOOVER INSTITUTE, STANFORD UNIVERSITY, CALIFORNIA, USA
Manifesto of the British Workers' National League (1916).

AT THE LONDON METROPOLITAN ARCHIVE
London County Council, Bridges Committee, Minutes, Agenda's, and Presented Papers (1893-1910).
——— Parks and Open Spaces Committee, Minutes (1893-1907).
——— Technical Education Board, Minutes and Agendas (1893-1904).
Metropolitan Asylum Board, Minutes (1898-1904).
——— Children's Committee, Minutes (1898-1904).
Poplar Board of Guardians, Minutes (1893-1907).

AT THE MODERN RECORDS CENTER, UNIVERSITY OF WARWICK
Amalgamated Stevedores Labour Protection League, *Annual Reports.*
Board of Trade Papers.
Dock, Warf, Riverside & General Workers Union, Annual Reports & Minutes of Annual Delegate Meetings, (1890-93).
The Great Dock Labourers' Strike of 1889, Manifesto & Statement of Accounts, (1890).
Tillett/Mackay Papers.

AT THE LABOUR HISTORY ARCHIVE & STUDY CENTRE, MANCHESTER
Labour Protection League, No. 4 Branch, Minute Book, (1880-83).
Labour Representation Committee/Labour Party, Correspondence, (1903-1920).

AT THE TUC COLLECTION, LONDON METROPOLITAN UNIVERSITY
Amalgamated Society of Engineers, *Quarterly Reports 1913-1918.*
London Trades Council, Minute Books (1887-1900).
TUC Annual Reports (1908-1918).

AT THE WORKING CLASS MOVEMENT LIBRARY, SALFORD
Gasworkers' & General Labourers' Union, Minute Book, (1889). Yearly Report & Balance Sheets, (1889-94), and Cash Book, (1889-94).

OTHER COLLECTIONS
Arthur Balfour Papers, British Library.
John Burns, Trade Union Collection, University of London.
Fred Butler Papers, in the possession of Sheila Moilliet, Ontario, Canada.
Will Crooks Papers, in the possession of Sue Spear, Mylor Bridge, Falmouth, Cornwall.
Herbert Gladstone Papers, British Library.
Bruce Glasier Papers, Liverpool University.
David Lloyd George Papers, House of Lords Record Office and the NRO.
Ministry of Munitions Papers, NRO.

J. Ramsay MacDonald Papers, NRO.
Walter Long Papers, British Library.
Labour Representation Committee and Labour Party, *Annual Reports 1900-1921* (1906-8 missing), and the Woolwich Labour Representation Association, *Annual Reports (1903-1916)*, in possession of Author.
Parliamentary Recruitment Committee 1914-16, British Library.

OFFICIAL PUBLICATIONS
Royal Commission on Labour, Cd. 6078/ 1892.
Board of Trade Labour Department, Agencies and Methods for Dealing with the Unemployed, Cd. 7182/ 1893-4.
Royal Commission on Labour: Minority Report 1893-4, by William Abraham MP (Mabon), Michael Austin MP, James Mawdsley MP, and Tom Mann.
London County Council: Census of London 1901, LCC Publication No.627/ 1903.
London County Council: Report of the Conference on the Lack of Employment in London, November 1903.
Report of Poplar Labour Colony, 1904.
 Transcript of the Shorthand Notes taken at the Enquiry ordered by the Local Government Board into the Administration of the Poor Law in the Poplar Union, Cd. 3274/1906.
Report to the President of the Local Government Board on the Poplar Union, by J. S. Davy, Cd. 3240/ 1906.
Report of the Conference appointed to Examine the Shops and Machinery at Woolwich Arsenal, other than the Danger Buildings and Torpedo Factory, in order to consider whether any article not now made in the Ordinance Factories can appropriately be made there with this Machinery (Henderson Report), Cd, 3514/ 1907.
Report of the Government Factories and Workshops Committee, (Murray Report) Cd. 3626/ 1907.
Royal Commission on the Poor Laws and the Relief of Distress, Vol. XIX, Cd. 4795/1909, *Report on the Effects of Employment or Assistance given to the Unemployed since 1886 as a Means of Relieving Distress outside the Poor Law*, by Cyril Jackson and the Rev. J. C. Pringle.
Royal Commission on the Poor Law and Relief of Distress, vol. XXXVII, Cd 4499/1909, Report by Russell Wakefield, Francis Chandler, George Lansbury, and Sidney Webb.
Royal Commission on the Poor Law and Relief of Distress, Minutes of Evidence, Cd 5066/1910.
Report Upon The Present Disputes Affecting Transport Workers in the Port of London and on the Medway together with Minutes of Evidence of the Enquiry, Cd, 6229/ 1912.
Board of Trade, Seventeenth abstract of labour statistics, Cd. 7733/ 1914-16.
Parliamentary Debates, forth series (1903-1908), and *Hansard*, fifth series, House of Commons (1909-1921).

NEWSPAPERS AND PERIODICALS
East End Advertiser
East End News
East London Advertiser
Eastern Post
Clarion
Daily Chronicle
Daily Graphic
Daily News
Daily Sketch
Fabian News
Illustrated London News

ILP News
Justice
Kentish Independent
Labour Leader
Morning Leader
Municipal Journal
Nation
Nineteenth Century
Nottingham Daily Express
Review of Reviews
Shipping Gazette
The Clare Market Review
The Speaker
The Star
The Times
The Toynbee Record
The Western Daily Mercury
Times Weekly
Yorkshire Daily Post
Westminster Gazette
Woolwich & District Labour Journal
Woolwich & District Labour Notes
Woolwich Gazette
Woolwich Pioneer& Labour Journal

FABIAN TRACTS

W. L. Phillips, *Why are the Many Poor*, Tract No. 1, (1884).
S. Webb, *Facts for Socialists*, No. 5, (1887).
——— *Figures for Londoners*, No. 10, (1889).
——— *Reform of the Poor Law*, No. 17, (1890).
S. W. Group, *Questions for Guardians*, No. 20, (1890).
G. B. Shaw, *Fabian Election Manifesto*, No. 40, (1892).
John Burns, *The Unemployed*, No. 47, (1893).
J. F. Oakeshott, *Humanising the Poor Law*, No. 54, (1894).
S. Webb, *Labor in the Longest Reign (1837-1897)*, No 75, (1897).
E. R. Pease, *How Trade Unions Benefit Workmen*, No. 104, (1900).
S. Webb, *The Education Act, 1902*, No. 114, (1903).
H. Bland, *After Bread, Education*, No. 120, 1905).

CONTEMPORARY BOOKS, PAMPHLETS AND ARTICLES

A. H. D. Acland and B. Jones, *Working Men Co-operators*, (1893).
J. Adderley, *In Slums and Society*, (1916).
C. Addison, *Politics from Within 1911-1918*, 2 vols. (1924).
Wm. C. Anderson, *The Great Strike Movement of 1911 and Its Lessons*, (1912).
——— *What Means This Labour Unrest?* (1912).
W. Barefoot, 'Will Crooks' Personality: The Secret of his Power', *Pioneer*, (10 June 1921).
W. Beveridge, 'Emergency Funds for the Relief of the Unemployed: A Note on their Historical Development', *The Clare Market Review*, (May 1906).
——— *Unemployment: A Problem for Industry*, (1910).

BIBLIOGRAPHY 265

H. Bland, 'The Outlook', in G.B. Shaw (ed.), *Fabian Essays in Socialism*, (1889).
C. Booth (ed.), *Labour and Life of the People: East London*, vol. 1, (1889).
─────── *Life and Labour of the People of London*, (1902).
H. H. Champion, *The Great Dock Strike*, (1889).
W. Chance, *The Better Administration of the Poor Law*, (1895).
G. D. H. Cole, *Labour in Wartime*, (1915).
─────── *Trade Unionism and Munitions*, (1916).
W. Crooks, *An Address on the Unemployment Problem*, (1905).
─────── *Mr. Percy Alden. M.A.: His Public and Civic Life*, (1904).
─────── 'My Early Struggles', in *Great Thoughts*, (1917).
─────── 'Piety in the Home', *in Labour and Religion*, (1910).
─────── *The British Workman Defends His Home*, (1917).
W.T.Davies and W.B.Neville, (eds.), *The History of the RACS Ltd 1868-1918*, (1921).
J. T. Dodd, *The Unemployed and the Powers of the Guardians of the Poor*, (1903).
East End News. 'Poplar's Most Popular Boy: An Appreciation', (7 June 1921).
Enemies of the Red Flag, *Socialism and the Osborne Judgement*, (1910).
F. Engels, *The Condition of the Working-Class in England*, (1892).
J. F.B. Firth, *Municipal London*, (1876).
─────── *London Government and How to Reform It*, (1881).
─────── *The Reform of London Government and the City Guilds*, (1888).
J. F. B. Firth and E. R. Simpson, *London Government under the Local Government Act*, (1888).
V. Fisher, "Democritus", *Labour and Democracy: Being a Series of Open Letters to the Labour Party*, (1916).
J. Gunning, *Hollesley Bay: Farm Colony Experiment*, (1907).
J. Keir Hardie, *The Party Pledge and the Osborne Judgement*, (1911).
G. Haw, *From Workhouse to Westminster*, (1907).
─────── *The Life Story of Will Crooks, MP*, (1916).
History of the Ministry of Munitions 1918-22, 8 vols. (1922).
E. G. Howell and M. Wilson, *West Ham*, (1907).
Joint Committee on Labour Problems after the War, *The Munitions Acts and the Restoration of Trade Union Customs*, (1916).
─────── *The Restoration of Trade Union Customs after the War*, (1916).
B. Jones, *The Next Parliamentary Election: A Labour Representative for Woolwich: Report of the Meeting at the Assembly Rooms...: address, etc.* (1892).
J. Lloyd, *London Municipal Government: History of a Great Reform 1880-1888*, (1910).
J. Ramsay MacDonald, *The New Unemployment Bill of the Labour Party*, (1907).
─────── *War and the Workers: A Plea for Democratic Control*, (1915).
The Pioneer, 'Will Crooks' Life Story: A Sketch of his Remarkable Career', (11 February 1921).
─────── 'Will Crooks and His Work for Woolwich: A Retrospective Over Twenty Years', (10 June 1921).
T. Mann and B. Tillett, *The "New" Trades Unionism*, (1890)
J. Morley, *Life of Gladstone*, vol.III, (1903).
W. Mornington and F. V. Lampard, *Our London Poor Law Schools*, (1898).
W. V. Osborne, *My Case. The causes and effects of the Osborne judgement*, (1910).
─────── *Trade Union Funds and Party Politics*, (1910).
E. R. Pease, *The History of the Fabian Society*, (1916).
W. P. Ryan, *The Labour Revolt and Larkinism*, (1913).
P. Snowden, *Labour in Chains: The Peril of Industrial Conscription*, (1917).
─────── *Socialism and Syndicalism*, (1911).
H. E. Sturge, 'Hollesley Bay', in the *Toynbee Record*, (March 1908).

G. Taylor, 'England's Revolutionary Strike', in *The City Club Bulletin* (Chicago), vol. IV, no. 19, (October 1911).
B. Tillett, *The Dock Labourers' Bitter Cry, An Address by a Docker*, (1889).
S & B. Webb, *The History of Trade Unionism 1660-1920*, (1920).

REFERENCE WORKS

J. M. Bellamy and J. Saville, (eds.) *Dictionary of Labour Biography*, 7 vols. (1972-1984).
W. Chamberlain, *Industrial Relations in Wartime: Great Britain, 1914-1918. Annotated Bibliography of Materials in the Hoover Library on War, Revolution, and Peace*, (1940).
C. Cook, with others, *Sources in British Political History 1900-1951*, vol. 1: *A Guide to the Archives of Selected Organisations and Societies*, (1975), vol. 2: *A Guide to the Papers of Selected Public Servants*, (1975), vol. 3 and 4: *A Guide to the Private Papers of Members of Parliament*, (1977), vol. 6: *First Consolidated Supplement*, (1985).
F. W. S. Craig, *British Parliamentary Election Results 1885-1918*, (1974).
────── *British Parliamentary Election Results 1918-1948*, (1977).
V. F. Gilbert, Cumulative Index to the *Bulletin of the Society for the Study of Labour History* (1986-1989) and the *Labour History Review* (1990-1995), (1998).
────── *Labour and Social History Theses: American, British and Irish university theses and dissertations in the field of British and Irish labour history, presented between 1900 and 1978*, (1982).
T. Hogg (ed.), *Arsenal Who's Who*, (n.d).
R. Harrison, G. Woolven, R. Duncan. *The Warwick Guide to British Labour Periodicals 1790-1970*, (1977).
C. Hazlehurst and C. Woodland, *A Guide to the Papers of British Cabinet Ministers 1900-1964*, (1996).
C. Tagg and L. Glenister, *London Laws and Byelaws*, (1908).
C. Silvester, *The Literary Companion to Parliament*, (1996).
A. Marsh and J. Ryan, *Historical Directory of Trade Unions*, (1987).

SECONDARY SOURCES
Published in London unless otherwise stated

R. J. Q. Adams, *Bonar Law*, (1999).
────── *Arms and the Wizard*, (1978).
R. J. Q. Adams and P. P. Poirier, *The Conscription Controversy in Great Britain 1900-18*, (Ohio 1987).
P. Adelman, *The Rise of the Labour Party 1880-1945*, (1986).
────── *Victorian Radicalism*, (1984).
C. Addison, *Four and a Half Years*, 2 vols. (1934).
W. H. G. Armytage, *A. J. Mundella 1825-1897*, (1951).
H. H. Asquith, *Memories and Reflections 1852-1927*, 2 vols, (Boston 1928).
J. Attfield, *With Light of Knowledge: A Hundred Years of Education in the Royal Co-operative Society 1877-1977*, (1981).
Rodney Barker, *Education and Politics 1900-1951*, (Oxford 1972).
W. Barefoot, *25 Years History of the Woolwich Labour Party*, (1928).
Barrow and Bullock (eds.), *Democratic Ideas and the British Labour Movement 1880-1914*, (Cambridge 1996).
F. Bealey and H. Pelling, *Labour and Politics 1900-1906: A History of the Labour Representation Committee*, (1958).

F. Bealey (ed.), *The Social and Political Thought of the British Labour Party*, (1970).
Lord Beaverbrook, *Politicians and the War 1914-1916*, (1928).
J. Belcham, *Industrialization and the Working Class*, (1990).
R. Bellamy, *Victorian Liberalism*, (1990).
C. Benn, *Keir Hardie*, (1992).
G. L. Bernstein, *Liberalism and Liberal Politics in Edwardian England*, (1986).
W. Beveridge, *Power and Influence*, (1953).
E. F. Biagini and A. J Reid (eds.), *Currents of Radicalism: Popular radicalism, organised labour and Party
politics in Britain, 1850-1914*, (Cambridge 1991).
A. Bird and H. Nabb, *Stoking up the Past*, (Bristol 1989).
D. Blaazer, *The Poplar Front and the Progressive Tradition*, (Cambridge 1992).
N. Blewett, *The Peers, The Parties and the People: The British General Elections of 1910*, (Toronto 1972).
H. Bloch and G. Hill, *The Silvertown Explosion 1917*, (1997).
W. J. Braithwaite, *Lloyd George's Ambulance Wagon*, (1957).
N. Branson, *George Lansbury and the Councillors' Revolt: Poplarism 1919-1925*, (1979).
A. Briggs and J. Saville, (eds.), *Essays in Labour History*, (1960).
———— *Essays in Labour History 1886-1923*, (1971).
K. D. Brown, *Labour and Unemployment 1900-1914*, (Newton Abbot 1971).
———— *Essays in Anti-Labour History*, (1974)
———— *The First Labour Party 1906-1914*, (1986).
T. Brown, *Trade Unions or Syndicalism*, (1943).
J. Charmley, *Churchill: The End of Glory*, (1993).
W. Churchill. *The World Crisis*, (1931).
D. Clark, *Colne Valley; Radicalism to Socialism*, (1981).
P. Clarke, *Lancashire and the New Liberalism*, (Cambridge 1971).
———— *Liberals and Social Democrats*, (Cambridge 1978).
F. S. Clayton, *John Wilson of Woolwich*, (1927).
H. A. Clegg, A. Fox and A. F. Thompson, *British Trade Unions since 1889*, vol. 1, (Oxford 1964), vol. II, 1911-1933, (Oxford 1985).
K. Coates and T. Topham, *The Making of the Labour Movement*, (Nottingham 1994).
C. Cook and J. Stevenson, *Modern British History 1714-1987*, (1988).
G. D. H. Cole, *Short History of the British Working Class Movement*, vol. III, (1927).
G. D. H. Cole and R. Postgate, *The Common People*, (1946).
M. Crick, *The History of the Social Democratic Federation*, (Keele 1994).
G. Crossick, *An Artisan Elite in Victorian Society: Kentish London 1840 -1880*, (1979).
G. Dangerfield, *The Strange Death of Liberal England*, 1935, (1997).
J. Davis, *Reforming London*, (Oxford 1988).
R. E. Dowse, *Left in the Centre*, (1966).
R. Ensor, *England 1870 - 1914*, (1936).
J. Fair, *British Interparty Conferences: A Study of the Procedure of Conciliation in British Politics 1867-1921*, (Oxford 1980).
D. Feldman and G. Stedman Jones (eds.), *Metropolis: London, Histories and Representations Since 1800*, (1989).
B. Fryer, and S. Williams, *A Century of Service 1889-1993*, (1993).
A. G. Gardiner, *John Benn and the Progressive Movement*, (1925).
D. Lloyd George, *War Memoirs of David Lloyd George*, vol. I, (1938).
M. Gilbert, *Winston S. Churchill*, vol. III, 1914-16, (1971).
R. Gray, *The Aristocracy of Labour in Nineteenth-century Britain c. 1850-1914*, (1981).

J. Grigg, *Lloyd George: The Peoples Champion 1902-1911*, (1978).
────── *Lloyd George: From Peace to War 1912-1916*, (1985).
────── *Lloyd George: War Leader 1916-1918*, (2002).
E. Halevy, *Imperialism and the Rise of Labour*, (1929).
────── *The Rule of Democracy 1905-1914*, (1952).
V. Halperin, *Lord Milner and the Empire*, (1952).
J. Harris, *Unemployment and Politics*, (Oxford 1972).
────── *William Beveridge*, (Oxford 1977).
W. Harry, *The Royal Arsenal Woolwich*, (n.d.).
A. Haworth and D. Hayter (eds.), *Men Who Made Labour*, (2006).
C. Hazlehurst, *Politicians at War*, (1971).
J. Hinton, *Labour and Socialism, A History of the British Labour Movement 1867-1974*, (Massachusetts 1983).
E. J. Hobsbawn, *Labour's Turning Point 1888-1900*, (1948).
────── *Labouring Men*, (1986).
O. Hogg, *The Royal Arsenal, Its Background, Origin and Subsequent History*, (1963).
B. Holton, *British Syndicalism 1900-1914*, (1976).
E. Hopkins, *Working-Class Self-Help in Nineteenth-century England*, (New York 1995).
D. Howell, *British Workers and the Independent Labour Party*, (Manchester 1983).
A. W. Humphrey, *The Workers' Share*, (1930).
J. Jacobs, *London Trades Council 1860-1950*, (1950).
D. James, *Class and Politics in a Northern Industrial Town: Keighley 1880-1914*, (Keele 1995).
D. James, T. Jowitt, and K. Laybourne (eds.), *The Centennial History of the Independent Labour Party*, (Halifax 1992).
E.F.E. Jefferson, *The Woolwich Story 1890-1965*, (1970).
J. B. Jefferys, *The Story of the Engineers*, (1945).
K. Jefferys (ed.), *Leading Labour*, (1999).
R. Jenkins, *Sir Charles Dilke*, (1958).
────── *Asquith*, (1964).
────── *Mr. Balfour's Poodle*, (1954).
────── *Churchill*, (2001).
C. Job, *London's Arsenal*, (1945).
Y. Kapp, *Eleanor Marx*: vol. II, *The Crowded Years, 1884-1898*, (1976).
G. Kichman, *Fly a Flag for Poplar*, (1975).
W. Lax, *Lax of Poplar*, (1927).
B. Lancaster, *Radicalism, Cooperation and Socialism: Leicester working-class politics 1860-1906*, (Leicester 1987).
G. Lansbury, *Looking Backwards and Forwards*, (1935).
────── *My Life*, (1928).
K. Laybourn, *The Rise of Labour*, (1988).
F. M. Leventhal, *Arthur Henderson*, (Manchester 1989).
J. Lovell, *Stevedores & Dockers*, (1969).
F. S. L. Lyons, *Ireland Since the Famine*, (1971).
S. MacCoby, *English Radicalism 1886-1914*, (1953).
────── *English Radicalism: The End?* (1963).
────── (ed.), *The Radical Tradition*, (1952).
N & J. Mackenzie, (eds.), *The Diary of Beatrice Webb*, vol. 2, 1892-1905, (1983), vol. 3, 1905-1924, (1984).
────── *The Diaries of Beatrice Webb*, (2000)
D. M. Smith, *Mazzini*, (Newhaven 1994).

D. Marquand, *Ramsay MacDonald*, (1977).
A. Marwick, *The Deluge*, (1991).
L. Masterman, *C. F. G. Masterman*, (1939).
R. M. Martin, *The Lancashire Giant*, (Liverpool 2000).
A. M. McBriar, *Fabian Socialism and English Politics 1884-1918*, (Cambridge 1962).
R. McKibbin, *The Evolution of the Labour Party 1910-1924*, (Oxford 1974).
R. Miliband, *Parliamentary Socialism*, (1964).
B. Millman, Managing Domestic Dissent in First World War Britain, (2000).
H. Moncrieff, *Roots of Labour*, (Coventry 1990).
A. J. A. Morris, *Edwardian Radicalism 1900-1914*, (1974).
F. Morison, *War on the Great Cities*, (1937).
A. L. Morton and G. Tate, *The British Labour Movement*, (1979).
D. J. Newton, *British Labour European Socialism and the Struggle for Peace 1889-1914*, (Oxford 1985).
R. Page Arnot, *South Wales Miners*, (1967).
S. Pankhurst, *The Home Front*, (1932)
H. Pelling, *A Short History of the Labour Party*, (1961).
——————— *Origins of the Labour Party*, (1954).
——————— *Popular Politics and Society in Late Victorian England*, (1968).
——————— *Social Geography of British Elections 1885-1910*, (1967).
——————— *The Challenge of Socialism*, (1968).
P. Piorier, *The Advent of the Labour Party*, (1958).
R. Price, *An Imperial War and the British Working Class*, (1972).
W. Ramsey, *The East End then and Now*, (1997).
R. Rhodes, *An Arsenal for Labour*, (1998).
M. Rose, *The Relief of Poverty 1834-1914*, (1974).
T. Rothstein, *From Chartism to Labourism*, 1983.
P. Rowland, *The Last Liberal Governments: The Promised Land 1905-1910*, (1968).
——————— *The Last Liberal Governments: Unfinished Business 1911-1914*, (1971)
P.K. Russell, *Liberal Landslide: The General Election of 1906*, (Newton Abbot 1973).
P. Saint (ed.), *Politics and the People of London*, (1989).
L. J. Satre, *Thomas Burt, Miners' MP, 1837-1922*, (Leicester 1999).
M. Savage, *The Dynamics of Working-class Politics: The Labour Movement in Preston 1880-1940*, (Cambridge 1987).
R. J. Scally, *The Origins of the Lloyd George Coalition*, (Princetown 1975).
J. D. Scott, *Siemens Brothers 1858-1958*, (1958).
R. Shannon, *The Crisis of Imperialism 1865-1915*, (1976).
H. Snell, *Men, Movements and Myself*, (1936).
P. Stafford, *A Match to Fire the Thames*, (1961).
P. Stansky (ed.), *The Left and the War: The British Labour Party and World War 1*, (Oxford 1969).
G. Stedman Jones, *Outcast London*, (1971).
——————— *Languages of Class*, (1983)
T. P. Stevens, *Father Adderley*, (1943).
D. Stevenson, *Armaments and the Coming of War: Europe 1904-1914*, (Oxford 1996).
M. Stocks, *The Workers Education Association*, (1953).
R. Storey (ed.), *Tom Mann: A Bibliography*, (Warwick 1993).
R. B. Stucke (ed.), *Fifty Years of the Woolwich Labour Party*, (1953).
A. J. P. Taylor (ed.), *Lloyd George: Twelve essays*, (New York 1971).
——————— *English History 1914-1945*, (Oxford 1975).

P. Thane (ed.), *The Origins of British Social Policy*, (1978).
E. P. Thompson, *William Morris: Romantic to Revolutionary*, (1955).
N. Thompson, *Political Economy and the Labour Party*, (1996).
P. Thompson, *Liberals, Radicals and Labour: The Struggle for London 1889-1914*, (1967).
W. Thorne, *My Life's Battles*, (1925)
H. Tracy, *The British Labour Party*, 3 vols. (1948).
C. Tsuzuki, *H. M. Hyndman and British Socialism*, (Oxford 1961).
D. Tanner, *Political Change and the Labour Party 1900-1918*, (Cambridge 1990).
B. Tillet, *Memories and Reflections*, (1931).
H. H. Tiltman, *James Ramsay MacDonald: Labour's Man of Destiny*, (New York 1929).
D. Torr, *Tom Mann*, (1936).
――――― *Tom Mann and His Times*, vol. I, (1956).
J. Wilson, *A life of Sir Henry Campbell – Bannerman*, (1973).
T. Wilson, *The Downfall of the Liberal Party*, (1966).
――――― (ed.), *The Political Diaries of C. P. Scott 1911-1928*, (1970).
J. M. Winter, *Socialism and the Challenge of War*, (1974).
C. J. Wrigley, *David Lloyd George and the British Labour Movement*, (1976).
――――― *Lloyd George and the Challenge of Labour*, (1990).
――――― (ed.), *Warfare Diplomacy and Politics*, (1986).

ARTICLES

F. Bedarida, 'Urban Growth and Social Structure in Nineteenth Century Poplar', *The London Journal*, vol.. 1, (1975), pp. 159-188.
G. Bernstein, 'Liberalism and the Progressive Alliance in Three Constituencies, 1900-1914: Three Case Studies', *History Journal*, 26, 3 (1983), pp. 617-640.
K. D. Brown, 'Conflict in Early British Welfare Policy: The Case of the Unemployed Workmen Bill of 1905', *Journal of Modern History*, 43, (1971), pp. 613-29.
J. Chamberlain, Pauperism and Distress: Circular Letter to Boards of Guardians, 15 March 1886, in W. Chance, *The Better Administration of the Poor Law*, (1895), Appendix J, pp. 242-3.
W. Crooks, 'The Prospects and Programme of the Labour Party', *National Review*, vol. 46, (1906), pp. 621-32.
G. Clifton, 'Members and Officers of the LCC, 1889-1965', in A Saint (ed.), *Politics and the People of London*, (1989), pp. 1-26.
J. Davis, 'The Progressive Council, 1889-1907', in *Politics and the People of London*, pp. 27-48.
F. Dilnot, 'The Old Order Changeth', in C. Silvester, *The Literary Companion to Parliament*, (1996), pp. 228-230.
R. Douglas, 'The National Democratic Party and the British Workers' League', *Historical Journal*, xv, 3, (1972), pp. 533-552.
J. Gillespie, 'Municipalism, Monopoly and Management: The Demise of 'Socialism in One County', 1918-1933', in A. Saint (ed.), *Politics and the People of London*, (1989), pp. 103-125.
R. Harrison, 'The War Emergency Workers' National Committee 1914-1920', in A. Briggs and J. Saville (eds.), *Essays in Labour History 1886-1923*, (1971), pp. 211-59.
C. Hazlehurst, 'Asquith as Prime Minister, 1908-1916', *Economic History Review*, (1970), pp. 502-30.
B. Keith-Lucas, 'Poplarism', *Public Law*, (Spring 1962), pp. 52-80.
S. E. Koss, 'The Destruction of Britain's Last Liberal Government', *Journal of Modern History*, vol. 11, No. 2 (June 1968), pp. 257-77.

K. Laybourn, 'The Rise of Labour and the Decline of Liberalism: The State of the Debate', *History*, 80 (June 1995), pp.207-26.
B. Lancaster, 'The Rise of Labour', *Labour History Review*, 57, 3 (1992), pp. 97-100.
J. Lawrence, 'Popular politics and the limitations of party: Wolverhampton 1867-1900', in E. Biagini and A. L. Reid (eds.), *Currents of Radicalism: Popular radicalism, organised labour and Party politics in Britain, 1850-1914*, (1991), pp. 65-85.
J. G. Little, 'H. H. Asquith and Britain's Manpower Problem, 1914-1915', *History*, 269, (July 1997), pp. 397-409.
M. Mansfield, 'Flying to the Moon: reconsidering the British labour exchange system in the early twentieth century', in *Labour History Review*, 66.1, (Spring 2001), pp. 24-40.
D. E. Martin, 'The Instruments of the People'?: The Parliamentary Labour Party in 1906, in David E. Martin and David Rubinstein, (eds.), *Ideology and the Labour Movement*, (1979), pp. 125-146.
P. C. Mathew, R. I. McKibbin and J. A. Kay, 'The Franchise Factor in the Rise of the Labour Party', *Economic History Review*, (1976), pp. 723-752.
R. I. McKibbin, 'James Ramsay MacDonald and the Problem of the Independence of the Labour Party, 1910-1914', *Journal of Modern History*, vol. 42, 2, (1970), pp. 216-35.
K. O. Morgan, 'The New Liberalism and the Challenge of Labour: The Welsh Experience, 1885-1929', in K. D. Brown, (ed.), *Essays in Anti-Labour History*, (1974), pp. 159-182.
S. Pennybacker, 'The millennium by return of post', in D. Feldman and G. Stedman Jones (eds.), *Metropolitan : London*, (1989), pp. 129-162.
D. Powell, 'The Liberal Ministries and Labour 1892-1895', *History*, 68 (1985), pp. 408-426.
────── 'The New Liberalism and the Rise of Labour', *History Journal*, 29, 2 (1986), p. 369-393.
W. Purdue, 'The Liberal and Labour Parties in North-East Politics 1900-14: The Struggle for Supremacy', *International Review of Social History*, vol. XXXV1, (1981), pp. 1-24.
N. Raynsford MP, 'Will Crooks 1852-1921, in D. Haworth and D. Haytor (eds), *Men Who Made Labour*, (2006), pp. 47-52.
A. J. Reid, 'Old Unionism reconsidered: the radicalism of Robert Knight, 1880-1914', in E. Biagini and A. Reid (eds.), *Currents of Radicalism*, pp. 214-243.
G. Rose, 'Locality, Politics and Culture: Poplar in the 1920s', *Society and Space*, (1988), pp. 151-168.
P. A. Ryan, 'Poplarism' 1894-1930, in Pat Thane, *The Origins of British Social Policy*, (1978), pp. 56-83.
F. Sainsbury, 'The Silvertown Explosion', *Newham History Society Occasional Papers*, No. 2, (November 1988), pp. 25-44.
P. Saint, 'Technical Education and the Early LCC', in *Politics and the People of London*, pp. 71-91.
J. Saville, 'Trade Unions and Free Labour: The Background to the Taff Vale Decision', in A. Briggs and J. Saville (eds.), Essays in Labour History, (1967), pp. 317-350.
J. P. Taylor, 'The Great War — The Triumph of E. D. Morel (II)', in Stansky, *The Left and War: The Labour Party and World War 1*, 1969, pp. 306-13.
J. Shepherd, 'Labour and parliament: the Lib.-Labs. as the first working-class MPs. 1885-1906', in *Currents of Radicalism*, pp. 187- 213.
J. O. Stubbs, 'Lord Milner and patriotic labour 1914-1918', *English Historical Review*, 87, 4, (1972), pp. 717-54.
D. Tanner, 'Ideological debate in Edwardian labour politics: radicalism, Revisionism and socialism', in *Currents of radicalism*, pp. 271-293.
P. Thane, 'Non-Contributory Verses Insurance Pensions 1878-1908', in P. Thane (ed.), *The Origins of British Social Policy*, pp. 84-106.
────── 'The Working Class and State 'Welfare' in Britain, 1880-1914', *History Journal*, 27, 4 (1984), pp. 877-900.

E. P. Thompson, 'Homage to Tom Maguire', in A. Briggs and J. Saville, (eds.), *Essays in Labour History*, (1960), pp. 276-316.

C. Townsend, 'The British Policy in Ireland, 1906-1921', in D.G. Boyce (ed.), *The Revolution in Ireland, 1871-1923*, (1988), pp. 173-192.

P. F. Tyler, 'The origins of labour representation in Woolwich', *Labour History Review*, vol. 59, Part 1, (1994), pp. 26-33.

———— 'Will Crooks and the origins of independent Labour representation in Poplar, 1888-1892', *Working Class Movement Library Bulletin*, 10, (2000), pp. 13-19.

———— 'Will Crooks MP, Local Activist and Labour Pioneer', *Greenwich Industrial History Society*, Issue 30, (2003).

D. Weinbren, 'From gun carriage to railway carriage; the fight for peace work at the Woolwich Arsenal 1919-22', *Labour History Review*, vol. 63, Part 3, (1998), pp. 277-297.

T. Wilson, 'The Coupon and the British General Election of 1918', *Journal of Modern History*, vol. xxxvi, (n. d.).

C. Wrigley, 'In The Excess Of Their Patriotism: The National Party and Threats of Subversion', in C. Wrigley (ed.), *Warfare Diplomacy and Politics*, (1986), pp. 93-119.

THESIS

D. W. Crowley, 'The Origins of the Revolt of the British Labour Movement from Liberalism 1875-1906', (PhD. London 1952).

J. Frankis, 'Industry and Politics in an Armaments Town', (MA. Greenwich, 1991).

D. T. Jones, 'The Well Hall Estate, Eltham, London, SE9', (Open University Project, 1975).

J. R. Orens, 'The Masses and the Music Hall: a study of Stewart Headlam's Radical Anglicanism', (PhD. Columbia University, New York, 1977), at THLHL.

J. M. Stevens, 'The London County Council under the Progressives 1889-1907', (MA. Sussex, 1966).

D. Thom, 'Women Munition Workers in the Woolwich Arsenal', (MA. Greenwich, 1970).

———— 'The Ideology of Women's Work, 1914-1920', with particular reference to the NFWW and other trade unions, (PhD. Greenwich, 1982).

P. Thompson, 'London Working-Class Politics & the Formation of the London Labour Party 1885-1914', (DPhil. Oxford, 1964).

P. F. Tyler, 'Will Crooks MP, local activist and Labour pioneer: Poplar to Woolwich 1852-1921', (PhD. University of North London, 2002).

D. Weinbren, 'The "Peace Arsenal" scheme: the campaign for non-munitions work at the
Royal Ordnance Factories, Woolwich after the First World War', (PhD. Greenwich, 1990).

INDEX

Abbey Wood Club 102
Abrahams, William 210
Adams, Major William
  138,139,164,165,169-72
Adams, R.J.Q 197
Adamson, W 172
Adderley, Rev. James 24
Addison, Dr 201,202
Adelman, P 30,36
Admiralty 156,199
adult suffrage 191,192
Adult Suffrage Society 191
aged and infirm 59,62,66
Alden, Percy 84
Aldermen 45,46,53
Amalgamated Society of Engineers
  102,105,114,176,185,203,205
Anderson, W. C 184,218
armaments 43,155,156,175,177,185,
  198-200
Army Council 156
  demobilisation 78,81,219
Army/Navy Estimates 12,128,147,175
Arsenal Gates and meetings
  9,106,107,113,135,138,164
Arsenal, the 13,100-2,104,107,110,117,
  118,128,138,140-7,155,156,170,174-
  6,185,197-205,220
  discharges 12,140-8,150,
  156,165,166,192,219,220
  Shop Stewards Committee
  205,206,219,220
  strike 183,185,186
  wages 112,113,172,175,219
  women workers 205,208,209
  workers 10,137,143,145,
  164-6,172,179,209
  workers' direct action 146

Askwith, Sir George 185,186
Asquith, Herbert
  13,151,155,164,168,174,178,179,185,
  186,192,194,195,205,207,218,220
Australia and New Zealand 160,162,184

Backbench MPs 13
Baker, H.T 199
Balfour Government 8,87,88,93,94,
  136-8,140
Balfour, Arthur 88-90,94,96-8,220
Balfour, Gerald 93,94,97
Balkans, the 185
ballot 39,105,109,171
Banbury, Sir F 177
Bangor 132,134,135
  Liberal Association 134
Banner, Robert 36,103,105-7
Barefoot, William 10,103,108,114,119,
  121,134,137,138,,157,198,203,205,
  206,208,210,215,216,219,221
Barnard Castle 120,126
Barnes, George 114,144,145,
  154,205,210,219
Barnett, Canon 5
Bartley, Sir George 94
Battersea 30.44
  Labour League 45
Bazalgette, Edward 48
Bealey, Frank 125,133
Bell, Richard 112,121,133,134
Bellsham, Councillor Job 81
Benn, John 134
Bentinck, Lord Henry 209
Beresford, Lord Charles
  104,108,111,112,118
Beveridge, William 5,76,84,86,98
Bevir, Mark 35

Biagini, E. F 2
Binnie, Alexander 49
Birrell, Augustine 140
Bishop, George 110,121
Black, W.F 86
Blackburn 138
Blackwall Tunnel and schemes
    7,10,26,42,45,47-9,
    52,54,61,73,100,117,158
Bland, Hubert 32,107
Blewett, Neal 157,162,163,
    168,169,172,173
    The Peers, the Parties and the People 157
Board of Trade 11,74,77,85,177,180,209
Board of Works 75,79,101
Boards of Guardians 8-10,19,26,33,37-9,
    42,69,72,74,75,78,80,82,85,86,148
Boer War 77,100,107,128,196
Bonfield, Margaret 164,191,192,209
Booth, Charles 17,18,101
borough councils 64,65,86,141,222
Bowerman, Charles 220,221
Brace, William 207,210
Bradford 132,139
Branson, Noreen 5
Bridges Committee 7,46,47,49.50-52,54
Bright, John 2,20
British Workers' League 13,209,210
British Workers' National League 209
Broderick, William 128,129,147
Bromley 39,44,48,53,54,
    64,71,72,75,76,81,98,172
    Recreation Ground 54
Bromley St Leonard 48,57
Brooks, Stopford 81
Brown, Harry 36
Brown, Kenneth D 2,94,97,149
Browning Settlement 166,167
Brownlie, J.T 205
Brunner Mond and Co 209,212
    explosion 212,213
Bryant and May 17,18,25
Bullivant, William 26,27,35
Burns, John 1,6,44,45,50,54,
    62-4,72,73,82,83,93,106,114,128,
    149-51,154,155,160,186
Burrows, Herbert 106
Burt, Thomas 4
Butler, Fred 107,221
Buxton, Sydney 23,35,38,39,
    47,48,54,72,165

by-elections 106,111,112,115,118,120-2,
    125,126,133,134,140,148,153
    (1903) 112,118,120-2,125
Camberwell Green 61
Cameron, Alexander 216-8
Campbell-Bannerman, Henry 96,127,
    137,147
Canadian-Pacific Railway 160,162
Carrington, F brewer 28
Carson, Edward 189
casual labour 67,86,188
Cecil, Lord Hugh 179
Census (1901) 17,67
Chamberlain, Joseph
    69,78,87,127,136,138
    Pauperism and Distress 69,71,72,79
Chambers, Tom 106
Chance, Sir William 93
Chandler, Rev. Arthur 72-4
Chaplin, Henry 60,75
Charity Organisation Society 74,105
Chartism 2,127
Chesterton, G.K 57,223
children of the poor 5,13,19,
    26,61,62,117,128,131,148,167,
    187,188,211
    food for 187,188
Chinese labour 131,136,138
Churchill, Winston 159,160,196
Clarion, The 159,173
Clark, David 28
clergy 24,30,81
Clitheroe 120,121
Clynes, John 77, 91, 159, 161, 184, 218
Coal Tax abolition 42
Coalitions 13,194,195,200,207,210, 211,
    217-9,221
Cole, G.D.H 31,180
Collectivism 34,49,53,140,215
Colne Valley 28,163
Comradeship 105,106
conscription 3,205,207,208
    Bill 207
Conservatives 9,23,53,64,65,78,93,
    110-12, 121,126,127,132,135,138,140,
    163,165,166,169,191,217,218
Constitution, new (1918) 214-6
constitutional crisis 12,173
Cooper, Ben 54,72,81
Coopers' Union 20,36,110,132,148,167
cost of living 164,180

Cowes 204
craft unions 34,36
Crilly, Daniel 165,189
Crooks, Will 1-223
  and Arsenal work 199
  and 'college' 6,7,9,22
  25,31,33,45,47,49,55,72,73,106,116
  and bombing tragedy 212-4
  and Parliament, Crooks election to
  9,10
  and Poplar enquiry 9,141
  and war effort 194,203
  apprenticeship and trade 20,21,28,30
  as Mayor of Poplar 7,22,54,179
  as MP 5,26,46,53,80,
  90-2,107,111,125-53,203
  Colonies tour 160-2
  complaints against 132-5
  death and funeral 221
  duty and mission 3,25 26
  early years 18-21
  Empire tour 183,184,188,193
  family 18-21,58,98,
  161,209,212,219,223
  funding 7,34,35,
  37,110,114,117,133,167.
  health 14,22,28,90-2,116,
  128,136,142,147,148,160,161,
  167,203, 209,211,212,214,216-9
  honesty, commitment, loyalty
  13,14,57,61
  ideological makeup 22
  legacy 222
  main role 174
  meetings attendance and travel 62,
  90-2
  patriotism 13,194-6,201,208
  political outlook 32,39,40,46,132
  religious values 3,4,10,24,192,210
  resignation 14,176,178,219
  temperance 110,111,167,187
  world cruise 12,160-2,184
Curran, Pete 38,49,91,92,102,103,161

Daily Chronicle 46
Daily Express, The 163
Daily Mail, The 177,178
Daily News 97,114,199
  East End Relief Fund 81,82
Daily Sketch 213
Dangerfield, George 140,157,179
Darley, A.H 161
Davis, John 45,53
Davis, Mary 192

Davy, Chief Inspector James S 62,64,67
  Report 65,67
death threat 76
depression, trade 18,23,68,77,
  78.84,115,151,153
Derby 96,112,121
Derby, Lord 205
  Scheme 205,207
Despard, Charlotte 191
Devlin, C 161
Devonport 132,134,135,166
Devonport, Lord 183
dignity, importance of 8,59,161
Dilke, Sir Charles 186
Dilnot, Frank 178
dilution 205-8
disenfranchised poor 83,171,174
distress, causes and relief 79,81-3,
  85-8,93,97,98,150,151,153,154,188
District Board system 7,41,42,75,76
Dock Strike 1889 18,22,27,28,
  30,58,67,102
dockers 18,102,103,174,180,182-4,223
  Union 33,36,46,57,67
docks and dockyards 17,21,27,28,
  113,155,180
Dockworkers' Union 37
Douglas, R 209
Drage, Geoffrey 112,113,115,138,170
  Old Age Pensions 115
drink question, the 187
Duncan, C 143
Dunston Farm 83
Dunton Wayletts Farm 77

East End News 27,38,39,42,43,74,78,212
East End of London 4,17,23,25,32, 37,
  37,49,55,67,68,72,73,84,132,212
East India Docks 6,17,20,22,25-7,73,87
education 3,8,11,12,14,
  24,30,55,59,73,104,106,107,115,117,
  118,127,130,131,137,148,186-9,223
  (Administrative Provision) Bill 188
  (Provision of Meals) Bill 149,187
  Act (1902) 111,127
  Bill 118,119,140
educational reform 210
Edward VII, King 98,142,146,167-169
  death 169
eight-hour day 9,27,37,45,104
elections 26,29,25-7,64,65,
  108,111,112,114,116,118,120,132,
  137,138,148,158,166-9,180,217,
  221,217,218

electoral reform 13,193
  register 78,137
Emmott, Lord Alfred 183
Empire Tour 183,184,193
Empire, the 3,209,210
  and war 3
employment 11,18,61,73,142,147
  relief 84,86,88
Engels, Frederick 107
engineers 34,101-3,117,207
Entwistle, John 185
Erith 100,106
Escreet, Canon 83

Fabians the 2-4,6,24,27,28,30,31,33,
  35-7,44,49-51,63,106,107,111,167,
  184,191
  and the Poplar Labor League 31
fair day's pay 29
  day's work 29
  wages 7,8,49-53,61,73,95,106
Fair, John 140,168
farms and farm colonies 26,62-4,75-7,
  82-4,89,94,95,98
feeding the poor 188
Fels, Joseph 83,84,89
Fennel, Edwin 108
First World War 3,13,140,172,
  189,192,194-6,199,204,208,
  211-13,216,217
fiscal reform 88,89,138,139,153
Fisher, Admiral John 197,198,200
footway tunnel 26,117
Ford, George 56
foreshores 74,83
Forest Gate Schools District 59,60
Fowler, Henry 70,71,72,79
Fox, Tom 184
franchise, the 10,73,78,88,191,215,217
Free Churches 110,115,118,164
Free trade 10,118,131,134,
  136,137,139,153,163
  and Labour Union, speech on 134
  in land 31
Funding and finance 84,86,87,
  90,93,98,114,117,132.133,149,183,
  186,220

gas and water control 26,42
Gasworkers' Union 27,34,36,50,
  71,102,104,171
Gee, Captain Robert 221

General Election (1892) 32
  (1903) 164
  (1906) 126,140
general elections 35,39,45,46,104,
  137,158,159,162,216
  (1910) 12,153,162,163,165-73,192
  (1918) coupon, the 14,211,217,218
Germany and the Germans 2,14,202,
  208,210,213,214,217
Gill, A 91
Gladstone, Herbert 119,120,125-7
Gladstone, William 2,23,31,165
Gladstone/MacDonald entente 126
Gladstonian Liberalism 31
  parties 32,39
Glasier, Bruce 105,133
Goldstone, F.W 172
Gorton 11
government workers: holidays and
holiday pay 211
  housing 211
  minimum wage 175,190
  pay and conditions 128,129
  wages 211
  war bonuses 211
Graham, Alf 33,35,39,51
Grant, Corrie 58,63,130
Graphic, The 95
Green, W.H 221
Grey, Sir Edward 127
Grigg, John 157,163,164
Grinling, Charles 88.105,106,
  109,110,113,120
Grosvenor, Hon. Richard 26,27

Hackney 32,81,132
Halbury, Lord 183
Haldane, Richard 142-7,156,175
Halévy, Elie 77
Hammill, Fred 30,36,106
Hardie, Keir 1,11,37,93-7,105,
  107,114,120,121,127,129,133,139,144,
  149,160,161,184,191,210
Hare, Rev. Marmaduke 72
Harney, George Julian 2
Harris, J 69,78,84,85,98,151
  Unemployment and Politics 69
Harvey, G.A engineers 100
Harvey, William 178
Haw, George 3,4,20,55,
  57,69,73,90,93,98,193,195
  Who is Will Crooks? 115
  Workhouse to Westminster 69

INDEX

Hazelhurst, Cameron 197
Helps, Jack 33
Henderson, Arthur 2,3,93,95,96,
  114,120,131,134,144,147,151,158,
  161,164,165,178,184,191,193,195,
  207,208,210,214,215,217,218,220-222
  Committee 142,172
Herbert, Jesse 125-7
Higgins, John 165
Hills, A.F 75
Hobsbawm, Eric J. 35,36
Hodge, John 11,119,159,184,195,210
Holland, Canon Scot 73
Hollesley Bay colony 62-4,76,84,89
Holton, Bob 180,182
Home Office and Home Secretary
  61,209
House of Commons 11-222 *passim*
House of Lords 12,13,140,153,154,
  162-6,168-71,178,189,190
  constitutional position 163
  veto 157,159,168,169,
    170,172,173,178
housing 24,45,111,154,219,223
  reform 115
Howell, David 37,139
Hughes, Colonel 104,108,112
Hughes, Edwin 101
Hughes, William 209
Hull 148
humane assistance 62,63,65
Hutchinson, Henry 63
Hyndman, Henry Mayers 106

ILP News 119
implements of peace 143,145,147
Independent Labour Party 7,24,30,31,
  34-8,46,85,86,94,102-5,107,111,114,
  119,120,126,132,135,139,191,214,209,
  218
Independent Labour Representation
  6,7,9,10,23,26,28-31,33,37,44,80,
  101-6,108,127,132,222
industrial conciliation 181,183
  conscription 196,197
  relations 4,28,176,222
  unrest 13,151,180
Ireland 13,23,92
Ireland, Church of 21
Ireland, Home Rule for 10,12,13,
  23,24,31,53,113,127,138,164,
  165,168,169,170,172,175,179,
  186,189-92,209

Irish National Party
  163,164,168,169,172,189,190
Isle of Dogs 17,26,52,54

Jackman, Frank 221
Jarrow 163
Jenkins, J 143
Jenkins, J.H 155
Jenkins, Roy 157
Job, C 206
Joint Registration Committee 108,109
Jones, Ben 103,104,111
Jones, Ernest 2
Jones, Rev. Jenkins 108
Jowett, Fred 139,218
Juvenile Offenders' Bill 61

Kaiser, the 196
Kaye, Harry W 26,37,57
Keith-Lucas, B 69
Kennedy, Rev. H.A 33,71
Kentish Independent 206
King, McKenzie 162
King's Prerogative 169
  Speech 92,150,154,155,210
  Speech Motion 129,154
Kingsway-Aldwych junction 98
Kitchener, Lord 194,198,205
Knee, Fred 107

Labour Associations 110,120,222
Labour: candidates 35,37-9,46,
  65,79,106,109,110,119,126,
  132,167,168,173,216-8,221
  colonies 76,84,89
  movement 1,24,58,73,94,
    105,117,118,223
Labour Disputes Bill 174,175,180,181
Labour Exchanges 5,70,79,155,160,223
  Bill 159,160
Labour Government, 1924 194
Labour Journal 115,118
Labour Leader 86,126,135
Labour Party 1-216 *passim*
  conferences 207,217
  consolidation 11,121,222
  constitution (1918) 194
  National Executive Committee
    157,178,184,191,193,195,210,
    214-7,220
  platform, independent 132
  policy 12
  programme 38

propaganda 127
Recruiting Committee 205
Reorganisation Conference 215
unrest 13,180-6
women's suffrage 191
Labour Protection League 27,102, 117,141,185
Labour Representative Committee 10,11,46,85,91,92,94,96,104,108,110, 111,114,117,119-21,125-7,131-3, 135,137-9,149,178,222
Constitution 110,132-4
Labour, Ministry of 11,210
Labour, Royal Commission on 67
labour, skilled 17,36,95,100,117,197,198
labour, unskilled 17,67,68,74,196
labourers 36,50,72,117
Labourism 2,110,196,222
Laindon 62,76,82,83
Lananton, John 27
Lancashire 139
Lancaster, Bill 29
land reform 149-51,155,158
Lansbury, George 1,8,9,57-60, 62-6,69,71,76,83,87,88,96,98,222
Lansdowne, Lord 140,190
Laurier, Sir Wilfred 162
Law, Andrew Bonar 190,194,217,218
Lawrence, J 40
Lax, William 17
Laybourn, Keith 6
LCC Bridges Committee 117
contracts 50
Education Committee 56
election 1892 33,34,38,45
elections 26,29,37,39, 42,65,103,132,165,166,167
Progressivism 37
Works Committee 56
Works Department 52,53,222
Ley, Henry 39
Lib/Lab pact 139
Liberal and Radical Association 38
Liberal Associations 29,38, 39,41,45,120,134
Liberal candidates 27,45,46,126,149,173
Liberal concessions 125,126
Liberal Government 5,11,53,62,98, 137,140,153,164,168,172,182,195, 197,200
downfall 197
Liberal Party and Liberals 2-222 *passim*
schism 22,23
Liberal Unionists 112

Liberal/Radical Progressives 41
Liberal/trade union alliance 23
Liberalism 2,29,37,101,126,127,131,140
Liberals, Old 135
Liberty and Property Defence League 53,113,115
Lib-Lab pact 132,158,173
Licensing Bills 11,129,130,157
Liddington, Jill 191
Liverpool 21,85,91,92,96,131
Liverpool Mercury 134
Local Government (County Council) Act (1888) 7,25
Local Government Board (LGB) 9,18, 47,48,53-8,65,67,69,72,75,77,80, 84-7,92,93,95,129,150,153,154,174, 186-9,211,222
London County Council (LCC) 7,8,22, 25,27,28,31,33-5,39,41,42,44-9,51, 54-6,58,67,73,81-3,94,106,107,109, 111,118,121,132,167,192
London School Boards 50,107,114
London School of Economics 63,116
London Society of Compositors 50
London Trades Council 30,33, 70,72,103,105
London Unemployed Districts 86
London Unemployment Fund 8,84,86,88
London unemployment problem 89,93
Long, Walter 60,84-8,90,92-4
unemployed scheme 86,89,90,93,98
Lloyd George, David 3,13,134,153, 157,168,175,192,194,196,200,202,206, 212,214,217,218,220,221

Macarthur, Mary 191
Macdonald, J. A 71
MacDonald, James Ramsay 1,2,46,63,82, 83,91,93,94,97,105,111,114,119,120, 125,127,131-4,137,138,148 150,157,160,161,173,181,184, 191,195,218,221
MacDonald/Gladstone agreement 11,120,121,125,126,173
Mackintosh, Alexander 190
Macnamara, T.J 63
Macpherson, J.T 164
Mahon, John Lincoln 103
Main, Councillor Alex 83
Manchester 97,140
Mann, Tom 1,6,22,49,106,116
Mansion House scheme 72,84,86
Marsland, W 181
Marx-Aveling, Eleanor 103,106

Marxism 23
Matchgirls' Strike 18,25
Mayor, first Labour 108
Mazzini, Joseph 2,3,24
McBriar, A.M 35,51
McCarthy, Tom 33
McDougall, Sir John
  26,27,35,38,45,54,61,82
McKenna, Reginald 155,156,175
McKibbin, Ross 162,163,214,216-8
McNeill, Swift 165
Merthyr Tydfil 96,121,139
Metropolitan Asylums Board 7,42,
  60-2,91
Metropolitan Board of Works 7,27,
  41,47-9,75
Metropolitan Community Poor Fund 59
middle class 4,17,23,33,36,79,191,217
Middleton, Jim 91,92,125,126,138
Miliband, Ralf 216
  Parliamentary Socialism 216
military service: legislation 3,13,207,213
  compulsory 205-7
Mills, Jack 206,216,220
Milner, Lord 209,210
miners 163,182,210,223
miners' national strike 180,182
minimum wage 175-8,182,192,222
Morgan, K.O 139
Morning Leader 25
Morpeth 4
Morris, William 103
Mundella, A.J. 11,74,83
Municipal Alliance 62-5
Municipal Journal 52
Municipal reforms 26,28,49,65
Municipal Socialism 51,53
munitions 13,140,142,
  143,145,147,192,196-8,200-5,209,219
  legislation 200-2,205,207,208
Munitions, Ministry of 11,197,200-2,
  205,206,209
Murray Committee 140
  *Government Factories and Workshops
  Committee Report* 140,146,147,198

National Federation of Women Workers
  209
National Insurance 175,179
National Liberal Federation 31,32
National Transport Workers' Federation
  182,183
National Union of Women's Suffrage
  Societies 191

Navvies, Bricklayers' Labourers and
  General Labourers' Union 50
Navy, the 153,155,174,190
New Unionism 2,6,18,22,
  25,27,28,103,180,222
Newcastle 132,181
  Programme 31,32
  resolution 119
Newton 172
Nineteenth Century 73
nonconformity 2,100,101,139
North and North-East 100,126,223
North Wales Quarrymen's Union 134
Norwich 132,133,135
Nottingham 105
Nottingham Daily Express 130

O'Donnell, Frank Hugh 108
O'Grady, J 139
O'Malley, William 190
old age pensions and pensioners 5,11-13,
  24,64,104,115,117,118,
  127-9,148,151,152,211,223
one man, one vote 31,127
Orbell, Harry 36,184,221
Ordnance: Department 197
  factories 140-2,145-7,
  156,175,198,202,209
Osborne judgement 162,163,
  170,179,180,183
Outdoor/out relief 62, 64. 69,129, 150

Pankhurst, Emmeline 191
Parish of All Saints, Poplar 42
Parker, James 139,210
Parks and Open Spaces 7,26,41,42,
  53-5,72
Parliament, special session 88,89,
  90,96,98
Parliament Act/Bill (1911) 172, 175, 178,
  189
Parliament, Members of : salaries 175,
  179
Parliamentary grant 150,151
Parliamentary Labour Party 142-4,
  154,164,184,195,208,211
Parliamentary Recruitment Committee
  195,205
pauperism 8,9,66,69,78,152,155
pay, low 11,14,18,22,
  128,129,186,188,189,222,223
Pearson, S. and Son 48-50
Pearson, Sir Wheatman 48

Pease, Edward 4,33,36,107,
 133,167,173,174
Pelling, Henry 32,104,125,133,180
Pellitier, Sir H. 161,162
Pennybacker, Susan 2,52
 A Vision for London 52
People's Budget 11,12,157-60,
 163,164,168,169
Philanthropic Coopers 30,33
Piggott, John 54
Pioneer 63,108,143,153,
 159,161,162,165,168,170,171,185,198,
 199,202,203,206,212
Plumstead 101,102,106,171,184
 Conservative and Unionist
  Association 158
 Radical Club 102,107,166,178
Poor Law 5,8,10,12,18,
 23,57,58,62,64,65,69,85,90,94,97,128,
 148,150-3,155,161,187,188,211,222
 administration
 26,42,62,79,80,128,186,187
 Commission (1909) 151
  Minority Report 159
 reform 1,10,19,39,186,187
 relief 23,78,149
 Royal Commission on 85
 school 19
 system 19,20,62,65,94,129
 Unions 88,91
 Poor Rates 26,42,63
poor, the 12,17,18,21,
 23,62,68,72,92,128,148,152,154,155,
 159,177,179,181,186,187,222
Poplar 1,4-7,10,14,17,18,21-3,25,28,
 30-32,34,35,37,39,43-5,47,48,52-5,
 57,61,65,72,73,76,80,84,87,91,96,98,
 102,150,155,161,166,174,191,211,
 212,219,221-3
 relief 18,25,76,77,
 79,82,84,129,148,152,189
Poplar Board of Guardians 5,7-9,
 18,19,22,59-64,69,74-7,79,
 81-4,86,88,91,93,94,98,222
Poplar: Board of Works 70-2
 Borough Council 79,83,91,98
 Council 82,83,161
 Enquiry 62-6,141
 Joint Committee 88
 Labour Party 32,36-8
  Committee 49
 Election Committee 26,31-3,
 35,37,39,44,50,70-4,107
 Relief Committee 73-5

 Poplar Fabians 9,28,31-3,36,106
Poplar hospital 141,211-13,221
Poplar Labor League 30,31,
 44,51,107,111,117
Poplar Liberal Radical Association
 6,24-7,30,33,35,38,39,42,44,111
Poplar Poor Law policy 60,65,66
Poplar Technical Institute 26,56
Poplar trade union and labour movement
 8,29,30,38,44,47,49,106,161
Poplar trade union and socialist alliance
 29
Poplar Union 57,60,62,64,67,77
Poplar workhouse 58,60,80
Poplar working class 29,47
Poplarism 5,69
Port of London 68,182,183
Portsmouth 96,166
Postgate, R 31
Pound, John 86
poverty 4-6,10,14,
 17,18,20,22,24,26,72,81,82,87,92,97,
 112,140,142,152,177,222,223
 issues 186,188
 relief 189
 state responsibility for 149,150,
 160,222
 working class 68
Press, the 168,177,221
Price, Richard 77
private contractors 156,175,185,197-202
Progressive and Labour platform 35
Progressive Association 105,109,120
Progressive candidates 25,26
Progressives, the 7,27,31,34,35,39,42,
 45-7,49,52,53,61,65,69,70,81,105,111,
 120,127,135,165,222
Progressivism 45,126
Progressive and Labour programme 45
propaganda, Labour 114,115
property owners 57,168,191
Protectionism 118,136
Public Enquiry 1906 9

quarrymen 223
Quelch, Harry 106
quinquennial valuation 43,44

Radical Association 39,41,45
Radical clubs 102,104,114
Radical liberalism 3,6,20,196
Radical Liberals 27,71,103,126,135,186
Radicalism 2,3,7,10,22-4,29,30,32,34,
 37,45,47,51,127,140,192

INDEX

Radicals and Radical Party 23,24,26, 29-35,37-40,44,46,76,78,90,93,111
railways and railwaymen 17,30, 34,117,180
rate aid clause 92,93,97
rate support relief 79
rates and ratepayers 25,26,41-5, 47,49,53,57,61,62,68,72,75,79, 89,90,92,93,98,115,130,150,151
Raven, Sir Vincent 209
reclaiming land 74,75,83
recruitment campaign 13,203-6
Redistribution Bill 96
Redmond, John 168,179,189,190
Redmond, W.A 189,190
register reform 42
registering supporters 108,109
Reid, Alastair J 2,34
relief schemes 80,84,85,90
religion 13,29,113,117
Representation of the People Bill 214,215
Review of Reviews 46,153
RGF 140,146,201
Richards, T.F. 133,143
Right to Live March 146
Right to Work scheme 150,151,154,158
Ritchie, Charles 48,61
river improvements and work 81,83
Roberts, George 133,178, 184,195,207,210
Robertson, J.M 177
Rogers, Isaac 111,133
Rosebery, Lord 48
Rotherhithe 52
Rowland, Peter 168,172
Royal Arsenal Co-operative Society 101,102,104-7,118,142
Royal Carriage Department 185
 Factory 146
Royal Gun Factory 100,140,198
Royal Laboratory 140,146
Royal Ordnance Factories 197
Rundell, William, Joshua 43
Russell, A. K 139
Ryan, W.P 69

Sainsbury, Frank 212
Saint, Andrew 55
Salisbury, Lord 35,77,93
Salvation Army 81,84
Saville, John 28
Scheu, Andreas 106
school meals 12,130,131,148,149,223

Scotch Education bill 96
Scott, C.P 195,197
Seamen's Union 114,180
Second Home Rule Bill 165
Shackleton, David 2,3,91,120, 121,128,134,147
Shaw, George Bernard 4,35,36,105
Shell Scandal 11,13,195,197-203
Shenfield 81,82,84
Shepherd, John 5,31
 George Lansbury 5
Shipbuilding 17,171,203,204,223
Shipwrights and Union 114,155,171
Siemens Brothers 100,113,114
Silver's India Rubber, Gutta Percha and Telegraph Works Ltd 102
 Silvertown 102,117,171,209
 disaster 212
Simon, Sir J 201
Slater, Dr Gilbert 107,142,144
Smith, F.E. 196
Smith, Professor William 112
Smiths and Hammermen 117
Snell, Harry 106,221
Snowden, Philip 105,133, 138,200,201,218
social democracy 36,45
social radicalism 186,187,223
social reforms and reformers 2,5,10, 14,20,21,24,25,29,32,41,62,64,72,82, 84,106,109,127,136,138,152-4, 157,186-8,222
Socialist Democratic Federation 23,24,31,37,76,79,84,103,104,107
Socialist League 103,104
Socialists and socialism 2-4,10,23-5, 29,36,49,53,73,93,103,105,106,113, 119,120,126,140,153,157,158,161, 163,177,191,209,210
soldiers 13,211,219
South Africa 81,136,138,184
 war 141
South, Matilda 21
South, Thomas 21
Southwark 98
Speaker, The 126
Stafford, Ann 29
Standard, The 107,165
Stansky, Peter 194
Star, The 46
Stead, W.T 46
Steadman, Bill 30,36,82,83,88,144
Steelsmelters 119
Steer, Jim 106

Stephenson, J 91
Stepney 84
Strikes and strikers 18,22,27,
    28,58,67,102,103,180-3,185,186
Stubbs 209,210
suffrage, adult 170,193,194,210
suffragettes 98,191,192
    hunger strike 192
    war effort 192
Sunderland 172
super-tax 157
sweatshop system 17,18,22
Syndicalism 180

Taff Vale decision 115,127
Tanner, Duncan 32,125,126,139,215
    Political Change and the Labour Party 125
tariff reform and reformers 87-9,
    111,117,118,126,127,136,138,153,154,
    157-9,163,164,169,173,177
taxation 45,78,87,136,157-9,164
Taylor, A.J.P 214
Taylor, J.W 139
Tea Operatives' Association 18
Technical Education Board (LCC)
    76,55,56,63
Technical Institute 56
temperance 11,13,37,110,
    111,114,154,164,167,170,187
Tennant, Jack 201
Testimonial Funds 220
Thames Communication (Blackwall) Act
1887 47
Thames Communication 42,47,49
Thames, river 7,17,26,
    47,49,52,61,68,69,83,171,223
Thom, Deborah 206,208
Thomas, J. H 218
Thompson, Paul 4,5,24,46,102,109,193
    Socialists, Liberals and Labour 4
Thorne, Will 49,102,106,134
Tillett, Ben 6,18,22,24,
    30,31,36,46,49,106,107,116,183
Times, The 3,64,79,80,118
Tootill, Robert 210
Tories 7,31,37,39,
    44,47,53,101,111,121,126,137,141,
    145,147,159,169,171,172,176,178,187,
    190,208,215,222
    candidate 164-6
    democracy 101
    government 5
    Progresssives 105

scaremongering 165,166
    working class 110,119,126,127,168

Toynbee, Arnold 23
trade and labour unions 70,71
Trade Union Act 183
trade union and labour movement 1,5,6,
    7,13,24,25,31,33,45,70,72,81,85,91,95,
    109,116,178,205-8,216,221
Trade Union Bill 113,133
Trade Unionism 2,29,53,
    73,104,107,151,185,201,207
trade unions and trade unionists 1,4,10,
    13,21,22,24,26,28,30,31,34-36,
    45,80,82,101,103,106,108,110,118,
    119,129,135,139,142,154,155,179,180,
    181, 186,191,194-6,197,201,207,
    214,216,218,222
    organisation 26,30,102
    interests 117,118,182
    meetings 7,47
Trades Council 104,105,107-9,
    120,135,141,206,207
Trades Union Congress 4,85,142,
    150,175,181,207,220
    Parliamentary Committee 85
transport industry 182
Treasury 179,205
Trotter, W.R 161
Turnbull, Jim 106

unemployed 5,7,8,21,22,
    24,47,62,64,66,128,150,223
    Special Committee 71,72
    state responsibility for 93,94,98
    work schemes 11,69-71,98
Unemployed Workmen Bill and Act
    (1905) 8,84,85,92-9,
    149-52,159,160,222
Unemployed Workmen Bills (1907-8) 11
unemployment 1,5,6,8,10-12,14,17-19,
    22,23,53, 57,59,67-9,72,75,83,92,
    112,127,130,131,136,140,148-51,
    153-5,158-60,174,180,186,187,189,
    222,223
    and the Poor Law 67-99
    distress caused by 69,70-3,76-8
    insurance 159,160,179
    question (parliament) 84,85,88
    rate 77,84,96,136,153
    registers 42,81,98,150
    relief 8,68,69,150

Unionists 35,53,111-15, 118,126,138,163,164,168,169,172,173, 79,189,195,208,209
United Irish League 115,164,165,189,190
United Society 110

Verville, A. 161
Vestries 7,41-4,46,70,72,101
veto resolutions 168
Victoria, Queen 52
votes and voters 25,26,29, 32,37,39,44,53,79,101,108-10,115,131,137-9,148,163,164,170-2
votes for women 12,191

wage rates 71,72,95,113,117,145,175
wage, minimum 12,49-51,129,170
wages 12,45,47,50,59, 77,98,102,107,128,141, 142,145,164,179,180,203,205,206,219
Wales 139,223
Wales, Prince of 52
Walker shipyard 204
Wallace, Graham 36
Wallace, J. Steward 37
Wallas, Graham 4
Walsh, S 195
War Office 10,11,13,140,141, 144-7,156,175,176,179,197-203
War Services Bill 206,207
Wardle, G 143,184
Webb, Beatrice 63,64
Webb, Sidney 4,34-36,63,82,116
welfare 5,184,223
Wemyss, Lord 54,113
Westminster, 1st Duke of 26
Wilkie, Alex 114,155
Williams, J 139
Wilson, Havelock 114
Wilson, Trevor 197,217
Wilson, W.T 149
women workers 208,209
Women's Enfranchise Bill 131,214
Women's Social and Political Union 191,192
Wood, Sir Howard Kingsley 218
Wood, Thomas MacKinnon 61

Woolwich 1,2,4,5,7,10, 12,17,24,30,37,45,47,65,66,74,80,91, 100-122 *passim*,127,132,135,140,142,143,150,156, 162,164,170-2,174,189,191-3, 203,204,211,215,222,223
Woolwich Board of Guardians 83,88,121,192
Woolwich borough council 101,143
Woolwich by-elections 7,11,106-8, 111,125,126,221
Woolwich District Trades and Labour Council 103, 104, 108, 110,129,207,221
Woolwich Dockyard 141,219
Woolwich election campaign 137,169,171
Woolwich Ferry 46,50,106,117
Woolwich ILP 36
Woolwich Labour election campaign (1910) 164
Woolwich labour movement 9,106,137,214
Woolwich Labour Party 36,103, 121,192,216-17,220,221
Woolwich Labour Representative Association 103,110,113-5, 117,120,121,132,135,145,167, 170,189,192,207,208,215,222
workhouse 2,8,19,22,26,58-61, 76,129,152,154,177,181,187
  country 83
  dietary scale 80
  management corruption 58
working class, the 2,9,11,12,14,19,22-4,28,29 36-8,53,55,61,70,87,92,101,104,106, 111,112,117,121,141,157,166,164,173, 180,189,191-3,196,200,201,207,214, 217,223
  educational rights 118,119
Workingmen's clubs 100,102
Workmen Unemployment Act 73
Workmen's Compensation Act (1897) 13
Wrigley, Chris 45,197,207,209

yard labourers 102,103
Yorkshire 126,139
Yorkshire Daily Post 130
Young Italy movement 2

www.ingramcontent.com/pod-product-compliance
Lightning Source LLC
Chambersburg PA
CBHW061434300426
44114CB00014B/1683